Burst of Breath

Burst of Breath

Indigenous Ritual Wind Instruments
in Lowland South America

EDITED BY JONATHAN D. HILL &
JEAN-PIERRE CHAUMEIL

UNIVERSITY OF NEBRASKA PRESS
LINCOLN & LONDON

Publication of this volume was assisted by
a grant from the Centre d'Enseignement et
de Recherche en Ethnologie Amérindienne
(EREA), Laboratoire d'Ethnologie et Sociologie
Comparative, at the Centre National de la
Recherche Scientifique (CNRS), Université de
Paris X.

∞

Library of Congress Cataloging-in-Publication
Data

Burst of breath: indigenous ritual wind
instruments in lowland South America / edited
by Jonathan D. Hill and Jean-Pierre Chaumeil.
p. cm.
Includes bibliographical references and index.
ISBN 978-0-8032-2092-8 (pbk.: alk. paper)
1. Indians of South America—Music—History
and criticism. 2. Wind instruments—South
America. 3. Indians of South America—Rites
and ceremonies. I. Hill, Jonathan David,
1954– II. Chaumeil, Jean-Pierre.
ML3575.A1B87 2011
788'.1908998—dc23
2011037139

Set in Sabon.

We dedicate this book to our friend and colleague Maria Ignez Cruz Mello (1962–2008), whose death was a terrible loss for the community of scholars interested in the anthropology of indigenous Amazonian musical and other cultural practices. No act of commemoration or dedication can fill the void left by the death of such a creative scholar who was still in the early postdoctoral years of her career and who undoubtedly had so much more to contribute to ethnomusicology and anthropology. The pairing of Maria Ignez's work with that of her widower, Acácio Tadeu de Piedade, is one of the greatest strengths of *Burst of Breath*, since it will mark the first time that anthropology will have achieved a truly cross-gendered documentation and analysis of indigenous Amazonian music—both vocal and instrumental, women's and men's—written by husband-and-wife fieldworker/collaborators who are (or were, sadly, in the case of Maria Ignez) also both highly accomplished musician-composers as well as recent doctorates in social anthropology. It is our sincere hope that by dedicating *Burst of Breath* to the memory of Maria Ignez Cruz Mello and publishing her superb essay on the complex and highly creative synergy between Wauja women's iamurikuma singing and the men's sacred flute music, we will have planted a seed that will inspire generations of researchers to emulate her skillful blending of musical creativity and ethnographic inquiry.

Contents

Illustrations

Images

Map

Tables

Overture

JONATHAN D. HILL AND JEAN-PIERRE CHAUMEIL

This book aims to produce a broadly comparative study of ritual wind instruments (flutes, trumpets, clarinets, and bullroarers) that are subject to strict visual and tactile (but not auditory) prohibitions and that are found among indigenous peoples in many areas of Lowland South America. The type of prohibition can vary from one group to another but primarily affects certain categories of persons more than others, which is why these wind instruments are often described, however inadequately, as "sacred" or "secret" instruments. Although there have been intensive studies of this kind of instrument and their music, understood as ritual objects and voices that condense a myriad of different relations in specific contexts, there have been no attempts to bring these isolated studies together into a more global, comparative perspective that goes beyond more documented areas, such as northwestern Amazonia and the Upper Xingu region and that integrates a diversity of approaches from anthropology, ethnomusicology, ethnolinguistics, and museum studies. Here we have assembled recent and ongoing research in these fields from a variety of ethnographic contexts (northwestern Amazonian, Upper Xingu, Guianas, Orinoco, Mato Grosso, and others) where we find sacred wind instruments played in pairs or trios.

The chapters are organized into two sections. Part 1, "Natural Sounds, Wind Instruments, and Social Communication," contains six essays that explore the complex ways in which ritual wind instruments are used to introduce natural sounds into human social contexts and to cross the boundary between verbal and nonverbal communication. The interplay of lexicality and musicality in the playing of sacred wind instruments is often regarded as a privileged means for human communication with, or impersonations of, mythic beings, such as the spirit-owners of forest animals, fish, birds, and plants. Part 1 explores the highly diverse ways in which indigenous South American peoples (Yagua of Peru, Kamayurá of Brazil, Wakuénai of Venezuela, Curripaco of Colombia, Piaroa of Venezuela, and Nambikwara of Brazil) have developed these interminglings of musical sound and verbal form and meaning to construct unique cultural poetics of ritual power. At the same time, the essays demonstrate how these culturally specific ways of integrating sounds and meanings are closely associated with animals, birds, fish, and other natural species. Flutes, trumpets, and other wind instruments are often named after natural species, and their sounds are said to be directly connected to the eating, mating, and other behaviors of animals.

The general theme of "seeing" versus "hearing" cuts across the entire spectrum of naturalized, lexicalized musical sounds and is prevalent throughout Lowland South America. In many cases, women and uninitiated children are forbidden to *see* ritual flutes and other aerophones yet are allowed or even required to *hear* the music of these instruments and are in some cases even expected to "converse" with them. Keeping instruments out of women and children's sight but not their hearing also allows male flute players to use the sounds of their instruments to disguise their voices, the sounds of which would easily allow women to identify the men who made it.

The essays in part 2, "Musical Transpositions of Social Relations," explore some of the ways in which ritual wind instruments and their music enter into local definitions and negotiations of

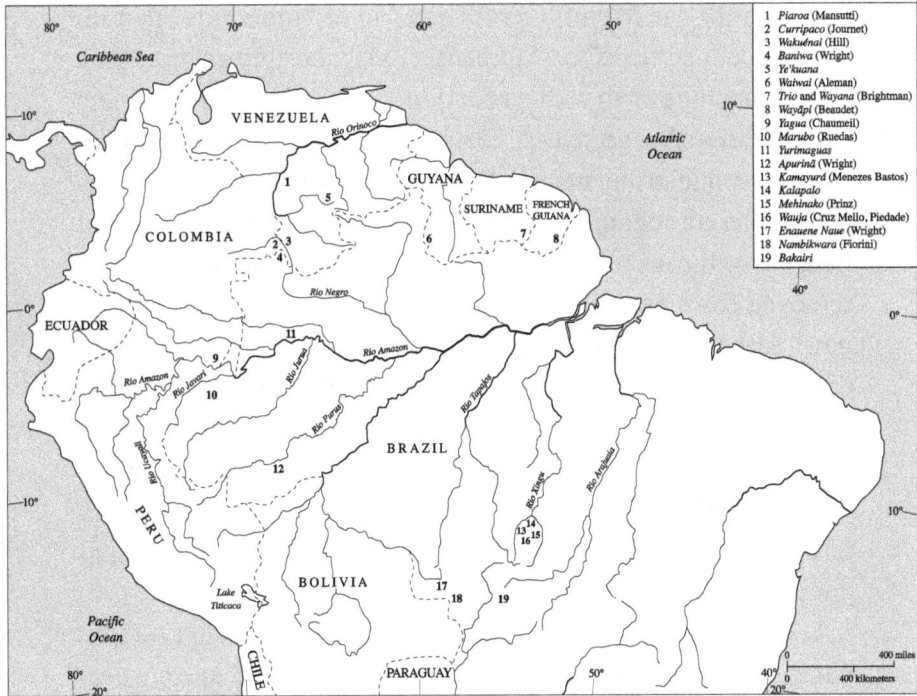

1	*Piaroa* (Mansutti)
2	*Curripaco* (Journet)
3	*Wakuénai* (Hill)
4	*Baniwa* (Wright)
5	*Ye'kuana*
6	*Waiwai* (Aleman)
7	*Trio* and *Wayana* (Brightman)
8	*Waýãpi* (Beaudet)
9	*Yagua* (Chaumeil)
10	*Marubo* (Ruedas)
11	*Yurimaguas*
12	*Apurinã* (Wright)
13	*Kamayurá* (Menezes Bastos)
14	*Kalapalo*
15	*Mehinako* (Prinz)
16	*Wauja* (Cruz Mello, Piedade)
17	*Enauene Naue* (Wright)
18	*Nambikwara* (Fiorini)
19	*Bakairi*

MAP 1. Indigenous communities in Lowland South America covered.

relations between men and women, kin and affine, and insiders and outsiders. Starting with case studies among the Trio, Wayana, and Waiwai of Guiana, a comparative sociological perspective emerges through three studies of ritual flute music and women's ritual singing among the Wauja and Mehináku in the Upper Xingu region of Brazil; the Marubo of Brazil; and four Arawak-speaking groups in widely separate regions of Brazil. The playing of aerophones in ritual and secular contexts is frequently associated with shamanic powers of curing and purification; relations between mythic ancestors and their human descendants, both living and dead; and relations between kin and affines. Although for the most part ritual flutes and other aerophones are used to evoke concepts of stability and continuity through celebrating natural and social processes of rejuvenation, the adoption of "Inca" flutes among the Marubo serves as a foil of "otherness" that indirectly defines "true" or "authentic" Marubo cultural practices.

We conclude with a short section, or "Coda: Historical and Comparative Perspectives," consisting of two essays, a study of sacred wind instruments in a European museum and a commentary on the ethnographically based studies in parts 1 and 2. What happens to the meaning of ritual wind instruments that have been removed from an indigenous social milieu and placed in museums? Although such preservation of sacred artifacts could be understood as a simple process of alienating them from their original meanings, the study of sacred instruments collected in the northwest Amazon by early twentieth-century German ethnologists and placed in the Museum of Ethnology in Vienna, demonstrates a more complicated process in which sacred meanings are still highly salient.

Several generations of anthropological researchers in Lowland South America have reported on the importance of wind instruments and their music in collective rituals and ceremonies. Yet only in the last thirty or so years have anthropologists trained as ethnomusicologists gone into the field with the specific goals of recording indigenous music and understanding how the production of musical sounds is situated in people's everyday social and economic activities, their forms of political organization and history, and their ways of conceptualizing nature and cosmos. A 1993 overview of the ethnomusicology of Amazonia concluded that "substantial works on the topic can be counted on the fingers of one hand" (Beaudet 1993: 527, our translation) and included two studies of vocal music among Gê-speaking peoples (Seeger 1987; Aytai 1985), one survey of Nambikwara music (Halmos 1979), and two works on music of the Tupí-speaking Kamayurá (Menezes Bastos 1978, 1989). By 2000, this list had grown to include major new studies of music among the Warao (Olsen 1996), Arawak-speaking Wakuénai (Hill 1993), and Tupí-speaking Wayãpi (Beaudet 1997). In addition to this growing number of book-length studies, an increasingly rich literature on specific genres of indigenous Amazonian music began to appear in scattered journals and edited volumes (Avery 1977; Beaudet 1989, 1992, 1999; Canzio 1992; Chaumeil 1993; Graham 1986; Hill 1979, 1986, 1987, 1994; Menezes Bastos 1995, 1999; Seeger 1979, 1991). Building on this new generation of ethnomusicological research in specific localities, *Burst of Breath* fills a major gap in existing literature by advancing a comparative perspective on the widespread uses of aerophones across widely dispersed regions of Lowland South America.

Indigenous Ritual Wind Instruments in the History of Western Imagination

Carrying out research on the ritual role of wind instruments in Lowland South America inevitably implies an interest in the ideas and representations found in the accounts by the first European observers. We know, in fact, to what extent these "instruments of the shadows," as C. Lévi-Strauss (1966) termed that group of instruments played mostly at night, influenced the first chroniclers of the conquest as well as later eyewitnesses in their views of American Indian religion. In the course of history, there were many interpretations of such ceremonies. They have captured the attention of travelers and missionaries alike since the seventeenth century and, more recently, that of ethnographers. The first descriptions saw these rituals as a "religion of the devil" or a false religion at the service of evil forces—an appraisal destined to discredit at once the indigenous beliefs in view of the nascent evangelizing project.[1] The name *Yurupari* (*jurupari*) has often been given to these rituals, since they were already known in many parts of Amazonia as "Yurupari feasts" during colonial times. The term refers to a mythical hero's name of Tupí-Guaraní tradition and was adopted by the first missionaries, who rendered its meaning as "the devil" in the Catholic religion. Thus any rituals using wind instruments prohibited to women were systematically described in the literature as " Yurupari feasts" or "feasts of the devil."

We owe to the Jesuit Samuel Fritz the first precise accounts of the existence of such ritual performances in the Amazon at the end of the seventeenth century, namely, the ritual of Guaricaya among the Yurimaguas. In Fritz's accounts of these rituals, we find the main characteristics that, beginning in the nineteenth century, were reported in the " Yurupari feasts" of the northwest Amazon: secret flutes, visual prohibition for women, ritual flagellation, etc. (Porro 1996, 137–41). Let us read what the missionary wrote:

> Remarkable is the fact, that I at this time found out in this village of the Jurimaguas, which is that in a revelry that they were making, I, from the ranch where I was lying, heard a flute played, that caused me so great terror, that I could not endure its sound. When they left off playing that flute I asked what it meant, and they answered me, that they were playing in this manner, to Guaricaya, that was the Devil, who from the time of their ancestors came in visible form, and took up his abode in their villages; and they always made him a house apart from the village within the forest, and there they brought him drink and the sick that he might cure them. Finally enquiring with what kind of face and form he came, the chief, named Mativa, answered: "Father I could not describe it, only that it is horrible, and when he comes all the women with their little ones flee, only the grown-up men remain, and then the Devil takes a whip that for this purpose we keep provided with a leather lash made of the hide of a Sea-Cow, and he flogs us on the breast until much blood is drawn. (Edmundson 1922: 61)

This description emphasizes an element that we encounter today in many Amazonian cultures: the curative power of the flutes (see the Wauja, this volume). This fact suggests a direct and ancient relationship between shamanism and the flute rituals, whose "breath" or music (or the simple act of seeing them) had the power to cure certain illnesses. Among the contemporary Kalapalo, it is said that many people (including some women) have been cured of serious illnesses by the sacred flutes:

> In the Kalapalo village, several individuals are designated *kagutu oto*, by virtue of having been cured by the playing of trumpets during a severe illness. These persons are responsible for announcing when the trumpets are to be played, seeing that there are men to play them, keeping the *kuakutu* (trumpets) in repair, making payment to both players and specialists, and storing the trumpets in their houses when they cannot be played. (Basso 1973: 61)

Among the Bakairi, in contrast, the sacred flutes aid shamans in contacting their own helper spirits: "The spirit that then appeared to him [a shaman apprentice] instructed him how to make a flute which he kept in the sacred flutes house, and gave him a special tune by which he could always call his spirit helper. The novice had then to prove himself by curing some sick person or by finding lost property. If he were successful he became a recognized shaman" (Oberg 1953: 75).

In the first half of the eighteenth century, the Jesuit José Gumilla wrote about the sacred flute rituals. He related it this time to the funerals held by the Saliva of the Orinoco basin. His testimony is remarkable because it establishes the relationship between the flutes and the treatment dispensed toward the dead and because of his precision in describing the instruments, of which he left us a curious graphic representation (Gumilla 1758: 303–10, and plate facing page 303; Mansutti Rodríguez 2006: 11–12). In 1782, another missionary, Jesuit Felipe Salvador Gilij, connected the flute ritual among the Maypure with a kind of "cult to the serpents" (Gilij 1987: 234–38), although later sources talk about a cult toward plants. Alexander von Humboldt, the first scientist to travel to the Arawak region of the Upper Orinoco, described the use of the *botuto* trumpets as part of the ritual of propitiating fruits. According to him, the shamans would often play the sacred instruments under palm trees to secure their fertility (Humboldt 1822: 336–39). Humboldt also saw the cult of the botuto as the locus for a possible political transformation of these societies toward hierarchical or more complex models. Humboldt's study of the Arawak ritual flutes is important in that it initiated studies in the field. As it is well known, Humboldt was acknowledged as the most influential scientist of his time. His works were long considered one of the main sources of scientific knowledge on South America. They were also thought to have had a great impact on the development of modern anthropology, at least in North America, in the early twentieth century. Humboldt's pioneering work inspired a series of investigators of Amazonia throughout the nineteenth century, especially the German naturalists Carl Friedrich von Martius and Johann Baptist von Spix, and later the German ethnologists Karl von den Steinen, Paul Ehrenreich, Max Schmidt, Konrad Theodor Preuss, Theodor Koch-Grünberg, and Curt Nimuendajú—all of whom followed Humboldt's steps in becoming interested in indigenous music and ritual.

The first reference to the cult of the Yuruparí as such comes from the writings of Alfred Russell Wallace, who traveled on the Vaupés River in 1850 and 1852 and witnessed the ritual (Wallace 1853). After his testimony, the description of this cult on the part of travelers, missionaries, and ethnographers that explored this region became commonplace (Hugh-Jones 1979: 4–5; Orjuela 1983: 45–69). Koch-Grünberg (1909–10), in particular, became notable in this field when he undertook several trips to Amazonia between the years 1898 and 1924 that allowed him to witness several Yuruparí ceremonies. The recordings of flute music and songs that he made during these trips are the earliest sound recordings from the region.[2]

During this same period, the outpouring of scientific interest in sacred wind instruments from Amazonia and other regions of the American tropics spilled over into western literature and popular culture. Oscar Wilde, for example, included a very detailed listing of indigenous musical instruments from Latin America in his novel *The Picture of Dorian Grey*.

> He collected together from all parts of the world the strangest instruments that could be found, either in the tombs of dead nations or among the few savage tribes that have survived contact with Western civilizations, and loved to touch and try them. He had the mysterious *juruparis* of the Rio Negro Indians, that women are not allowed to look at, and that even youths may not see till they have been subjected to fasting and scourging, and the earthen jars of the Peruvians that have the shrill cries of birds, and flutes of human bones such as Alfonso de Ovalle heard in Chili, and the sonorous green jaspers that are found near Cuzco and give forth a note of singular sweetness. He had painted gourds filled with pebbles that rattled when they were shaken; the long *clarin* of the Mexicans, into which the performer does not blow, but through which he inhales the air; the harsh *ture* of the Amazon tribes, that is sounded by the sentinels who sit all day long in high trees, and can be heard, it is said, at a distance of three leagues." (1926: 200–201)

Despite the exoticism and romanticism in Wilde's literary account of Latin American musical instruments, his list demonstrated a relatively precise knowledge of these artifacts and their social and geographic origins.

Many interpretations of these musical instruments and the ceremonies in which they are played have since been put forth, each one evidently answering to the pressing questions and views common to the times when they were raised, without nonetheless exhausting the theme of the flute rituals. People have seen this ritual as a cult of the ancestors (Goldman 1963), albeit suspecting a certain Andean influence, as well as a rite of passage related to the context of an "initiation into a secret men's cult" (Hugh-Jones 1979: 7), or simply as a ritual of masculine domination associated in one way or another with the institution of "the men's house" (Schaden 1959: 149–63). Rejecting all these theses, Reichel-Dolmatoff (1989) proposed his version of the Yuruparí as a rite oriented first and foremost toward the promulgation of exogamy. Recently, the first native ethnographic account of the distinct types of the *dabacuri* flute rituals belonging to the Desana were published by two Desana authors, an accomplishment that entails, without a doubt, the most comprehensive and detailed study of the flute rituals among the Desana (Diakuru and Kisibi 2006).

Nowadays, the tendency is not to consider the flute rituals as a cult of the ancestors or as a symbol of masculine domination, but more as a ritual of growth and fertility that associates both masculine and feminine elements. But more than any other cultural manifestation, the flute rituals could not be extricated enough from the dominant paradigms or prejudices that marked all the distinct historical times, from its definition as a religion of the devil until the more recent interpretations about fertility. In spite of the lack of agreement, it seems there is at least a point of consensus among authors concerning the hypothesis of the Arawak as the center and main axis of diffusion of the sacred flute ceremonials in Lowland South America.

We should remind ourselves that in South Americanist studies, the theme of secret flutes and associated rituals has played an important role in the great classifications by cultural areas in the 1950s, as in the case of the *Handbook of South American Indians* (1946–50). In the model adopted by the editor of the *Handbook*, Julian Steward, the demarcation between the so-called northwest Amazonian tribes and the Montaña tribes follows in a certain way the line marking the presence of this presumed cult of the sacred flutes.

Instrumentarium Amazonia

Before entering into a more detailed consideration of the religious and other meanings of ritual wind instruments and their music, we begin with a brief summary of the instruments themselves. Following the lead of Curt Sachs and Erich von Hornbostel (1914), musical instruments can be classified into four broad families according to the manner in which they produce sound. Membranophones, or drums and related instruments, create sound through vibration of a membrane caused by striking or rubbing. Cordophones are stringed instruments on which sounds are produced through striking, rubbing, or plucking a stretched cord. Idiophones, such as rattles and log drums, produce sound by striking or rubbing solid materials without the use of strings or membranes placed under tension. Aerophones are wind instruments in which sound is produced by the passage of a stream of air across the edge of an orifice or through a valve.

A complete survey of indigenous South American musical instruments is provided in *Musical and Other Sound Instruments of the South American Indians: A Comparative Ethnological Study*, by Karl Izikowitz. It is immediately clear that aerophones and idiophones are the two families of instruments most highly developed among indigenous South American peoples. As for cordophones, Izikowitz (1970: 201–206) lists only simple musical bows from Patagonia and eastern Peru and some violins introduced among the Warao, lowland Quechua, and a few other groups by missionaries during the colonial period. However, it appears that the geographic distribution of musical bows and European violins is somewhat broader than Izikowitz believed and extends across an arc from southern Bolivia, where the Weenhayek use musical bows and the Guaraní play violins, and as far north as the Shuar of eastern Ecuador (Beaudet, personal communication, 2007).[3] Likewise, membranophones are relatively scarce in South America, and "The great majority of them are nothing but copies of European military drums" (Izikowitz 1970: 165). Percussive or struck idiophones, however, are much more numerous and well developed in South America and include many kinds of wooden drums, jingle and hollow rattles, and stamping tubes (Izikowitz 1970: 7–160). Aerophones, or wind instruments, are still more numerous and diversified than the percussive idiophones and include many kinds of valve instruments (trumpets and clarinets) and an even larger variety of flutes (Izikowitz 1970: 207–410).

The family of aerophones breaks down into three broad groups, called "free" aerophones,[4] valve instruments, and flutes. Our primary interest is in exploring wind instruments through which a stream of air is directed into a closed space and made to vibrate either through a valve (clarinets and trumpets) or by splitting the air column against the edge of an orifice (flutes). The case studies include examples of most of the major kinds of valve instruments and flutes listed in Izikowitz's typology: "simple" and "complex" trumpets, clarinets without stops, flutes without airducts (both with and without stops), and duct flutes (with and without stops).

The most common form of valve instrument in Lowland South America is the trumpet, or a hollow, often tubular resonator with a relatively large aperture into which the lips are tightly compressed and a stream of air causes the lips to vibrate in a valve-like manner. Simple trumpets, or single tubes lacking separate mouthpieces, include the bark trumpets found mainly north of the Amazon River and made by wrapping bark spirally into cone-shaped resonators held together by a framework of sticks attached to the outside of the resonators. In *Burst of Breath*, we find these bark trumpets among the Wakuénai/Curripaco/Baniwa of the Upper Rio Negro region (see essays by Hill, Journet, and Wright), the Yagua (see Chaumeil), and Apurinã (Ipuriná) (see Wright and Augustat). Complex trumpets, or ones in which a separate mouthpiece or embouchure is attached to a tubular resonator, are represented by *surubí* (catfish) trumpets of the Wakuénai/Baniwa/Curripaco. In these unique trumpets, a woven basketry tube is covered with melted resin and then attached to a separate mouthpiece (see Hill). Other complex trumpets are the Piaroa trumpets using clay vessels as resonators (see Mansutti Rodríguez) and "roarers," speaking tubes or megaphones used in rituals among the Yagua (see Chaumeil) and Wayana (see Brightman). Figure 1 shows the geographic distribution of complex trumpets in Lowland South America.

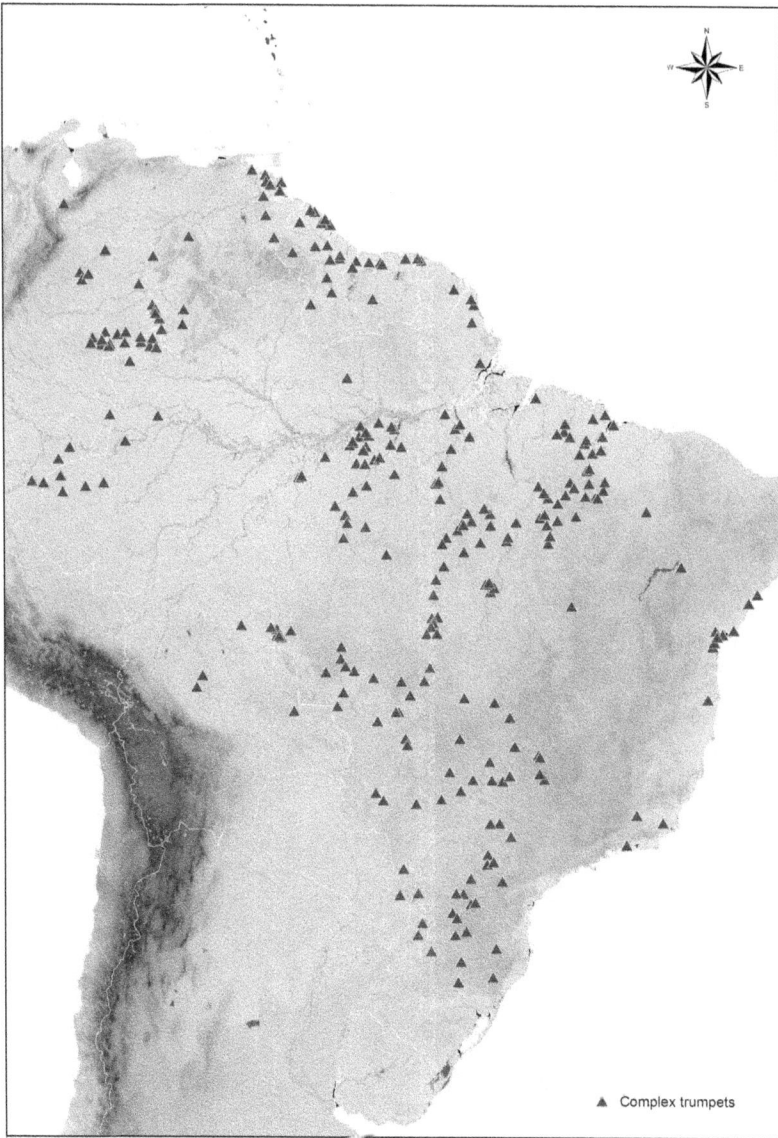

1. Geographic distribution of complex trumpets in Lowland South America.
Courtesy of Love Erikson.

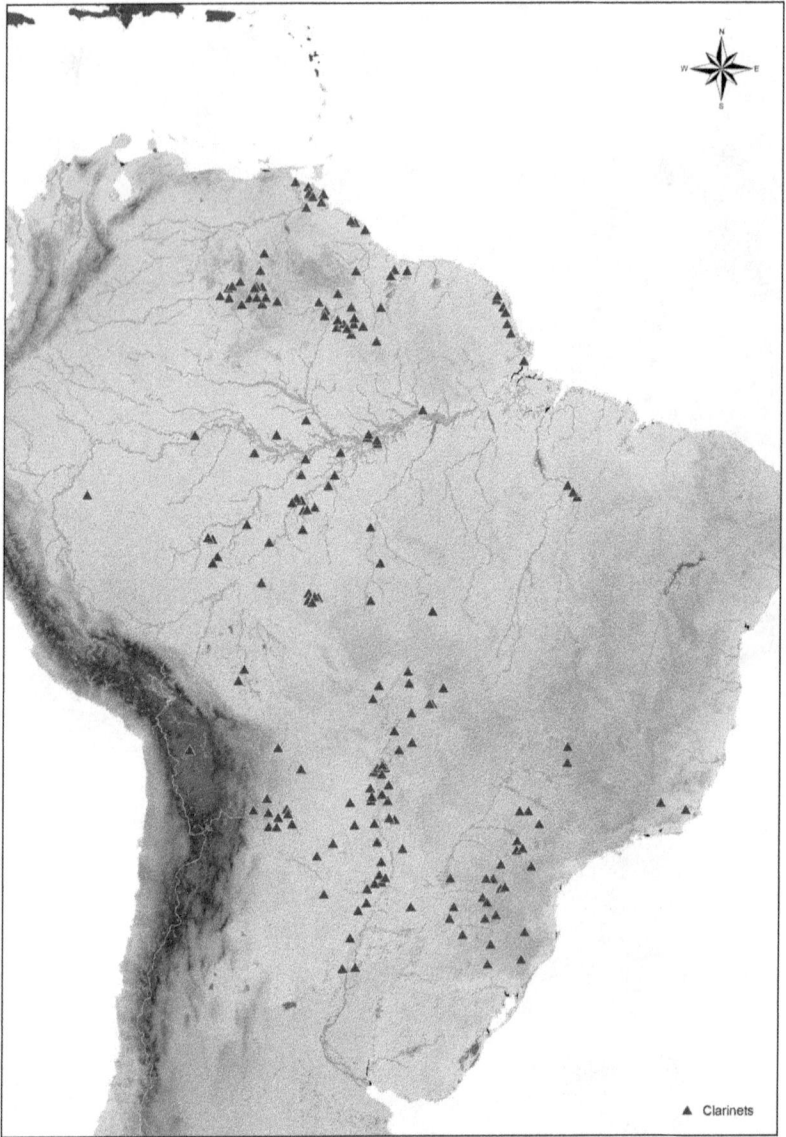

2. Geographic distribution of clarinets in Lowland South America. Courtesy of Love Erikson.

Clarinets, or valve instruments in which sound is produced by the passage of air across a single reed, are less common in Lowland South America than trumpets. Large clarinets up to two meters in length and without finger holes are found among the Ye'kuana and many Carib- and Tupí-speaking groups across the Guyana Shield region of northern South America; along the Jari and Oyapock rivers in northeastern Brazil; and along the Tapajos and Xingu rivers in Central Brazil (fig. 2). These large clarinets come in two varieties: idioglottal instruments in which the reed is built into the mouthpiece, and heteroglottal instruments in which the reed is fastened over the sound orifice in the mouthpiece. *Burst of Breath* includes only one example of these large clarinets, the *waitakala* idioglottal clarinets played in Wayana intercommunal ceremonies (see Brightman). Although clarinets are less common than trumpets and flutes in Lowland South America, their wide distribution across northern, central, and southern regions supports the conclusion that the large clarinets called *turé* originated in the central Amazon basin (Beaudet 1989: 108).[5]

Flutes, or wind instruments in which a stream of air is split against the edge of an orifice causing vibration of an air column within a closed space, are by far the most diverse group of aerophones in Lowland South America (fig. 3). The section on flutes takes up 143 out of 202 pages devoted to aerophones in Izikowitz's book.

> We have seen that there are such a large number of flute types in South America that one almost receives the impression that the Indians experimented more with this group of instruments than with any other. Every known type of flute construction in the world was also known to the Indians. Within the main types there is an infinite variation of form, due to the various materials used." (Izikowitz 1970: 409)

The essays in *Burst of Breath* bear ample testimony to the validity of Izikowitz's words written more than seventy years ago.

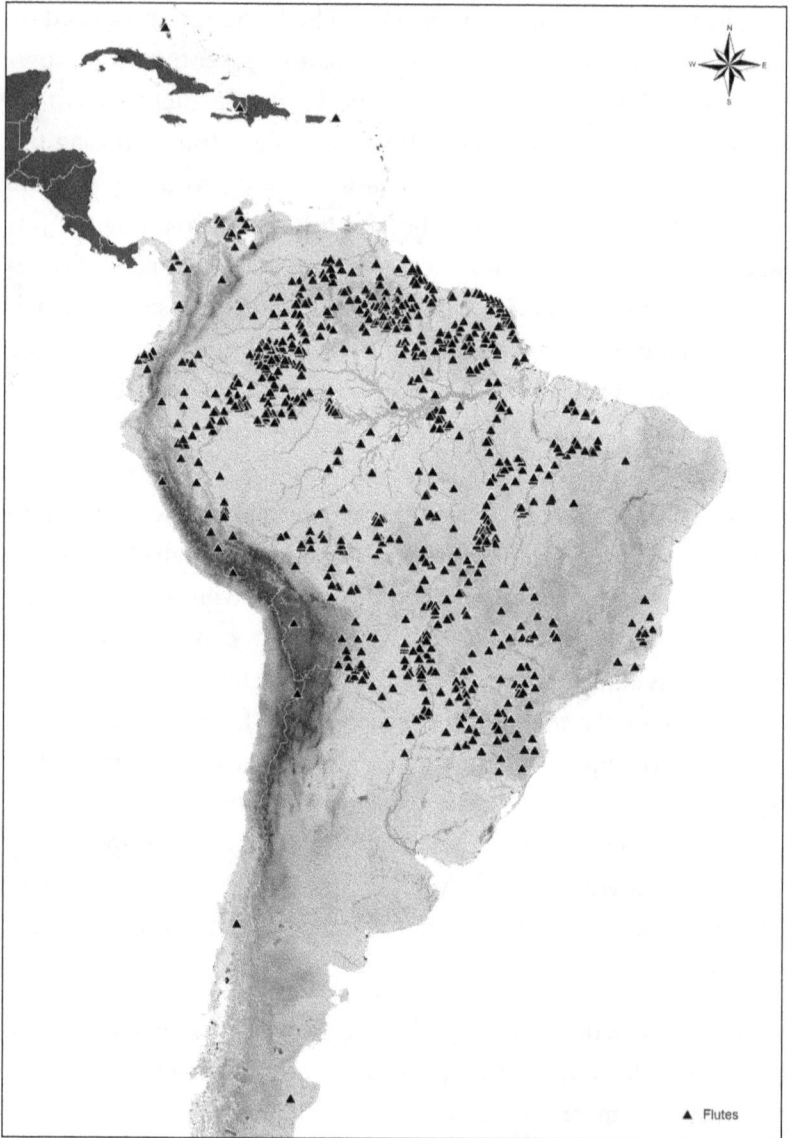

3. Geographic distribution of flutes in Lowland South America. Courtesy of Love Erikson.

Flutes can be divided into two groups: those into which an air current is directly blown without ducts and those in which airducts are used to channel the flow of air. Both groups can be made with or without stops, resulting in a quadrupartite taxonomy: (1) flutes without ducts and without stops, (2) flutes without ducts and with stops, (3) duct flutes without stops, and (4) duct flutes with stops. From an organological perspective, the essays in *Burst of Breath* lead to the conclusion that most of the "sacred" or otherwise centrally important flutes in Lowland South America are duct flutes rather than flutes without ducts (fig. 4). This is not to say that there are no examples of sacred flutes in the latter category but rather that there are fewer examples and that most of the sacred flutes are duct flutes. The Nambikwara, for example, make ductless, straight, bamboo end flutes with four stops and regard these as highly sacred instruments (see Fiorini).

Different kinds of duct flutes, both with and without stops, feature prominently in this book. The large pairs of ceremonial flutes called *máwi* (or *yapurutú*) among the Wakuénai/Curripaco/Baniwa are duct flutes *without* stops and with partly covered sound orifices (see Hill). The sacred flutes of Kuwái, the primordial human being of myth, among the Wakuénai/Curripaco/Baniwa are duct flutes *with* stops with partly covered sound orifices. Duct flutes with stops and with partly covered sound orifices also describe the Wawitihó flutes played in Yagua male initiation rituals (*ñá*) (see Chaumeil). In the Upper Xingu region, the sacred *yaku'i* flutes of the Kamaiurá and *kawoká* flutes of the Wauja and Mehináku are plug flutes with stops, or those in which a deflector (or plug) blocks nearly the entire proximal end of the flute's bore except for the airduct (see Piedade, Cruz Mello, and Prinz).

The elaboration of different aerophones—especially flutes, but also trumpets and clarinets—by indigenous peoples of Lowland South America is related to the great diversity of animal species to which the instruments' sounds and meanings are verbally

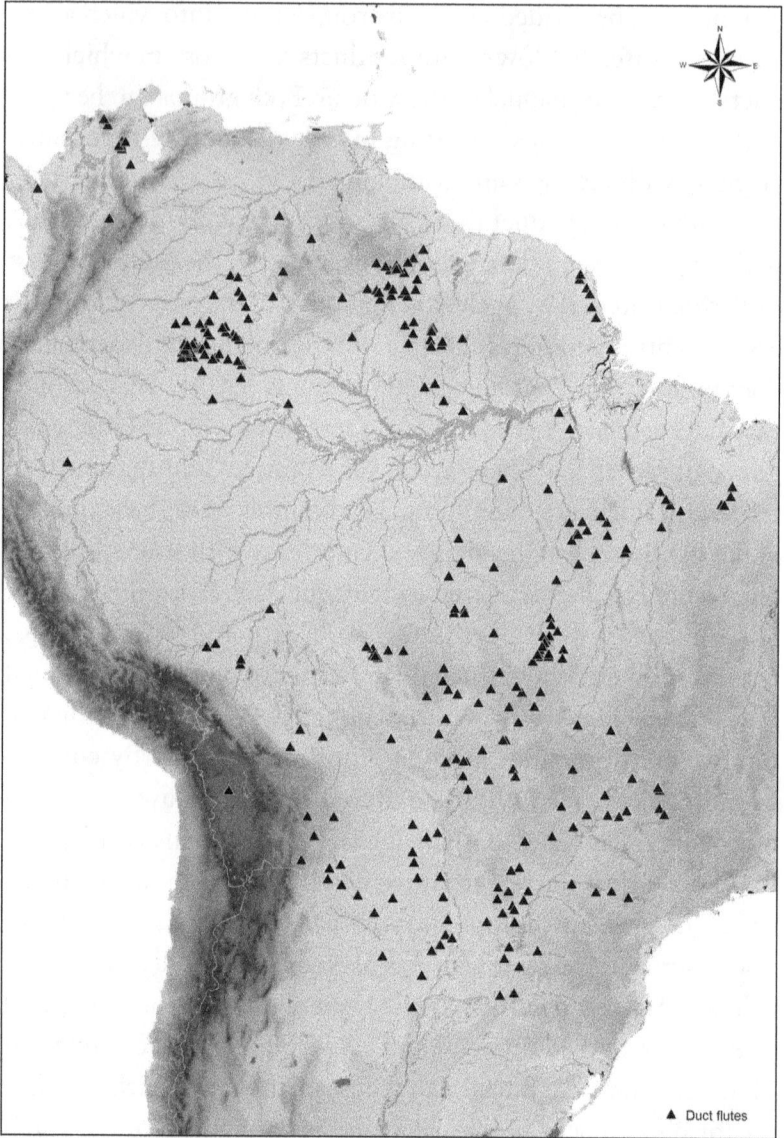

4. Geographic distribution of duct flutes in Lowland South America.
Courtesy of Love Erikson.

connected. The roaring of jaguars, the grunting of peccaries, the rumbling of catfish, the singing of birds and frogs, and many other natural sounds can all be ritually (re)introduced into human social worlds through these instruments. The instrumentarium Amazonia is to some degree also an instrumentarium zoologica Amazonia that ties specific peoples and local animal species into musico-choreographic configurations.[6] Animals are not only good to eat and think but play, sing, and dance into being in rituals.[7] Given the diverse range of natural sounds, spirit beings, and human discourses that are being produced with this instrumentarium Amazonia, it is hardly surprising that we find such an impressive variety of aerophones in Lowland South America.[8]

The preponderance of aerophones across such widespread geographic areas is no doubt also connected to the ancient migratory pathways and trade relations of specific Amazonian peoples and language groups. It is possible, or even likely, for example, that the spread of sacred flute complexes is closely linked to the migratory and trade routes of Arawak-speaking peoples across the Amazon basin and its tributaries (see Piedade).[9] Likewise, Beaudet's 1997 study of the geographic distribution of clarinets in Lowland South America finds a close link between these instruments' locations and the migratory movements of Tupí-Guaraní and Carib-speaking peoples.

Nevertheless, the elaboration of aerophones cannot be understood as merely the reflection of natural diversity and historical processes of human occupation. Instead, we must interpret this musical inventiveness as a basic feature of indigenous ways of constructing the world as a soundscape, or worldviews that privilege sound over vision. But to explain the predominance of aerophones rather than other families of instruments, we must turn to indigenous understandings of breath and breathing as expressions of life force and aerophones as ways of channeling breath into collective activities designed to ensure the continued fertility of animal nature as well as the regeneration of human social worlds.

Shamanic Musicologies

The fact that ritual wind instruments and in a more general sense "air-tubes" such as blowguns, mythic bones, hair-tubes, and in some cases hollow palm branches in indigenous Lowland South America are connected to, or perhaps even grounded in, the central importance of shamanic breathing has been known for some time to ethnologists and ethnomusicologists working in the region.

> The whistle is itself a space used to manipulate and transform breath. All Waiwai laymen may perform acts of magical blowing, but only the shaman uses magical whistles to summon helper spirits. "This use of an implement has presumably replaced the simpler form of ordinary blowing from the mouth" (Fock 1963: 116). Efficacy is bestowed on breath in a new way by introducing it into a different container. The use of the whistle, then, is a more effective and magical variant of blowing one's breath. (Sullivan 1988: 446)

In this Waiwai example, ritual aerophones are understood as an augmented or amplified form of shamanic breath or a transformation of it from a barely audible level of sound into a much louder sound that carries over long distances. The breath that is emitted in bursts but transformed into musical sound by compression into a closed space, whether musical wind instruments or other hollow tubular structures, beyond the cavity of the mouth and lips is more powerful than shamanic breath itself.

Ethnologists and ethnomusicologists have begun to focus on this connection between shamanic breath and ritual wind instruments. A musical ethnography of sacred singing and chanting among the Wakuénai of the Upper Rio Negro region (Hill 1993), for example, called attention to the significance of blowing, or the exhalation of voiced, aspirated sounds ("h-h-m-m-m-f-f-") made visible in the form of tobacco smoke. Master chanters (*malikái limínali*) are referred to as "blowers" (*sopladores*) in regional Spanish, and they refer to their ritual art as "to blow tobacco smoke" (*ínyapakáati dzéema*). It is through the exhalation of audible, visible breaths that the invisible power of spirit beings named in sacred singing and chanting is "materialized" and brought to bear on people, food, tools, and the rest of the experiential world.

A more recent study of instrumental music among the Wayãpi of French Guiana (Beaudet 1997) took this idea a step further and was the first to explore the proposition that the prevalence of aerophones in Wayãpi rituals and ceremonies "is linked to other equally important breathing manifestations in the region, typically those related to shamanism" (Menezes Bastos and Piedade 2000: 151). In this book, connections between shamanic breathing and the collective playing of aerophones are no longer simmering but have reached the boiling point. For just as shamanic breathing and blowing of tobacco smoke provide a means for using sounds—the privileged sense mode for mediating relations between spirit and human worlds—to make the invisible into the visible, so also does the playing of aerophones use sounds to make the invisible into the visible, at least for the initiated adult men who make and play these instruments.

The special relationship of shamans and other ritual specialists to the world of spirits—animal spirits, spirits of the dead, ancestor spirits—allows them to see these spirits, which remain invisible to nonspecialists. The hierarchical relationship between shamans who can see *and* hear (and converse with) invisible spirits versus nonspecialists who can only hear them serves as a template for, or perhaps even generates, the more collectivized relationship between initiated men who can see the sacred wind instruments and women and children who must hear the instruments' sounds but never see the instruments themselves. In effect, the men's seeing, making, and playing of sacred flutes and trumpets transports them into a shamanic realm of power that allows them to participate directly in processes of mythic creation, destruction, and transformation. Yet in order for this collective male journey through shamanic spirit worlds to happen, there must also be an audience of women and uninitiated children for whom the spirit beings remain invisible. The sounds of the flutes and trumpets add another layer of secrecy to the ritual journey by preventing women and children from being able to identify men's voices. Sacred wind instruments thus act as auditory masking devices that, together with strict prohibitions regulating who can see them, allow people to harness and give public expression to the power of shamanic breath in ways that suppress individual identities in favor of the collectively shared beings of mythic creation.

The role of sacred wind instruments as auditory "masks" becomes dramatically clear in cases where men make and wear masks in the same ritual moments when they make and play sacred wind instruments. Among the Wauja of the Upper Xingu region, a set of sacred kawoká flutes and masks must be made to commemorate the shamanic curing of individuals who have recovered from life-threatening illnesses believed to have been caused by *apapaatai* spirits. A number of these dangerous spirits are enacted in special masked dances, but "the mask of the kawoká is the flute, or firstly, the group of sacred flutes whose music is their epiphany" (see Piedade). The ensemble of masks and flutes are not merely representations of, or performances about, apapaatai spirits but "a very part of the ritually activated being" (Piedade 2004), or a collective singing-and-dancing-into-being of the powerful spirit beings of myth (Basso 1985). The Wauja conflation of flutes and masks makes perfect sense as a way of allowing groups of men to directly enact shamanic healing powers that require men to mask their identities in ways that privilege hearing over seeing.

The Wauja complex of kawoká flutes and masked dances provides an unusually vivid illustration of how shamanic breath and the playing of sacred flutes are two manifestations of the same ritual powers. The shamanic healer effects a return from death to life in individual Wauja, whose magical recoveries then become sources of collective ritual power to regenerate nature and society through the playing of kawoká flutes and dancing as spirit beings, or masks. A hypothesis that emerges from the chapters of *Burst of Breath*, building on Piedade's suggestion that the spread of sacred flute and trumpet complexes in South America is closely linked to the migratory and trade routes of Arawak-speaking peoples across the Amazon basin and its tributaries, is that these kinds of very tightly integrated relations between shamanic healing and sacred aerophones are found principally among Arawak-speaking peoples (see Wright, this volume). Among the Wakuénai/Curripaco/Baniwa of the Upper Rio Negro region, for example, the integration of shamanic chanting and singing, on the one hand, and the playing of sacred flutes and trumpets in collective rituals on the other is fully explained in a lengthy cycle of myths about the primordial human being, Kuwái. In the first part of the cycle, the body of Kuwái is said to emit powerful word-sounds that travel far away, creating the various species of animals, fish, and birds, and opening up the world for the first time (see Hill). It is this world-opening concatenation of words and sounds that becomes the template for shamanic singing and chanting in rites of passage at childbirth and puberty as well as in curing rituals. After teaching the sacred chants and songs to the first chant-owner, Kuwái is pushed into a bonfire, and the world of the first creation shrinks back to its original, miniature size. Trees and vines that grow from the ashes of Kuwái sprout up and, when felled by the trickster-creator (the father of Kuwái), become the sacred flutes and trumpets whose sound opens up the world for a second time. So whereas the first part of the myth cycle establishes the basis of shamanic breath as a world-creating synthesis of words and sounds, the second part asserts the power of sacred flutes and trumpets to re-create these shamanic powers through collective rituals. The integration of shamanic powers and sacred instrumental music is so complete that we can refer to them as shamanic musical configurations or analytical units in which shamanic and musical spheres are systematically linked together.

The case studies in this book demonstrate that shamanic musical configurations are not all cut from a single cloth and that they can take a variety of forms in which shamanic breath and the music of sacred wind instruments are less directly integrated than they are among the Wauja and Wakuénai/Curripaco/Baniwa. Among the Wasusu (Nambikwara) of Brazil, for example, we find that people "still stop the ends of the taboca with leaves when they pick them in the forest to make new flutes, so that the breath of the souls won't blow out and away" (see Fiorini). The use of sacred wind instruments among the Yagua of Peru displays two interesting parallels with shamanic breathing practices: (1) the privileging of sound over vision and other sense modes and (2) the theme of corporeal dissociation. Yagua shamans first establish contact with spirit beings by hearing their voices "becoming louder yeee EEEE as spirits get closer" (see Chaumeil). Only later do these spirits become visible to shamans, first as animal spirits and then in more human forms.[10] Corporeal dissociation, or experiencing a splitting apart of bodily flesh from bones as a step toward their reintegration, is a basic feature of Yagua shamanic practices. In male initiation rituals, this same process is generalized to groups of young men in relation with the sacred flutes and trumpets, which are perceived as the inner structure, or "bones" (ndu), of the hunting spirits. In this way, the young initiates experience the presence of the spirit entities in the form of a fragmented body (the flutes, that they "see" for the first time, embody the "voices" and the "bones" of the spirits), while the Yagua shamans experience the same process, but in their own body during their apprenticeship, and directly, not through a spirit instrument as in the male initiation. If we are right, the male initiation appears, here, as an indirect or attenuated form of shamanic experience. The process of corporeal dissociation would further demonstrate the shamanic nature of the flutes.

Another variety of shamanic musical configurations is found among Carib- and Tupí-speaking peoples of northeastern South

America. Among the Wayana of French Guyana, the playing of clarinets and flutes during intercommunal ceremonies is not directly rooted in shamanic breathing, yet there are important intertextual linkages between the two spheres established in myths and native musicologies. In studying these linkages, Marc Brightman finds a basic analogy in which "flutes are to blowing as death is to fertility." Flutes and clarinets are "bones" (sometimes literally, as in the flutes made from tortoise claws, armadillo claws, or animal bones) that signify death, but when men blow air through them to make music, their breath transforms death (cessation of individual organismic life) into fertility (collective renewal of nature and society).

The hollow, tubular shape of ritual wind instruments and their capacity for transforming the sounds of rapidly exhaled breaths into musical tones makes them ideal tools for conceptualizing and acting out various transformations within the overall scheme of shamanic journeys from life to death and back again. In the Wayana case mentioned above, ritual wind instruments act as "energy transformers" (Rivière 1969), and convert affines into kin metaphorically if not literally" (see Brightman). The significance of tubular structures in Lowland South America has also been linked to the prevalence of male and female genitalia—penises, breasts, wombs, birth canals, and umbilical cords—as symbols that ensure the flow of life by allowing passage of food, water, air, sound, semen, blood, children, and other vital substances. "Like rivers, anacondas, palm trunks, and flutes, the human body and its various parts—vocal apparatus, gut, bones, and genitals—are all tubes" (Hugh-Jones 2001: 252). Ritual wind instruments belong to this family of tubular structures that transform energy, sustain life, and convert potentially dangerous "others" (e.g., affines) into fully socialized members of local kin-based communities (on this subject, see Chaumeil 2001). Ritual wind instruments are thus symbols of the ability to build connections, or enduring social ties, between the living and the dead, mythic ancestors and human descendants, humans and animals, men and women, kin and affine, indigenous peoples and nation-states, and so on. These sacred flutes, trumpets, and clarinets are the skeletal inner structure of the social body that binds together men, women, animals, spirits, and others into coherent universes of meaning and discourse.

The case studies in this book demonstrate several ways in which these "musical skeletons," or shamanic musical configurations, can be put to use in the building and transforming of social ties. For one thing, the ritual wind instruments themselves are frequently treated as human bodies (or body parts) that must be offered food and drink or that serve as socially appropriate ways of publicly asking local hosts for food or drink. In more specifically musical and choreographic terms, ritual wind instruments dramatize the building and transforming of social ties by being played together by groups of men in ensembles. Many of the flutes and all of the trumpets and clarinets in Lowland South America are what Izikowitz (1970: 215) calls "natural" instruments, or simple blowpipes lacking stops, or finger holes. The instruments' relatively simple technology means that they require ensembles of players to work together to produce complex melodies or other kinds of sound texturing, since single instruments played in isolation can only produce a single primary tone and the natural overtone series through harder and softer blowing. One of the clearest ways of using multiple instruments to build social ties is through the technique of alternation, or the hocket style of playing in which two or more instrumentalists play their notes in succession to produce a single melodic line of notes. The hocket style of playing is found widely in Lowland South America (see Hill 1979, 1987, 2004; Beaudet 1997; essays by Brightman, Hill and Chaumeil, this volume) and is quite prevalent in panpipe music throughout the Andean highlands.

The building of social ties by combining sounds is also accomplished through performances in which several instruments are played in unison to create complex blocks of richly textured sounds. Such orchestrations of wind instruments are important in the clarinet suites played among the Wayãpi of French Guyana (Beaudet 1997) and serve to create more stable, heterophonic chunks of sound that contrast with more dynamic solo passages in which melodic variations are employed to produce a sense of movement and change. Likewise, we find the playing of numerous sacred flutes and trumpets, each representing different animal species and body parts of the primordial human being (Kuwái) among the Wakuénai/Curripaco/Baniwa in Venezuela, Colombia, and Brazil to be a process of building stability and unity among groups of men, who collectively reconstruct the body of Kuwái by playing music together. Listening to these ritual flutes and trumpets played in unison gives the impression of standing in front of an impenetrable wall of sounds ranging from the booming bass of the four-meter-long jaguar bone (*dzáwiñapi*) trumpets to the shrill chirping of toucan (*dzáate*) flutes and everything in between.

In other contexts, however, these same blasts of sound, or bursts of breath, from multiple wind instruments are used not to build unity and stability in groups of men but to transform, or transport, them into the realm of mythic creation. In these settings, we find groups of men playing instruments at their highest volume, not in unison or delicate overlapping, but as sounds competing to be heard over one another in cacophonous, heterophonic blasts that serve as auditory "portals," acoustic thresholds or "looking glasses" that socially mark the movement from everyday social worlds into the realms of mythic creation. In Yagua male initiation rituals, for example, the arrival of hunting spirits follows a general pattern of trumpets followed by flutes, resulting in an alternation between more rhythmical and more melodic voices. There is no clear ordering of instruments within the ritual but "a will to produce a somewhat cacophonic ensemble of dissonant sounds and voices," or "a multiplicity of 'dissonant' sounds and voices" that subverts the orderliness of human discourses and narratives into a 'language' of the spirits by separating the constitutive elements of language that would only be found harmoniously together in humans" (see Chaumeil). The ritual use of "cacophony" and "dissonance" serves to mark the transition to a mythic space-time that is prior to and larger than the specific worlds of meaning that can be carved out through human language. Likewise, in *pudáli* ceremonial exchanges among the Wakuénai/Curripaco/Baniwa, groups of men playing *máwi* and *déetu* flutes, *kulirrína* trumpets, and *píti* whistles emit bursts of cacophonous sound to signify their social transition into the primordial space-time of the mythic trickster-creator (Made-From-Bone), thus letting their hosts know that the time has arrived to make formal speeches of offering and accepting the gift of smoked fish and game meat (Hill 1987). In a general sense, musical cacophony is a powerful way of giving material form to the idea of the mythic primordium as an unfinished time with no clear distinctions between humans and animals, men and women, and living and dead.[11]

Echoing the solitary journeys of wandering shamanic loners across the cosmos in search of their patients' lost souls, musical expressions of movement and transformation often take the form of theme and variation played in duets or larger ensembles of wind instruments. Wayãpi clarinet suites, for example, consist of thematic solos, which are variable and different for each specific piece, and blocks of sound that do not vary and that are played by larger ensembles of clarinetists (Beaudet 1997; Menezes Bastos and Piedade 2000: 149). Wayãpi musicians have created approximately 230 solo themes, which together with dance movements are imitative of many animal species (Menezes Bastos and Piedade 2000: 147–48). These 230 themes are organized into eight distinct suites, or arrangements, of several pieces into an ideal order. Each suite has its own stock of thematic solos. The exact number and order of thematic solos within each suite is not fixed, and there is variation between one performance of a suite and the next. Improvisation on thematic solos is allowed in some of the suites but not in others. The repertoire of eight suites thus provides a general structure that allows a great deal of variability in arrangements at the level of specific performances but that anchors this melodic variability with invariant blocks of sound played by groups of instrumentalists.

Similar processes of theme and variation, always balanced by stabilizing phrases and tones that do not vary, are evident in the music of sacred kawoká flutes among the Wauja of the Upper Xingu region in Brazil. Unique phrases are learned in dreams, played only by the master flautist, and make use of a "set of operations of motific variation," "such as augmentation, diminution, transposition, inversion, inclusion, exclusion, and duplication" (see Piedade). These unique phrases are regarded as more powerful than the standard phrases, which are played by all three flutists (the master flutist and his two apprentices) and contain little or no variability. Meanwhile, Wauja women make use of the same principles of theme and variation against the background of invariant phrases and a tonal center in the special genre of songs, called *kawokakuma*, performed in female-controlled iamurikuma rituals. Variations are created through "transposition, a small alteration of interval or rhythm at the beginning or end of the motif, an addition or exclusion of a note, or others" (see Cruz Mello). It is important to remember that these parallel uses of theme and variation in Wauja men's sacred flute music and women's ritual singing directly participate in shamanic rituals designed to cure individuals who are believed to have been afflicted by apapaatai spirits. In other words, Wauja sacred flute music and its female counterpart form a complex of ritual actions, or a shamanic musical configuration, that produces social movements and transformations rather than mere reaffirmations of existing social ties.

A final example of theme and variation comes from the pudáli ceremonial exchanges among the Wakuénai/Curripaco/Baniwa of the Upper Rio Negro region. In the final stage of pudáli ceremonies, after the gift of cooked food has been distributed for consumption among guests and hosts alike, women from the host village are free to dance with visiting male flutists. Unlike the standardized and highly repetitive máwi flute duets played by large ensembles of flutists in the opening stage of pudáli, flute duets played in the final stage of the ceremony are highly improvisatory pieces in which a single theme is subtly altered to make dozens of shorter and longer variants with slightly different melodies (see Hill). Although these performances are not directly rooted in shamanic ritual practices in the same manner as the music played on sacred flutes and trumpets in male initiation rituals, the use of theme and variation in pudáli ceremonies is nonetheless concerned with social movements and transformations that unfold when groups of kin and affines from different communities come together to exchange and consume food and drink together and to celebrate the abundance of nature as the source of human social regeneration.

The Well-Tempered Aerophone

If we have explored in the second part of the book some of the ways through which the sacred flutes and their music mediate the relationships of men and women, relatives and affines, "us" and "them," we are particularly interested in this section in what these wind instruments produce or represent (and not only relate or mediate), in other words: in their existence as persons or "actors." As actors or persons, we are interested not only in these instruments' being and acting, their personalities, sensibilities, individualities, and idiosyncrasies, but also in their wants and desires. Several essays in this volume emphasize this "agentive" dimension (or agency) of the ritual flutes, especially as it concerns "the domestication of predation" (in the terms of Wright, this volume), or "the control of affinity" (in the words of Brightman, this volume).

To say that an entity is a person is, first and foremost, to grant it the quality of a member of a community or a given collectivity

(Taylor and Viveiros de Castro, 2006: 152). In this respect, it is important to notice that in many Amazonian cultures, the ritual flutes often constitute what could be called "a kinship group": a group organized around a network of kin terms and relations (affinal or consanguineal) and generational bonds (usually extending themselves, in a more or less standard way, between the second ascending generation and the first descending one: G+2/G-1). In some cases, these collectivities form specific groups of beings like the Kamayura's "yaku'i people" (see Menezes Bastos), where the relationship with the instrument spirits is expressed in terms of a generational class (or age set). Thus such relation can obtain from consanguinity or affinity, like that between brother/sister, senior/junior, husband/wife, man/woman (when the instruments are played in pairs), or a husband and his two wives (when they are played in trio).

On the other hand, in a much more generalized way, the instrument spirits are perceived as having a body that has to be taken care of, adorned, and nourished. They can be treated as complete bodies, but may often be described as embodying the arms, legs, bones, penis, etc.—the body parts of mythical personae or spiritual entities. Among the Wakuénai, for instance (Hill, this volume), the sacred flutes are parts of Kuwái's body, and that body produces music (Hill thus emphasizes the notion of "*corps musiquant*"). Among the Kalapalo (Basso 1985, 304–305, cited in Prinz, this volume): "the mouthpiece of the flute is called a 'vagina,' and when the flutes are stored at the house of the sponsor, it is said that they 'menstruate.'" The theme of male menstruation in relation to the flutes is a classic topic in Amazonia (see, for example, Fiorini and Menezes Bastos, this volume). As regards the Nambikwara, M. Fiorini emphasizes: "The flutes are not only bodies; they are the tracheas and the esophagus of spirits and the fact that the Nambikwara often blow tobacco or *chicha* through them makes that even more explicit."

Like any other entity with a given "body," the instruments are painted and copiously adorned with palm or plumes, but above all, they are invariably fed with distinct foods or substances (manioc beer, tobacco smoke, etc.). As a common theme, the ritual flutes are perceived as entities that are voraciously hungry and insatiably thirsty. The importance of food and of alimentary regimes in Amazonian cultures has been carefully documented in recent years, particularly in relation to the processes of familiarization or the construction of kinship (Taylor and Viveiros de Castro 2006; Fausto 2007). If offering foods to the spirits is tantamount to transforming them into relatives (in the same manner that the shaman becomes related to spirits by means of sharing, amongst other things, his alimentary habits during certain types of fasts), it is important to notice that in many cases, these varieties of food are of a special type (near, unfermented beer, as in the Yagua case). Spirits, like people, have their preferences and culinary customs; that is, they do not eat any kind of food at any one moment. There is an emphasis here on the theme of food exchange between humans and spirits, the latter of which, once they are satiated and contented, guarantee to human beings the abundance and availability of fish and meat. This exchange must involve the active participation of women, knowing that the preparation of foods—and especially that of manioc beer—is exclusively women's work. Without this participation, it is clear that the flutes would remain "silent." Also, on the theme of exchange, we look at how, in some cases (Wayana, Wakuénai/Curripaco), flutes or other instruments (like trumpets and clarinets) are used by guests as a way to politely ask their hosts for manioc beer and other drinks, as a kind of ritualized dialogue between groups of men and women. Similarly, we will look at the exchange of flutes or trumpets themselves (e.g., the catfish or *surubí* trumpets among the Wakuénai/Curripaco) as tokens of larger processes of giving and receiving between communities of people.

As persons, each spirit instrument has other characteristic attributes, such as proper names (frequently taken from names of natural species: animals, birds, plants, etc., or stars), as well as their own voices, with various qualities and modulations of sounds that evoke certain "states of spirit" (or sensible states), from compassion to anger, or else from happiness to sadness. Thus, among the Piaroa, Worá's voice is deep, repetitive, and evokes discipline and the norm, Chuvo's voice is sweet and discreet and it seduces; whereas Buoisa's voice is ridiculous, grotesque, scandalous, and expresses an unbridled sexuality (see Mansutti Rodríguez). Among the Nambikwara, the extremely beautiful tunes of the flutes evoke people's innermost desires (see Fiorini). We should also note that the instrument spirits are not usually played by themselves, but in groups, and often with an almost daily frequency, as in the Mundurucú case: "The frequent playing of the *karökö* is accepted as a necessary part of the ordinary round of village life" (Murphy 1958: 65). It is also customary that each instrument has its own specific character and particular sensibility: they must be treated with great care and consideration (whether inside or outside the flutes house), and must be played with great verve during male initiation rites.

Finally, as we have stated, the instrument spirits are rarely played in isolation, and their voices are often juxtaposed or combined in what we could apparently call a "dissonant cacophony," although it would be better to refer to this aspect as a form of "polyphonic music." In fact, to speak of a "cacophonous" mode can be disputed in the sense that it implies, a priori, a referential "harmony," which could perhaps reveal our own bias, one that does not necessarily correspond to the point of view and the aesthetic sensibility of indigenous musicians (see Beaudet). Nevertheless, we could also see in these particular musical worlds not only an entry point to the realm of spirits and myth (Hill, this volume), but also the expression of a certain precategorical way of thinking, that is, a form of thinking about cultural elements as a continuum, before they become part of distinctive categories (the universe where the figure of the trickster appears frequently associated with this kind of sound production). In this sense, perhaps it would be appropriate to question once again the opposition of "seeing"/"hearing" in relation to the ritual flutes: not exactly as if they were two discontinuous and autonomous processes, but in relation to an indigenous definition of sensorial experience where such domains (as well as others, like the sense of smell) are closely intertwined (the first contact with the spirits is auditory rather than visual). Most of the Amazonian ethnographic data calls in fact for a transformational continuity in sensorial experience (Gebhart-Sayer 1986; Keifenheim 1999; Lagrou 2007). In light of this, we could say that women and noninitiates find themselves, in the face of the spirit instruments, in a partial and limited sensorial state (restricted to hearing), appropriate to their social condition. We could compare this kind of experience to that of a shaman, capable of simultaneously seeing and hearing the spirits, whereas nonspecialists normally can only hear them (without seeing them).

Last but not least, the notion of "copy" should hold our attention. Among the Kamayurá, for example (Menezes Bastos, this volume), the flutes are perceived as copies (*ta'angap*) of certain water spirits, *mamaé*. Their condition as copies, however, apparently does not affect their "agentive" potential, since they can incarnate the spirits as well as share with them the same ontological nature. We thus see that the notions of "copy" and "original," when applied to cultural artifacts, make for a complex subject of study in these cultures. The question of the copy is equally of interest in view of the discussion put forth by C. Augustat (this volume) about the acquisition and the exhibition of these sacred instruments by museums. These instruments are often described in their cultures as gifts from mythical heroes whom they frequently incarnate, as we have shown, as a body or a part of the ancestral body. As such, these instruments are inalienable possessions that hypothetically cannot be exchanged, even if during the ritual they obviously produce exchanges between human beings or between humans and nonhumans. Otherwise, these "sacred" objects are susceptible to becoming simple merchandise in the hands of unscrupulous foreign collectors whose sole purpose may be gathering the maximum number of them for sale or for the museum. Often, as C. Augustat points out, indigenous peoples will make an effort to supply collectors with mere copies (as in the case of P. Ehrenreich among the Apuriña in 1888), or else they will give in to their demands while keeping the fact under the utmost secrecy and out of the sight of onlookers (as in the case of T. Koch-Grünberg among the Baniwa). Moreover, the acquisition of the flutes is generally the result of a decision made by a single indigenous individual (for political reasons), more often than the decision of an entire community, as shown in the case reported by C. Augustat of a Yuruparí instrument collected between 1972 and 1973 by F. Trupp and W. Ptak, and preserved at the Vienna Museum. We could also cite the case of the flutes appropriated by Father Coppi on the Vaupés River in 1883. It is thus probable that the interest manifested by the first travelers and anthropologists in these instruments has raised their value in the eyes of indigenous peoples. Based on her own experiences with the Piaroa, C. Augustat suggests, nonetheless, that the "sacred" character of such objects can be preserved (from the perspective of indigenous peoples) even if their material manifestations were transformed into merchandise. This double perspective in relation to such objects should therefore become a subject of great concern for the institutions that have preserved them, especially at the moment of their display in museums. On one hand, there is a need to satisfy the desire for knowledge by the public (how one should present these objects and what one should say about them becomes a question here), and, on the other hand, there is a necessity to respect the indigenous contexts in which such objects acquired their meanings and significances.

Musical Transformations in a Globalizing World

Whether the study of indigenous Amazonian wind instruments includes the acquisition of these artifacts for preservation and display in museums or merely the recording of their sounds in field situations, researchers inevitably become entangled in similar kinds of complex questions about the meaning and value of this special class of objects. One solution to this conundrum is to focus on specific moments of acquisition of sacred objects and to analyze these moments of exchange as movements between different regimes of value rather than simple losses of meaning and value (see Augustat). Ethnomusicologists and other researchers who document and interpret the ritual uses of sacred wind instruments and associated sounds and meanings must also come to terms with the multitude of ways in which indigenous musical traditions are changing as indigenous peoples navigate contemporary identity politics in South America.

Collective musical performances often form a central part of indigenous ways of expressing and recovering cultural identities in situations where these have been ignored, suppressed, or denigrated by outsiders. Using indigenous languages to speak to national or international audiences is a powerful symbol of authenticity that generates symbolic capital for leaders of indigenous movements (Graham 2002), but it pales in comparison with the expressive and practical force of entire communities of Xavante, Kayapó, and other Gê- and Tupí-speaking peoples of Central Brazil as they collectively sang- and danced-into-being an indigenous alliance in opposition to the proposed building of a hydroelectric dam on the Xingu River at Altamira in 1989 (Graham 2002; Turner 1991). What are the processes of musical changes that unfold in such moments of history and across such massive movements between radically different regimes of value? How do indigenous musical practices change when the purpose of performing music is no longer primarily that of connecting a community of people to ancestor spirits or other symbols of the origin of their social world but also to create, with ever-increasing urgency, new political and interpretive spaces for such sacred connections to persist in the globalizing nation-states of South America?[12]

Our primary goal here is to explore the historical and social meanings of sacred wind instruments within indigenous Amazonian communities and worldviews, for it is only through understanding how sacred wind instruments and their music are situated in specific social worlds that we can begin to address questions about how indigenous musical practices have transformed across a myriad of historical and contemporary forces. In any case, there is no suggestion here that shamanic musical configurations of Lowland South America—with their concern for coupling transformation, improvisation, and creativity to continuity, community, and persistence—are in any way static or ahistorical practices. Even in the earliest stages of interethnic contact with representatives of national societies, sacred wind instruments are capable of becoming dynamic sources of power, as they most certainly did when a group of Kamayurá men in the early 1950s deliberately showed the sacred *yaku'i* flutes to a chief's wife because she was having an affair with a powerful white outsider (see Menezes Bastos). Over longer periods as indigenous Amazonian peoples have adjusted to permanent interethnic relations within and against the national societies of South America, the meanings and uses of sacred wind instruments have changed in diverse, sometimes surprising, ways.

Among the Waiwai of southernmost Guyana, for example, men's flute playing was traditionally an important expression of manhood in which flute music provided a central way of demonstrating shamanic powers to attract game animals as well as sexual prowess in attracting women as lovers. Yet the younger generation of Waiwai men have abandoned the playing of flutes, "stating without exception that it is 'hard to blow'" and instead "have embraced a new medium in the form of battery-powered cassette players" in ways that largely reproduce the social purposes of flutes (see Alemán). Although some things have been lost and have undergone permanent change in this process of replacing flutes with boom boxes, other things have been gained as the younger generation of Waiwai men are coming of age in, and actively engaging with, a world filled not only with natural sounds and shamanic songs but also with a diverse soundscape of Guyanese and Brazilian popular music as well as American gospel and country music. Where this process will ultimately end up is impossible to predict, but it is clear that by shifting from flutes to boom boxes, these young men are re-creating a distinctively Waiwai social world under radically different historical conditions than those lived by their fathers and grandfathers.

Generational shifts of this kind are taking place in villages, towns, and cities across Lowland South America as indigenous peoples move from oral traditions to literacy and from word-of-mouth to the Internet in a matter of years. The many ways in which indigenous peoples accept, reject, and modify these new technologies and the access to their own and other musicalities that come along will be a rich field of study for ethnomusicologists and other researchers. Some indigenous groups, like the Suyá and Kamayurá of Central Brazil, refuse to allow any recordings of their traditional music to be placed on the Internet in digital formats, even for purely academic purposes of research and preservation (Anthony Seeger and Rafael Menezes Bastos, personal communications, November 2008). Other peoples like the Baniwa (Coripaco) of Brazil and the Wakuénai (Curripaco) of Venezuela have actively sought to have recordings of their narrative and musical traditions made available on their own websites or in research archives, such as the Archive of the Indigenous Languages of Latin America at the University of Texas (www.ailla .utexas.org).[13] The Baniwa-Coripaco of Brazil established a school in 2005, called the Escola Pamaali, for training young people in their indigenous cultural traditions. According to their website, the school is designed to provide youths with education in a location that is closer to their home communities and that would be a means for recovering and valorizing their culture. The object of the school is to "form persons who can live within and outside of their community without losing their own individual identity" (*www.pamaali.wordpress.com*, translation mine). Recovery of traditional genres of collective music and dance, as well as sacred shamanic song and chant, figures prominently in the school's activities.

The Pano-speaking Marubo of western Brazil demonstrate that indigenous communities can absorb new forms of musical expression from historical contacts with other indigenous peoples without abandoning their own specific ways of making music. Marubo elders claim that the end-blown flutes made of plastic and played by younger men are not Marubo but foreign (*nawa*), or "Inca," a phenomenon that apparently results from interactions between Marubo and Quechua-speaking men who worked together during the Rubber Boom of the late nineteenth and early twentieth centuries. The Marubo have institutionalized the generational differences between elders and youths by allowing youth to "incorporate nawa elements into Marubo rituals, while a core set of ritual actions organized by elders remains central to the Marubo self-definition" (see Ruedas). In contrast to the Waiwai process of replacing flutes with boom boxes, the Marubo institutionalization of generational differences allows for the addition of new musicalities—Inca-style flutes made of plastic and cassette recordings of Brazilian dance music—to the elders' tradition of singing and drumming during ceremonial feasts celebrating the making of a new hollowed-out log drum (*ako*). At the same time, however, the Marubo ability to absorb new musicalities resembles the Waiwai replacement of flutes with boom boxes in as much as it, too, results in a culturally specific way of engaging with the changing global soundscape.

Across Lowland South America, indigenous peoples have developed a rich variety of sacred and ceremonial wind instruments—clarinets, trumpets, and especially flutes—and have attached a mind-boggling array of culturally specific meanings to these wind instruments and their musical sounds. In all of the case studies presented here, these wind instruments, their sounds, and their meanings are central to indigenous ways of reproducing their social worlds by connecting them to natural processes of regeneration. Understood in these terms, ritual wind instruments are not merely aesthetic expressions of cultural differences or folkloristic remnants of a supposedly pristine indigenous past but dynamic symbolic practices of interpreting and engaging with the contemporary world we all share.

Notes

1. This demonization of indigenous religion has continued for a long time, and it certainly lasts until today in some places with the arrival of the fundamentalist evangelical missions. In order to understand certain mechanisms in use by missionaries in their project of deconstruction of Indian religion, a document written in 1883 by the Franciscan Iluminato José Coppi is of special interest to us. Coppi talks about the profanation of the Yuruparí flutes by missionaries living among the Vaupés Indians.

2. Several of these recordings, collected between 1911 and 1913, have been released on a CD-ROM in Berlin (Koch and Ziegler 2006).

3. The broader distribution of musical bows is alluded to in Anthony Seeger's statement that "Cordophones [are] rare in traditional indigenous music, with the possible exception of musical bows" (1986: 175, our translation).

4. Free aerophones, such as bullroarers, produce sound in the open air by whirling a wooden blade on the end of a string.

5. Izikowitz's conclusions that the large clarinets (or *toré*) "can hardly be old" and that "the clarinet may be a post-Columbian culture element in South America" (1970: 265) were based on the relatively small number—a dozen or so—of references to these instruments at the time of his research in the 1930s. Since then, ethnographers have reported the use of clarinets in many other indigenous societies of Lowland South America (Beaudet 1989: 98).

6. Beaudet 1997) develops a concept of "musical configuration" as an analyt-

ical unit "through which the musical and social spheres are systematically (because not mechanically) linked together" (Menezes Bastos and Piedade 2000: 150).

7. Note, too, how all these animal sounds are produced by humanly fashioned plant materials; how this arises from the myth of Kuwái's death and rebirth in the form of plant species made into flutes and trumpets; and how plants are used by the Wakuénai for making blowguns, fish traps, and flutes, suggesting that flutes and their music are in one sense merely part of the cultural tool kit, fashioned from plants, for transforming animals—fish and game—into products of human consumption and exchange—cooked meat.

8. Waiwai shamans make a direct, almost literal connection between ritual wind instruments and the animal species that they are designed to call. "The yaskomo [shaman] often employs an aid in summoning his helping spirit: he blows on a ant-eater claw to call the ant-eater, or uses a special kidney-shaped whistle when the harpy eagle is to be summoned" (Fock 1963: 116).

9. It is important to note, however, that the subandine branch of Arawak-speaking groups, such as the Yanesha, Asháninka, Mojos, and Matsiguenga, have apparently never used this kind of sacred flute.

10. The transposition of auditory patterns into visual designs is also a basic feature of shamanic curing rituals among the Shipibo-Conibo, a Pano-speaking people living along the middle Ucayali River in eastern Peru (Gebhart-Sayer 1985).

11. Drawing upon Clastres's 1972 ethnographic accounts of Guayakí male initiation rituals, Lawrence Sullivan finds an important connection between the use of cacophonous sounds in ritual performances of music and moments "of transition from one state of being to another that occurs by means of a symbolic death. . . . The singing contest between the three groups eventually escalates to a climax of violent, cacophonous chaos" (1988: 282).

12. For a case study of this kind of musical and social change expressed through collective performances of ceremonial flutes and other instruments, see Hill 1994. The duality of power patterning (Whitten 1988) evident in these performances is not a completely novel phenomena, since the playing of sacred and ceremonial wind instruments was undoubtedly prevalent in the way local indigenous communities negotiated their political and economic relations with "others" (e.g., affines, distant members of the same ethnolinguistic group, or members of different ethnolinguistic groups) long before the arrival of European colonizers in Lowland South America.

13. Digital recordings of all narratives and musical performances discussed in "Soundscaping the World" (see Hill, this volume) can be accessed in the "Kurripaco" collection (KPC001,-002, and-003) at www.ailla.utexas.org.

References Cited

Avery. 1977. "Maimandé Vocal Music." *Ethnomusicology* 21, no. 3: 359–77.

Aytai, Desidério. 1985. *O Mundo Sonoro Xavante.* Coleção Museu Paulista, Etnologia, vol. 5. São Paulo: Universidade de São Paulo.

Basso, Ellen. 1973. *The Kalapalo Indians of Central Brazil.* New York: Holt, Rinehart and Winston, Case Studies in Cultural Anthropology.

———. 1985. *A Musical View of the Universe: Kalapalo Myth and Ritual Performances.* Philadelphia: University of Pennsylvania Press.

Beaudet, Jean-Michel. 1989. "Les *turè*, des Clarinettes Amazoniennes." *Latin American Music Review* 10, no. 1: 92–115.

———. 1992. "Musique et alcool en Amazonie du Nord-Est." *Cahiers de sociologie économique et culturelle* 18: 79–88.

———. 1993. "L'Ethnomusicologies de l'Amazonie." *L'Homme* 126–28: 527–33.

———. 1997. *Souffles d'Amazonie: les Orchestres "tule" des Wayãpi.* Collection de la Société Française d'Ethnomusicologie, III. Nanterre: Société d'ethnologie.

———. 1999. "Polay, uwa : danser chez les Wayãpi et les Kalina. Notes pour une ethnographie des danses amérindiennes des basses terres d'Amérique du Sud." *Journal de la Société des Américanistes* 85: 215–37.

Canzio, Ricardo. 1992. "Mode de Fonctionnement Rituel et Production Musicale chez les Bororo du Mato Grosso." *Cahiers de Musiques Traditionnelles* 5: 71–96.

Chaumeil, Jean-Pierre. 1993. "Des Esprits aux ancêtres. Procédés linguistiques, conceptions du langage et de la société chez les Yagua de l'Amazonie péruvienne." *L'Homme* 126–28, nos. 2–4: 409–27.

———. 2001. "The Blowpipe Indians: Variations on the Theme of Blowpipe and Tube among the Yagua Indians of the Peruvian Amazon." In *Beyond the Visible and the Material: The Amerindianization of Society in the Work of Peter Rivière*: ed. Laura Rival and Neal Whitehead, 81–99. Oxford: Oxford University Press.

Clastres, Pierre. 1972. *Chronique des Indiens Guayakí.* Paris: Plon.

Coppi, Iluminato José. 1883. "Breve historia de las misiones franciscanas en la provincia amazonense del imperio brasilero con la que se describe hechos importantes e singularmente el culto directo que estas tribus indianas dan al diablo." Manuscrito depositado en el Museo Luigi Pigorini de Roma.

Diakuru (Américo Castro Fernandes) and Kisibi (Durvalino Moura Fernandes). 2006. *Buerí Kâdiri Marîriye: Os ensinamentos que nâo se esquecem.* Sâo Gabriel da Cachoeira: FOIRN-UNIRT, Coleçâo Narradores Indígenas do Río Negro, vol. 8.

Edmundson, George, ed. 1922. *Journal of the Travels and Labours of Father Samuel Fritz in the River of the Amazons between 1686 and 1723.* London: Hakluyt Society.

Fausto, Carlos. 2007. "Feasting on People: Eating Animals and Humans in Amazonian." *Current Anthropology* 48, no. 4: 497–530.

Fock, Niels. 1963. *Waiwai: Religion and Society of an Amazonian Tribe.* Nationalmuseets Skrifter, Etnografisk Raekke, 8. Copenhagen: National Museum.

Gebhart-Sayer, Angelika. 1985. "The Geometric Designs of the Shipibo-Conibo in Ritual Context." *Journal of Latin American Lore* 11, no. 2: 143–75.

———. 1986. "Una terapia estética: Los diseños visionarios del Ayahuasca entre los Shipibo-Conibo." *América Indígena* 46: 189–218.

Gilij, Felipe Salvador. 1987[1782]. *Ensayo de historia americana,* vol. 2. Caracas: Biblioteca de la Academia Nacional de la Historia.

Goldman, Irving. 1963. *The Cubeo Indians of the Northwest Amazon.* Urbana: University of Illinois Press.

Graham, Laura. 1986. "Three Modes of Shavante Vocal Expression: Wailing, Collective Singing, and Political Oratory." In *Native South American Discourse,* ed. Joel Sherzer and Greg Urban, 83–118. The Hague: Mouton de Gruyter.

———. 2002. "How Should an Indian Speak? Amazonian Indians and the Symbolic Politics of Language in the Global Public Sphere." In *Indigenous Movements, Self-Representation, and the State in Latin America,* ed. Kay Warren and Jean Jackson, 181–228. Austin: University of Texas Press.

Gumilla, José. 1758. *Histoire naturelle, civile et géographique de l'Orénoque,* vol. 1. Avignon: Chez la Veuve de F. Girard.

Halmos, Istvan. 1979. *The Music of the Nambikwara Indians (Mato Grosso, Brazil).* Budapest, Akademiai Kiado (*Acta Ethnographica Adademiae Scientarum Hungaricae*) 28, nos. 1–4: 205–350.

Hill, Jonathan. 1979. "Kamayurá Flute Music: A Study of Music as Meta-Communication." *Ethnomusicology* 23: 417–32.

———. 1986. "Myth, Spirit-Naming, and the Art of Microtonal Rising: Childbirth Rituals of the Arawakan Wakuénai." *Latin American Music Review* 6, no. 1: 1–30.

———. 1987. "Wakuénai Ceremonial Exchange in the Northwest Amazon Region." *Journal of Latin American Lore* 13, no. 2: 183–224.

———. 1993. *Keepers of the Sacred Chants: The Poetics of Ritual Power in an Amazonian Society.* Tucson: University of Arizona Press.

———. 1994. "Musicalizing the Other: Shamanistic Approaches to Ethnic-Class Competition in the Upper Rio Negro Region." In *Religiosidad y*

Resistencia Indígenas hacia el Fin del Milenio, ed. Alicia Barabas, 105–28. Quito: Abya-Yala.

——. 2004. "Metamorphosis: Mythic and Musical Modes of Exchange in the Amazon Rain Forests of Venezuela and Colombia." In *Music in Latin America and the Caribbean: An Encyclopedic History. Volume 1: Performing Beliefs: Indigenous Cultures of South America, Central America, and Mexico*, ed. Malena Kuss. Austin: University of Texas Press.

Hugh-Jones, Stephen. 1979. *The Palm and the Pleiades: Initiation and Cosmology in Northwest Amazonia*. Cambridge: Cambridge University Press.

——. 2001. "The Gender of Some Amazonian Gifts: An Experiment with an Experiment." In *Gender in Amazonia and Melanesia: An Exploration of the Comparative Method*, ed. Thomas A. Gregor and Donald Tuzin, 245–78. Berkeley: University of California Press.

Humboldt, Alexandre de. 1822. *Voyage aux régions équinoxiales du nouveau continent fait en 1799, 1800, 1801, 1802, 1803 et 1804*, vol. 7. Paris: Chez N. Maze, Libraire.

Izikowitz, Karl Gustav. 1970 [1934]. *Musical and Other Sound Instruments of the South American Indians: A Comparative Ethnographical Study*. Göteborg: Elanders Boktryckeri Aktiebolag; reprint, East Ardsley, UK: S. R.

Keifenheim, Barbara. 1999 "Performative Viewing and Pattern Art among the Cashinahua Indians (Peruvian Amazon Area)." *Visual Anthropology* 12, no. 1: 27–48.

Koch, Lars-Christian, and Susanne Ziegler, eds. 2006. *Theodor Koch-Grünberg: Gravações em cilindros do Brasil (1911–13)*. Berlin: Berliner Phonogramm-Archiv., text + CD-ROM.

Koch-Grünberg, Theodor. 1909–10. *Zwei Jahre unter den Indianern: Reisen in Nordwest-Brasilien, 1903–1905*. 2 vols. Stuttgart: Streker & Schröder.

Lagrou, Els. 2007. *A Fluidez da forma: arte e alteridade entre os Kaxinawa*. Rio de Janeiro: Top Books.

Lévi-Strauss, Claude. 1966. *Mythologiques 2. Du miel aux cendres*. Paris: Plon.

Mansutti Rodríguez, Alexander. 2006. *Warime: la fiesta. Flautas, trompas y poder en el noroeste amazónico*. Ciudad Guayana: Fondo editorial de la Universidad Nacional Experimental de Guayana.

Menezes Bastos, Rafael José de. 1978. *A Musicológica Kamayurá: para uma Antropologia da Comunicação no Alto Xingu*. Brailia, FUNAI.

——. 1989. *A Festa da Jaguatirica: uma Partitura Crítico Interpretativa*. PhD diss., São Paulo.

——. 1995. "Esboço de uma Teoria da Música: para além de uma Antropologia sem Música e de uma Musicologia sem Homem." *Annuário Antropológico* 93: 9–73.

———. 1999. "Apùap world hearing: A Note on the Kamayura Phono-Auditory System and on the Anthropological Concept of Culture." *The World of Music* 41, no. 1: 85–96.

Menezes Bastos, Rafael, and Acacio Piedade. 2000. "Souffles d'Amazonie: Les Orchestres "tule" des Wayãpi." *British Journal of Ethnomusicology* 9, no. 1: 143–56.

Murphy, Robert. 1958. *Mundurucu Religion*. Berkeley: University of California Press.

Oberg, Kalervo. 1953. *Indian Tribes of Northern Mato Grosso, Brazil*. Washington: Smithsonian Institution, Institute of Social Anthropology, publication no. 15.

Olsen, Dale. 1996. *Music of the Warao of Venezuela: Song People of the Rain Forest*. Gainesville: University of Florida Press.

Orjuela, Héctor H. 1983. *Yurupary: Mito, leyenda y epopeya del Vaupés*. Bogotá: Publicaciones del Instituto Caro y Cuervo LXIV.

Piedade, Acácio Tadeu de C. 2004. *O Canto do Kawoká: Música, Cosmologia, e Filosofia entre os Wauja do Alto Xingu*. Tese de Doutorado em Antropologia. PPGAS/UFSC.

Porro, Antonio. 1996. *O povo das águas: Ensaios de etno-história amazônica*. Petrópolis: Editora Vozes.

Reichel-Dolmatoff, Gerardo. 1989. "Biological and Social Aspects of the Yurupari of the Colombian Vaupés Territory." *Journal of Latin American Lore* 15, no. 1: 95–135.

Rivière, Peter. 1969. "Myth and Material Culture: Some Symbolic Interrelations." In *Forms of Symbolic Action*, ed. R. F. Spencer. Seattle: University of Washington Press.

Sachs, Curt, and Erich von Hornbostel. 1914. *Systematik der Muiskinstrumente*. Berlin: ZE, vols. 4 and 5.

Schaden, Egon. 1959. *A mitologia heroíca de tribos indígenas do Brasil: Ensaio etno-sociológico*. Rio de Janeiro: Ministerio da Educaçáo e Cultura

Seeger, Anthony. 1979. "What Can We Learn When They Sing? Vocal Genres of the Suyá Indians of Central Brazil." *Ethnomusicology* 23: 373–94.

———. 1986. "Novos horizontes na classificaçâo dos instrumentos musicaís." In *Suma etnológica brasileira*, tomo 3, ed. B. Ribeiro, Petrópolis.

———. 1987. *Why the Suyá Sing: A Musical Anthropology of an Amazonian People*. Cambridge: Cambridge University Press.

———. 1991. "When Music Makes History." In *Ethnomusicology and Modern Music History*, ed. S. Blum, P. Bohlman, and D. Neuman, 23–35. Urbana: University of Illinois Press.

Steward, Julian, ed. 1946–50. *Handbook of South American Indians.* 6 vols. Washington: Smithsonian Institution, Bureau of American Ethnology, Bulletin 143.

Sullivan, Lawrence. 1988. *Icanchu's Drum: An Orientation to Meaning in South American Religions.* New York: Macmillan.

Taylor, Anne-Christine, and Eduardo Viveiros de Castro. 2006. "Un corps fait de regards. Amazonie." In *Qu'est-ce qu'un corps?* ed. Stéphane Breton, 148–99. Paris: Musée du quai branly—Flammarion.

Turner, Terence. 1991. "The Social Dynamics and Personal Politics of Video Making in an Indigenous Community." *Visual Anthropology Review* 7, no. 2: 68–76.

Wallace, Alfred Russell. 1853. *A Narrative of Travels on the Amazon and Rio Negro, with an Account of the Native Tribes.* London: Reeve.

Whitten, Norman E., Jr. 1988. "Historical and Mythic Evocations of Chthonic Power in South America." In *Rethinking History and Myth: Indigenous South American Perspectives on the Past,* ed. Jonathan Hill, 282–306. Urbana: University of Illinois Press.

Wilde, Oscar. 1926 [1891]. *The Picture of Dorian Grey.* New York: Modern Library.

First Movement

Natural Sounds, Wind Instruments,
and Social Communication

1. *Speaking Tubes*

The Sonorous Language of Yagua Flutes

JEAN-PIERRE CHAUMEIL

Translated by José Antonio Kelly Luciani

Recent anthropological literature on Amazonia has shown that one of the specific ways of communicating with spirits (or with some categories of spirits) entails the choice of a nonverbal sound medium (most commonly an acoustic register, the tone of a voice, whistling, and music) rather than a linguistic one (the possible combination of the two forms notwithstanding). This is typically the case of the Yagua of the western Amazon, who are the main focus of this essay.[1] In fact, Yagua shamans impose on themselves several voice-deforming exercises in order to reach a very high pitch they say corresponds with the way spirits "speak." Their chants always begin with whistling sounds, which could be interpreted as "tuning into" the acoustic frequency of the spirits. The content of the chants, which varies little from one to the next, seems here to be less relevant than the tone or the register of the voice in which they are sung.[2]

Curiously, the study of sound types and acoustic registers employed in exchanges with spirits (mythical beings, animal masters, and other entities) has up to now received little attention on the part of specialists. The purpose of this essay is to portray the process of interaction with spirits through an analysis of the complex play of musical forms and other vocal expressions produced by the ritual flutes of the Yagua. According to the Yagua, the entities incarnating these instruments (representing "the voice" and "the bones" of certain spirit categories) play a significant role, not only in the management of natural resources (hunting, gathering, and fishing) but even more so in the growth and fertility of beings and things in the world.

An analysis of the types of sounds and acoustic registers employed in communicating with nonhumans should allow us a better characterization of these modes of interaction and the types of relations (or of actions) that these sounds induce. With the objective of reflecting on the nature and status of these sonorous "discourses," we will also be drawing on data from other Amazonian cultures. In doing so, we are following the path opened by several Amazonianist colleagues who study the musical repertoires of aerophone rituals, particularly the work of Rafael Menezes Bastos, who also contributes to this volume.

I

Perhaps one of the most salient features of communication with entities we call "spirits" is the use of special linguistic forms, sometimes referred to as "ritual," "secret," or even "esoteric" languages, that, being different from the language spoken in everyday circumstances, are normally unintelligible to most people. There are several means by which these differences are marked: using different languages or archaic words (that have fallen into disuse), or using stylistic procedures and other modifications that affect the *lexico* (metaphor), the syntax, or the morphology of words (by adding syllables or suffixes, the use of repetition, parallelism, mythical references, etc.). All these are well-known procedures generally referred to in the literature as the "spirit languages" used by shamans and ritual specialists (see, for example, Civrieux 1974, on the "magic language" of the Kariña of the Venezuelan Guiana). It would seem to be that what is being stressed is above all the act of communicating rather than the content of a dialogue (which varies in degree of intelligibility). As Cédric Yvinec (2004: 35) suggests, it is the fact that this discourse is different from human language that matters, not the information it may communicate. In the end, the message is that one "is communicating."

It is also common for this "language of the spirits" to be perceived as a radically different one, reinforcing its distance from common language. In these cases, this language can be a matter of "pure sounds" (blowing sounds, noises, and other sound effects) or music (Yvinec 2004: 57). References to these musical or sound effects occur frequently in myths and tales of encounters with ancestral entities and spirits. In Yagua mythology, for instance, we can find formulae (a kind of acoustic code) introduced by the teller that could almost be understood as a "sonorous language" constitutive of these encounters and that seem to be reinforcing the reality or the presence of such entities: for example, *ró róno ró óóó* (indicates the voice of the Palm Grove spirits), *núñunútapu núñunútapu* . . . (reproduces the voice of the spirits of *Colpa*, sites where animals go to lick salt), *trananá* (the voice of Thunder), *tsi iii* (the voice of Wind), *fi fi fi fi fi* (whistles associated with the voice of the forest spirits whose arrival is announced with the exclamation *pó!*), etc. It is also in this fashion that the spirit Norón (yagua equivalent of the ancient Tupi's Kurupira spirit) "deafens" and "disorients" his victims—usually individuals wandering in the forest—by means of strident whistles *fi fi fi* and the banging *tó tó tó* sounds of his percussion on tree trunks (Chaumeil 2000). The ability to control and resist the effect of powerful sounds is presented in the myth of the twins as conditioning human social order: the twins must learn to dominate the powerful "breath" of the flutes of their dead parents so as to avoid defeat and secure victory over their enemies (Chaumeil 2001: 87). In similar fashion, Yagua hunters must learn "the language of animals" to locate their prey. The ability to imitate the call of a female or offspring of an animal in order to hunt it is called "to make the animals sing," *uñachanu awanu teetaú* (Chaumeil 1993: 416–17). For example, when tracking howler monkeys, the hunter imitates the call of the young *owé owé owé,* to which the parents (male and female) quickly respond *úu úu úu hum hum*, looking for their young and approaching the hunter instead. In the case of the panguana bird (*Crypturellus undulatus*), the hunter imitates the threatening call *kokóbweno kokóbweno* thought to be a generic threat used by enemy animals (an onomatopoeia that also designates the panguana bird itself, *kokóbweno*). The bird is supposed to respond with the same call, indicating its desire for combat and hence walk toward the hunter. In shamanism, the typical sound of the *chacapa* (rattle made of a bundle of dry leaves) *che che che*, used by the shaman in curing sessions, has a particularly soothing effect on spirits, who indicate their satisfaction by replying with a *fu fu fu fu* sound.

We could continue multiplying examples (and by the way demonstrate the need for a detailed study of onomatopoeic expression within Amazonian anthropology), yet what we want to highlight here is the importance of the acoustic code in relationships with spirits, even more so when we consider that each class of spirit is often conceived of as having a "voice" of its own. We will return to the possible meaning of this multiplicity of "voices."

II

The Yagua maintain at least two levels of formal relations with spirits both requiring a specialized apprenticeship, namely, shamanism and the flute ritual. We will briefly comment on the first, for it is to the second that we will devote most of our attention in this essay.

A large part of the shamanic initiation ritual consists of familiarizing oneself with the spirits and, above all, learning (reproducing) their "language" or, more specifically, their "voice," *mbayántu niquieyanu*. In the majority of cases, the initiate uses concoctions of hallucinogenic plants (where *Banisteriopsis caapi* vine is the main ingredient) to enter into audible and visual contact with vegetable spirits. Once contact is attained, this allows for a "linguistic" exchange—an exclusive prerogative of shamans—

with these renowned entities who are known to be the real owners of shamanic chants and powers. Even when vegetables are conceived of as "mute," *ne niquie*, those who know how can enjoy their beautiful whistled melodies. In fact, each category of vegetal spirits is known to possess a chant to which a specific tone of voice corresponds. Shamanic chants, which always begin with acute whistles, are primarily meant to reach the very high acoustic frequencies of the spirits, in such a way that their efficacy depends less on their content or the meaning of their words than on an indigenous theory of sounds and sonorous language. To reach these tones, Yagua shamans spend months performing vocal exercises and scraping their tongues with the sharpened blade of a shell in order to transform their voice and extract, as they say, the phlegm, *worapóndi*, the "foam" of the tongue that, in ordinary circumstances, hoarsens the voice. The diversity of the registers reached contrasts with the similarity in content of these incantations. These registers constitute the usual mode of communicating with the spirits that "emit" and "receive" on the same frequencies, not unlike the way a two-way radio functions. This acoustic language—a sort of metalanguage shared by shamans and plants— acquires a semantic value, producing meaning as it emits sounds.

Two notions are worthy of further comment. The first is that among the Yagua, shamanic chanting is conceived of as a veritable physiological capacity, inasmuch as its efficacy is conditioned by a physical procedure (the scraping of the tong). The second is that it is possible to obtain (control) another's agency and knowledge (whether spirits or any other being) by imitation, that is, identically reproducing their acoustic frequency. Hence the secret character of shamanic chants is always a source of tension between shamans competing for control over spirits.

Let me comment on two more aspects regarding shamanism that will be of use to us later on. During the most intense episode of initiation, shaman initiates undergo a process of bodily dissociation or fragmentation, experiencing the separation of their extremities and of flesh from bones only to recombine later on (a classical phenomenon found in many descriptions of this type of experience). This scheme of corporeal dissociation—which we will find again in our discussion of the ritual flutes—seems to be a constitutive aspect of the encounter and relationships with spirits in numerous Amazonian societies (on this subject see Yvinec 2004). The other interesting aspect refers to the field of the senses. If we refer to what various Yagua shamans have told us about their specific initiations (Chaumeil 2000), we notice that the first contact with the spirits is auditory rather than visual: always beginning with a series of noises and voices, becoming louder *yeeeee EEEE* as spirits get closer. Only later do the zoomorphic, and then anthropomorphic, images become discernible along with the first chants: vocal sequences that we also find in the flute ritual to which we will now turn our attention.

III

Until recently the Yagua used to celebrate each year, during the fruiting period of the *Bactris gasipaes* palm, a grand male initiation ritual called *ñá*. Without entering into too much detail, this ritual—in many ways reminiscent of the Yuruparí ritual characteristic of northwestern Amazonia—could last several weeks and hence required enormous preparation in terms of procuring food and drink reserves (particularly game and manioc beer) and creating artifacts (Chaumeil 2000–2001).

Male initiation consisted precisely of presenting young men—those pertaining to the clan of the "owner" of the feast—for the first time with the hunting spirits represented by five pairs of aerophones, the sight of which, in accordance with a rather classic standard in Amazonia, is strictly forbidden to women and noninitiates. (For more details on these instruments, the interdictions they are subject to, and their distribution in Amazonia, see Piedade 2000; Mansutti 2006; Chaumeil 1997 and 2007.) In the Yagua case, there are three types of instruments: bark trumpets, speak-

5. Owner of the feast offering unfermented manioc drink to the spirit instruments. Photo by Jean-Pierre Chaumeil.

ing tubes, and duct flutes with stops and with a partly covered sound orifice, always played in pairs in hocket style (on this subject see Hill 2001: 64). These instruments embody the "voice," *niquiejada*, and the "bones," *ndu*, of the hunting spirits that regulate this activity. In this way, they are understood as autonomous entities, different from the animal masters, each with its own character, voice (although all spirits understand each other, for they "share the same language"), odor, sensibility, and way of being played, with the added peculiarity of also being considered as great drinkers. (They are always thirsty!) During the ritual, the instruments are hence "fed" large quantities of manioc beer that spills over from their "mouths" (the mouthpiece of the tubular instruments) in exchange for the game that their intervention has allowed. The lack of this beverage (which is a female product) enrages the spirits, who then will not "deliver" more animals. The instruments are also beautifully "decorated" with headdresses and paint, exhibiting the motifs of the clan of the owner of the feast. Several authors have commented on the very sensitive personality of the ritual flutes, which can easily feel disrespected. It is because of this sensitivity that, according to Murphy (1958: 63), the sprits of the *karökö* flutes among the Mundurucu get angry if they are not frequently "fed" and "played"; similarly among the Cubeo Hehénewa, the flutes must be treated with considerable care and respect (Goldman 2004: 224).

Among the Yagua, every type of spirit-instrument is associated with a relatively precise category of animals. The main instrument, Rúnda (a pair of bark trumpets), called *yatí*, "leader," is related to birds and terrestrial fauna, in particular with the *ndusu*/kachuno monkey (*Lagotrix lagotricha*).[3] Rúnda has three forms of vocal expression or "voices," each having two modalities, one of a lower tone than the other, which are produced in alternate fashion:

Strident cries *hú hu hú hu hú hu* (representing its "laughter");

A rhythmic series (march) of grave sounds, associated with the "voice of Thunder," in which one can identify "words" (that is, the human vocal system transformed by the instrument): for example, *hihihihu hihihihu*, "I am arriving," or *wiwi hihi hihi*, "I am leaving";

Reiterated roars ended by gurgling sounds *huwuwuwuwo oooo*, meaning "I am requesting to drink manioc beer," where the gurgling specifically means "I am already drinking" (see Chaumeil 1993: 409–20, for further details).

These voices form sequences (that can be repeated at will) following this pattern beginning with the cries and ending with the gurgling sounds (the latter played standing up). Whilst the Rúnda exhibits a fundamentally binary musical pattern, the tempo increases considerably at the end of the second sequence, forming more complex rhythmic structures that the Yagua liken to a "speech."

The second spirit-instrument, Wirisihó (a pair of speaking tubes) also called *rimitiu'*, "the old one" (because it is represented as a hoarsely voiced elder), is associated with chelonians and caimans. It has the reputation of coming with turtles, which in this context are called *wichótu*, meaning "stool"—the allegoric name given to this turtle due to the resemblance between the shape of the turtle's shell and the stool. The usual name of this turtle is *notiu*. This spirit-instrument produces two sound sequences likened to the "jaguar's voice" that are audible from a large distance:

Series of five or six grave sounds followed by five or six produced one tone higher;

Successive roars (the instruments are played standing up) amongst which, nonetheless, the rudiments of words can be discerned, for example *tititititiri*, "I am going to begin walking," or *yiwó yiwó wó wooo*, "I am walking." Wirisihó is in essence rhythmic, and his voice is an evocation of the manner of walking of the mythical jaguars, *wu wu wu wu*. However, the name could well be derived from *wirisi*, the name of a species of fish locally known as *carachama*, and distinguished by its shell-shaped scales.

The three other spirit-instruments, Wawitihó, Yurihó, and Sipató (three pairs of identical yet different sized duct flutes with stops and with partly covered sound orifices), are associated with aquatic fauna and certain species of terrestrial animals. The melodic sounds they produce contrast with the vibrating, hoarse, and chopped sounds of the preceding instruments. The "music" of these flutes consists of long concatenations of rising and descending notes played alternatingly in hocket style by the "male" flute (the longer one) and the "female" flute (the shorter one). Wawitihó is reputed to arrive with peccaries and fish species and is given the responsibility of organizing the handling of the meat in the ñá ritual. He has up to three vocal manifestations, varying from a free melodic phrase to a quasi-rhythmic one:

A *wawa wawa wawa* signals the arrival of the spirit;

Rising and descending *wuwuwuwuwuwuwuwuwu* expresses the spirit's happiness;

A *meme meme meme* indicates his departure.

The Yagua refer to these sonorous manifestations with the word *chacún* (Powlison and Powlison 1976; Powlison 1995). The name Wawitihó is perhaps derived from *wawitiu*, a class of hawk. If this were the case, the chacún onomatopoeia would then correspond to the "voice" of the hawk. We would hence be faced with another example of the distinction noted by Stephen Hugh-Jones for the Tukano (Hugh-Jones 1979: 146) between, on the one hand, the sounds of bark trumpets associated with the noise of thunder and the roar of the jaguar, and on the other hand, the sounds of flutes associated with the call of birds. This identification of the "voices" of the ritual flutes with the "cries" of different animal species is relatively common in Lowland South America (see, for example, Mansutti 2006 on the Piaroa and Hill 2004 on the Wakuénai).

On their part, Yurihó and Sipató produce only one sound sequence melodically similar to that of Wawitihó. The Yagua refer to them with the *yuri yuri yuri* and *sipa sipa sipa* onomatopoeias. The term *sipa* designates the grated manioc-based drink given to the hunting spirits as a farewell beverage. Sipató spirit receives this name because it drinks enormous amounts of grated-manioc juice. This is indicated by its voice, which constantly demands this beverage, *sipa sipa sipa*. Occasionally, Sipató can appear as the wife of Rúnda in which case a linguistic marker for the feminine form is added, Sipatónda. The name for the Yurihó spirit comes from the term *yuri*, which probably refers to ancient enemies of the Yagua, historically located to the north of their territory, who are the subject of several series of ritual songs. It is said that Yurihó comes with the howler monkey (*kánda*), which is allegorically referred to in the flute ritual as *ramanujú*, or "ayahuasca vine" (*Banisteriopsis caapi*), by analogy between the shape of the monkey's tail and the hallucinogenic vine.

The musical arrangement of the instruments is, as far as we can tell, relatively free. There is apparently no synchronization between the instruments: the voices can be superimposed, played as a solo, or even used to initiate a "dialogue" (deformed voice) usually touching on sexual topics (generally addressed to the women enclosed in the house holding the feast, who are very much entertained by this kind of humor coming from the spirits) like the following example illustrates:

Wirisihó tells *Wawitihó*: (sequence of sounds interpreted as)
"I have seen you with your sister"
(implicitly meaning "making love")

Wawitihó responds: (another sound sequence)
"Where have you seen me? Are you trying to trick me?"

Wirisihó: "Of course, your sister came to see me."
(implicitly meaning "I have also had sex with her")

As far as we can tell, there is no form of segmentation or correspondence between notes and words, as has been noted by Jonathan Hill (1993: 84–85) in the case of the Wakuénai.

While the play of musical forms seems to be relatively open, there is an order for the arrival of the instruments to the village. They come in a line always headed by Rúnda, then Wawitihó (with the other flutes behind), and Wirisihó at the end (due to having the most powerful voice and the slowest pace). Let us recall that the instruments are fabricated in a secret place in the forest. This idea of an order being part of the modalities of interaction with spirits, a theme that surely deserves further studies, has also been highlighted by various authors (Arhem et al. 2004; Diakuru and Kisibi 2006).

IV

The flutes and trumpets intervene in the first part of the ritual and accompany the initiated men in their different activities, always bringing meat (but also fish and fruit) from the forest, while the women and the noninitiate men are enclosed in the house holding the feast. A very curious sonorous dance then commences between men and women, between "seeing" and "hearing." When the women hear the instruments approaching (their "voices" can be heard more than an hour before their arrival), they vigorously beat their mortars (used to grind manioc) with pestles to an irregular beat, letting the hunting spirits know they have prepared them a hefty provision of manioc beer. These noises can also be heard from a long distance and can last more than an hour, which is why women must also exercise for several days to achieve the necessary endurance (just like men must do for playing the flutes). On the outside, the spirits respond to the women's noises by beating (each with their characteristic noise) the roof of the feast house with sticks and pieces of meat, informing the women that they bring plenty of game. This exchange between the sexes takes place only at the level of sounds: to the "voices" of the instruments (including the sexually loaded "conversations" we referred to above) women respond with their yelling alongside the cries of children fearful amid all the commotion. More than a mere passive "dialogue" marking the separation of sexes, we could think of these sonorous sequences (banging, yelling, etc.) of women as a feminine counterpart or complement in the flute ritual complex, as much for their intensity and duration (including the apprenticeship and training phases) as for the heterophony of the sounds produced. It is as if the visual interdiction between spirits and women (which applies both ways, for neither do the spirits "see" the women, even when they "hear" them) needed to be compensated by an excess of sound production and exchange between them. This interpretation resonates with those found in other contemporary studies of ritual in the lowlands. Instead of opposing, as it has always been done, male rites on the one hand, to female rites, on the other, the tendency now is to see them as two expressions of the same ritual complex (see, for example, Mello 2005 and this volume, Piedade 2004, or Prinz, this volume).

Now, the object of male initiation is precisely to "see"—and not just to "hear"—the instruments, so as to learn to reproduce

6. Spirit instruments beating the roof of the feast house with pieces of game to reassure the enclosed women that there will be plenty of meat. The women respond by beating their manioc mortars, indicating there will also be plenty of manioc beer. Photo by Jean-Pierre Chaumeil.

(imitate) their "voices" as well as to fabricate them (reproduce their "bodies"). This is a long and progressive process (children beginning at five or six, until ten years of age) of familiarization with the flutes, the "breath" of which is considered far too dangerous for the young (as it was for the mythical twins that had to control the deadly breath of the first flutes of their dead parents in order to reestablish the social order). Before being exposed for the first time to the gaze of the spirits, the young initiates undergo rigorous fasting (previously they were given hallucinogenic beverages) and their eyes are covered with cloth. They then listen for the first time for the "voices" from outside of the feast house, a highly emotive and frightening moment. The young become accustomed as the "voices" approach, and it is only then that they are allowed to see and touch the spirit-instruments and their adornments, thus discovering their "real" corporeal appearances

7. Child being painted just after having seen the flutes and trumpets for the first time. Photo by Jean-Pierre Chaumeil.

in the shape of the flutes and trumpets (that is, as pure "bones" and "voices"). From then on, and in time, they will learn to recognize and distinguish the sounds, components, and odors typical of each spirit.

An interesting parallel now becomes apparent between shamanic initiation and the male initiation, in that both reveal the scheme of corporeal and sensorial dissociation or decomposition as a constitutive feature of the encounter with spirits. In both cases of initiation, the learning process exhibits the same "hierarchy" of the senses. Contrary to what happens in everyday life, the senses operate here not simultaneously but successively, one after the other: the sense of audition tends to play a role before those of sight, smell or touch. The idea, often suggested to be universal, of a precedence of vision over the other senses seems in this case to lose validity. Both shaman and initiate reproduce (imitate) the "voice" of the spirits: the former adopting, as we have seen, the most ample repertoire of acoustic registers possible, the latter, the widest range of musical variations on the flutes. The theme of corporeal dissociation is also present in both cases, even if under a different guise. While the shaman experiences the fragmentation of his body during his initiation (bones and flesh become separated), in the case of the initiation rite, it is the spirits themselves that appear (to the young initiate) "reduced," if one can say such a thing, to mere "bones" (flutes and trumpets). If, as it has been suggested, corporeal dissociation is a constitutive aspect of the relationship with spirits, this would further demonstrate the dual nature of the shaman, being at once human *and* spirit, but also indicate the shamanic nature of the flutes.

V

By way of conclusion, we would like to show how the theme of fragmentation, which is thought to be characteristic of the spirit world (Yvinec 2004), when applied to the field of language, finds another expression in the vocal production and the manner of speech of the five hunting spirits. We have seen that the main spirit, Rúnda, has three vocal manifestations: cries, rhythmic succession, and roars ending in gurgling sounds. After the episode of cries (his "laughter"), Rúnda always continues with a classic binary structure that opposes masculine and feminine sounds (instruments are paired as "male" and "female")—that would be the basic linguistic configuration, to put it some way—to later produce more complex rhythmic and melodic structures, and then return to roars and gurgling sounds (the gurgling sounds seems always to break the previous melody as if wanting to prevent the spirit language from coming too close to human language). Wirisihó performs a series of alternating (male/female) sounds and successions of roars, whilst Wawitihó (the same as Yurihó and Sipató) produces melodies of enchained rising and descending notes, contrasting with the hoarse sounds of the preceding instruments.

If we now consider the order of arrival of the hunting spirits, the binary structure of the bark trumpets opens the march, followed by the flutes' melodic phrases, and closing the sequence we find the successions of sounds and roars of the speaking tubes. We could perhaps see in the "language" of the spirits a desire to alternate between rhythm and melody. However, we have seen that in the course of the ritual, the musical arrangement is relatively free, without much synchronizing, showing rather a will to produce a somewhat cacophonic ensemble of dissonant sounds and voices.[4] It would seem as if this multiplicity of "dissonant" sounds and "voices" were an effort to separate off the constitutive elements of language that would only be found harmoniously together in humans. This would be the differentiating mark of the language of spirits. Comparing Wakuénai shamanic chanting with the music of their ritual flutes, Jonathan Hill (2004: 16) showed that the heterophony found both in sounds and instrumental melodies, as in the shamanic voices, served as an entry into the space of spirits and myth. If the hypothesis of a decomposition of the human language in "sounds" in the exchanges with spirits has any validity, it would resonate with the phenomenon of dissociation in the corporeal and sensory fields, which we have seen in the preceding pages.

This scheme of fragmentation could be, as Yvinec (2004) notes, one of the constitutive aspects of communication with nonhumans. If so, it would allow us to explain, among the Yagua and elsewhere in Amazonia, the utmost importance given to sonorous language in such processes, informing us more broadly about the complex relations between musicality and lexicality for many lowland indigenous populations.

Notes

1. The Yagua are considered the last representatives of an isolated linguistic family (Peba-Yagua) thought to be spoken initially by three subgroups (the Peba, the Yagua, and the Yameo). They are swidden horticulturalists who today live in the Peruvian and Colombian Amazon. The Yagua presently number about four thousand.

2. On this topic see Seeger 2004: 51 on the relationships among the different vocal art forms performed by the Suyá of Mato Grosso (Brazil); from speech (with a priority of text over melody) to ritual song (with a priority of melody over text). See also the contribution of Marc Brightman in the present volume.

3. The common names of animal species are never used in the context of the flute ritual. Allegoric names, generally of vegetable origin, are used instead (Chaumeil 1993: 412–14). This being so, in a ritual context the kachuno monkey is designated by the term *ndusu*, literary meaning "bag," by analogy to the way the female monkey carries her offspring hanging like a bag on her back. In the above cited article, we have provided several examples of allegoric names that must be used when soliciting the aid of spirits in hunting, lest one induce an absolute confusion among the spirits and return home empty-handed. This kind of allegoric language—which is used in reference not only to game but also to ritual objects and the actors of ritual themselves—is maintained throughout the duration of the flute ritual.

4. The issue of the apparent lack of synchronization, concordance, or some degree of "order" in the musical expression of spirits merits a more detailed inquiry than what we have been able to draw from our field recordings. It could also be the case that what appears "cacophonic" for humans is, from the point of view of spirits, a "harmonious" language. This interpretation would be in keeping with a wider inversion scheme where animals, for example, take the form of vegetables from the perspective of spirits, and where the unfermented beverages offered to the spirits as part of the ritual farewell are seen by the latter as fermented drinks. I thank Acácio Tadeu de Camargo Piedade for bringing this point to my attention.

References Cited

Arhem, Kaj, L. Cayón, G. Angulo, and M. Garcia, eds. 2004. *Etnografía Makuna: Tradiciones, relatos y saberes de la Gente de Agua.* Bogotá: ICANH/Acta Universitalis Gothoburgensis.

Chaumeil, Jean-Pierre. 1993. "Des Esprits aux ancêtres: Procédés linguistiques, conceptions du langage et de la société chez les Yagua de l'Amazonie péruvienne." *L'Homme* 126–28, nos. 2–4: 409–27.

———. 1997. "Les os, les flûtes, les morts: Mémoire et traitement funéraire en Amazonie." *Journal de la Société des Américanistes* 83: 83–110.

———. 2000. *Voir, savoir, pouvoir: Le chamanisme chez les Yagua de l'Amazonie péruvienne.* Genève: Georg éditeur.

———. 2000–2001. "Le masque et le placenta: Notes sur les costumes-masques yagua." *Bulletin de la Société Suisse des Américanistes* 64–65: 97–105.

———. 2001. "The Blowpipe Indians: Variations on the Theme of Blowpipe and Tube among the Yagua Indians of the Peruvian Amazon." In *Beyond the Visible and the Material: The Amerindianization of Society in the Work of Peter Rivière*, ed. L. Rival and N. Whitehead, 81–99. Oxford: Oxford University Press.

———. 2007. "Bones, Flutes, and the Dead: Memory and Funerary Treatments in Amazonia." In *Time and Memory in Indigenous Amazonia: Anthropological Perspectives*, ed. C. Fausto and M. Heckenberger, 243–83. Gainesville: University Press of Florida.

Civrieux, Marc de. 1974. *Religión y magia Kariña.* Caracas: Universidad Católica Andrés Bello.

Diakuru (Américo Castro Fernandes) and Kisibi (Durvalino Moura Fernandes). 2006. *Bueri Kãdiri Marîriye: Os ensinamentos que não se esquecem.* São Gabriel da Cachoeira: UNIRT/FOIRN, Coleção Narradores indígenas do Rio Negro, vol. 8.

Goldman, Irving. 2004. *Cubeo Hehénewa Religious Thought: Metaphysics of a Northwestern Amazonian People.* New York: Columbia University Press.

Hill, Jonathan. 1993. *Keepers of the Sacred Chants: The Poetics of Ritual Power in an Amazonian Society.* Tucson: University of Arizona Press.

———. 2001. "The Variety of Fertility Cultism in Amazonia: A Closer Look at Gender Symbolism in Northwestern Amazonia." In *Gender in Amazonia and Melanesia: An Exploration of the Comparative Method*, ed. T. Gregor and D. Tuzin. Berkeley: University of California Press.

———. 2004. "Metamorphosis: Mythic and Musical Modes of Ceremonial Exchange among the Wakuénai of Venezuela." In *Music in Latin America and the Carribean: An Encyclopedic History*, 1: 25–48. Austin: University of Texas Press.

Hugh-Jones, Stephen. 1979. *The Palm and the Pleiades: Initiation and Cosmology in Northwest Amazonia.* Cambridge: Cambridge University Press.

Mansutti, Alexander. 2006. *Warime: la fiesta. Flautas, trompas y poder en el noroeste amazónico.* Ciudad Guayana: Fondo Editorial de la Universidad Nacional Experimental de Guayana.

Mello, Maria Ignez Cruz. 2005. "Iamurikuma: Música, Mito, e Ritual entre os Wauja do Alto Xingu." PhD diss., Universidade Federal de Santa Catarina.

Menezes Bastos, Rafael José de. 1999. *A musicologia Kamayura: Para uma antropologia da comunicação no Alto Xingu*. 2nd ed. Florianópolis: Ed. da UFSC.

Murphy, Robert. 1958. *Mundurucu Religion*. Berkeley: University of California Press.

Piedade, Acacio Tadeo. 2000. "Antropologia da música dos aerofonos masculinos nas terras baixas da América do Sul." *XXIV Reunião Annual da* ANPOCS/GT4-*Etnologia Indigena*.

————. 2004 "O Canto do Kawoká: Música, Cosmologia e Filosofia entre os Wauja do Alto Xingu." PhD diss., Universidade Federal de Santa Catarina.

Powlison, Esther, and Paul Powlison. 1976. *La fiesta Yagua, Jiña: una rica herencia cultural*. Yarinacocha: Instituto Lingüístico de Verano, Comunidades y Culturas peruanas 8.

Powlison, Paul, ed. 1995. *Diccionario Yagua-Castellano*. Lima: Ministerio de Educación-Instituto Lingüístico de Verano, Serie "Lingüística peruana" no. 35.

Seeger, Anthony. 2004 [1987]. *Why Suyá Sing: A Musical Anthropology of an Amazonian People*. Urbana: University of Illinois Press.

Yvinec, Cédric. 2004. "Les formes de communication avec les non-humains en Amazonie amérindienne." Paris, diplôme de DEA, EHESS.

2. *Leonardo, the Flute*

On the Sexual Life of Sacred Flutes among the Xinguano Indians

RAFAEL JOSÉ DE MENEZES BASTOS

The other great branch of sympathetic magic, which I have called Contagious Magic, proceeds upon the notion that things which have once been conjoined must remain ever afterwards, even when quite dissevered from each other, in such a sympathetic relation that whatever is done to the one must similarly affect the other. Thus the logical basis of Contagious Magic, like that of Homoeopathic [*sic*] Magic, is a mistaken association of ideas; its physical basis, if we may speak of such a thing, like the physical basis of Homoeopathic Magic, is a material medium of some sort which, like the ether of modern physics, is assumed to unite distant objects and to convey impressions from one to the other.

—Sir James George Frazer, *The Golden Bough* (1922)

What exactly do we mean when we speak of "sacred flutes" or "rituals"? Answering this question is not easy. Difficulties arise from the fact that we are not dealing merely with flutes. Or better, we are not referring merely to the aerophones typologically identified by the number 421 in the Hornbostel-Sachs's 1914 system—a system for classifying musical instruments that most anthropologists and ethnomusicologists have never taken seriously, in spite of its descriptive attributes.[1] We are not dealing only with flutes, since depending on the ethnographic case, sacred flutes may include not only aerophones of various types but also, as in the Xinguano (Kamayurá) case studied here, some types of idiophones (globular and other types of rattles, etc.) and various kinds of aerophones (flutes, trumpets, clarinets, bullroarers).[2] But it is not only for organological reasons—always of strategic interest for the comprehension of musical systems-that the question above is not at all easy to answer: the snag in analysis hinges upon the adjectives *sacred* or *ritual*, sometimes replaced by *secret* or others, qualifiers that are inadequate for capturing the nature of the instruments under consideration.[3]

The theme of the sacred flutes has moved me since the beginning of my research in the Upper Xingu (Menezes Bastos 1978 [1999a]). In this essay I will rethink an episode involving the sacred flutes, the Kamayurá who make and play these instruments, and the famous Villas-Bôas brothers, Orlando, Cláudio, and Leonardo, who founded the Xingu National Indian Park. In a previous work (Menezes Bastos 1989), I analyzed the exegeses of the Tupían Kamayurá and the Arawak Yawalapití from the then Xingu National Indian Park about this saga involving the Villas-Bôas brothers.[4] Over time, I have become increasingly convinced that this episode is crucial for understanding both the universe of the sacred flutes per se in Lowland South America and, more generally, how mythic and ritual themes and models having to do with the flutes and the senses are used to shape, retell, and understand the not-so-distant past of interethnic or colonial relations. In my previous published account (Menezes Bastos 1989), I described the episode with only a single footnote. Twenty years later, I find myself still thinking over the subject matter at times. In this article, I will summarize my thoughts.

In 1981, Takumã, chief of the Kamayurá in that period, narrated the aforementioned episode with reference to the arrival of the Villas-Bôas brothers in the headwater region of the Xingu River. The episode took place sometime between 1947 and 1953. Takumã was then an adolescent who was in his period of puberty seclusion; today he is about seventy-five years old. As I wrote in my 1989 work, the narrative discloses a rather unpleasant side of the relations between the Kamayurá and the Villas-Bôas brothers, which challenges the accuracy of the asexual rhetoric through which the brothers have always presented their saga to the world.[5] The episode presented here portrays the sacred flutes in action or as agents. By revisiting its analysis, my intent is to contribute to the anthropology of Lowland South America in topics related to the sociocultural construction of the senses, gender, and power. Additionally, I will make a brief excursion into the problematic of indigenous Amazonian constructions of myth and history.

The following transcription of Takumã's narrative is divided into five parts:

Some Savage Sentiments

1. "So I remained at the Xingu, with Leonardo.[6] I remained there. I remained there for many years [ten years]. So my father called me back to the village.[7] In the village, I entered seclusion [puberty seclusion]. I remained secluded for an extremely short time [two months], and soon I came back to Xingu.[8] Leonardo had called me back. I remained there. . . . Then my father called me back to the village again. Soon Leonardo came to the village to take me to remain with him. So I remained, I remained . . . with Leonardo. That time, Leonardo lent me a rifle. Later, he gave me another one, a .44. Then I remained with him, I remained, remained. . . .

2. "It was then that, later on, Leonardo took the wrong path.[9] He had maintained sexual relations with [some] Kamayurá women. He was jealous in relation to the other caraíbas[10] living in the area, always telling them: 'People, you must not have sexual intercourse with the Indians. You can transmit illnesses to them.' Orlando Villas-Bôas also proceeded in this manner. Leonardo was angry at the other caraíbas. He wanted to order all of them to go away from the Indian area. But how? The Villas-Bôas would remain alone. Then Leonardo called me and said: 'Takumã, you must tell the women not to enter the workers' houses, because they can transmit illnesses to them.' So I went to

talk to the women. They told me: 'No, we haven't been to the houses of the caraíbas.' So I remained talking [with the Kamayurá women], talking, talking. . . . It was then that Leonardo took the wrong path. The others saw it. Everybody saw it. . . .

3. "He maintained sexual intercourse with Skin of Secluded. She was my father's wife. My father was married to Skin of Secluded. She was a *manga'uhet.*[11]

4. "Then Skin of Secluded saw the *yumi'ama'e* [the sacred flutes].[12] At Leonardo's house, we had left a trio of yumi'ama'e. Skin of Secluded, when she went wooing with Leonardo, entered and saw the flutes. So they all [the Kamayurá men] said: 'Let's rape Skin of Secluded.' My father was very sad. My father knew that Leonardo was in love with Skin of Secluded.

5. "Then, on another day, we played the flutes. Skin of Secluded was at Leonardo's. Both of them were lying in a hammock with a mosquito net. Skin of Secluded was in the mosquito net. Nobody knew that. Then the men played the yumi'ama'e flutes. Leonardo didn't like it: 'Why did you play that?' He argued with the Kamayurá men. He uttered bad words, spoke over and over. . . ."[13] Then Leonardo took a gun and said: 'I'm going to kill you, Takumã.' I replied: 'You may kill me.' He pointed the rifle to my face. My father said: 'Go on. . . . Whoever kills my son may kill me as well. . . . Why are you jealous about your people? . . . You are wrong, Leonardo. . . . I don't want Skin of Secluded anymore. . . . You may marry her.'"

What I would like to highlight right away from this impressive narrative is the double identification—caused by contamination—produced in the event:

1. Between "the flutes house" (*tapùy* in Kamayurá) and Leonardo's house; and

2. between the flutes and Leonardo himself.

This identification—and that is the reason I call it contamination, in a movement that aims at evoking *The Golden Bough*—is not a pure mental equation (in this case, metonymic), since it has taken place in the empirical world: placing the flutes inside Leonardo's house concretely transformed it into a "flutes house." From that moment on, things started to happen that forced Leonardo into the position, or perspective, of an individual of the *yaku'i* species.[14]

Note that the act of placing the flutes in Leonardo's house has been done intentionally, most probably as commanded by Kutamapù. Aware of the affair between Leonardo and Skin of Secluded, he felt that the Kamayurá were victims of nothing less than an act of war on the part of Leonardo—a classical act of wife-stealing. It is also important to remember that the affair under analysis was continuous, public, and marked by exclusiveness—in terms of Skin of Secluded's "loyalty" toward Leonardo. In addition to being a great chief, Kutamapù was a powerful and respected *payé*, or shaman, who was acting as the group's legitimate representative.

However, the chain of transformations did not stop at that point. Once these identifications, or contaminations, had been established, the village men were placed in the position of a yaku'i community. So the ferocious revenge took place, and the men as a community of yaku'i spirits raped Skin of Secluded, who had unwittingly positioned herself as the prey of this community of spirits. Unaware and unwilling, Skin of Secluded went repeatedly to a tapùy (flutes house), as she visited Leonardo's house. The tapùy is by all means prohibited to women among the Kamayurá and the Xinguano in general, precisely because it is the yaku'i flutes house. Even worse, by visiting that house on a daily basis, Skin of Secluded would threaten its power by seeing the sacred flutes themselves.

A second point to emphasize from this gruesome episode is cumulative in relation to the previous one: the collage triggered between Leonardo and

1. jealousy (to the Kamayurá, it is a feeling that has to do with accumulation, in the case of women),[15]

2. lack of discretion (as Leonardo had frequent, scandalous sexual relations with a married woman and, even worse, with one of the chief's and great shaman's wives), and

3. violence, which was at first verbal, since Leonardo "uttered bad words" or swore. Afterward it became physical, expressed as a death threat with a gun, aimed prominently at Takumã, the Kamayurá chief's oldest son and the first in the succession lineage. This violent ethos became evident in an even more drastic manner to the Kamayurá, from the moment when Leonardo—who for them was in the position of a flute, or of an individual of the yaku'i species—argued with much anger (in the fifth and last part of the narrative) over the way the men's playing of the sacred flutes took place at his house, which had been empirically transformed into a flutes house, as noted above. Leonardo, a flute, complained in anger over the performance of "his" own music. This complaint reached its summit when he threatened to shoot Takumã.

This collage gives the final touch to the identification that the Kamayurá projected onto Leonardo Villas-Bôas, which rose above the level of a witch, or someone whose antisocial power can be eliminated from society through expulsion or even execution. Neither was Leonardo identified merely as a human war enemy. Rather, in this episode he had come to be regarded as more than a declared enemy and had attained the level of a *mama'e*, or spirit, a tremendously dangerous being that possesses incomparable power and that is potentially extremely violent. In the episode in question, Leonardo came to be identified as an individual of the horrendous *mama'e yaku'i* species or yumi'ama'e, the sacred flutes, an individual at whose house these flutes *must be* played and not angrily rejected (according to item 5 in the narrative). Note that to play *for* these mama'e has the purpose of controlling them, as their yaku'i music is itself shamanic music

(Piedade 2004). So Leonardo was equated with an individual of the yaku'i species absolutely beyond Kamayurá control and in frank combat with them. At the time of the Kamayurá's arrival in the Upper Xingu region sometime during the eighteenth century, the "flutes house" was an institution in which warriors were recruited (Menezes Bastos 1995). The institution played this role until the suppression of warfare in the region in the mid-twentieth century, with the imposition of *pax xinguensis* by the Villas-Bôas brothers. Note that the mama'e are controlled only by shamanism, which is monopolized—particularly among the Kamayurá—by its principal shaman, the chief himself (Menezes Bastos 1984–85, 2001).[16]

A third and final point about the episode that I would like to make is the violent and obdurate nature of the revenge that the Kamayurá men—in the position of a community of flutes—carried out against both Leonardo and Skin of Secluded. The act of revenge against Leonardo occurred in response to his jealousy, indiscretion, violence, and extreme lack of reciprocity. Due to his possessive desire to have Skin of Secluded, Leonardo lost the lover he had stolen from the chief and he was even forced to leave the Kamayurá village. Skin of Secluded, the involuntary author of the original violation, was gang-raped and expelled from the village. Note that she was not contaminated by anything coming from the episode here under study. Rather, she was put in the position of a prey of the yaku'i flutes due to her violation of the principle of their invisibility to the women.[17]

It is important to make clear that the revenge in question was *not* triggered by the Kamayurá chief's jealousy or excessive sexual desire for Skin of Secluded. On the contrary, the revenge was motivated by Leonardo's radical rejection of Kutamapù, the group's legitimate representative, and the Kamayurá in general, since Leonardo wanted Skin of Secluded for himself alone. It was also motivated by the Indians' refusal to tolerate violence and the extreme negation of reciprocity surrounding the affair between Leonardo and Skin of Secluded.

In regard to this third aspect, it is also important to understand that male and female marital infidelity in the Kamayurá world does not usually cause anything more than a minor disturbance. Most of the time, punishments in such cases are limited to the betrayed spouse mildly beating an unfaithful partner. The Kamayurá always stress the fact that the difference between them and the "civilized" ones is that the latter are seen as overreacting to cases of adultery.[18] However, in mythology these punishments tend to be portrayed with great and dramatic intensity, provoking catastrophes and ruptures (i.e., origins).[19] Thus, the events that transpired during Leonardo's adulterous affair with Skin of Secluded unfolded as if they had a mythic pertinence, which would trigger (as it did) at least two major ruptures or origins: Kutamapù's forced divorce due to Skin of Secluded's rape and ostracism; and Leonardo's enmity in relation to the Kamayurá, with its eventual generalization to the Villas-Bôas brothers as a whole (Menezes Bastos 1989).

What would be the relation between this impressive episode and my object of analysis? How may the study of the sacred flutes in the lowlands contribute to the broader ethnological concerns about power relations, sociocultural constructions of the senses, gender, and of world constitution in general?

The Kamayurá Sacred Flutes

The Kamayurá sacred (or ritual) flutes (yaku'i or yumi'ama'e) are aerophones classified as duct flutes with deflectors (see Izikowitz 1935: 332–40).[20] They are about one meter long and have four digital orifices, or stops.[21] In most cases, they are played by a *maraka'ùp* (music master) and two assistants or apprentices. When played in solo, the flute is always played by a virtuoso master. The flutes are regarded as spirit beings, called yaku'i, which are believed to constitute the ego of a kin group of the kindred

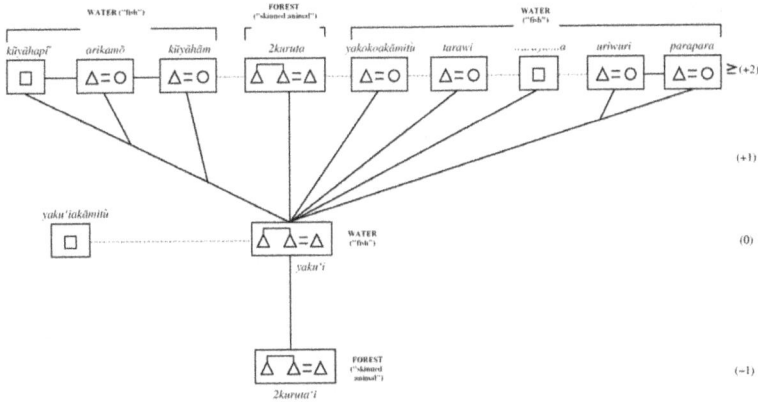

8. The Kamayurá sacred flutes and their kindred.

type (ego-oriented), called *yaku'iare'ùy* or *yumi'ama'eare'ùy* (literally something like "similar to yaku'i" or "people of yaku'i") in Kamayurá. It is a relatively large group, which encompasses eleven more musical instruments, all of them having the ontological nature of mama'e (fig. 8).[22]

In the +2 generation of the kindred cited, there are the following:

The trumpet-type aerophones *kuyahapi*, *arikamo*, and *kuyaham*, whose environment is the water. They are regarded as similar to fishes.[23]

The *kuruta* flutes, similar to the yaku'i, since they have duct and deflector. Their environment is the forest, and they are seen as similar to skinned animals.

The *yakokoakamitù* globular rattles.

The *tarawi* clarinet-type aerophones.[24]

The *warayumi'a*, a kind of slit-drum.

And the *uriwuri* and *parapara* bullroarers.

The last five instruments are also identified as aquatic beings (fishes).

In the o generation, that of the yaku'i themselves, are found the *yaku'iakamitù*, jingle rattles made with *pequi* fruits that are tied to the right ankle of dancers. The original environment of these two instruments, as well as the yaku'i flutes', is water, and they are said to be similar to fishes.

In the-1 generation, there are the *kuruta'i* flutes, which, like the yaku'i and the *kuruta*, have ducts and deflectors. Their environment is the forest, and they are identified as "skinned animals." This kindred lacks the +1 generation.[25]

The yaku'i flutes reside mainly, but not exclusively, in the tapùy, where they are customarily stored. This house is located on an important spot in the Kamayurá village, which is itself a mapping of cosmography. Placed in the center of the village, the flutes house is one of the original places of the cosmos par excellence, a place where the creation of the cosmos is enacted. The flutes house is also consistently referred to by the term *hoka'ù*, which means "water's house," and *hotatap*, which means "fire's house." At the same time, the flutes house is an exclusively masculine space among the Kamayurá and other Xinguano people, which is why it is also known as a "men's house." As already mentioned above, women are prohibited, under threats of being raped, from entering the masculine space of the flutes house.

The front side of the flutes house possesses two doors and faces west. These doors are called *apùy* (nostrils). At its back side, facing east, there is only one door, called simply *okenap* (door). Among the Kamayurá, sexual relations are monitored and are the object of diligent vigilance through the smell they give off, as well as through the scent that male and female fluids exude (which includes especially menstrual blood). Considering that the flutes house (tapùy) is the quintessentially masculine space for the Kamayurá, and keeping in mind that the political manifestation of this masculinity is expressed through the capacity of controlling sexuality typically through its scents, it is not at all surprising that for the Kamayurá this house itself is, in terms of local cosmography, a "big nose" that senses all things. So the flutes house can be said to be a "pan-osphresic" place (from the Greek *pan-osphré-tikós*), instead of a "pan-optical" one (from *pan-optikós*) (Fou-

9. The Kamayurá yaku'i flutes house. Photo by Rafael José de Menezes Bastos.

cault 1977). Figure 9 shows the Kamayurá tapùy as it appeared in 1974, with a house under construction in the right background.

According to native oral history, the flutes house presents itself as one of the basic distinctions of the Kamayurá Apùap subgroup, known as "the real Kamayurá," and classified precisely as the people of the *tapùyatapiã* type ("whose villages have tapùy"). According to written historical reports about the Kamayurá, the tapùy was a great structure where the male community's secret rites took place. The flutes houses were related to the sacred flutes and to the other instruments that constitute their kindred. According to these same reports, the tapùy was the place where young men undergoing initiation during puberty were secluded, and in former times these rites of passage were always collective and not individual as they are practiced today (see Menezes Bastos 1995).

The yaku'i cannot be seen by the women, yet the women diligently hear and listen to the flutes' music.[26] Among the Kamayurá, the yaku'i flutes are not the only rituals that are visually—

but not auditorily—prohibited to women. The Payemeramaraka, "ritual of the shaman's community," can never be seen by women (see Menezes Bastos 1984–85). Furthermore, I once experienced an episode in the Kamayurá village in 1981, which was connected to a peccary hunt where the animals' corpses were deposited on the village plaza. The women (and the children) were visually isolated from that, locking themselves in their houses, fearing that men would transform themselves into mama'e. While the women secluded themselves indoors, the men on the village plaza outside engaged in a dramatic discussion of the "xinguanization" of the Kamayurá, or the historical process whereby their ancestors had transformed from invaders of the region who were accustomed to killing and eating game animals into Xinguano Indians who no longer eat skinned animals (Menezes Bastos 1995).[27] Among the Kamayurá, these gender-based visual prohibitions point to an absolutely imperative female duty: that of visually (and evidently tactilely) avoiding the mama'e universe. This duty is specifically based in the women's fear, a real fright, in relation to men transforming themselves into mama'e, which would bring an end to this world, the end of the "social contract," which is always so fragile for them.[28] On the other hand, these prohibitions are based on the Kamayurá conception that to be seen causes disempowerment to the object being seen, empowering the subject who sees (Menezes Bastos 1990). Among the Kamayurá, human control of the mama'e is only possible through shamanic intervention, a male-controlled monopoly of ritual power under the guidance of the chief, who also serves in the role of principal shaman.

However, the women are prohibited not only from seeing the sacred flutes but also from knowing the identities of the men who are playing them. When men play the instruments, they conceal themselves inside the tapùy. When playing them outside on the village plaza, all house doors are shut, and women and children must remain secluded inside. When playing the yaku'i, men must not bathe by immersing in the river but only by pouring water from bowls over themselves. Nor are they allowed to have sexual intercourse, and they are also subjected to several other prohibitions, which evoke women's behavior when having their period. These practices evoke comparable practices that surround the playing of sacred musical instruments in the Upper Negro River (see Hugh-Jones 1979; Hill 1993; and Piedade 1997). In both regions, ritual prohibitions are indications of a symbolic male menstrual period that expresses power on a political plane instead of a biological one and that is also comparable to practices in New Guinea.[29]

The ritual flutes—and their kindred—are important themes in the Kamayurá and Xinguano mythology. Briefly I relate some of the most important references to them in this mythology.[30]

1. The flutes in question are *ta'angap*, that is, copies made of wood, of the subaquatic mama'e with the same name. These copies, which conserve the original ontological nature of mama'e, have been produced by Ayanama, one of the Kamayurá demiurges.[31]

2. Once upon a time, these flutes were exclusively under women's rule. Therefore, there was a complete inversion of what occurs nowadays: women used to go fishing, men used to plant manioc and look after children. The flutes house was exclusively under women's command, so that men were forbidden to enter there. To sum up, during that time, the constitution of the Kamayurá world was the opposite of what it is today from a gender-oriented point of view.

3. Discontented, the men started a revolution in which they took the flutes from the women and constituted the world as it is today. In order to accomplish this revolution, Morenayat, "the owner of the Morena," another Kamayurá demiurge, threatened the women, playing the horrendous *uriwuri* and *parapara* bullroarers, which are also *ta'angap*, copies, of their respective mama'e, being themselves mama'e.[32] From that time on, the world was constituted as it is now. Its maintenance is implemented out of fear, fright, and horror, which the women attribute to the universe of the ritual flutes and of the

mama'e in general. I emphasize that only men, among the Kamayurá and Xinguano, are allowed to be shamans.

Since the beginning of my studies in the Upper Xingu, I have worked on the assumption that the senses, much beyond the fact of being invariable bio-psychological organs, are—as is the body, according to Marcel Mauss—the very first objects of cultural construction (see Menezes Bastos 1999a). From this idea, I elaborated the notion of *world hearing* (Menezes Bastos 1999b) to describe those indigenous cosmologies in which there is a clear preeminence of the sense of hearing, in contrast with what happens in other indigenous cosmologies (see Lagrou 1995) and in the western world, where seeing seems to be the most important sense. The Kamayurá are a people to whom the notion of *world hearing*—much more than *world seeing*—suits them perfectly. Like the Gê-speaking Suyá living in the northern region of the Xingu Park (Seeger 1975), the Kamayurá use a single verb, *anup*, to refer to both hearing and comprehending. It belongs in a hierarchically superior position to that of the verb *tsak*, which means "to see" but also points to the nexus "to understand." In this way, it may be said that, among the Kamayurá, "to see" assumes an analytical form of perception and knowledge of the realms of intellect and explanation. Note that "to see" too often is taken as a sign of a highly antisocial means of empowerment, as in the case of the witches and, even worse, in the case of the mama'e, among whom are the yaku'i flutes and many other components of their kindred, especially the kuyahapi, arikamo, and kuyaham horns. These horns have neither ears nor nose, only ferocious eyes and mouths that devour instead of simply eating (fig. 10).[33]

In contrast with the sense of seeing, the word for hearing evokes a more synthetic form of perception that is located in the domains of sensibility and comprehension. Furthermore, the exaggerated capacity of hearing is interpreted by the Kamayurá as an index of virtuosity typically associated with musical and verbal arts.[34]

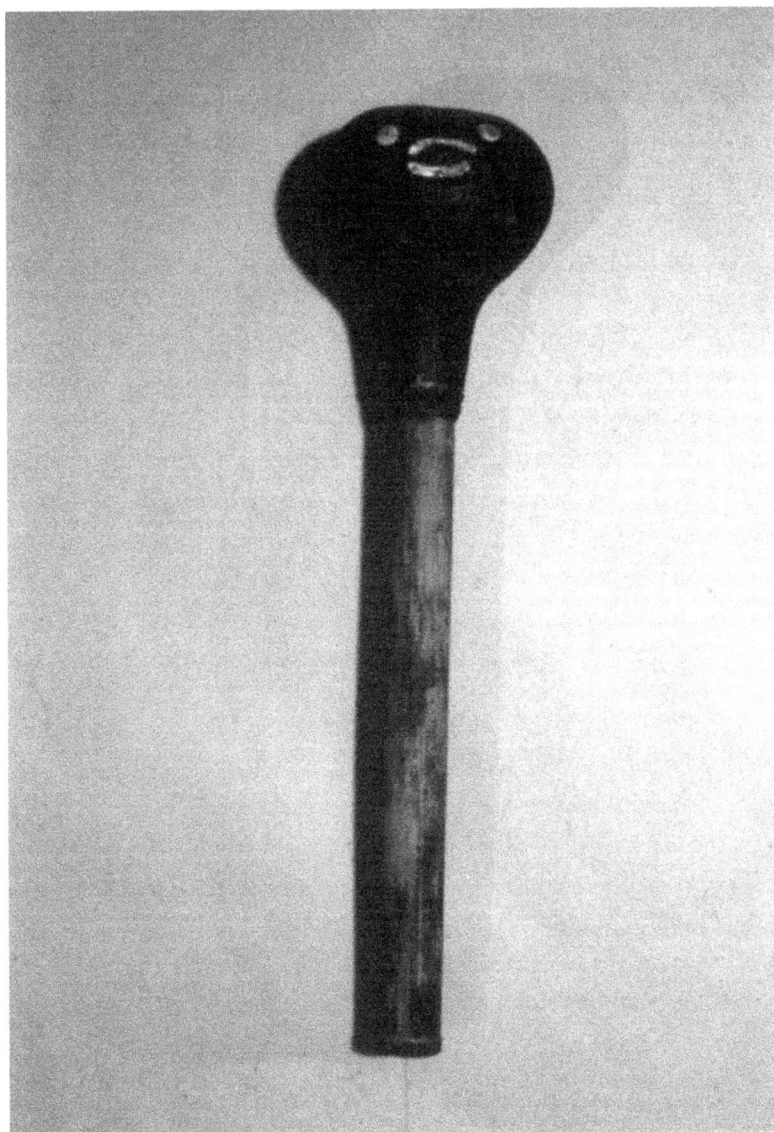

10. The Kamayurá kuyahapi horn. Photo by Rafael José de Menezes Bastos.

Previously I commented that the episode here described had a mythical pertinence for the Kamayurá. In saying so, I wanted to highlight the fact that for them—and for those engaged in trying to comprehend them—the episode was embedded with an original and modeling nature, which included prototypical catastrophes or, more precisely, origins and principles. If the Kamayurá concept of "myth" (*moroneta*) meets its vocational role in ruptures (undoubtedly opposed to the kind found in westerners' thinking), history serves the practical role of establishing continuity between past and present. To the Kamayurá, everything runs as if the past (the distant, unrecoverable, or lost one) exists only in myth. Unlike history, where there are only present times, more or less "presentified" by questioning (Sousa 1981), mythic narratives for the Kamayurá act as a kind of cyclotron that seeks reminiscences or emanations from the past.[35]

As noted above, the episode in question provoked two major ruptures or catastrophes, which established the following origins:

1. Kutamapù's divorce and Skin of Secluded's ostracism, dramatically mediated by her rape.

2. Leonardo's transformation into an enemy to the Kamayurá, which is the germ of the Villas-Bôas brothers as a whole becoming more and more irreversibly distanced in relation to the Kamayurá. From this moment on, the Kamayurá, in contrast to the Yawalapití, started to direct their contact with the world of the whites to the Xingu Detachment, an establishment kept during that time by the Brazilian Air Force in the Jacaré region (see Menezes Bastos 2004a).

If we believe the pretense that Kutamapù's jealousy of Leonardo was the prime mover of events, we would see the referred jealousy as the cause for demanding that the yaku'i trio be placed at Leonardo's house. Following this logic, Kutamapù coldly expected the men's revengeful reaction toward the violation of the rule prohibiting women from seeing the sacred flutes. However, this interpretation of the episode would reduce it to a mere crime of passion, an interpretation that makes no sense from the Kamayurá point of view. From a native perspective, the interpretation of the episode starts from the fact that the chief's (or great shaman's) and the Kamayurá men's reaction to the affair most directly responded to the radical denial of reciprocity with which Leonardo established his relations with Skin of Secluded and, through her, with the Kamayurá. Seen in this way, the sacred flutes are beings imbued with distinction, agency, and subjectivity. When Skin of Secluded violated the inviolable, the basis for the constitution of the Kamayurá world, she triggered a sequence of transformations that unfolded within the ferocious ethics of the sacred flutes, released from human control: Leonardo's house transformed into a flutes house, Leonardo himself turned into a flute who refused his own music, and the Kamayurá men became a yaku'i collectivity. This is exactly how the Kamayurá relate the episode today, following the patterns largely found in their mythology, which are for them the universal way of explaining ruptures.

Notes

A previous version of this text, delivered at the round table "Anthropology and Aesthetics: Art as Gnosis and Worldview" in the twenty-fifth meeting of the Brazilian Anthropological Association (Goiânia, June 11-14, 2006), was published in Portuguese in *Antropologia em Primeira Mão*, no 85 (2006). Another version, also in Portuguese, was issued by *Revista de Antropologia* 49, no. 2 (2006). The preliminary draft of the present English version was done by Alinne Fernandes. Thanks to Jonathan Hill for reading it and making suggestions. Thanks also to the anonymous reviewers of the text. I am solely responsible for it.

1. In Hornbostel-Sachs's system, number 421 corresponds to the "edge (aerophones) instruments or flutes." In short, this system has as basic nexuses the discrimination between the elements (strings, air columns, membranes, etc.) and the processes (for strings, strumming, percussing, playing with a bow, etc.) responsible for sound generation. As can be seen, timbre is included at a fundamental level of this classification. See Izikowitz 1935 for a classic study about the organology of indigenous South America based on the model of Hornbostel and Sachs, and see Menezes Bastos and Piedade 2000 for a brief discussion of it.

2. In Hornbostel-Sachs's system, idiophones are those instruments which contain the sound-producing elements within their own (in Greek, *idio-*) bodies.

3. See Piedade 2004 for a paradigmatic work about flutes in the Upper Xingu region among the Arawak-speaking Waurá (or Wauja). See also Barcelos Neto 2004 and Mello 2005. As far as I know, the first text includes the most complete study with a comparative approach of the flutes under analysis in Lowland South America. See Menezes Bastos 2006a and 2006b for a state-of-the-art account of the anthropology of music in the region.

4. The literature about the Xinguano and Upper Xingu in general is immense. See Heckenberger and Franchetto 2001 for an updated global account.

5. Denouncements by the Suyá, Kayabí, and Trumaí included in Menezes Bastos (2004a) are characterized likewise. The Yawalapití's evaluation of the Villas-Bôas brothers is completely different from the Kamayurá's, being highly positive (Menezes Bastos 1989, 1990, 1995).

6. Xingu in the Portuguese spoken by the Kamayurá is the region called Yakarep (Jacaré in Portuguese—"alligator" in English). It is close to the Indian post now located at Diauarum. It was there that the Brazilian Air Force later maintained a now-deactivated base. Leonardo was the youngest of the Villas-Bôas brothers. He died in 1961, due to heart problems. His name was given to the former Indian post Capitão Vasconcelos in acknowledgment of his role in creating the Xingu National Indian Park.

7. Takumã's father was the great chief and shaman Kutamapù. At that time, the Kamayurá village was situated at the mouth of the Tuatuari River, in a territory that the Kamayurá themselves recognize as Yawalapitian. See Menezes Bastos 1995.

8. At this point, Takumã complains about the upheavals that constrained the perfect fulfillment of his period of puberty seclusion from his living with Leonardo Villas-Bôas. He displays explicitly the shock between his father's and Leonardo's points of view with respect to the duration of his seclusion. His father, seeking to make Takumã a chief, wanted it to be long. Leonardo was conditioning it to be short. If, in the Kamayurá Portuguese in the context of the narrative, ten years represents a long duration, two months represents a very short one. The greater or shorter duration of one's puberty seclusion points to the best or worst care of his father in relation to the formation of his son. This is especially important in the case of the formation of the chiefs.

9. In Kamayurá Portuguese, *errar o caminho* means "take the wrong path." This expression, with all the piety that characterizes it, is used by Takumã in a subtle and highly efficient way toward Leonardo's moral condemnation under the point of view of the values themselves managed by him in his pedagogy of interethnic contact. Toward the condemnation and—with charity—the forgiveness!

10. These other *caraíbas*—the word that the Xinguano use in Portuguese to

mention the white men in general—were the workers of the Roncador-Xingu expedition to the region of the headwaters of the Xingu River, under the chieftainship of the Villas-Bôas brothers.

11. *Manga'uhet*: "immediately ex-puberty secluded woman." Kutamapù, Takumã's father, had three wives by that time. Skin of Secluded was the youngest.

12. Yumi'ama'e (or yaku'i) are the Kamayurá sacred flutes.

13. "To utter bad words," meaning to swear (*ye'eng nikatuite*) is an antisocial verbal behavior, innate to the witches. It is highly against Xinguano etiquette.

14. See Viveiros de Castro (1986: 625) for a seminal statement about the question of the agents' position, or perspective, in Indian thought.

15. To read about jealousy among the Kamayurá, see Menezes Bastos (1990).

16. One of the main tasks—and privileges—of the principal shaman among the Kamayurá is the detection of the witches and of the species of mama'e involved in the production of deaths (Menezes Bastos 1984–85).

17. Then she moved to Bananal Island, where she married an eminent Karajá chief. During my field work periods of 1974 and 2000 among the Kamayurá, Skin of Secluded visited the village, being a guest of Takumã's house. On the first occasion she accompanied her husband. On the second, she went alone. I did not note then any restriction from the Kamayurá to her and her husband. Sonia Regina Lourenço, a doctoral student under my supervision, presently is doing research about the Javaé Indians of Bananal Island (see Lourenço 2006 for her proposal). The Javaé and Karajá live very close on this island. She is including in her study a brief account of Skin of Secluded's life among the Karajá.

18. The Kamayurá understand that the spouses of ego—feminine or masculine—can be sexually shared, but only in secret (Menezes Bastos (1990).

19. The narrative of Leonardo and Skin of Secluded can be classified as a *moroneta*, "myth." It most immediately evokes the origin myths of the ritual of *Yawari* (Menezes Bastos, R. and H. 2002: 140, Menezes Bastos 2004b: 96) and of *Pequi* (Agostinho 1974a, 109–12), among others. For the Kamayurá, *moroneta* is the universal form of explanation of origins (see Menezes Bastos 1978, 1993, 2001).

20. According to my 1999a text. See Piedade (2004) for, as already said, a paradigmatic study on these flutes among the Xinguano Aruak speaking Wauja. It is worth noting that among the Kamayurá the flutes in question are *not* thought to be masks, as seems to be in the case of the Wauja, according to Piedade, and also according to studies by Barcelos Neto (2004) and Mello (2005). Undoubtedly, the Xinguano—and not only in terms of their forms of thinking about the sacred flutes-are neither simply equal (or similar) nor simply different (see my text of 1995).

21. Of course, I cannot post a picture of them here, as I did thoughtlessly in my 1999a text. As to recordings of their music, I also cannot include them with the text because the music of the sacred flutes is very sensitive for the Kamayurá and they expressly asked me not to disseminate them. One of the points of their sensibility in relationship to this dissemination is that they fear other Xinguano Indians will steal their music by recording it in their heads.

22. This diagram is in my 1999a text (228).

23. In this type of aerophone, the sound is produced through vibration of the player's lips due to air pressure.

24. In the case of the clarinets, the sound is created in a reed, which vibrates with the air the player produces. About clarinets in the lowlands, which Izikowitz wrongly believes to have a European origin, see Beaudet 1997 and Menezes Bastos and Piedade 2000. The acoustic differences involving flutes, trumpets, and clarinets, as well as the other instruments, are extremely interesting for Kamayurá organology.

25. This omission of the +1 generation might point to the nexus that only interests the referred kindred, the ancestors (+2 generation and superior), the children (-1), and the siblings of ego (and ego, of course). It must be noted that in Kamayurá thought, the authorship (or signature) of ego's genealogical substance belongs to his or her ancestors, being only transmitted by the +1 generation (see Menezes Bastos 1990).

26. See Mello 2005 for an important study on this matter among the Wauja. It involves the music of the male sacred flutes and relevant parts of the female vocal repertoire. According to this study, the women listen to the flutes to record their melodies in their heads, transposing them; or better, transforming them into models, for their vocal music, particularly that of the iamurikuma ritual. Note that the mental recording of music is said by the Kamayurá to be similar to "our" recording machines.

27. Xinguanization (see Menezes Bastos 1999a) is estimated to have begun in the eighteenth century. For the contemporary Kamayurá, xinguanization is understood in terms of important changes in some crucial cultural domains, such as the adoption of the pan-Xinguano taboo against killing and eating game animals, with the exception of some kinds of monkeys, which can be eaten by old people (see Menezes Bastos 1990, 1995, 2001).

28. The myth that is the basis of the iamurikuma ritual presents this risk in its original form—the transformation of men into mama'e, provoking the same transformation among women, and thus the end of the sociality of this world (see Mello 2005). I have already dealt with the frailty of the human "social contract" among the Kamayurá in some previous works, among them 1990, 1993, 1995 and 2004b. On shamanism in Upper Xingu, see my 1984–85 article.

29. According to Hogbin 1970. The referred comparison is in Menezes Bastos 1999a: 223–29. See Piedade 2004 and some other texts present in Gregor and Tuzin 2001 for recent approaches on the matter.

30. For the mythology in question, see Agostinho 1974a, 1974b: 159–201, and Villas-Bôas 1975. Agostinho 1974a: 113–27 collects some narratives specifically on the flutes and their kindred. See Serra 2006 for a comparative study about Xinguano mythology, with central attention to the Kamayurá's. On this study, Serra raises the inclusion of the incest prohibition rule into the feminine prohibition of seeing the sacred flutes (167).

31. The notion of *ta'angap* is extremely rich and complex as that of mimesis. I have dealt with it in many texts, among those 1984–85, 1990, and 2001.

32. *Morena* is the region where the world was originated, according to the Kamayurá. It is near the Yakarep.

33. This picture was taken indoors by me and is in my 1978 text. Note that the horn's mouthpiece is made with teeth of piranha, which is an especially ferocious species of fish.

34. To stress this, note that virtuosity in music is directly linked to the already mentioned capacity of the mind to record music in high fidelity as "our" machines do.

35. *Questioning*, as a matter of fact, seems to be one of the original nexuses of the Greek word *history*.

References Cited

Agostinho, Pedro. 1974a. *Mitos e Outras Narrativas Kamayurá*. Bahia: Universidade Federal da Bahia.

———. 1974b. *Kwarìp: Mito e Ritual no Alto Xingu*. São Paulo: EPU/Editora da Universidade de São Paulo.

Barcelos Neto, Aristóteles. 2004. "Apapaatai: Rituais de Máscaras no Alto Xingu." PhD diss., Universidade de São Paulo.

Beaudet, Jean-Michel. 1997. *Souffles d'Amazonie: Les orchestres tule des Wayãpi*. Nanterre: Société d'ethnologie.

Foucault, Michel. 1977. *Vigiar e Punir: História da violência nas prisões*. Petrópolis: Vozes.

Gregor, Thomas A., and Donald Tuzin, eds. 2001. *Gender in Amazônia and Melanesia: An Exploration of the Comparative Method*. Berkeley: University of California Press.

Heckenberger, M., and B. Franchetto, eds. 2001. *Os Povos do Alto Xingu: História e Cultura*. Rio de Janeiro: Editora da Universidade Federal do Rio de Janeiro.

Hill, Jonathan. 1993. *Keepers of the Sacred Chants: The Poetics of Ritual Power in an Amazonian Society*. Tucson: University of Arizona Press.

Hogbin, H. Ian. 1970. *The Island of Menstruating Men: Religion in Wogeo, New Guinea*. Scranton PA: Chandler.

Hornbostel, E. M., and Curt Sachs. 1961 [1914]. "Classification of Musical Instruments." *Galpin Society Journal* 14: 3–29.

Hugh-Jones, Stephen. 1979. *The Palm and the Pleiades: Initiation and Cosmology in Northwest Amazonia*. New York: Cambridge University Press.

Izikowitz, Karl Gustav. 1935. *Musical and Other Sound Instruments of the South American Indians*. Göteborg: Eleander Boktryckeri Aktiebolag.

Lagrou, Elsje M. 1995. "Compulsão Visual: Desenhos e Imagens nas Culturas da Amazônia Ocidental." *Antropologia em Primeira Mão* 9.

Lourenço, Sonia Regina. 2006. "A Dança dos Aruanãs: Rito, Mito, e Música entre os Javaé da Ilha do Bananal-to." PhD diss., Universidade Federal de Santa Catarina, Programa de Pós-Graduação em Antropologia Social. Available at www.musa.ufsc.br.

Mello, Maria Ignez Cruz. 2005. "Iamurikuma: Música, Mito e Ritual entre os Wauja do Alto Xingu." PhD diss., Universidade Federal de Santa Catarina. Available at www.musa.ufsc.br.

Menezes Bastos, Rafael José de. 1978. *A Musicológica Kamayurá: Para uma Antropologia da Comunicação no Alto Xingu*. Brasília: Funai.

———. 1984–85. "O 'Payemeramaraka' Kamayurá—Uma Contribuição à Etnografia do Xamanismo no Alto Xingu." *Revista de Antropologia* 27–28: 139–77.

———. 1989. "Exegeses Yawalapití e Kamayurá da Criação do Parque Indígena do Xingu e a Invenção da Saga dos Irmãos Villas-Bôas." *Revista de Antropologia* 30–31–32: 391–426.

———. 1990. "A Festa da Jaguatirica: Uma Partitura Crítico-Interpretativa." PhD diss., Universidade de São Paulo.

———. 1993. "A Saga do 'Yawari': Mito, Música e História no Alto-Xingu." In *Amazônia: Etnologia e História Indígena*, ed. E. Viveiros de Castro and M. Carneiro da Cunha, 117–46. São Paulo: Universidade de São Paulo.

———. 1995. "Indagação Sobre os Kamayurá, o Alto-Xingu e Outros Nomes e Coisas: Uma Etnologia da Sociedade Xinguana." *Anuário Antropológico/1994*: 227–69.

———. 1999a. *A Musicológica Kamayurá: Para uma Antropologia da Comunicação no Alto Xingu*. 2nd ed. Florianópolis, Brazil: Editora da Universidade Federal de Santa Catarina.

———. 1999b. "Apùap World Hearing: On the Kamayurá Phono-Auditory

System and the Anthropological Concept of Culture." *World of Music* 41, no. 1: 85–96.

———. 2001. "Ritual, História, e Política no Alto Xingu: Observações a Partir dos Kamayurá e do Estudo da Festa da Jaguatirica (Jawari)." In *Os Povos do Alto Xingu: História e Cultura*, ed. B. Franchetto and M. Heckenberger, 335–57. Rio de Janeiro: Editora da UFRJ.

———. 2004a. "'Cargo Anti-Cult' no Alto Xingu: Consciência Política e Legítima Defensa Étnica." *Antropologia em Primeira Mão* 71. Also see www.antropologia.ufsc.br.

———. 2004b. "The Yawari Ritual of the Kamayurá: A Xinguano Epic." In *Music in Latin America and the Caribbean: An Encyclopedic History*, ed. Malena Kuss, 1: 77–99. Austin: University of Texas Press.

———. 2006a. "Música nas Terras Baixas da América do Sul (Primeira Parte)." *Antropologia em Primeira Mão* 86.

———. 2006b. "Música nas Terras Baixas da América do Sul (Segunda Parte)." *Antropologia em Primeira Mão* 89.

Menezes Bastos, Rafael José de, and Acácio Tadeu de Camargo Piedade. 2000. "Beaudet: Souffles d'Amazonie: Les Orchestres 'Tule' des Wayãpi (review essay)." *British Journal of Ethnomusicology* 9, no. 1: 143–56.

Menezes Bastos, Rafael José de, and José de Hermenegildo. 2002. "A Festa da Jaguatirica: Primeiro e Sétimo Cantos. Introdução, Transcrição e Comentários." *Ilha: Revista de Antropologia* 4, no. 2: 133–74. Also available at www.antropologia.ufsc.br.

Piedade, Acácio Tadeu de Camargo. 1997. "Música Yepamasa: Por uma Antropologia da Música no Alto Rio Negro." Master's thesis, Universidade Federal de Santa Catarina. Also available at www.musa.ufsc.br.

———. 2004. "O Canto do Kawoká: Música, Cosmologia e Filosofia entre os Wauja do Alto Xingu." PhD diss., Universidade Federal de Santa Catarina. Also available at www.musa.ufsc.br.

Seeger, Anthony. 1975 "The Meaning of Body Ornaments: A Suyá Example." *Ethnology* 14, no. 3: 211–24.

Serra, Ordep. 2006. *Um Tumulto de Asas: Apocalipse no Xingu—Breve Estudo de Mitologia Kamayurá*. Salvador: Editora da Universidade Federal da Bahia.

Sousa, Eudoro de. 1981. *História e Mito*. Brasília: Editora da Universidade de Brasília.

Villas-Bôas, Orlando, and Cláudio Villas-Bôas. 1975. *Xingu: Os Índios, seus Mitos*. 2nd ed. São Paulo: Edibolso.

Viveiros de Castro, Eduardo. 1986. *Araweté: Os Deuses Canibais*. Rio de Janeiro: Jorge Zahar.

3. Soundscaping the World

The Cultural Poetics of Power and
Meaning in Wakuénai Flute Music

JONATHAN HILL

In this essay I will document and analyze two complementary
processes of creating musical soundscapes among the Arawak-
speaking Wakuénai of the Upper Rio Negro region in Venezuela.[1] The first of these can be called "cultural soundscaping" and
is concerned with the creation of local identities through employ-
ing the power of mythic ancestors and primordial human beings
to socialize animal nature. The second musical process of "natural soundscaping" is a naturalizing of social being, or a production of "otherness," through movements of flute and trumpet players away from the socializing space of mythic ancestral
power into more naturalized places of animals, deceased humans,
and "other people."

In previous works (Hill 1993, 2004), I have demonstrated how
these two complementary processes of sound-and-meaning production arise from the interplay of language and music, or lexicality and musicality, in the genre of ritually powerful sung, chanted,
and spoken speech (*malikái*) performed in rites of passage and
shamanic curing rituals.[2] "Cultural soundscaping" privileges
the classificatory, or taxonomic, power of verbally constructed
categories of powerful mythic beings over the more dynamic,
transformative effects of musicality and musical sounds, which
are understood as creations of and/or journeys through mythic-
historical times and spaces. Cultural soundscaping transforms

and constrains the explosive creativity of musical sounds into lexical categories of spirit names and is a logocentric process of constructing images of continuity, gradual change, and an ideal of perfect transmission of cultural knowledge and linguistic forms across the generations of time separating mythic ancestors from living human descendants. In contrast to the logocentrism of cultural soundscaping, natural soundscaping privileges the dynamic, transformative power of musicality and musical sound over the more stable lexical categories of powerful mythic beings and the stabilizing process of cultural soundscaping. Natural soundscaping, which I also refer to as "musicalization" (Hill 1993, 1994), transposes verbally constructed meanings into musical sound as a way of creating naturalized social being through movements away from and back to the center of mythic space. Musicalization is about the creation of an expanding world of culturally differentiated peoples and geographically distinct places as musically dynamic processes of transformation, movement, displacement, and discontinuity.

The twin processes of cultural and natural soundscaping can also be understood as complementary ways of using musicality and musical sounds to link the human life-world as a verbally constituted community to the Upper Rio Negro's rich diversity of fish, forest animal, plant, and other nonhuman life forms. Whereas cultural soundscaping uses "language"—verbal categories, naming processes, and speech—as a symbolic template for musical performance, natural soundscaping draws its inspiration from sounds and behaviors—especially eating and reproductive ones—of fish, amphibians, insects, and other nonhuman life forms. Natural soundscaping is a mimetic process in which natural behaviors are "reintroduced" into the human social world in both material and symbolic ways as a means of renewing and regenerating the social world through exchanges of surplus foods and the creation of alliances and intermarriages.[3] In short, there is a recursive relation between people and the riverine ecology of the

Upper Rio Negro in which the nonhuman world is imbued with social meanings through cultural soundscaping and, at the same time, reintroduced into the social world as a process of naturalization, or natural soundscaping.

The Wakuénai, or Curripaco, as they are known in Colombia and Venezuela, are northern Arawak-speaking peoples living along the Isana and Guainía rivers and their tributaries at the headwaters of the Rio Negro. They form part of the larger region of fishing and horticultural societies of northwestern Amazonia and organize themselves into internally ranked, named, localized phratries consisting of five older-to-younger brother patrisibs. Daily subsistence activities revolve around fishing and bitter manioc cultivation, with some hunting and much gathering of plant materials from the surrounding forests. Their subsistence economy can be summed up in the phrase "Let the fish and game come to us." Human communities, fishing traps, and gardens are set up along riverbanks to take advantage of seasonal spawning runs and migratory movements of fish and game. The timing of ritual and ceremonial activities is closely related to the natural movements of fish and game animals and to seasonal changes between periods of relative scarcity when river levels are rising and times of relative abundance when they are falling (Hill 1984, 1989). The integration of musical performances, fishing, and hunting finds concrete expression in the fact that the same species of palm, called *máwi* (*Astrostudium schomburgkii*), is used for making ceremonial flutes (*máwi*), fish traps, and blowguns (see fig. 11).

The Place of Musical Performances in Mythic Narratives

Wakuénai narratives about mythic times can be arranged into three groupings, starting with "The Primordial Times" (Úupi Pérri), continuing through "The World Begins" (Hekuápi Ikéeñuakawa), and concluding with "The World Opens Up" (Hekuápi Ihméetakawa).[4] This ordering is not a simple, linear chronology. Although the arrangement of narratives tends to move from

11. Bundles of máwi palm tubes harvested while the men fell trees for new manioc gardens during the dry season. Máwi and other ceremonial flutes of pudáli are made from separate tree trunks that have been hollowed out. Photo by Jonathan Hill, September 1981.

earlier, undifferentiated times to later periods of cultural separateness, there are many "strange loops" and cultural practices, such as shamanic curing rituals and *pudáli* ceremonies, that allow for movements backward and forward in mythic space-times.

"The Primordial Times" include ten narratives that describe the origins of the trickster-creator (Iñapirríkuli, or Made-From-Bone), sickness, and death. This grouping of narratives centers around the figure of the trickster, whose struggles against various adversaries resulted in the creation of natural and social worlds. Overall, "The Primordial Times" was a period of unceasing violence between Made-From-Bone and his animal-affines in which the trickster anticipated the treachery and deceit of other beings and skillfully manipulated words and other signs as tools for deceiving and defeating these adversaries. The trickster always managed to find ways to cope with difficult, even life-threatening, situations, not by directly confronting adversaries but through self-concealment and use of secret knowledge to imagine a future way to break out of present dangers.

"The World Begins" encompasses six narratives that explain the origins of night and sleep, cooking fire, manioc gardens, peach-palm fruits, and the musical dancing of pudáli and *kwépani* ceremonial exchanges. The beginning of ceremonial music (*mádzerukái*) marks a turning point in Wakuénai mythic history, for Made-From-Bone and his younger brother Káali created mádzerukái as a way to teach their children how to give and receive food and other things from their affines in a nonviolent, respectful manner.

Musical sounds and performances occupy a special place in Wakuénai mythic narratives, since it was through the invention of mádzerukái that Káali transformed the unceasing cycles of violence, fear, and hostility of "The Primordial Times" into relations based on respect and reciprocity between communities of people (Hill 2009). An indigenous theory of music, or musicology, thus arises in the first place from the principle that collective musical dances provide the primary means for socializing the relations between communities of people who are in the process of creating, or celebrating, affinal alliances through exchanges of male and female labor, food and drink, and other material goods.[5] This musicalization, or musical socialization, of affinal relations between communities of people is a process of creating a naturalized social space in which human interactions are densely interwoven with the sounds and behaviors of fish and other animal species.

The final section of narratives, or "The World Opens Up," outlines the conception, birth, and life cycle of the primordial human being, Kuwái. The cycle of myths about Kuwái describes the origins of individual male and female humanness, the human life cycle, the passage of generational and historical time, and the ritual practices for controlling all these developmental and temporal processes. In addition, "The World Opens Up" includes several narratives about the origins of witchcraft, shamanic curing, the afterlife, and modernity.

During the life of Kuwái, musical word-sounds acted as the life force that created all the animal and plant species of the Upper Rio Negro region and that "opened up the world" into an expanding universe of distinct peoples and places. The second defining principle of an indigenous musicology, or "musical naming power," emerges from the mythic figure of Kuwái as a being whose body "speaks" with words, music, and animal sounds.

> "karrú, napirrikú," pidaliaku, "núnuka nukathinátaka nahliú hnaha nudakenai," pidaliaku.
> ("No, Iñapirríkuli, I've come to show myself to them, my grandsons," said Kuwái.)
> "námaka pida nakáapaka Kuwái," pidaliaku.
> ("They want to see Kuwái," he said.)

> "imée hnua ikatsa Kuwái kee hnua," pidaliaku Iñapirríkuli isriú.
> ("because I am the real Kuwái," he said to Iñapirríkuli.)
> "phímaka watsa kuameka kákuka hnua," pidaliaku.
> ("You are going to hear how I speak, my sound," he said.)

kamena kákukani Iñapirríkuli isriú. dapa, máaliawa, phiume hna
Kuwái, phiume kákuka lidaki.
(And he began to "speak," or make sounds, for Iñapirríkuli:
paca, white heron flutes, everything of Kuwái, all the sounds of
his body.)

kamena liúkakawa dzakalérikohle. kamena likapéetaka hna
iénpetipe.
(Kuwái arrived in the village and began to show himself to the
boys.)

kamena kákukani hnéemakaru liaku phiume hekuápiriko.
tsúukatua hekuapi.
(He began to "speak" the word-sounds that could be heard in the
entire world. The world was still very small.)

kamena kákukani. "heeee," pidaliaku. limáliatsa pida hiekuita
lihméetawa hekuapi.
(He began to say, "Heee." The sound of his voice ran away and
opened up the world.)

Through a nearly total blurring of the boundary between words
and sounds, or lexicality and musicality, this episode of mythic creation fuses verbal acts of naming and classification together with
musical processes of singing and chanting. This fusion of meaning and sound forms a hypercreative process of musical naming
power, "the powerful sound that opens up the world" (*kémak-
ani hliméetaka hekwápi*), or the power to verbally sing and chant
the world into being.

The integration of verbal and musical arts into a single creative
life force means that any attempt to interpret ritual singing and
chanting must start from an understanding of the verbal processes
of spirit-naming and the different ways of integrating them with
musical processes.[6] The myth of Kuwái as "the powerful sound
that opens up the world" also generalizes the act of speaking to
include the entire proto-human body. Kuwái "speaks" with all
the parts of his body—feet, hands, back, neck, arms, legs, and

penis—not just his speech organs. And each body part is said to be a species of fish, bird, or forest animal, each making its own unique sounds and contributing to the sound of the voice of Kuwái as it travels far away and opens up the world. Kuwái is thus an anthropomorphic being whose body is at the same time a zoomorphic synthesis of animal species, a duality that allows for relating the second principle of indigenous musicology back to the first principle, or the use of musical sounds to create a naturalized social space.

In the following discussion, I will focus on the genre of ceremonial dance music, or mádzerukái, as a social means for constructing the space-times of mythic creation through making and playing flutes and trumpets in collective dances.[7] During my fieldwork with the Wakuénai in the 1980s, I learned that the term *mádzerukái* encompassed all instrumental and vocal music performed during two very different kinds of ceremonial exchange, pudáli and kwépani. Wakuénai musicians told me that there was a strict taboo against playing music of pudáli in the context of a kwépani ceremony and vice versa.[8] Nevertheless, my attempts to elicit distinct names for these two subgenres of mádzerukái were fruitless, so I have distinguished between them as pudáli and kwépani subgenres of mádzerukái, respectively.

The pudáli subgenre of mádzerukái outlines a complex, elaborate process of musicalization, or natural soundscaping, in which musical sounds and associated dance movements are employed in various forms of imitating natural sounds and animal behaviors. Performances of mádzerukái in pudáli are celebrations of natural abundance and resulting surpluses of fish and game meat that allow for exchanges and feasting between affinally related groups. The flutes and trumpets made for and played in pudáli are, for the most part, made and played in public with women and children present and participating as dance partners to male instrumentalists.[9]

Sharply contrasting with the openness and inclusivity of pudáli, the kwépani subgenre of mádzerukái requires the strict exclusion of women and uninitiated children from the adult men's making and playing of flutes and trumpets. These instruments are considered to be highly powerful and potentially dangerous, since they are considered to be different parts of the body of Kuwái, the primordial human being of myth. Kwépani, or "Kuwái-dance," is an exclusively male activity of reassembling the body of Kuwái by making and playing sacred flutes and trumpets.[10] Most of these instruments also have animal namesakes—*maaliáwa* (white heron), *dzáate* (toucan), *dápa* (paca), *molítu* (a species of small frog), and so on. Although women and children are strictly prohibited from *seeing* these musical instruments, they are allowed or even required to *hear* the music of these instruments and, as I will show below, are in some cases even required to "converse" with these musical instruments.[11] Kwépani ceremonies are at basis a construction of the hierarchical linkages of continuity between mythic ancestors and groups of living male descendants through transforming musical sounds into "language," or speechlike patterns of sound.[12]

Both pudáli and kwépani subgenres of mádzerukái include two distinct, yet unnamed, sub-subgenres (see fig. 12). Pudáli ceremonies come in two-part cycles: (1) an opening, male-owned ceremony in which a male leader (*púdalímnali*) organizes the amassing and transporting of a gift of smoked fish and game meat to another community and (2) a closing, female-owned ceremony in which a female leader (*púdalímnarru*) supervises the production of a large quantity of processed manioc pulp and its presentation to the guests of the opening ceremony (Hill 1983, 1987). In terms of musical performances, the main difference between male- and female-owned pudáli ceremonies is the playing of large *kulirrína* trumpets named after striped catfish in male-owned ceremonies versus the use of *wáuna* dance stamping tubes and singing of *waanápani* songs in female-owned ceremonies. The kwépani subgenre of mádzerukái is also performed in two ritual contexts:

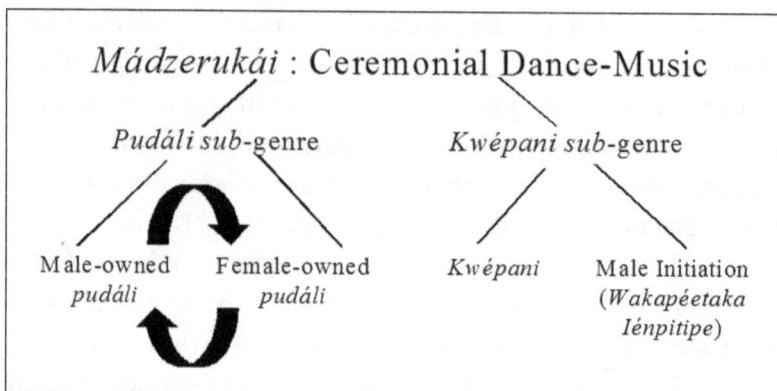

```
        Mádzerukái : Ceremonial Dance-Music
              /                          \
      Pudáli sub-genre           Kwépani sub-genre
       /            \             /            \
Male-owned   Female-owned    Kwépani    Male Initiation
  pudáli        pudáli                   (Wakapéetaka
                                          Iénpitipe)
```

12. Subgenres and sub-subgenres of *mádzerukái*.

(1) kwépani ceremonial exchanges of wild palm fruits and (2) male initiation rituals (called *wakéetaka iénpitipé*, or "we show our children).

Molítu: A Frog for All Seasons

Cultural soundscaping, or "logocentrism," is without question most clearly illustrated in men's performances on small flutes called molítu during kwépani ceremonies and male initiation rituals. Before presenting some examples of the musical "talking" of the molítu flute players, it is important to note that the molítu frog has two distinct meanings. On the one hand, the molítu frogs are said to have constituted an army of male warriors who accompanied the trickster-creator, Iñápirríkuli, in his pursuit of Ámaru and the women after they had stolen the sacred flutes and trumpets of Kuwái. As mythic symbols of men's ability to regain control of the sacred flutes and trumpets from women, molítu frogs are embodiments of masculinity and male-controlled ritual power. Accordingly, as ritual flutes played in the kwépani subgenre of collective dance music, molítu signifies that most masculine of body parts, the penis of Kuwái. So when men use the molítu flutes to "talk" with women during sacred ceremonies and rituals, they are

Constellation: Mákwa -pidánia | Kéwe -dápani | Máarinai | Zúrunai | Dziaka | Várupan -hnúme | Wáriperi | Upitaina | Kaku -dzudi | Iñéwia | Umáinai

River Level: falls about half-way — rises rapidly — falls to lowest annual level — rising to highest annual level — stationary

Fishing: abundant — scarce — very abundant, dry season expeditions — super -abundant — very scarce — scarce

Agriculture: cutting new gardens — extending old gardens — burn & plant — weed & clean new gardens

Weather: fairly dry, gusty winds — rainy — relatively dry & sunny — heaviest rains — heavy rains — thunderstorms

Molitu frog Käaliéni: sings — sings — sings

Months (bottom axis): Sep | Oct | Nov | Dec | Jan | Feb | Mar | Apr | May | Jun | Jul | Aug | Sep

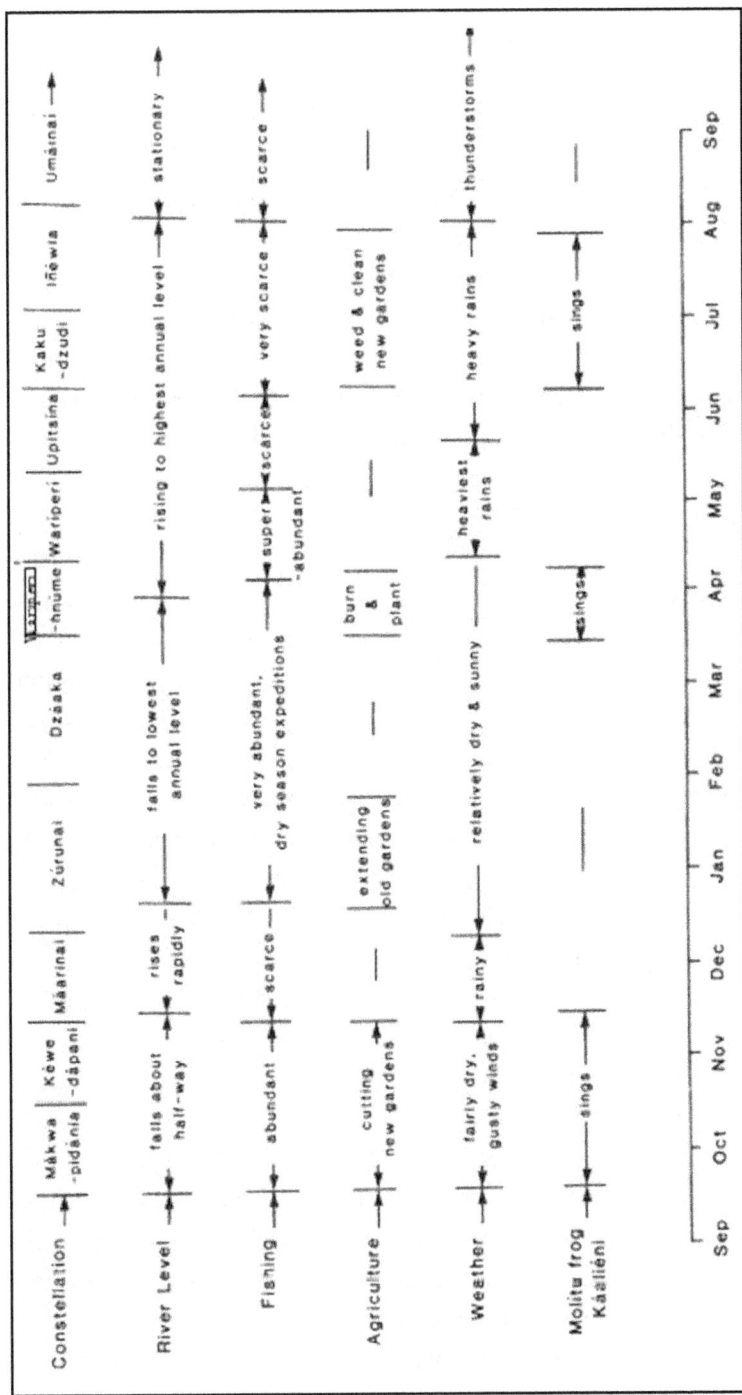

13. Annual cycle of fishing and gardening activities showing periods of molitu frog's singing.

also giving voice to the prototypical human penis. On the other hand, as a species of frog, the molítu is regarded as one of Káali's children (*Káaliéni*) and forms part of the process of musicalization in pudáli ceremonies. The singing of the molítu frog is said to "tell" men and women when it is time to select and clear forest lands for new manioc gardens, when to burn the felled vegetation, and when to plant new gardens. Thus the same frog species that serves as a "talking flute/penis" in kwépani is also a natural acoustical sign for regulating the timing of seasonal horticultural activities through its singing (see fig. 13). The multivocality of molítu frogs thus spans the entire spectrum of cultural and natural soundscaping, or the semiotic space between spoken language and musicalized speech.[13]

In both kwépani (Kuwái dance) ceremonies and male initiation rituals, men playing molítu flutes "converse" with women, who are secluded inside a special house so that they can *hear* but not *see* the men playing sacred instruments outside. As pointed out elsewhere in this volume (see chapter by Nicolas Journet), the secrecy that surrounds the sacred flutes and trumpets of Kuwái applies primarily to the sense of vision. Women know about these instruments, can hear their music, and "converse" with men playing the molítu flutes; but they must never see either the instruments or the men who play them. Clearly the secrecy of the sacred flutes is an avowed one in which both men and women are required to participate in a ritual reconstruction of the secret. Having said this, there is another sense in which the auditory mode parallels and heightens the visual secrecy of the molítu and other sacred flutes and trumpets. The flutes' "voices" are not only invisible to the women but also serve to disguise, or mask, the individual identities of male flute players. The molítu flute thus allows men to cross the symbolic divide between the sexes by suppressing men's voices as distinct social identities and transposing them into a mythic realm of collective identity—viz., that of the primordial human being, whose body is collectively assembled by groups of men playing a variety of flutes and trumpets, each of which represents a different part of the body of Kuwái. In kwépani and male initiation rituals, the playing of sacred flutes and trumpets is ultimately about the subordination of individual identities to collective ones based on gender and, in turn, the encompassing of both men and women as groups within the hierarchical relations of power between mythic ancestors and their human descendants.[14]

During kwépani and male initiation rituals, women are secluded inside a special house and perform drinking songs, called *pákamarántakan*, in which they dialogically joke with one another. When they hear the molítu flute being played outside, the women continue their drinking songs by addressing questions to the molítu flute. The sound examples referred to here were recorded by Felix Oliveros during a male initiation ritual held in March 1985. (See the complete list of sound examples at the end of the chapter.) In their songs, the women address the molítu flute in *lingua geral* as "*mawá*" rather than in Curripaco as *molítu*. They are asking if the molítu flute players would like to have some fermented manioc and fruit drinks. The following transcriptions are based on spoken demonstrations that I elicited during my fieldwork in 1981.[15]

> Molítu: *Mu, mu, mu. Mu-tu-r-ru.*
> Women: *Pímaka píra turúru, Molítu?*
> (Do you want to drink liquor, Molítu?)
> Molítu: *Oh-hon, mu, óh-hon.*
> (Yes, *mu*, yes.)

Pregnant women also ask molítu flutes about the sex of their unborn children, as in the following transcription (also from my fieldwork in 1981):

> Women: *Mawá? Kwáka ruénipe sruátaha kewédani?*
> (Molítu? What sex will her unborn child have?)

Molítu: "*Í-na-rru-á-tsa*," "*Í-na-rru-á-tsa*," *mu.*(female, female)
Women: *Kwámi?*
(What?)
Molítu: "*Í-na-rru-á-tsa*"
(Female)

In this example, the molítu flute "speaks" by using different stress patterns to indicate "male" or "female." "*Í-na-rru-á-tsa*," or female, is conveyed by making five notes in succession, with *lengthening* and stress on the first and fourth notes or "syllables." "*A-tsiá-tsa*," or male, is communicated through a pattern of three notes in succession with lengthening and stress on the second, or middle, note.

In addition to their use in musical "dialogues" between male flute players and female singers (sound ex. 1), molítu flutes are also played together with other flutes and trumpets of Kuwái, such as the massive "jaguar bone" trumpets representing the voice of mythic ancestors in male initiation rituals (sound ex. 2) or with trios of *waliáduwa* flutes at the end of male initiation rituals (sound ex. 3).[16] Sometimes the molítu flute will add its voice to the ritual speeches, or advice, that fathers and other elders give to young men during initiation rituals (sound ex. 4). In all three of these examples, the molítu flute appears to be added to men's speeches or other instrumental playing as a way of calling attention to, or poeticizing, the importance of their verbal or musical "messages." There do not appear to be any cases where men address or converse with molítu flutes in the same style as the women's song dialogues with molítu flute players.

Pudáli: Gender Complementarity and the Musicalization of Intercommunal Exchange

As I noted above, pudáli ceremonies are two-part cycles in which an opening, male-owned gift of smoked fish and game meat is reciprocated in a later ceremonial offering of processed man-

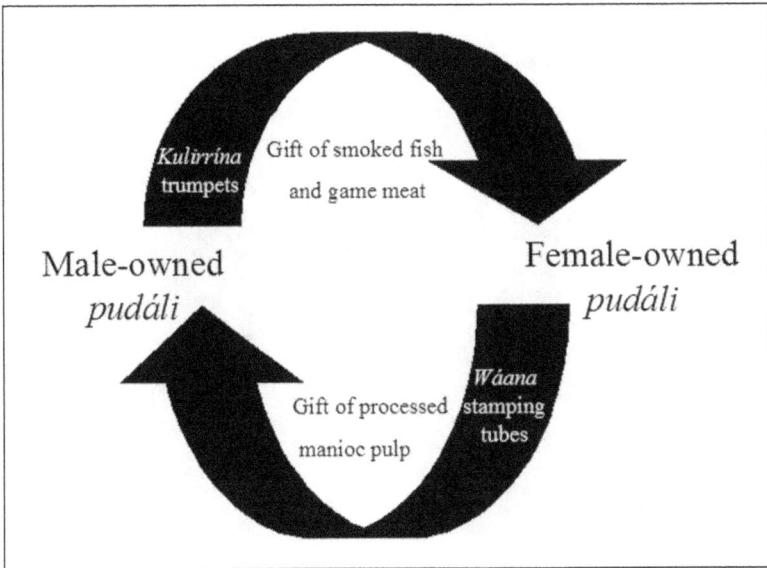

14. Pudáli: Gender complementarity and the musicalization of intercommunal exchange.

ioc pulp organized by a female leader (*pudalímnarru*) (see fig. 14). Although there are important differences between male- and female-owned pudáli ceremonies, they share a common tripartite organization that moves from standardized flute music played in large ensembles around the offering of food to smaller, individualized flute duets based on improvisatory theme and variation after the redistribution of the food gift. Guests arrive bearing a large offering of smoked fish and game meat in the late afternoon and form ensembles of male flute and trumpet players with female dance partners who circle around the gift of food while their hosts watch from a respectful distance.

There is a standardized duet played on pairs of long máwi flutes during the opening dances of pudáli (sound ex. 5). Máwi flutes are made in "male" and "female" pairs. The male flutes are the height of a man, whereas the female flutes are four finger widths shorter (up to a man's eyebrows).[17] These máwi flutes must be

15. Men playing kulirrína trumpets and máwi flutes with their female dance partners during the "catfish trumpet festival" of 1981. Photo by Jonathan Hill, October, 1981.

made from separate máwi tree trunks that have been hollowed out. The flutes have no finger holes and so can only produce a series of overtone intervals rather than smaller, melodic intervals. However, when played in a hocket style, pairs of male and female flutes tuned approximately one whole tone apart can be made to produce a great variety of melodic patterns, each based on the interweaving of male and female notes.[18]

In male-owned pudáli ceremonies, the standard opening duet of máwi flutes is played together with several kulirrína trumpets (see fig. 15) (sound ex. 6).[19] Kulirrína trumpets are named after a species of large striped catfish (*kulírri* or *raiao*), and the sounds of these trumpets are said to replicate the sound of a river or stream filled to the brim with spawning, migrating *bocachico* (*Leporinus Sp.*) fish, a phenomenon that occurs each year at the very beginning of the long wet season when rivers and streams first flood their banks, allowing the *Leporinus* fish to migrate into newly flooded forests to spawn. Large quantities of these fish are captured in weirs placed at the mouths of streams when they attempt to return to the river's main channel. There are three distinct dancing formations of kulirrína trumpet players and máwi flute players during the opening performances of pudáli, each named after a different species of bocachico fish.[20] During the opening performances, hosts watch from a distance and must not participate in their guests' dances. At the end of these opening performances, the male leader of the guests, or *pudalímnali*, makes a formal speech offering the gift of food to the host's headman (*pantímnali*), who stores the food inside his house during the night.

During the night, hosts invite guests inside to drink manioc beer and sing *pakamarántakan*, or drinking songs. From time to time, guest men go outside to play small flutes, called *déetu* (coconut palm weevil).[21] The men surround the host's house and play their déetu flutes up under the rafters to "ask" their hosts for manioc beer. The host's headman comes outside and silences the déetu flute players one by one, offering them each a large quantity of manioc beer, which they are expected to drink until vomiting. These late-night performances are an important transition between the large, standardized performances of the opening dances and the more individualized, improvisatory musical dances of the following day. The guests' sucking and vomiting of fermented drinks from their host's house implicitly evokes shamanic curing rituals, in which the sucking and vomiting of disease-causing agents (e.g., splinters or poison) serve as a basis for reversing illnesses. More explicitly, the feeding behavior of déetu (a shiny black weevil with very long proboscis) is also the moment when these insects lay eggs in the pith of felled palm trees as they suck the tree's oozing sap. The déetu performances of pudáli symbolically encompass natural eating and reproductive behaviors in a single musical performance.[22] The déetu flutes are not made in male and female, or longer and shorter, pairs, so the instruments produce only a single rising and falling set of overtone intervals rather than the melodic patterns of larger máwi flutes (sound ex. 7).

During the last hours of the night when the first grayish light of dawn appears on the eastern horizon, guests and hosts go outside to perform special kulirrína trumpet dances named after the black resin (*maíni*) used to coat the trumpets' woven resonators. The low, somewhat mournful rumbling sound of the kulirrína trumpets is played without the more spirited sounds of máwi flute duets. At the end of this performance, the guests give their kulirrína trumpets to the hosts as reminders of their obligation to sponsor a female-owned ceremony in several weeks' time.[23]

After daybreak, the hosts redistribute the gift of smoked fish and game meat among host and guest families, beginning a day of feasting, drinking, and dancing in which guest men are permitted to dance with host women and vice versa. The day of feasting provides a setting for young men to demonstrate their creative and improvisatory skills as máwi flute players. Among the many improvisatory duets with animal names played in the final stage of pudáli, the one called *dzawírra* after a species of small fish (*viejita*, Span.; *cicholasoma* species), was the most popular in Wakuénai villages along the lower Guainía River in Venezuela and Colombia at the time of my fieldwork in 1980–81. The following description of dzawírra dances is based on three performances of the same duet in the Dzáwinai village where I carried out six months of fieldwork in 1981. I made a musical transcription and analysis of the dzawírra duet while living in the village, and this exercise gave me my first clear understanding of the improvisatory theme and variation style of performance. After reaching this understanding, I experimented with the idea of theme and variations by learning to perform and dance the dzawírra duet with Wakuénai men and women. These practical experiences as a participant in máwi flute duets confirmed the results of my transcription and analysis of dzawírra.

The dzawírra duet begins with a pair of male flute players dancing in a circle. The men support their instruments with the outside arms and embrace one another aroung the shoulders with the inside arms. After completing one full circle, two women join them. Suddenly, the two dancers on the inside of the circle stand still, and the other couple continues on for a few more paces, turns around to face the motionless couple, and then approaches them from the front-right side. They approach until the flute in front of them crosses underneath that of the couple who stands still. Then they back off and approach again.[24] On the third approach, the flute player who is standing still raises his instrument up high to allow the other couple to pass underneath. He continues to play the flute in this raised position while the other couple dances in small, counterclockwise circles around him and his partner. Immediately following this sequence, the roles are reversed, and the couple that had been moving in small circles stands still. The couple that had been standing still then goes through the series of approaching and backing-off motions before being allowed to pass several times under the raised flute of the other couple. After the role reversal has been completely acted out, the two couples rejoin and dance in a clockwise direction to the place where the dance had begun on one side of the dancing area. The end of the duet comes with the usual high-pitched screeching sounds of the two flutes when overblown with maximum force (sound ex. 8).

According to the Wakuénai, the dzawírra duet portrays a female dzawírra fish protecting a nest of eggs against an enemy. They point out that the dzawírra fish stays with its nest until the eggs are ready to hatch, whereas most other fish species simply lay eggs and abandon them. The approaching and backing-off motions of dancers in the dzawírra duet are said to represent a process of asking the mother fish's permission to "dance" in a circle over her nest. Similarly, the raising of the máwi flute is said to be the mother fish's sign of giving her approval to the outside intruder to enter the nest. Although the indigenous explanation centers around the theme of protection against predators, it also evokes a sexual theme of male fish asking permission to "dance" in the female's nest. The spawning runs of fish are generally referred to with the word meaning "to dance" (-*irrápaka*), and the emphasis on fish nests and eggs in the dzawírra duet expresses a concern for natural processes of reproduction and their relevance as models for social behavior in the ceremonial context of pudáli.

The dzawírra duet uses the sexual symbolism of the male aggressor versus the female protector to construct the idea of a natural, presexual reproductive process in which gender is reversible and exchangeable. Keeping in mind that Wakuénai musical performers attribute male gender to the longer máwi flute and female gender to its shorter counterpart, the sexual meaning of the dzawírra duet is not simply that of a juxtaposition of male and female genders in which two male flute players alternately play the role of male aggressor. Instead, the dzawírra duet expresses a total blurring of male and female genders by acting out the transformations of male aggressor into *male* protector and of female protector into *female* aggressor. This same collapsing of genders into presexual imagery is evident in the symbolism of dance, since both the aggressor and protector roles are acted out by pairs of male and female dancers. One couple acts out the male aggressor and protector roles, while the other couple performs the reciprocal transformation of female protector into female aggressor. The reversible, exchangeable concept of gender that the dzawírra duets construct is so complete that it can be seen as an expression of transsexuality or androgyny (Drummond 1981), a concept of spontaneous generativity that preconfigures the dichotomy between male and female genders.

Natural Soundscaping, or the Fugue of the Five Sexes

The dzawírra duet is also a powerful, metaphorical performance of the idea of the precultural, or a collapsing of culturally separate, human identities into a primordial oneness of natural and social orders. As with the idea of the presexual, the idea of the precultural does not arise suddenly in the opening stage of pudáli but through a series of collective representations that gradually transform the symbolic boundary between human society and nature. In the opening dances of pudáli, the human-to-animal connection is metaphorically expressed through the playing of kúlirrína trumpets to imitate the sound of a river full of migrating, spawning *Leporinus* fish. Male and female genders are construed as separate, yet highly interdependent, categories of personhood through the attribution of "male" and "female" genders to longer and shorter máwi flutes that must be played together in a hocket style to create melodic patterns. The naming of trumpet dances after species of *Leporinus* fish also helps to establish the metaphorical connection between humans and animals, or fish, and this naming practice is in turn part of the more general metaphor of "dancing = spawning" that pervades all stages of pudáli ceremonies. In addition, the construction of the kúlirrína trumpets out of male and female elements (e.g., mouthpiece and resonator, respectively) extends the metaphorical comparison between human sexual reproduction, gestation, and birth and the behavior of a natural species of large catfish. Kulirrína trumpets embody the concept of "ambisexuality," or maleness and femaleness welded together into a single sound-producing object.

In the late-night transitional period of pudáli, the metaphorical connectedness of humans and animals begins to take ascendancy of the cultural separateness of humans. In the déetu flute performances, male flute players directly embody the natural reproductive and feeding activities of déetu insects by "sucking" fermented drinks out of their host's house. In these performances, the connection between humans and animals is much more direct and iconic than the symbolic evocation of fish spawning behavior in kúlirrína trumpet dances, which depends upon mediation through naming of dances, the musical sound of the trumpets, and the material construction of the trumpets. In déetu flute performances, the "sucking" behavior of adult déetu insects is directly evoked through the guest men's activity of surrounding the host's house and raising their flutes up into the rafters to "suck" out alcoholic beverages. Déetu flutes are made in only one length and are not categorized by gender. The flutes thus convey the idea of "nonsexuality," just as their use in performances imitates a nonsexual form of reproduction through eating, depositing eggs, and metamorphosis.

Finally, the dzawírra and other flute duets of the last stage of pudáli make use of the same direct, iconic embodiment of the natural reproductive behavior of nonhuman species, but they carry the process one step further. In the dzawírra duet, it is not just *male* flute players who directly evoke animal reproductive behavior but *pairs* of male flute players and female dance partners who act out the protection of the nest of eggs and its penetration by an outside aggressor.

The presexual and the precultural are densely interwoven in the course of ceremonial performances, since it is the reproductive behavior of nonhuman (fish and insect) species which is focalized in each of the three stages of pudáli. To sum up, the presexual emerges in the transformation of gender reciprocity into representations of nonsexual and ambisexual reproductive modes, ending up with the imagery of the total interchangeability of gender in the dzawírra flute duets. The precultural begins with the metaphorical comparison, mediated by musical sounds and instruments, between fish spawning runs and human sexual reproduction in the kúlirrína trumpet dances. This indirect, symbolic relation between humans and animals is transformed in the déetu flute performances into an iconic representation of insect behavior by male flute players. Finally, the dzawírra duet gives direct, iconic representation of human-to-animal relations in the form of pairs of male flute players and female dance partners.

Conclusions

In Wakuénai rituals and ceremonies, musical sounds and musicality are densely interwoven with lexical sounds and meaning, on the one hand, and with sounds and behaviors of natural life forms—fish, amphibians, birds, insects, and forest animals—on the other. This integration of a specifically human world constructed through verbal discourse and the natural world of animal and plant species is rooted in mythic narratives about the primordial times and the special role of musical performances as ways for living humans to access and exercise mythic power. The primordial world described in mythic narratives is a state of being in which the distinction between humans and animals is blurred or even nonexistent, with animals "speaking" and humans transforming into animals. Sacred flutes and trumpets that re-create both the different parts of the primordial human being's body and a diversity of natural species are ideally suited to produce sounds that are at once proto-human "voices" of the mythic ancestors and the sounds of various animal species. Although less overtly sacred and powerful, ceremonial flutes and trumpets are equally appropriate vehicles for imitating the sounds and behaviors of animal species as a way of creating a musical and choreographic space for building and reaffirming peaceful social relations between kin and affines.

Musicalization, or natural soundscaping, is a process of movement or journeying back and forth across different "places," regions of the cosmos, or categories of social being. However, this traveling is understood not as a simple movement from one preexisting place to another but as the creation, or "opening up," of political, social, economic, life-cycle, ritual, and other historically situated space-times. As such, musicalization is a process of making history; of encountering other peoples, species, and beings; and of experiencing that otherness within an overall process of returning to individual and collective identities. Soundscaping, whether cultural or natural or both, is about the movement of musical sounds away and across the rivers and forests, the opening up of a fully human world of men and women, children and adults, and the multitude of natural plant and animal species inhabiting the equatorial Amazonian rivers and rainforests of the

Upper Rio Negro. Perhaps the clearest example of this active construction of a shared historical space-time comes at the very end of male initiation rituals when the last group of male flute players departs from the village while playing a continuous melody on three waliáduwa flutes. The three flute players never miss a beat as they dance slowly down to the river's edge and embark in a canoe. From time to time, the flutes' sweet melody is punctuated by shrill blasts of a molítu flute player. The sound of the sacred flutes continues for several minutes and gradually fades into the distance, letting everyone in the village hear the sound of Kuwái and the mythic ancestors as they move across the landscape, opening up the world for a new generation of men (sound ex. 9).

Sound Examples

1. Molítu flute "conversing" with women singing drinking songs (*pákamaránatakan*), male initiation. (www.ailla.utexas.org, KP C002R002I005.mp3, 23':29"—26':49").

2. Molítu flute and ancestor trumpets (*dzáwiñápa*), male initiation. (www.ailla.utexas.org, KPC002R002I003.mp3, 16':50"—24':31").

3. Molítu flute together with waliáduwa flutes, male initiation. (www.ailla.utexas.org, KPC002R002I007.mp3, 14':14"—14':43").

4. Molítu flute and men speaking to male initiants. (www.ailla .utexas.org, KPC002R002I008.mp3, 9':19"—10':33").

5. Máwi flutes in standardized, opening duet of pudáli ceremonies. (www.ailla.utexas.org, KPC001R043I001.mp3).

6. Máwi flutes played together with kulirrína trumpets. (www .ailla.utexas.org, KPC001R068I001.mp3).

7. Déetu flutes. (www.ailla.utexas.org, KPC001R068I001.mp3).

8. Improvisatory máwi flute duet named after dzawírra fish; from third and last stage of pudáli, after redistribution of food offering. (www.ailla.utexas.org, KPC001R005I021.mp3).

9. Waliáduwa and molítu flutes departing village at end of male initiation (www.ailla.utexas.org, KPC002R002I019.mp3, 7': 35"—9': 54").

Notes

1. The term *soundscape* was popularized in Murray Schafer's *The Tuning of the World* (1977), which was reissued as *The Soundscape: Our Sonic Environment and the Tuning of the World* (1994).

2. My understanding of malikái has been strongly influenced by Joel Sherzer and Greg Urban's approach to indigenous discourse genres in *Native South American Discourse* (1986). Paul Friedrich's definition of poetry as the creation of "felt consubstantiation between language music and mythic meaning" (1986) has also been very helpful in exploring the many ways in which musicality and lexicality interact within performances of malikái. Apart from my own works on the "poetic polarity" in malikái singing and chanting among the Wakuénai of Venezuela, Laura Graham's excellent study (1986) of three modes of Shavante discourse—ritual wailing, ceremonial dance songs, and political oratory—is one of the only ethnographic studies in Lowland South America that directly focuses on interactions between musicality and lexicality.

3. For a parallel, yet strikingly different, ethnographic study of ritual performances of music as a process of reintroducing nature into society, see Anthony Seeger's analysis (1979, 1987) of *akía* (shout songs) among the Suyá of central Brazil.

4. From June through December 1998, I conducted a field study with the Wakuénai of Venezuela on their narratives about the trickster-creator, Iñapirríkuli or Made-From-Bone. The research was funded by grants from Southern Illinois University's Office of Research and Development Administration, National Endowment for the Humanities, and Wenner-Gren Foundation for Anthropological Research. In December 1998, I presented a Spanish and Curricarro compilation of these narratives to the Office of Indigenous Affairs at the Ministry of Education in Caracas, for use in its bilingual intercultural education program. An English translation and interpretation of the narratives is available in *Made-from-Bone: Trickster Myths, Music, and History from an Amazonian Community* (Hill 2009).

5. See the essay by Marc Brightman (this volume) for a comparable ethnographic study of ceremonial flutes as "energy transformers" that allow Wayana communities to convert affines into kin.

6. I have written about these musical naming processes in *Keepers of the Sacred Chants: The Poetics of Ritual Power in an Amazonian Society* (Hill 1993). Wakuénai chant-owners emphasize the priority of verbal art when teaching ritually powerful singing and chanting (malikái) to apprentices, who must first memorize the categories of spirit names and all the specific names that belong within each category.

7. Mádzerukái consists primarily of instrumental dance music but also includes some collective singing as well as more personalized song dialogues, called *pákamarántakan*. I do not have space to discuss these varieties of collective and individual singing here.

8. However, there are rare yet highly significant exceptions to this rule (see Hill 1994).

9. The moment at which men close the resonators of kulirrína trumpets over palmwood mouthpieces is an exception, since women of childbearing age are not allowed to see this action as it is believed that it could cause future, unborn children to become stuck inside their wombs.

10. The sacred wind instruments of Kuwái include three kinds of bark trumpets, called *dápa* (paca), *héemali* (fish species, *Cichla ocellaris*), and *dzáwiñapa* (jaguar bone). All three are examples of what Izikowitz (1970:223) calls "simple trumpets," or single tubes lacking separate mouthpieces, and are made by wrapping bark from *macanilla* palms around a frame of straight wooden poles. The various sacred flutes of Kuwái are all made from hollowed out macanilla palm logs and are examples of duct flutes with partly covered sound orifices and without stops (Izikowitz 1970: 337).

11. Flutes and trumpets played in kwépani are subject to strict visual restrictions and are not allowed to be photographed or filmed. My chapter, therefore, includes audio but not visual examples of these instruments.

12. The overriding significance of male continuity in kwépani ceremonies is also given material expression in the rule that all flutes and trumpets must be cut from continuous pieces of the same palm tree trunk without any gaps between the pieces.

13. It is significant that the Wakuénai say it is the molítu frog's singing that tells people when it is time to cut, burn, and plant new gardens, since the verbal message is being transposed into a natural musical realm of singing. In contrast, the use of molítu flutes in kwépani ceremonies is a transposition of the flutes' musical sounds into verbal messages, or "speech."

14. I have written in another publication (Hill 2000) about the interaction between gender and descent as organizational principles in the "fertility cultism" of northwestern Amazonia.

15. These verbal simulations (see www.ailla.utexas.org, KPC001R074.mp3) are an indigenous interpretation of the molítu flute performances that are quite different from the actual sounds made by molítu flute players in ritual performances. In listening to the recordings of the latter, it is impossible to discern such meanings, but one can infer the flute's intended meanings based on the context (i.e., the women's verbal singing and shouting of questions to the flute players).

Matos Arvelo (1912: 180) documented similar indigenous verbal interpretations of molítu flute performances among the Curripaco nearly a century ago.

16. In 2007 I collaborated with the Archive of the Indigenous Languages of Latin America (AILLA) at the University of Texas in digitizing and archiving all my cassette field recordings of Wakuénai musical performances and mythic narratives. The entire collection is available to researchers at www.ailla.utexas.org (after registering, search for "Kurripaco"). The list of sound examples provided at the end of this essay provides the exact collection, record, and item numbers in the AILLA web archive so that readers can easily find them.

17. The exact length of máwi flutes varies according to the height of the man who makes them, which also means that different pairs of "male" and "female" flutes will produce different overtone series. The male flute measuring 1.77 m, for example, produces the series G (below middle C)-D-G-B-F-G-(A)-(C), while its female companion (1.62 m long) produces an identical series of intervals only one whole step higher (i.e., A-E-A-C#-E-G-A-(B)-(D).

18. Máwi flutes are made from a palm called máwi (*Astrostudium schomburgkii*). Sections of these palms are soaked underwater so that the soft inner pith can be removed with a sharpened stick. A rectangular hole is cut near the proximal end of the flutes, and two palm leaves are lashed to the outside of the flute's barrel to partially cover the rectangular hole. A duct made of tree resins is placed inside the flute near the proximal end and directs air flow against the two palm leaves. In technical terms, máwi flutes are an example of duct flutes with partly covered sound orifices and without stops (Izikowitz 1970: 339).

19. Kulirrína trumpets are known as *surubí* in *lingua geral*. In 1927, Kurt Nimuendajú traveled through the northwest Amazon and concluded that these "catfish" (surubí) trumpets were the most distinctive material artifacts produced by Arawak-speaking "aniwa" of the Isana River (Nimuendajú 1950). In technical terms, the kulirrína are complex trumpets, or ones in which a separate mouthpiece or embouchure is attached to a tubular resonator (Izikowitz 1970: 232). The use of basketry covered with resins, waxes, and paints to make bell-shaped resonators is found only among Arawak-speaking groups of the Upper Rio Negro region.

20. *Táari* (white bocachico), *dúme* (spotted bocachico), and *dúpari* (red-tailed bocachico). See Hill 1987 for complete descriptions of the three dance formations.

21. Déetu flutes are identical to máwi flutes in construction but are considerably shorter (1.15 m). Like the máwi flutes, déetu flutes can be classified as duct flutes with partly covered sound orifices and without stops (Izikowitz 1970: 339).

22. The larva of déetu weevils grow into large, white, oily grubs, called *mútsi*, which are collected to be roasted and eaten. In the cycle of mythic nar-

ratives about the primordial human being (Kuwái), the trickster-creator lures Kuwái down to the ground to perform the first male initiation ritual by sending a messenger who entices him with a gift of mútsi grubs. Elsewhere (Hill 2004), I have written about the metamorphosis of white mútsi grubs into black déetu weevils as a model for understanding the interrelations between kwépani and pudáli ceremonies, respectively.

23. In female-owned pudáli ceremonies, the guests perform an elaborate song-dance called *dzudzuápani* (wheel dance) during the last hours before dawn. See Hill 1987 for a complete description of dzudzuápani and transcription of song texts.

24. There are strong similarities between the dzawírra flute dance and the *marake* ceremonies among the Wayana of southern French Guiana and southern Suriname (see Brightman, this volume).

References Cited

Drummond, Lee. 1981. "The Serpent's Children: Semiotics of Cultural Genesis in Arawak and Trobriand Myth." *American Ethnologist* 8, no. 3: 633–60.

Friedrich, Paul. 1986. *The Language Parallax: Linguistic Relativism and Poetic Indeterminacy*. Austin: University of Texas Press.

Graham, Laura. 1986. "Three Modes of Shavante Vocal Expression: Wailing, Collective Singing, and Political Oratory." In *Native South American Discourse*, ed. Joel Sherzer and Greg Urban, 83–118. The Hague: Mouton de Gruyter.

Hill, Jonathan. 1983. "Wakuénai Society: A Processual-Structural Analysis of Indigenous Cultural Life in the Upper Rio Negro Region of Venezuela." PhD diss., Department of Anthropology, Indiana University.

———. 1984. "Social Equality and Ritual Hierarchy: The Arawakan Wakuénai of Venezuela." *American Ethnologist* 11, no. 3: 528–44.

———. 1987. "Wakuénai Ceremonial Exchange in the Northwest Amazon Region." *Journal of Latin American Lore* 13, no. 2: 183–224.

———. 1989. "Ritual Production of Environmental History among the Arawakan Wakuénai of Venezuela." *Human Ecology* 17, no. 1: 1–25.

———. 1993. *Keepers of the Sacred Chants: The Poetics of Ritual Power in an Amazonian Society*. Tucson: University of Arizona Press.

———. 1994. "Musicalizing the Other: Shamanistic Approaches to Ethnic-Class Competition in the Upper Rio Negro Region." In *Religiosidad y Resistencia Indígenas hacia el Fin del Milenio*, ed. Alicia Barabas, 105–28. Quito: Abya-Yala.

———. 2000. "Varieties of Fertility Cultism in Amazonia: A Closer Look at

Gender Symbolism in Northwestern Amazonia." In *Gender in Amazonia and Melanesia: An Exploration of the Comparative Method*, ed. T. Gregor and D. Tuzin, 45–68. Berkeley: University of California Press.

———. 2004. "Metamorphosis: Mythic and Musical Modes of Exchange in the Amazon Rain Forests of Venezuela and Colombia." In *Music in Latin America and the Caribbean: An Encyclopedic History. Volume 1: Performing Beliefs: Indigenous Cultures of South America, Central America and Mexico*, ed. Malena Kuss. Austin: University of Texas Press.

———. 2009. *Made-From-Bone: Trickster Myths, Music, and History from an Amazonian Community*. Urbana: University of Illinois Press.

Izikowitz, Karl Gustav. 1970 [1934]. *Musical and Other Sound Instruments of the South American Indians: A Comparative Ethnographical Study*. Göteborg: Elanders Boktryckeri Aktiebolag; reprint, East Ardsley, UK: S. R.

Matos Arvelo, Martin. 1912. *Vida Indiana*. Barcelona: Casa Editorial Mauci.

Nimuendajú, Kurt. 1950. "Reconhecimento dos Rios Içana, Ayarí, e Uaupés. Relatorio Apresentado ão Serviço de Proteção ãos Indios do Amazonas e Acre, 1927." *Journal de la Société des Américanistes*, n.s., 39.

Schafer, R. Murray. 1977. *The Tuning of the World*. New York: Knopf.

———. 1994. *The Soundscape: Our Sonic Environment and the Tuning of the World*. Rochester VT: Destiny Books.

Seeger, Anthony. 1979. "What Can We Learn When They Sing? Vocal Genres of the Suyá Indians of Central Brazil." *Ethnomusicology* 23: 373–94.

———. 1987. *Why the Suyá Sing: A Musical Anthropology of an Amazonian People*. Cambridge: Cambridge University Press.

Sherzer, Joel, and Greg Urban, eds. 1986. *Native South American Discourse*. The Hague: Mouton de Gruyter.

4. *Hearing without Seeing*

Sacred Flutes as the Medium for an Avowed Secret in Curripaco Masculine Ritual

NICOLAS JOURNET

"The most useful science is the art of dissimulation," wrote a Jesuit philosopher in 1647 (and he added that "passions are an open door to a man's mind") (B. Gracian, maxime 98). He insisted that concealment and secrecy can be necessary in ordinary life and even more so in court life. Religions, too, use dissimulation, often mixed with mystery and ambiguity.

Because religions deal with death, destiny, and morals, they are accepted as containing mysteries even more than secrets. Initiation rituals, especially when participation is restricted, are often treated as if they were triggering mysterious forces and transmitting esoteric knowledge. They are frequently analyzed as a collection of symbols, and the ethnographer or the religious specialist undertakes to decode these symbols even more completely than any of the actors of the rite.

This essay begins by distinguishing among mystery, lies, and secrecy. A quick review of the topic (G. Simmel 1996, H. Bonello 1998, A. Petitat 1996) shows that religions may comprise all three categories. Mystery refers to an unrevealed truth supposedly unknowable or deemed so by some authority. Thus the difference between lies and secrets has little to do with intentionality. For example, within Christianity the Holy Trinity is a mystery that has been consciously instituted by the Church. Nevertheless, mystery always implies that truth is beyond the reach of ordinary human intellectual capacity, and its effectiveness relies on the belief that obstacles to revelation are either natural or supernatural, but not human. So dissimulation may use the mystery as a tool to enforce some secret; mystery relies on the belief that truth is out of range of the human mind. Secrecy is different; it is maintained by ignorance, threat, or even convention. Ignorance is fueled by lying, whereas threat is a public manifestation. Hence secrets are of different kinds. Some are like lies; others are publicly acknowledged as secrets and maintained as such, whether by threat or convention.

These distinctions are useful for understanding the numerous prohibitions that exist around sacred musical instruments in Amazonia. The particular example considered here is that of the Curripaco people of the Guainía River in Colombia. Sacred flutes and trumpets called *Kuai*—named for a mythic hero—are still sometimes exhibited in their villages for ceremonial purposes. In 1985, a male initiation ritual (*kapetiapan*) was performed in the village of Neeripan. Most of the ethnography in this essay comes from direct observation of that event. We will first describe the different kinds of precautionary measures that are required for both initiated and uninitiated persons when using the sacred flutes. Some of these measures are like the Polynesian *taboo*, and as such are imbued with supernatural beliefs. Others involve a deliberate restrictive arrangement toward women and children that requires dissimulation. Then we will turn our attention to analyzing the cognitively ambiguous kind of secret that is enacted in the flutes' prohibition.

Symbols and Food Avoidance

Scholars have frequently considered the symbolic dimensions of the prohibition of women from seeing Jurupari sacred flutes in the northwestern Amazon. In his analysis of the *He* concept among the Barasana, which is very close to the Curripaco Kuai semantic field, Stephen Hugh-Jones (1979) identifies the second most important ritual paraphernalia within the He ceremony as a wax gourd that men activate in the middle of the night. This gourd embodies a very strong and obvious female symbolism. Although this object is not formally forbidden to women, the wax gourd is exhibited along with a pair of sacred trumpets, and the moment when the wax is burned is considered to be a dangerous one, since it is associated with the idea of male menstruation. For obvious reasons, women are not welcome to witness such an event. It appears then that He ceremonies activate cosmic and sexual symbols, which acknowledge the strong gender separation that keeps at least half of the community out of the sight of the sacred flutes.

If such a point a view were to be applied to the Curripaco Kuai ritual, it would inevitably consider a word that Curripaco currently use to distinguish Kuai ceremonies from all other kinds of feasts. When speaking Spanish, Curripaco men use such words as *dangerous* and *mysterious* when trying to explain the specific climate in which kapetiapan is to be held. But the proper local word that applies is *kanupadaritsa*, an idiom that hardly can be translated better than "full of nupa." This last word is better described than translated.

Nupa, when associated with *Kuai*, designates all the substances whose contact or ingestion may be dangerous at any moment of the ritual period. The prototype of these nupa is prohibited food, particularly meat and capsicum pepper, but many other elements like the river water or the sound of sacred flutes may be labeled this way.

Papeeku rinupa is a formula that designates several ritual gestures consisting of spitting out food in determinate moments, flagellating a partner, jumping backward to avoid an invisible danger, slapping the river water with the hands, and waving a basket over a heap of fruits. It can be translated as "to throw out the nupa," and this operation is meant to diminish the dangerous attributes of the substance. When applied to a dish, papeeku rinupa authorizes its ingestion by the person who performs the gesture: thus it is an individual ritual of purification.

Pakanupaka is a verbal formula that designates the consequences of transgressing a prohibition. It is frequently described as a deadly bleeding, but it does not imply a real hemorrhage; rather, it designates the phenomenon of losing one's normal skin color when fainting.

Finally, nupa can also designate a personal allergy to or disgust for a specific substance without any reference to ritual context. A person who eats a specific food for the first time and gets sick will suspect that this food is probably a nupa to him or her. He or she will normally abstain from eating it in the future. In its ordinary sense, a nupa is merely something that one considers personally harmful.

In the ritual context of kapetiapan, *rinupa* is the general word used to refer to the food and behavior restrictions that young initiates and men follow when they are in the presence of the sacred flutes. These restrictions are not personal but collectively instituted by the presence of Kuai, and there are many reasons to think that the original model for these "allergies" is the mythic character himself. That is why Curripaco men refer to "his nupa" and never to "our nupa": food and behavior prohibitions are enforced as a way to be like Kuai, who is said to be extremely abstemious, eating nothing but "wind" and drinking nothing but manioc beer. By taking up his "allergies," participants in the ritual identify themselves with the mythic hero. By achieving commensality, they create a common humanity between Kuai and the ritual community, following a model that E. Viveiros de Castro (1996) has shown to be widespread in the Amazon area.

Comparatively, the concept of nupa appears to be very close to the more famous Polynesian *taboo* or *tapu*. It combines sacredness and danger; it is the specific attribute of a mythic hero; its causes exist in nature, but its use by men is largely symbolic (the adult men are not really afraid of transgressing food restrictions), and its consequences are specific and do not merge with human sorcery.

Taboo and Secrecy

All records of Jurupari feasts in the northwest Amazon nowadays agree that women and children are to be considered as active participants of the ritual. As we will see, they do interact in different ways with the men as they dance and play the sacred flutes. Women and children may not see the flutes or touch them, but they are required to listen to their sound. Such close involvement implies that women also are affected by the taboo dimension of the ritual, that is, the nupa dangers. Although they are not supposed to follow the same food restrictions as the men, they do not cook as usual and do not make a fire all night long.

During the ceremony, women live mainly on manioc tuber and leftover smoked fish. At determinate moments they may be directly affected by the nupa. For example, when preparing for kapetia-pan, men perform several *piamaka* rituals. These ceremonies consist of collecting large amounts of forest fruits or leaves or palm boards. Then men pile these offerings in the middle of the village plaza and play the Kuai flutes over the heap. As soon as they stop playing the flutes and dancing, they bring the instruments back to the river, protecting them from women's sight. Then, the women and children come close to the heap and make some comments. However, they abstain from touching the fruits or leaves until one of the women has performed a specific ritual gesture: she waves a large, flat basket over the heap, so as to "throw away the nupa." Touching or picking up the fruits before this operation is said to bring sickness and death. Immediately thereafter, fruits are collected, prepared with water and manioc gruel, and collectively drunk before dark. Leaves and palm boards are stored and used for fixing the ceremonial house. Thus we see that women and children may be affected by the taboo dimension of the sacred flutes' presence in the village.

However, evidence strongly suggests that the main and by far most critical prohibition that women have to follow, that of being barred from seeing the flutes, has no relation to this taboo dimension. Curripaco informants always have denied that women's exclusion has any relation to the sacred flutes' nature or significance. One of them clearly stated that women were barred only by men's will and for no other reason. There was no sense to speculate on Kuai's avoidance by women in terms of sacredness, nor any kind of allergy (nupa), be it natural or supernatural between the mythic figure and femininity. On the contrary, some men insisted that women were fully capable of handling the flutes, that they had done so in the past (this is an episode in all Jurupari legends), and that it was only because of men's meanness that they were kept away from the flutes. This kind of statement, although sporadically documented, has often been neglected because of such impressive prophecies as those that predict that, in case of sacrilege, men would immediately menstruate or that women would mysteriously be killed or die or, alternatively, that the sacred objects would lose their power and have to be replaced. Curripaco informants admitted that an inquisitive or clumsy woman would expose herself to the danger of getting sick or being assaulted. But they insisted that the cause would be human sorcery motivated by human jealousy; the figure of Kuai would not be involved in this sanction.

All this evidence leads to the conclusion that the prohibition against women and youngsters seeing the sacred flutes has neither natural nor supernatural significance: it is not even as symbolically grounded in the social division of labor. Curripaco men often state that women are unable to kill animals, but they have never suggested that women were unable to handle the sacred flutes. Thus the prohibition is not a taboo. It is a secret enforced by men, which has no fundamental symbolic relation to gender difference and has to be considered in its pragmatic and cognitive dimensions.

Lies, Secrets, and Dissimulation

Dissimulation is the common term encompassing different kinds of noncommunication (Bonello 1998: 35). Profound differences have been noted by social scientists as early as Georg Simmel, who in 1906 qualified common dissimulation as "passive," as opposed to "active" secrecy. Such dissimulation he considered necessary to social life. He noted that proper or essential secrecy "appears whenever the intention of dissimulating is confronted with the intention of unveiling." Although he does not theorize it, Simmel highlights the fact that secrecy exists also for those who do not share it and that it has a specific power to fascinate: it places the secret's owner "in the middle of a bright cloud that encompasses the surrounding persons" (Simmel 1996: 12).

As shown by Pascal Boyer, most ritual secrets are "active" secrets, in the sense that they must be known to exist by the people who are not admitted to share in the ritual. More recently, Michael Houseman (1993) has distinguished two kinds of secrecy policy used in initiation rituals:

> "Concealed secrecy" designates any situation in which not only specific information but its very existence is collectively concealed. For the outsider, the secret does not exist before it is disclosed. We may call it "true secrecy."

> "Exhibited secrecy" involves secrets whose existence is widely known, but whose precise content is not. As a consequence, this declared secrecy has two faces—one public, the other private—and both must be looked after so as to maintain the effectiveness of the secret. There exists a medium through which the secret is kept from the outer world.

Houseman has shown how among the Beti (Cameroon), masculine initiation uses both kinds of secrets in a progressive manner to give access to ritual details for the initiates. I will not try to apply such a sophisticated model to the Curripaco ritual. True secrecy exists in Kuai rituals, but it is clearly secondary to the extensive use of declared secrecy directed toward women.

One of the most interesting aspects of declared secrecy is its public face: what should those who do not have access believe about the sacred flutes? How are they kept ignorant about their true nature? Sacred Kuai flutes and trumpets are loud, melodious, and far-reaching instruments. They can be heard several hundred meters from their playing ground, and their tunes are very specific. One who has heard them once will recognize them apart from any other musical performance like social dancing and playing. Identification is certain and easy. The only restricted access to the flutes for women, children, and unrelated visiting persons is their sight. Hearing, smelling, and touching are not restricted, although evidence suggests that touching usually implies seeing. Thus the sacred flutes' secrecy has to be considered in its specific visual perspective.

Sensory Modes and Truth: A Look at Tatuyo Language

The Tatuyo are Tukano speakers who live on the Vaupés River in Colombia and share with the Curripaco the same ritual complex. Although Curripaco linguistics has not been fully studied, most of the classifier systems and worldviews are close to those of the Tatuyo. In a seminal article, Elsa Gómez-Imbert has shown how in Tatuyo language, the expression of truth is supported by verbal classifiers. Gómez-Imbert states that these semantic-syntactic forms are required when a speaker refers to past or present events that he thinks are real. The expression of a desire or a hypothesis is different. Without entering into linguistic details, according to Gómez-Imbert, there exist two classes and five categories of expression.

One class of verbal markers refers to indirect knowledge and comprises two categories:

1. citation: one has heard it from another person.

2. inference: one has seen an indirect indication of the event (footprint, mark, written report) and infers that it has probably happened.

Both 1 and 2 point out uncertain assertions for which the speaker does not engage his responsibility. Following Gómez-Imbert, citation is the less assertive form, and inference is a bit more credible. Likewise, auditive signals are less certain than visual ones.

The other class of markers is qualitatively more assertive. It comprises three categories and corresponding marks:

3. Distant perception: one has seen something from some distance and is not sure about it. Or it may have occurred some time ago. According to Gómez-Imbert, this marker compares to "it seems that."

4. Nonvisual perception: one has perceived something precisely but not visually. The event may simply have occurred out of the speaker's sight or be naturally invisible. For jungle dwellers, this situation is a daily experience. Animals are usually invisible but are frequently heard at a distance.

5. Modality of certainty: the speaker has witnessed what he is describing. Certainty, according to Gómez-Imbert, may be sensitive (visual) or intellectual (one maintains that he knows well what he is saying).

Categories 3, 4, and 5 are linguistic markers that deal with levels of truth. They constitute a three-step scale toward fully assured utterances. The difference between auditive and visual perception can be paired with the difference between a doubtful statement and a certain one. Citation and inference are not trustable modalities. The first deals with possible lies and the second with false inference, that is, sincere error (Gómez-Imbert 1982).

Evidentials in the Northwest Amazon

After Gómez-Imbert, other linguists have more extensively studied such grammatical particularities, usually described as "evidential systems," in the Vaupés-Rio Negro area. Their occurrences, number, conditions of use, and interpretation may vary among the various language families and dialects spoken in this region. Evidentials are lexical or grammatical means to specify the nature of the evidence on which a statement is based (Aikhenvald 2003a: 1). As an optional feature, evidentiality is universal, as every language in the world possesses lexical means to specify the source of knowledge that is at stake in a statement. Clauses like "I hear that," "I guess," "they say," and adverbs like "allegedly" exist everywhere.

However, not all languages have evidentiality as a grammatical category, and they may differ in how precisely they distinguish among sources of information. The simplest systems reviewed worldwide by Aikhenvald and Dixon (2003) consist of a distinction between indirect and direct sources (that is, hearsay and the others). More complicated systems may have up to seven markers and specify the kind of evidence: either sensory (visual, auditory), spatial (close, distant), or cognitively based (inferred, assumed, reported).

While they are not so common worldwide, such complex systems as the Tatuyo described by Gómez-Imbert have been found in various groups of the northwestern Amazon. Visual evidentials are present in several eastern Tucanoan languages of the Vaupés-Rio Negro area. Visual/nonvisual obligatory contrasts have been recorded in Tuyuca (Barnes 1984; Malone 1988), Barasana (Jones and Jones 1991), Tucano proper (West 1980), Desana (Barnes 1984; Miller 1999), and Cubeo (Morse and Maxwell 1999). The nonvisual evidence may be unspecified or—as in Tatuyo—frequently typified as a sensory experience, with auditory coming first: "the speaker heard, tasted, smelt, or felt the event or state" (Barnes, for Tuyuca, 1999: 214). The Tanimuka-Letuama (central Tucanoan) system seems slightly different. It has three evidential suffixes, and one of them specifies direct auditory information, as opposed to other inferred or hearsay modalities (Strom

1992: 90). As the latter are optional, the description permits us not to conclude that visual evidence is the default category but that is a possibility.

Another interesting point is that major language variations are no obstacle to the diffusion of morphosyntactic structures in the Vaupés-Rio Negro area. A sophisticated evidential system has been described by Aikhenvald among the Tariana, who are an Arawakan-speaking community living on the Brazilian banks of the Vaupés River. This system comprises five evidential markers (visual, nonvisual, inferred generic, inferred specific, reported) that combine with three tenses (present, recent past, remote past) (Aikhenvald 2003b: 133). There is no default category, so every statement must contain an indication of how the information was acquired (Aikhenvald 2003b: 134). In Tariana, the visual/nonvisual contrast is semantically similar to the Tuyuca system, but has no spatial close/distant distinction as in Tatuyo, and both evidential systems combine with tense variations.

The Tariana people have been living close to Tucanoan speakers for three to four centuries and do intermarry with them. As grammatical evidentiality is not often found in the Arawakan language family, Aikhenvald concludes that the Tarianas' fine-grained evidential system has been borrowed from Tucano. Nevertheless, she notices that several Arawakan-speaking groups living in the north Amazon and upper Orinoco do have a minimal nonobligatory system contrasting direct/hearsay statements. These are the Piapoco (Vaupés), the Achagua (Meta), and, in between, the whole array of Baniwa-Curripaco-speaking groups dwelling on the Içana and Rio Negro River banks with whom we are directly concerned in this chapter.

Whether or not a specific visual/nonvisual evidential contrast exists in Curripaco grammar is a question that is beyond the scope of this essay. Aikhenvald states that "the Baniwa-Kurripako dialect to the north and north-east . . . is the Tariana's closest relative outside the Vaupés" (Aikhenvald 1999: 385). However, she finds no evidence that a fine-grained evidential system exists in Curripaco and thus supports the idea that it does not. But absent a full description of Curripaco grammar, the question remains open. If, as noted by de Haan, evidentiality is "more of an areal feature than a genetic feature . . . given the ease with which it spreads from language to language" (n.d.: 1), we should be cautious in our conclusions.

Visual Evidentials and Epistemic Value

Aikhenvald states that among the Tariana, "the use of evidentials correlates with cultural stereotypes and with conventional attitudes to information" (2003b: 159). As an example, she notes that the visual/nonvisual markers apply to such modern media as television (visual) and telephone (nonvisual). The case seems quite obvious. But she also reports that evidentials are not only sensory or spatiotemporal markers; they have a different cognitive value as shown by a "number of epistemic extensions" (Aikhenvald 2003b: 161). Some of the best evidence she presents, like the evidence Gómez-Imbert offers for the Tatuyo people, concerns the way Tariana-speakers report dreams. Whereas shamanic visions are cast in the visual mode, ordinary people's nocturnal dreams are reported as nonvisual evidence. To Aikhenvald, visual evidentials in Tariana have an obvious epistemic value. The contents of shamans' dreams, which in fact are not proper visual experiences, are cast as visual because shamans are reliable sources of information. "Visual evidentials are associated with 'omniscience.' Shamans and evil spirits have access to supernatural knowledge and know it all" (Aikhenvald 2003b: 159). It appears that, for the Tariana, the visual mode is also the most authoritative. In sharp contrast, among devout Catholics, such a "true fact" as the presence of Jesus Christ in the Eucharist is definitely not a visual experience.

Gómez-Imbert, who disagrees with de Haan and other linguists' views of such grammatical entities as spatiotemporal or testimonial markers, strongly advocates labeling them "cognitive modalities" rather than evidentials. Significantly, she points out the modern use of the inferential mode among the Tatuyo, not only for reporting information from printed texts but also from photographs and drawings. Although the latter are images, they are not reported as visual information because they are not considered direct evidence. Nevertheless, printed texts and images are not cast as simple "hearsay" statements; as noted by Aikhenvald in Tariana, some "proof of the validity of the information can be seen as printed in the book" (Aikhenvald 2003b: 161).

There is evidence that the visual/nonvisual contrast has an epistemic value in Tatuyo as in Tariana. Gómez-Imbert states that in Tatuyo, the visual marker characterizes an event "fully perceived" by a speaker: "He has no doubt on the identity of the agent nor on the action itself" (2003: 120). Moreover, she notices that the visual cognitive modality encompasses "physically and psychologically evident facts, generally accepted truths (the sun is hot) and culturally admitted truths such as moral values and traditional behaviours and techniques" (2003: 121).

It appears then that in both languages, evidentials can be distributed on an epistemic scale running from the visual mode (encompassing the most valuable information) down to the "hearsay" mode, connoting the unreliability of the information. The nonvisual marker comes second in Tariana, and third in Tatuyo after the "visual long distant" marker. Although this ordering may be suspect, as an observers' construct, Aikhenvald and Gómez-Imbert classify visual and nonvisual markers close to one another because both are direct sensory experiences, whereas inferred and reported markers are indirect ones. In spite of their proximity, the epistemic value order in which the visual and nonvisual markers appear is unambiguous. A visually marked statement ought to be more fully authorized or reliable than a nonvisual sensory-based one. An auditive experience like hearing a voice in the night or a plane motor in a cloudy sky is not, in the

Tatuyo way, a "fully perceived fact." Paraphrasing Gómez-Imbert, we could write that it leaves some doubt "about the precise identity of the agent and of the action."

Evidentials and Jurupari Ritual

This discussion of linguistics and evidential systems among the Tatuyo and Tariana obviously raises many questions that are still vigorously debated among anthropologists and linguists. What kind of relation should be drawn between morphosyntactic structures, psychological categories, and cultural attitudes? Do we have to suppose a strict correspondence between visual/nonvisual discriminating evidential systems and ritual arrangements? Trying to discuss these points on theoretical grounds would lead us far beyond the aim of this essay. Gómez-Imbert, for her part, discusses the relation between language structure and experience. She concludes that grammatical categories are "fossilized psychological categories," and as such, "perception and conceptualization" are reflected in them. She adds that, functionally, evidentials should facilitate the expression of specific ideas (2003: 120). Aikhenvald does not discuss this point, but simply states, as noted above, that the use of evidentials "correlates with cultural stereotypes and with conventional attitudes to information." *Correlation* is one word we can appropriate to characterize the relation between the use of visual/nonvisual evidential markers in discourse and the enacting of a visual prohibition during Jurupari rites. Yet we still have a problem, as the existence of such a grammatical distinction is not confirmed in Curripaco language.

The point we will try to make thus diverges from the classical discussion about language-thought relation and is more an interpretative suggestion than an ethnolinguistic statement. Let us recall a few linguistic and ethnographic points:

1. Fine-grained evidential systems such as those considered above are rarely attested by linguists worldwide.

2. But they have been found in many (if not all) eastern Tucanoan dialects and also among the Arawak-speaking Tariana.

3. These groups are localized in the Vaupés basin.

4. Their closest northern neighbors are the Arawak-speaking Baniwa-Curripaco groups of the Içana and Upper Rio Negro basins.

5. The whole area (Vaupés–Içana–Upper Rio Negro) is marked by Jurupari ritual diffusion (Hugh-Jones 1979: 8). All these rites share the same model of visual but not auditive prohibition.

We suggest that looking at a Curripaco Jurupari performance with Tatuyo or Tariana "eyes" can shed light on the understanding of a visual/auditory ritually enforced contrast, whether or not it is marked in the Curripaco daily grammar. If such a distinction is a salient psychological category in this cultural area, we may admit it has been "fossilized" in different but parallel manners in different linguistic environments. Tariana and Tatuyo systems provide a useful model for categorizing distinctive aspects of the way Jurupari rituals deal with secrecy. We can now explore the meaning of a visual secret that simultaneously uses very obvious auditive signals to maintain its existence.

True Secrets are True Lies

As we will see, the visual prohibition of sacred flutes to women is the heart of the Curripacos' declared secret dimension. But there is evidence that the Curripaco also practice true secrecy as a first step into the ritual process. Enforcing a true secret consists in lying about the occurrence of a hidden event. That is what Curripaco men and women do in the first steps of the piamaka rites that precede the initiation rite and are dedicated to preparation of sacred instruments.

Every morning of these ritual days, men and women congregate on the village plaza and perform a good-bye ceremony. Women walk up to the men and ask out loud, "Are you going to the jungle?" Then they shake hands, and the men must say, "Yes, I am going to the jungle." This behavior is obviously part of the ritual because it is unusual. It is overtly performed to prevent any unauthorized person—youngsters and foreigners—from thinking that something special is happening. The loud good-bye is an attempt to deceive these people, although it is not a total lie. Men will go to the jungle, but they will not perform daily subsistence activities. "Going to the jungle" currently means going to hunt game animals, fibers, or fruits.

This ceremony is the main case of "true secret" performed in preliminary rites, using human voices and words. Actually, the lie requires that adult women be well informed of men's activities. The true secret is directed toward children and future initiates, as well as visitors who may be staying in the village or who appear unexpectedly. This is an aspect frequently neglected in ethnographic accounts of Jurupari rites: that the secret dimension of the ceremony is also directed toward people of both sexes who are not kin or members of the community. During piamaka preparations, men who travel on the river with sacred flutes or work in the forest collecting materials needed for the rite carefully avoid encounters with unrelated people—not only because of the eventual presence of women but also because they would be very annoyed to disclose the motive of their activities to the neighborhood. Discretion is the rule in this preliminary phase of the ritual, but it obviously ends as soon as the sacred orchestra begins to play; that sound acts as a warning signal to any unauthorized person.

Declared Secret: A Burst of Sound

Playing the sacred flutes on the village plaza forces women to abstain from stepping out of their enclosed shelter. As a precaution, a few days before the ceremony, men take special care to ensure the opacity of the clay and thatch walls of the women's house. For their part, women are very careful not to be exposed to the sight of the sacred flutes. Every time the flutes are played, moving up from the riverside to the village plaza at the beginning of ritual sessions, the women run away from the village to the nearby forest. They wait there until the music stops and the flutes are brought into the men's house. Then they walk back to their appropriate shelter and stay inside unless they are called out by men for mutual flogging. In these special moments, the flutes are played inside the men's house, but they can be heard very loudly on the village plaza. At night, as we will see, women "dialogue" with one of the sacred instruments. As a whole, the high level of acoustic communication contrasts sharply with the particular point of keeping the visual secret for women and children.

What they are supposed to believe about the ceremony has to accord with what they are allowed to perceive. They are in fact invited to perceive the sound of the flutes, the stomping of the men while they dance, the sound of collective singing, whistling, and shouting when the men welcome Kuai, and the voice of the shaman intoning his special chants. All these acoustic manifestations are supposed to indicate that the men are having a drinking, dancing, and flogging party with Kuai—the supernatural mythic hero whom the leader of the dancers addresses in a loud voice, calling him "our grandfather" (*wahwerim*).

Apart from chanting, shouting, and calling names, the men and the initiates try to keep silent or to speak in low voices so that the women cannot hear their conversations. They avoid joking and laughing. Any such sounds would reveal that the men are not as serious as they should be when dealing with such a dangerous entity.

These practices lead us to investigate the ambiguous fields of secrecy or what the uninitiated are supposed to believe. Women generally do not answer when asked about such topics as the sacred flutes or Kuai. They are not supposed to know about them. When men are queried, they state that women should ignore the exact nature of Kuai: they should think that it is an animal, or "a forest spirit" (*iupinai*), or a "dead person" (*niakaim*), but not a group of man-made musical instruments played by their husbands and fathers. Obviously, women do not believe such tales. Some of them may even know the names of the musical instruments and be able to identify their melodies when heard on a tape recorder. No doubt they have acquired this knowledge during the ceremony itself, probably from other women. This means that there exists a discreet tradition among women about the sacred flutes, whose real nature they do not ignore at all. As for the young boys and girls, the effect of the secret is notably different because they may be genuinely alarmed by what they hear during the ceremony. Before being introduced, young initiates may as well be convinced that something frightening is going to happen.

From a pragmatic perspective, the visual secret cast upon the flutes may be suspected to have important consequences: women cannot manufacture the instruments because they are not taught how, and women cannot play the sacred flutes because they are never shown how. But in truth visual secrecy is not a necessary condition: women could simply be prohibited from touching and playing the flutes, as they are prohibited from administering the Holy Communion in the Catholic Church but not barred from receiving it. A similar kind of prohibition exists among the Curripaco for a more profane sort of trumpet called *kulirina* whose sight is not prohibited to women, but about which men say that if a woman tried to play it, the trumpet would definitely be silent.

From a cognitive perspective, visual secrecy is a more coherent and specific device. It can be compared to the Tatuyo modality of "hearing without seeing." That is, it characterizes something about which one has strong suspicions, but uncertain knowledge as to its real nature. Visual secrecy ensures that the ritual flutes and trumpets remain something about which women and non-initiates may not be assertive, something they cannot talk about affirmatively to anyone else. From this perspective, visual secrecy would be directed not toward the exclusion of women as ritual agents—and they are not excluded as such—but toward controlling information that might become known outside the community through women.

Music as a Medium of Maintaining a Declared Secret

The sacred flutes' music has been considered in detail as a creative device by Jonathan Hill (1983). The music can also be considered as an emotional medium and as a means of communication within and without the ritual assembly. Here I will focus on its role as a medium supporting the existence of a declared secret. The prototype of the "hearing without seeing situation," as we have noted, is that of a person who is able to perceive an animal's noise or voice but not to see it distinctly. Curripaco men describe the sacred flutes' sound and melodies as ambiguous and misleading animal signals.

For example, the potent roaring of the *heemari* trumpets, whose name is that of a big ciclidae fish (*pavon*), mimics the slow movement of fins as the fish swims upriver in order to lay eggs. Another pair of trumpets, called *daapa* for a common rodent (*cuniculus paca*), produces a musical image of the stomping movements of this animal, especially the female, when attacked. The longest pair of flutes, called *maariawa* (from *maari*, the white egret), produces two melodies: first, a musical image of the bird's cry of anger, and then the musical evocation of a piece of human discourse saying, "You have eaten up my forbidden food, the fat palometa fish." Another flute, called *iaathe* (tucano bird), imitates the tucano's whistling.

The flute threesome called *waariadua* (young mother)[1] produces a melodious image of women's voices. Finally, there is an isolated flute called *muuritu* or *maawa* (depending on dialect) that evokes the voice of a garden toad and is the most articulated medium through which outsiders are allowed to dialogue with the sacred flutes.

Clearly, many of these musical signals are indexes of an animal's presence. But most of them are not musical analogies of naturally existing signals. The movements of a fish's fin do not produce any loud noise, nor does the stomping of a medium-sized rodent. (Jaguars do produce grunting sounds, but they are not half as loud as the trumpets' roarings.) Egrets (*Ardea alba*) generally do not croak; they do so only when disturbed. We assume that the flutes produce an angry egret's croak, and this burst of anger is followed by another tune that has a verbal translation: "You [the children] have eaten my taboo food, the fat palometa fish." This sentence refers to the legend of Kuai, the mythic hero. When hungry boys roasted and ate some of the fat fruits they had been sent to collect, Kuai could smell it and began angrily to sing these words. The substitution of "fat fish" for "fat fruit" exaggerates the boys' transgression.

The tucano flutes simulate the supposedly specific bird's call "when rain is coming soon." It may also refer to the myth. After Kuai has swallowed the boys, a rainstorm drenches the boys' village, and their father (Iapirikuri) guesses that some transgression has occurred.

The "young mother" (1) trio is the only non-animal named in the whole orchestra; it simulates the *inamanai* voices, that is, the group of women to which Amaru, Kuai's mythical mother, belongs. It produces a melodious tune and is always played when men flog each other, so that the sound of the whips is part of the melody.

Finally, *muuritu* or *maawa* refers to a common toad that can be heard by day in forest clearings and in people's gardens. This "toad" is the most human-like instrument because it is used as a playful medium for communication between those inside and outside of the ritual. During the night women periodically dialogue at a distance with this instrument. Muuritu is a very short, thick flute that is held in the left hand while the right hand modulates the sound. When all other instruments have stopped, the muuritu player produces a call three or four times that resembles the toad call. Then, if they wish, women shout questions to him in the night. They ask for beer and tobacco or inquire about marriage ("Will my daughter marry soon?") or about children ("Will the next be a boy?"). Then the toad player gives some kind of answer by pronouncing a short word into the instrument's mouth (yes, no, male, female). The toad's answers are kinds of oracular pronouncements, received with much joyful shouting and laughter.

If we now try to analyze the main characteristics of the sacred orchestra, we can identify at least three. First, most of these musical signals are animal indexes, although these indexes are not obvious. Some are overtly deceptive (the fish fin movement, the rodent stomping); others are more representational (the tucano's call), but have also a deceptive aspect (they announce a rain shower that does not exist). Two of the instruments are particularly interesting: the young mother and the toad. The former figures a group of human beings, the mythical women, and it does not talk (there are no words in their singing). The latter figures an animal that is supposed to talk. Whether or not it effectively communicates verbally is not clear to me. The flute player does pronounce words into the instrument's mouth, but these words are hardly understandable, at least to untrained ears. Furthermore, men use this instrument in a playful and deceptive way; according to the woman they talk to, they offer obscure or absurd answers. From that point of view, *waariadua* and muuritu are more deceptive than informative instruments. The signals they produce can be heard loud and clear, but these signals do not disclose their true nature. They are typical media for a declared secrecy that is half transparent and half opaque.

Second, besides triggering strong emotions like fear, pleasure, and attraction, the entire orchestra's sound is the medium through which the visual secrecy is declaredly maintained. One of the most salient of men's worries, when playing the flutes, is not to produce wrong notes, as they fear that such musical flaws will reveal their human nature. That may seem a very strange fear, because the instruments' secret is obviously a false secret. As one would expect, women know perfectly well what is going on outside on the village plaza and over in the men's house. Some may even be able to identify the instruments one by one when listening to a tape. Whether this is true for the whole ritual audience is not as obvious. Children and teens may really believe that something unnatural is going on. The initiates may come to the ceremony with very uncertain ideas about the exact nature of Kuai and be genuinely terrified by their first experience. They may also have experienced flogging once or twice when the men in Neeripan decided to whip every young child. (They stopped when a woman protested against flogging her baby.) Despite that incident, we have to keep in mind that flogging children is certainly not common among the Curripaco people, although mothers may threaten boys with caning when angry. Thus whips and flogging are exclusively associated with Kuai rituals and their dangers.

Finally, although no precise verbal mark for "hearing without seeing" has been identified in the Curripaco language, we have to acknowledge that the intention such a mark conveys is fully embodied by the kind of declared secrecy enacted in the kapetiapan rite. This secrecy consists both of visual avoidance and of acoustic communication imposed on the feminine half of the society. Hearing without seeing means that one cannot be assertive about the source of the sound. This truth modality contrasts with the modality of knowing something by sight and being able to assert its nature. Let us specify that these truth modalities should not be equated with objectiveness of the observed phenomenon; in Tatuyo, the visual truth mark applies to shamans' visions and to a person's dreaming as well as to fully conscious sight. Hearing without seeing also contrasts with not hearing at all, that is, ignoring that something is going on. This is the modality of true secrecy, which is briefly enacted in the first stages of the initiation ceremony. When groups of men leave the village to fetch such materials as tree bark, firewood, and whip sticks, they pretend to go fishing or hunting as usual. In a way they pretend that nothing special is happening, and they try to enforce this idea by avoiding noisy behaviors: no laughter and no loud conversations are expected during these collecting sessions. This "true secret" attitude is directed toward women and uninitiated persons, but even more toward any foreigner or outsider. This is an additional aspect of Kuai's secrecy that would require another chapter to analyze.

Notes

1. "The young mother" is a rough translation. The term *waariadua* has no simple meaning and refers to notions of renewal. See Hill 1983: 356.

References Cited

Aikhenvald, Alexandra Y. 1999. "Areal Diffusion and Language Contact in the Içana-Vaupés Basin, North-west Amazonia." In *The Amazonian Languages*, ed. R. M. W. Dixon and Alexandra Y. Aikhenvald. Cambridge: Cambridge University Press.

———. 2003a. "Evidentiality in Typological Perspective. In *Studies in Evidentiality: Typological Studies in Language*, ed. A. Y. Aikhenvald and R. M. W. Dixon, 54: 1–32. Amsterdam: John Benjamins.

———. 2003b. "Evidentiality in Tariana." In *Studies in Evidentiality: Typological Studies in Language*, ed. A. Y. Aikhenvald and R. M. W. Dixon, 54: 131–64. Amsterdam: John Benjamins.

Aikhenvald, Alexandra, and R. M. W. Dixon, eds. 2003. *Studies in Evidentiality. Typological Studies in Language*, vol. 54. Amsterdam: John Benjamins.

Barnes, Janet. 1984. "Evidentials in the Tuyuca Verb." *International Journal of American Linguistics* 50, no. 3: 255–71.

———. 1999. "Tucano." In *The Amazonian Languages*, ed. R. M. W. Dixon and A. Y. Aikhenvald, 207–26. Cambridge: Cambridge University Press.

Bonello, Henri. 1998. *Le Secret*. Paris: Presses Universitaires de France.

de Haan, Ferdinand. N.d. "Semantic Distinctions of Evidentiality." In *World Atlas of Language Structures Online*, chap. 77.

Gómez-Imbert, Elsa. 1982. "La Verdad de los Tatuyo." In *Primer seminario de antropología amazónica*. Bogotá: ICAN.

———. 2003. "Voir et entendre comme sources de connaissances grammaticalement explicites." In *Langues et cognition (Traité des Sciences Cognitives)*, ed. Claude Vandeloise, 117–33. Paris: Hermes Science Publications.

Gracian, Balthazar. 1980. *L'Homme de cour*. Paris: Champ libre.

Hill, Jonathan. 1983. "Wakuénai Society: A Processual-Structural Analysis of Indigenous Cultural Life in the Upper Rio Negro Region of Venezuela." PhD diss., Indiana University.

Houseman, Michael. 1993. "The Interactive Basis of Effectiveness in a Male Initiation Rite." In *Cognitive Aspects of Religious Symbolism*, ed. Pascal Boyer. Cambridge: Cambridge University Press.

Hugh-Jones, Stephen. 1979. *The Palm and the Pleiades: Initiation and Cosmology in Northwest Amazonia*. Cambridge: Cambridge University Press.

Jones, Wendell, and Paula Jones. 1991. *Barasano Syntax*. Summer Institute of Linguistics and the University of Texas at Arlington, Publications in Linguistics, publication 101. Dallas: Summer Institute of Linguistics.

Malone, Terrell. 1988. "The Origin and Development of Tuyuca Evidentials." *International Journal of American Linguistics* 54: 119–40.

Miller, Marion. 1999. *Desano Grammar*. Summer Institute of Linguistics and the University of Texas at Arlington, Publications in Linguistics, publication 132. Dallas: Summer Institute of Linguistics.

Morse, Nancy, and Michael Maxwell. 1999. *Cubeo Grammar*. Summer Institute of Linguistics and University of Texas at Arlington, Publications in Linguistics, publication 130. Dallas: Summer Institute of Linguistics.

Petitat, André. 1998. *Secret et formes sociales*. Paris: Presses Universitaires de France.

Simmel, Georg. 1996. *Secret et sociétés secrètes*. Paris: Circé.

Strom, Clayton. 1992. *Retuarã Syntax*. Summer Institute of Linguistics and University of Texas at Arlington, Publications in Linguistics, publication 112. Dallas: Summer Institute of Linguistics.

Viveiros de Castro, Eduardo. 1996. "Os Pronomes Cosmológicos e o Perspectivismo Ameríndio." *Mana-Estudos de Antropologia Social*, Rio de Janeiro, 2, no. 2: 115–44.

West, Birdie. 1980. *Gramatica Popular de Tucano*. Bogotá: Ministerio de Gobierno, Dirección General de Integración y Desarrollo de la Comunidad, División Operativa de Asuntos Indígenas, Instituto Lingüístico de Verano.

5. *Flutes in the* Warime

Musical Voices in the Piaroa World

ALEXANDER MANSUTTI RODRÍGUEZ

According to written sources from the colonial period, indigenous Arawak and Sáliva peoples living in the Orinoco basin were performing different forms of Yuruparí rituals at the time of contact with Europeans (Gilij 1965; Gumilla 1988; Humboldt 1991; Romero Moreno 1993). The Warime, a specific variety of Yuruparí rituals performed today among the Sáliva-speaking Piaroa and Wirö, is the most northern and eastern of the contemporary Yuruparí forms (Mansutti Rodríguez 2006). The main objectives of this chapter are to (1) describe the musical instruments played in Piaroa Warime rituals; (2) analyze the role they play in the ritual, the senses they privilege, and what they represent/re-create; and (3) evaluate the role that sacred flutes and other wind instruments play in the construction and transformation of hierarchical forms of social organization among the Piaroa. An overview of Piaroa history, the egalitarian organization of everyday social relations, and the shamanic basis of ritual hierarchy will lead into a more detailed demonstration of the fundamental role that sacred flutes and other musical instruments play in the episodic yet systematic construction of strongly hierarchical social relations.

The Piaroa, also known as Dea'ruwa, Huottoja and Uwotjuja, are an indigenous people of Sáliva linguistic affiliation who occupy the middle Orinoco between 3°50' and 6°22' of latitude. Their traditional habitat was the interfluve forest, although today they occupy sectors flanking the larger rivers (Mansutti Rodríguez 1990, 2002). Among the better known cultural attributes of this group are the Warime ritual, the control they exercise over their emotional expressions, the absolute prohibition of physical violence in their domains, and considerable shamanic prestige and renown (Overing 1986, 1989, 1990; Anduze 1974; Mansutti Rodríguez 1991, 2003).

During the sixteenth and seventeenth centuries, the Piaroa were surrounded by a complex system of Arawak-speaking peoples who occupied the lands along the Sipapo, Mataveni, Guaviare, Atabapo, Ventuari, and Upper Negro rivers (Mansutti Rodríguez 1991, 2003). The fact that the surviving Arawak societies of this vast region still practice collective rituals with a variety of sacred flutes and other wind instruments is a clear indication that these rituals were quite widely shared among Arawak-speaking peoples (Hill 1993; 2000 on the Curripaco; González Ñañez 1986 on the Guarequena; Vidal 2000 on the Baré and Curripaco; Wright 1998 for the Baniva). In light of this fact, it is reasonable to assert that the sacred flute ritual known as Warime among the Piaroa was nourished by, and in its turn nourished, an intersocietal, regional system of rituals that was spread throughout the Upper Orinoco region but that developed among the Piaroa in ways that reflected the "Guayanese" particularities of Piaroa social organization. The latter include the egocentric structuring of their social relations (Riviere 1984) and the absence of corporate groups. Both of these features set the Piaroa apart from the Arawak-speaking groups living in areas to the south, west, and north.

As late as the 1970s, the Piaroa lived in small, dispersed settlements of one or two extended families who cleared areas of humid tropical rainforest to build small communal houses, or *itso'de*. The population of such communities rarely exceeded thirty (Kaplan 1975). In contrast with neighboring societies, gender relations among the Piaroa were relatively cordial and lacking in recurrent physical violence. Although men's opinions tended to be dominant in decisions concerning issues affecting the entire community, such as its defense or relocation, women were active participants in deliberations about how to manage everyday activities.

Social hierarchies were quite simple and based principally on sex, age, place within kinship networks, and recognized abilities. Even after gaining status as an important leader, a man had a very limited capacity for imposing his opinions on other members of his community. The leader of the community is its founder or "owner of the house" (*itsoderuwa*), who is always a married man with at least one wife still living. At the leader's side is his senior wife, if having more than one, who is recognized as the primary feminine authority of the community. A team of male workers organizes itself around the leadership of the "house owner," and a parallel structure of female laborers surrounds his senior wife. The male teams are most frequently composed of the leader, some of his sons, and sons-in-law who are fulfilling their obligatory period of uxorilocal postmarital residence. The female teams consist of the senior wife, her daughters, some of her daughters-in-law, and the other wives. In order for these groups to work effectively as teams, there must be cooperation and agreement within them. If difficulties arise within a team, the individual who feels most affected has the option of leaving. The amicability of intracommunal relations among the Piaroa is conducive to egalitarian relations in everyday social life.

Intercommunal relations tend to become more complex. Within each region, the most important *itsoderuwa* is regarded as an "owner of the territory." These regional leaders are also called "owners of the people" (*tjujaturuwa*), and their leadership is recognized by the other house owners living in the region. They control access of strangers within their recognized territories. In spite of these powers, the regional leaders' actions have no impact whatsoever on the everyday lives of people who live in communities dispersed across their territories. They only have power within the shamanic domain, where they are responsible for coordinating and collaborating with other shamans in protecting the communities located within their region.

Shamanism is the only available means for transforming the loosely hierarchical organization of everyday social life into a structure that is vertical, rigid, and uncontestable. In effect, since the Piaroa world is one in which shamanic acts are the only instruments capable of creating realities, whoever has control of shamanic powers also has control over the world. The exercise of shamanic power is eminently masculine, whereas women are excluded from participating in rituals except through saying prayers (*meyeruwaju*).

Shamanism is the only institution among the Piaroa capable of generating solid hierarchies and authoritarian practices (Mansutti Rodríguez 2002, 2003). A house owner is powerful not only because he has organized the construction of a house but also because of his shamanic power to defend his house against enemy shamans and to maintain natural abundance in the local environment. Warime rituals are the most important manifestations of shamanic power among the Piaroa. Organizing Warime rituals depends upon social distinctions that produce hierarchy. Only shamans who have acquired the right to sponsor a Warime from another "owner of Warime" are capable of organizing a Warime ritual, whereas other shamans must await their invitation to a Warime ritual in order to serve as accompanists and to make it more appealing and powerful. The Warime presupposes and episodically constructs two other hierarchical segmentations: one between men and women and one between initiates and noninitiates (which is generally the same as the distinction between adults and children).

Among the men, power is concentrated in those individuals who are house owners, owners of prayers (*meyeruwa*), owners of blowing (*yuwawaruwa*), and who have also become owners of a Warime ritual and, along with this distinction, owners of the right to organize a Warime and to own its musical instruments. Power is also concentrated in women, but its magnitude and domain are not comparable to the masculine powers concentrated in the owners of Warime. The wife of the owner of Warime is called "owner of the sari" (*sariruwaju*), who embodies control of the fundamentally domestic domains, or house and food.

The distinctions between shamans who are owners of the Warime ritual and those who can only attend it, between men and women, and between adults and children fragment Piaroa social relations and crystallize them into separate parts. In these moments of ritual hierarchy, a single man, the owner of the Warime, has the power to decide what others must do, and the initiated men exercise power over what noninitiates can and cannot do. Any failure to comply with the norm can result in the death of the violators. In this way, an egalitarian society transforms itself into a community of clear and untransferrable hierarchies, and the owner of Warime acquires powers of life and death over his people. The exercise of shamanic power expressed in the Warime produces radical transformations in the Piaroa social organization, which is transported from one day to the next between egalitarian relations and a hierarchically differentiated cosmos.

The Piaroa Musical Instruments

The musical instruments used by the Piaroa can be classified as idiophones (*reré* shells and maracas) and aerophones, which include (a) ritual flutes and (b) common flutes. The ritual flutes are used only during the Warime complex, and all are end-blown (Izikowitz 1970). The common flutes are the *marana*, the *subiya*, and the *yemá iweka*. The Worá, Chuvo, Buoisa, Daa, Yajo, and Urema figure among those ritual flutes that will be documented in the following pages, and these flutes are all forbidden to the gaze of women and the uninitiated. The ritual flutes are in the first place to be understood as instruments of masculine power and segregation from the feminine domain. It is possible that more modalities of this ritual may exist, considering that the Piaroa Warime is the heir to many Yuruparí rituals that are no longer practiced

(Agerkoop 1983; Anduze 1974; Overing and Kaplan 1988; Morales et al. 1997; Signi 1988).

Worá is the mother of all Warime voices, and two musicians perform it simultaneously. It is a complex flute made up of three parts: two cylindrical tubes (approximately 2 cm diameter) and a clay pot used as a resonator. The tubes are placed in the mouth of the pot and blown alternately, producing a rapid succession of low deep tones.

Then there is Chuvo, a nose-blown flute created by Wajari, the Piaroa demiurge, to represent him. The voice of Chuvo is so beautiful that it provokes incestuous desires in his sister Chejeru, resulting in tragedies (Mansutti Rodríguez 2006). Chuvo is a voice loaded with eros, emitted by a flute with a single hole blown by the air expelled by one of the nasal openings. On the side that is blown, a ball of black wax is modeled to give it the form of a drum frame. The tonal range of this flute can be modified (Agerkop 1983).

The third important aerophone of Warime is Buoisa. It consists of a tongue of palm leaf placed between two pieces of cucurito wood (*Maximiliana regia* Mart.) that frame it. The Buoisa is played by placing it between the lips and blowing, thus causing the leaf to vibrate in the wooden frame. The Buoisa articulates sounds and speaks. In a Warime celebration, several Buoisa may converse about libidinous topics with different women who are present in the long house (*maloca*). Buoisa is Worá's husband, but he is not the father of the rest of the voices.

Worá, Chuvo, and Buoisa are the most important voices in Warime. Also present are Yajo, Daa, and Urema. Yajo represents the toucan (*Ramphastos aulacorhamphus*), considered the "owner of fruits" due to its wide range of diet and its insatiable appetite. It is a flute without holes whose tone can be modified. It awakens the Warime masked peccaries before dawn (Agerkop 1983). When the choir of musical voices comes out at night, it accompanies them circling the external wall of the maloca.

Daa represents the voice of the anaconda (*Eunectes marinus*). In this case, it is a complex voice that results from the simultaneous and alternate execution of two flutes, a male and a female, with different sized holes. The two performers stroll shoulder-to-shoulder sounding their flutes. Daa is part of the great orchestra of voices that integrates the Warime.

We have also Urema, the little toad. We have not seen it; however, Signi (1988) and Anduze (1974) reported it. According to Anduze, it is a lip whistle. We did not see it in the Warime of the Cataniapo River that we filmed (Chiappino 1993); Agerkop did not report it either in the Sipapo River (1983). It can be considered an optional instrument.

The last of the aerophones of Warime is a hummer made of a hardwood plate called Imu Chuvo; a string of moriche (*Mauritia flexuosa*) fiber is passed through a hole placed at one of the extremities. The instrument is swung around quickly by the string, so as to produce a sound similar to the song of the howler monkey (*Alouatta seniculus*).

The basic orchestra of a Warime is completed with a rattle, woven from the fiber of *tirite* (*Ichnosiphon spp.*), used by the main visible protagonists of Warime: the masked peccaries (*Tayassu pecari* or *Tayassu tajacu*). Their peculiar sound is produced by several hard-shelled fruits from a tree called *wiwito* (?) shaken in the woven rattle; it generates a dry sound and serves to mark the rhythm of the peccaries' songs. Their performance is in view of all the spectators.

This is the musical paraphernalia of Warime. Of the twelve instruments found among the Piaroa, including the reré shell and the shamanic maraca, eight are used exclusively during the Warime. Now let us see how these instruments are played.

Warime

The Warime can be rightfully sponsored only by the owner of Warime (*warimeruwa*). It is a right to which a man accedes after being chosen by the owner of Warime who can bequeath it.

An owner of Warime generally passes it on to his son, to his son-in-law, or to his brother. When the right to organize a Warime is inherited, the right to receive, to make, and to use the musical instruments and the masks that accompany it are also inherited.

When a shaman becomes an owner of Warime, he ascends in the traditional Piaroa power structure (Boglar 1976, 1999; Overing and Kaplan 1988). A warimeruwa is closer to being an owner of the people than any other shaman.

Warime is celebrated during a period of one to several months in the rainy season, a time of relative fecundity and abundance in local ecology. During this time, the following events occur:

> The domesticated environment is separated into two spaces: one hegemonic male space represented by the "men's house" or *ruwode*, and another, predominantly female, represented by the maloca.

> The beings Worá, Buoisa, Chuvo, Imu Chuvo, and *Yajo* are invited. Only adult men can see these beings, while women and children can only hear the beings' voices, which are all produced by musical instruments.

> Ojuodaa, the tapir-anaconda being that is the owner of the waters and their resources, is invited in the form of a canoe for fermentation.

> A masked dance is performed by peccaries (either white-lipped peccaries [*Tayassu pecari*] or collared peccaries [*Tayassu tajacu*]), a monkey, a bat, and Mara Reyo, the libidinous and ambiguous owner of the terrestrial and aerial animals.

> Manioc beer is drunk and subsequently vomited by men with the purpose of ridding themselves of negative feelings.

> A large amount of food is accumulated and consumed, marriages are arranged, and commercial exchanges are carried out.

> Rites of transition and fortification are performed such as passing the spine of a stingray through the tongue, applying biting ants and wasps, and whip lashing.

16. The ruwode, the house of men. Photo by Jean Chiappino.

The celebration begins at least one month before the arrival of the masked men, when the warimeruwa decides to build the ruwode. Inside the small, round house, of about two meters in diameter and two meters high (fig. 16), the initiated men meet to make masks, vests, and musical instruments or to mend those still in good shape. Women and children cannot enter the ruwode. They should be content to listen from outside to the persistent song of the peccaries: *Ju, ju, ju* (*Tayassu pecari* or *Tayassu tajacu*) and the frog's *bure*: *pruu, pruu, pruu* (*Leptodactylus knudzeni*) eventually accompanied by the voice of the howler monkey Imu Chuvo and Worá, who "speaks" every time that an important phase of the preparatory tasks of Warime begins or ends. To those listening from outside, the ruwode appears to be inhabited by Worá and Imu Chuvo accompanied by numerous peccaries and frogs preparing their celebration.

Preparations for the ritual are complex and require the formation of various teams of workers, some being of masculine orientation under the leadership of the owner of the Warime and others composed of women under the direction of the Warime owner's wife, or "owner of the sari (manioc beer)." The women dedicate their efforts to storing surplus foods and harvesting enough manioc to make sufficient quantities of manioc beer. Some of the men fix the showy masks in the ruwode and tune the instruments that produce the voices; others concentrate on carving the canoe for fermentation; others gather the basic materials for the masks, hunt, fish, and gather the food that will be consumed; and all the present shamans pray to defend themselves from attacks.

Worá, the main voice, sings when the men cut down the tree to be used for the canoe for fermentation and when they begin to carve an image of the head of Ojuodaa at each end of the canoe. She also sings when the men leave the village to search for sprouts of new leaves of Mauritia and the bark of marimu needed for the masks, when the hunters return and offer their prey, as soon as each mask is ready, when Ojuodaa is taken to the front of the maloca, after its interior is subjected to the direct action of fire, and when it is carried into the maloca to occupy its position of honor for the celebration (Chiappino 1993). Worá is a feminine voice that is prohibited to the women and that takes the leading role in a ritual that reaffirms men's power.

One month before the arrival of the masks to the celebration, the "musical voices" let themselves be heard after being invited by the Warime owner. Immediately prior to the first sound of these voices, most of the initiated men come outside of the maloca while the women and children, accompanied by a few men, enclose themselves inside the house. Soon the voices can be heard approaching the house and arriving just outside its walls, where they circle it in one direction and the other. While the musical voices are present, the community lives in an atmosphere of frenzy, seasoned by the intense and increasing activity provoked by the imminent arrival of the masks. This is a time of listening for those not initiated, women, and children.

Finally the masks arrive. This event marks the beginning of

17. The dialogue between the "owner of sari" and the warimetsa. Photo by Jean Chiappino.

the daytime domain of the sense of sight. The arrival occurs at dawn, soon after the ritual vomiting. The masks come out of the ruwode and move with short steps, one after the other, until arriving at the only entrance of the maloca. Once inside, a dialogue begins with the woman who is the wife of the owner of Warime (fig. 17). When the masked men enter, they emulate the speech of Wajari during the first Warime and a women answers, intoning an autobiographical text. The peccary's song re-creates the mythical times, and the female autobiography integrates history and myth. The circle of time closes by joining the re-creation of the original time with the woman's contemporary history. The masked beings represent the unalterable norm, and the woman represent the real history of hosts.

The daytime is the time to see. From dawn, the masks re-create a mythical event that occurred in the time when people could change their form and the animals had the same cultural powers as people. This is a dance of masked men in which the peccaries and Mara Reyo, the owner of the animals, play the main role, while a court of animals, including the white monkey and the bat, promenade through the maloca. In Warime, these masks, contrary to those used in the "ritual of fruits," never cease to be the "other" (Oyuela-Caicedo 2004).

It is during the day that women can show off their control of the domestic world and their capacity to produce and manage food and household. The women greet the masked dancers at the door, offer them manioc beer, and respond to them with songs. The women thus demonstrate that having lost the flutes to the men, they have successfully returned to the domestic domain, the space that their society has reserved for them. In short, the women's actions signify their agreement with the men.

In contrast, night is the time to listen, the time of the sacred voices. In relief of the masks, the musical voices Worá, Chuvo, Daa, Yajo, Buoisa, and Imu Chuvo come out to "speak" around the periphery of the palm frond–covered wall of the maloca. While the women and children are shut inside, listening to the orchestra, outside the concert of voices is playing, of which only those of the Buoisas emit words intelligible to the women.

In this manner, reproducing by day the visits of the masks and by night that of the voices of the invisible world, forbidden to women and children, the Warime develops, at times promoting transition rituals, at others healing sessions, and at others commercial and matrimonial exchanges, all in the context of a feast that expresses abundance and the capacity of the shaman to maintain a prolific environment.

Scripts, Voices, and Roles

Warime has a script that makes it recognizable. Though seen from the men's perspective of representation or from the women's perspective of re-creation, there are certain texts, a structure, a succession, a protocol, and several indispensable characters that must be respected. Without them, it is not a Warime. The characters can be divided into two classes: the masked beings and the musical voices. The access to both by women and children is regulated, but the regulations are more severe in the case of the musical voices than with the masks, even when it is the masks that preside over the most visible and dazzling events. In fact, the most sacred aspect of the Warime is the face of the musical voices; it is these that are manufactured in the strictest secret; to look at them is punished by death; it is they who put in play powers from the invisible world not represented by the masks or other visible instruments; they regulate life, and they can only be heard and never seen by women and uninitiated children; the transgression of this prohibition would result in death for the whole community. On the contrary, the treatment of the basic materials with which the masks are made is of public domain; their voices do not come from the invisible world but from the material world; they regulate neither life nor its fecundity, although their treatment implies severe regulations.

In effect, the Warime and its characters form part of a system, of a choreography that is consistent, on one hand, with a discourse about world vitality and the factors that put it in danger, and, on the other, with a northwestern Amazon cultural tradition of gender politics based on the differentiation of the access of men and women to the one social instrument for the concentration of power among the indigenous peoples of Lowland South America: shamanism.

This gender differentiation institutionalizes an instance of expropriation, since many Amazon societies that practice rituals with sacred flutes forbidden to women recognize that in the beginning of time these instruments belonged to them (Goldman 1963; González Ñañez 1986; Hill 1993; Wright 1998; Mansutti Rodríguez 2006). This also results in a segmentation of space, in which female power is consolidated in the interior of the maloca and in the culinary sphere, while the males control the shamanic domain. As a result, the event radically divides the role and the perception that men and women have of Warime: while men "represent" a ritual that happened in the times of origin, the women "re-create" this ritual and embody it as if it were happening again. The men act it; the women live it. This is a natural consequence of the fact that it is the men who perform the voices or who make them audible; they know that it is only through musical instruments that these beautiful sounds can be made and that in mythic times the women controlled the instruments before men took them away. Moreover, it is the men who wear the masks and who sing and act from within them.

Men, in consequence, represent the masks, they represent the voices of the special guests, and they represent Reyo, the owner of the animals of air and earth. Women, on the other hand, participate in the same way as in the original celebration Wajari made for his father-in-law, Kuemoi, with the beings of yesteryear materialized in the present. While the men perform as other characters, transforming themselves in the same manner as shamans, the women act as themselves.

Piaroa shamanism can be either constructive or aggressive. The constructive dimension is what allows shamans to imagine and create the world, what empowers them to maintain natural abundance within their regions. However, aggressive shamanism is what allows shamans to attack enemy shamans, both human and nonhuman, in order to prevent harmful attacks. In Warime rituals, both modalities of shamanism are present, but it is the creative shamanism that defines the ritual. It is not by chance that the three most powerful characters of the Piaroa cultural world are represented in the Warime: (1) Worá represents *Worajuwa*, the owner of agricultural products; (2) Ojuodaa is the owner of the water and the aquatic animals; and (3) *Mara Reyo* is the owner of the terrestrial and aerial animals. Ojuodaa is the recipient of fermented manioc; Mara Reyo comes as a masked figure to bring fruits and products of the hunt; Worá appears in the form of a deep, repetitive, and alternate voice. Ojuodaa can be seen but not heard; Mara Reyo can be heard and seen, and Worá is only heard and, although it can occur at any hour of the day, its time of visit is at night. Worá, who represents agriculture, is the only being of the powerful trilogy that can never be seen by women. It is a woman forbidden to women. With it, the vision of the female power that regulates the agricultural world is prohibited to women, precisely the social arena in which they have most quotidian control, precisely from where they originated. In this way shamanic control of the most feminine space, the agricultural sphere, is taken from women, impeding them to become more autonomous from men. In this way, women lose access to shamanic control of the very space whose effective control would allow them autonomy in the face of men.

This metaphor of the power expropriated from women also refers to the power of their own uteri, whose eventual misuse endangers the very reproduction of the group. This danger is mentioned in the myth reported by Goldman (1963) about the lazy women playing their Yuruparí flutes before they were expropriated by the men or to that of women, who celebrated rituals of female transition on their own, reported by Wright (1998). Reichel-Dolmatoff (1996) advances the idea that these rituals strengthen masculinity in patrilineal societies where women need to be weakened so that they will remain in the houses of their husbands. Maybe this ritual control also strengthens the men's power and their control over women in cognatic societies such as the Piaroa, where the oldest men are the authority figures of the domestic group.

On the other hand, if we consider the leading role played by Mara Reyo, Ojuodaa, and Worá and their power over the vital resources of the Piaroa people, it is easy to conclude that Warime is an event designed to renovate alliances with the beings that the shaman must consult regularly in order to keep his territory well stocked. In the Warime, masculine control of fertility and abundance, which were endangered by feminine control of the flutes and by the horticultural shamanic arts associated with Wora, is consolidated. In the end, the men control not only what is their own domain but also that which is related to natural fertility and which formerly belonged to the women. Warime can be considered, then, as a propitiatory ritual of total fertility and wealth controlled by men. It is also "communal ritual complexes in which wide ranking powers to fertilize nature are ascribed to a certain category of social actor upon whose ceremonial interventions others are dependent" and where "men have the ultimate say" (Whitehead 1986: 80).

The beings that attend the Warime are the same beings allied that the *meñeruwa* (the shaman who prays) invokes in order to enter the sacred mountains or *urou*, so as to fertilize the spirits of the resources, to multiply them, and to materialize them (Mansutti Rodríguez 1998). Moreover, the sounds the flutes produce symbolize the voices of the beings with whom Piaroa men are allied. The women perceive in this masculine representation the re-creation of the ancestral times; they greet the voices and masks, feed them, and offer them beverages. In this act, the women consolidate an alliance with the beings re-created in the masks and with the men who wear them. For that reason, the Warime re-inforces the women's domestic power, a power from which men benefit. As Hill says (2000: 47), "The dominant theme underlying ritual practices is the interdependence of men and women."

Worá represents the cultural art that distinguishes the Piaroa from other indigenous peoples: agriculture. Indeed, all indigenous peoples hunt and fish, but not all practice agriculture with the same dexterity. Agriculture is bequeathed to the Piaroa by two women associated with Wajari, the icon of mythical masculinity: Kuawayamu, his wife, and Chejeru, his sister. Men, who are heirs of a precultural state where survival depends on hunting and fishing, are at a disadvantage compared with women, who are heirs of the most sublime aspect of culture: agriculture. Feminine cultural arts make the difference between savagery and civilization in the cultural worlds of the Orinoco region. The expropriation of the shamanic control of agriculture from women is a strategic objective that precludes their domination over men.

Ojuodaa does not speak; he remains in silence at the middle of the maloca offering from her belly the manioc beer that the men will drink. Mara Reyo, the Piaroa equivalent of the Tukano Vai Mahse (Reichel Dolmatoff 1973; Mansutti Rodríguez 2002), does not speak either; he simply moves inside the maloca trying to capture women with his cane. In contrast, Worá is a chatterbox, although she does not articulate a single word. Once again, the metaphors refer to the real experience. In Piaroa society, men control their emotions while women laugh and scream, make jokes, and speak without contention. Worá is a female voice, as is Kuwé among the Warekena (González Ñañez 1986). The paradox is that, in a male-biased gender policy, the most important instrument is female.

Ojuodaa remains day and night in the maloca, Mara Reyo is a daytime visitor, and Worá goes out most of the time at night. Eventually she accompanies men by day in the outlying acts that make Warime possible. Every night, without fail, she goes out for a stroll, and her presence is felt, allowing her husband, Buoisa, and her son, Chuvo, who represents the voice of Wajari, to accompany her. They walk around the maloca hugging the walls.

While the voice of Chuvo is sweet and soft, Worá's is deep and vibrant, quick and repetitive, and Buoisa's is scandalous and the only one that articulates words. With these three instruments, the Piaroa orchestra creates an atmosphere of licentiousness; the others are barely heard. Sexual desire is expressed in the two male characters: Buoisa is grotesque, speaking clearly of the desires of women and how he satisfies them; Chuvo is discreet, reproducing Wajari's seduction of his sister *Chejeru* that caused so many misfortunes. Worá, in contrast, due to her cadence, the speed of her sounds, and the frenzy that she imposes, departs from all sexual allusion. Rather she evokes discipline, movement, and stability, making a sharp contrast with the images of disorder and restlessness that the men have of the women. The topics of the "language" of males and females are distinctive and serve to underline the difference of gender interests.

Worá, Buoisa, and Chuvo are not animals. Worá can be assimilated to Chejeru, the sister of the demiurge Wajari, who bequeathed to the Piaroa the arts of agriculture and the *meñé* prayers for curing illnesses. She is seen by Piaroa as an extraordinary benefactor, contrary to her brother Wajari, who in his rages and trickery created the Piaroa with teeth that rot quickly, provided raw materials that do not last, subjected people to fatal diseases, and made them susceptible to harassment by aggressive shamanism. In contrast, Puruna, the husband of Chejeru, creates the creoles, endowing them with good teeth, resistance to disease, long-lasting raw materials, and western medicine. Buoisa is sometimes assimilated to Buoka, Wajari's and Chejeru's older brother (Gheerbrant 1953), but that would imply ignoring Puruna and would institutionalize in the myth an incestuous relationship between Chejeru and her clumsy older brother. On the contrary, we postulate that the reading of the characters should be metonymic, in the plot. In this sense, Buoisa represents the unbridled male libido in the archetype of an old, impotent man taunted by the women. The importance of his figure is that he is always looking for sexual stimulation with all the women. This is his role.

The aerophones that represent animals play subordinate roles. Among them are Yajo, Daa, and Imu Chuvo. These are animals that control the shamanic arts. Remember that Yajo represents the toucan (*Ramphastos aulacorhamphus*), Daa the primordial anaconda (*Eunectes marinus*), and Imu Chuvo the grandfather of the howler monkeys (*Alouatta seniculus*). Yajo sings at dawn to wake up the warimetsa, emulating the animal that it represents. Daa is the only flute with both male and female aspects, both the same size but one is a little thicker than the other; therefore, it is the only one that emulates the pair of flutes characteristic of the

Arawak or Tukano Yuruparí. The flutes are played simultaneously by two men walking side by side. Imu Chuvó is the humming tablet that is the metaphor of the howler monkeys when they sing in the thickness of the forest. Peccaries, anacondas, toucans, and howler monkeys are all subject to predation by the Piaroa.

Other flutes like Akui, the small armadillo (*Dasypus novecinctus*), and masks like those of the jaguar (*Felis onca*), the tapir (*Tapirus terrestris*), and tarantula spiders (*Avicularia avicularia*) could appear in the Warime in minor roles; these characters represent the world of predation with their choreographies and sounds. In the context of the Warime, the parade of animal masks appear to comply with the same function as that of the so-called Dance of the Pijiguaos (*Bactris gassipaes*) or Dance of the Puppet, among many indigenous villages of the northwest Amazon, especially south of the Vaupés (Karadimas 2003; Oyuela-Caycedo 2004), where the sanctions for seeing the masks by children and women are less severe.

In Warime, the flutes are voices, but at the same time they are texts. Nobody can say what words Worá intones, but it can be said that her message is severe, systematic, repetitive, and fast. Her voice is not lovely; her voice imposes. Male voices, on the contrary, evoke other topics. The soft and parsimonious voice of Chuvo sounds continuously and can be heard speaking about seduction, discretion, and persistence in spite of being obscured by the sounds of Worá and Buoisa, and even of Daa, Yajo and Imu Chuvo. The text of Buoisa is that of the ridiculous, that of dissonant noise, the one that causes laughter. Although eros is present in his words, it only acts to diminish him. Men are in the flutes to speak of seduction and pleasure. Worá, the woman, evokes commitment and leadership. Even when women have lost the fight for real power in the world of men, the presence and the leadership of females in the magic world indicates how powerful they continue to be in the Piaroa imaginary.

Conclusions

The Piaroa Warime is clearly a form of Yuruparí, since it unites key elements distinctive of these rituals: sacred flutes that re-create voices of beings from mythical times and whose vision is forbidden to women, the death penalty for the women or communities where prohibitions are transgressed, consumption of copious amounts of food in times of abundance, male spaces with closed confraternities while domestic space is reaffirmed as a female space, and rites of passage and invigoration that take place during its execution. At the same time, what makes the Piaroa Warime a distinct form of Yuruparí is its egocentric orientation, which is expressed most clearly in the fact that it is acquired by specific individuals rather than corporate groups, such as lineages or clans. A single man exercises complete power over when to initiate the rituals and when to end them as well as the authority to organize special teams of workers. The Warime, we can conclude, is a form of Yuruparí ritual that has become "Guayana-ized."

It is evident that in the northwest Amazon there are several combinations of flutes and masks; also, the sacredness represented by the masks has fewer sanctions than that associated with the Yuruparí flutes. The combinations of instruments and levels of sacredness that generate powers are points in "a continuum of variability in the ways that specific societies have coped with the contradiction between ritual hierarchy and social equality" (Hill 2000: 2).

What is clear in all cases is the structural impact that these rituals have over social relations. When there is no Warime being held among the Piaroa, their communities maintain relatively egalitarian relations both internally and among themselves, only lightly inflected with flexible hierarchies that emerge in gender relations, the routines of everyday work, and preventive shamanic activities. In contrast, even the initial stages of preparing to hold the Warime ritual creates a vertical power structure, hegemonic voices, exclusive spaces, and rigid social norms that must be strictly observed. Piaroa society can thus be said to balance itself over the course of each year between one form of organization that is horizontal and egalitarian and another that is pyramidal and hierarchical. Within this process, the great significance of sacred flutes is the extraordinary symbolic weight that they carry as embodiments of that which is most inaccessible and highly prohibited. The flutes are the most important voices of the Warime.

The sound of sacred flutes enables the musical speech that legitimizes the exercise of gender power that can be seen in an egalitarian society such as the Piaroa, power that leads them to move back and forth annually between quotidian egalitarianisms and seasonal hierarchies. We are not exaggerating when affirming that the flutes of the Piaroa world are the voice of desire and the buttress of power.

Acknowledgments

To Ramon Castillo, Buré Marí, and Laureano Castillo. To Jean Chiappino. To Fundacion La Salle by its support to our research on Warime in 1989. To the FONACIT (old CONICIT), which financed the improvement to the CIAG, and Fundacite Guayana and the UNEG, which stimulated us to write this essay. Finally, to those who helped me in the translation: Michael Tancock, Nalua Silva Monterrey, Kay Tarble-Scaramelli, Jonathan Hill, and Juan Luis Rodriguez.

References Cited

Agerkop, Terry. 1983. *Piaroa: Venezuela*. Caracas: INIDEF.

Anduze, Pablo. 1974. *Dearuwa: Los dueños de la selva*. Biblioteca de la Academia de Ciencias Físicas, Matemáticas y Naturales, vol. 18. Caracas: Talleres Topográficos de la Dirección de Cartografía Nacional.

Boglar, Lajos. 1976. "Creative Process in Ritual Art: Venezuela." In *The Realm of the Extra Human*, 347–53. La Hague: Mouton.

———. 1999. "Warime: el poder de las máscaras." In *Orinoco-Parima: Comunidades indígenas de Venezuela. La Colección Cisneros*, ed. Juan Luis Delmont, 162–87. Alemania: Ostfildern-Ruit.

Chiappino, Jean. 1993. *Warime 89: Fête des masques dans une communauté Wotjuja*. Document audio-visuel. Paris: ORSTOM (IRD).

Gheerbrant, Alain. 1953. *L'Expedition Orénoque-Amazone*. Paris: Gallimard.

Gilij, F. Salvador, S.J. 1965. *Ensayo de historia americana*. 3 vols. Caracas: Biblioteca de la Academia Nacional de la Historia, nos. 71, 72, and 73.

Goldman, Irving. 1963. *The Cubeo: Indians of the Northwest Amazon*. Urbana: University of Illinois Press.

González Ñañez, Omar. 1986. "Sexualidad y rituales de iniciación entre los indígenas Warekena del Río Guainia-Río Negro, TFA." *Montalbán* 17: 103–38.

Gumilla, Joseph. 1988. *El Orinoco ilustrado y defendido, historia natural, civil, y geographica de este gran rio, y de sus caudalosas vertientes. Govierno, usos, y costumbres de los indios fus habitadores, con nuevas y utiles noticias de Animales, Arboles, Frutos, Aceytes, Refinas, Yervas, y Raices medicinales; y fobretodo fe hallaràn converfiones muy fingulares à N. Santa Fé, y cafos de mucha edificacion*. 2 vols. Valencia: Generalitat Valenciana.

Hill, Jonathan. 1993. *Keepers of the Sacred Chants: The Poetics of Ritual Power in an Amazonian Society*. Tucson: University of Arizona Press.

———. 2000. "Varieties of Fertility Cultism in Amazonia: A Closer Look at Gender Symbolism in Northwestern Amazonia." In *Gender in Amazonia and Melanesia: An Exploration of the Comparative Method*, ed. T. Gregor and D. Tuzin, 45–68. Berkeley: University of California Press.

Humboldt, Alejandro de. 1991. *Viaje a las regiones equinocciales del Nuevo Continente*. 5 vols. Caracas: Monte Avila Editores.

Izikowitz, Karl Gustav. 1970. *Musical and Other Sound Instruments of the South American Indians: A Comparative Ethnographical Study*. Yorkshire, UK: S. R.

Kaplan, Joanna. 1975. *The Piaroa: A People of the Orinoco Basin: A Study in Kinship and Marriage*. Oxford: Clarendon.

Karadimas, Dimitri. 2003. "La masque de la raie: Étude ethno-astronomique de l'iconographie d'un masque ritual miraña." *L'Homme* 165: 173–204.

Mansutti Rodríguez, Alexander. 1990. *Los Piaroa y su territorio*. Monografía no. 8. Caracas: Ceviap.

———. 1991. "Sans guerriers il n'y a pas de guerre: Etude sur la violence chez les Piaroa du Venezuela." Mémoire de DEA, Ecole des Hautes Etudes en Sciences Sociales (EHESS), Paris.

———. 1998. "Meñeruwas y empresarios: ambiente y desarrollo en tierras piaroas" (Meñeruwas and Managers: Environment and Development in Piaroa's Land), 199–204. In R. J. Carrillo, ed., *Memorias del IV Congreso Interamericano sobre el Medio Ambiente*, realizado en Caracas, Venezuela, entre el 8 y 11 de diciembre de 1997. Colección Simposia, 2:334. Editorial Equinoccio, Ediciones de la Universidad Simón Bolívar, Caracas.

———. 2002. "Le parcours des créatures de Wajari: Socialisation du milieu naturel, système régional et migrations chez les Piaroa du Venezuela." PhD diss., Ecole des Hautes Etudes en Sciences Sociales (EHESS), Paris.

———. 2003. "Piaroa: Los guerreros del mundo invisible." *Antropológica* 99–100: 97–116.

———. 2006. *Warime: La Fiesta: Flautas, trompas, y poder en el noroeste amazónico*. Ciudad Guayana: Fondo Editorial UNEG.

Morales, Severiano, Jesús Caballero, Laureano Castillo, and Alexander Mansutti. 1997. *Asi somos los Uwotjuja*. Caracas: UNICEF Venezuela.

Overing, Joanna. 1986. "Images of Cannibalism, Death, and Domination in a Nonviolent Society." *Journal de la Société des Americanistes* 72: 133–56.

———. 1989. "Styles of Manhood: An Amazonian Contrast in Tranquility and Violence." In *Societies at Peace*, ed. Signe Howell and Roy Willis, 79–99. New York: Routledge.

———. 1990. "The Shaman as a Maker of Worlds: Nelson Goodman in the Amazon." *Man* 25: 602–19.

Overing, Joanna, and M. R. Kaplan. 1988. "Los Wothuha (Piaroa)." In *Los Aborigenes de Venezuela*, ed. W. Coppens, 3: 307–411. Caracas: Monte Avila-Fundación La Salle de Ciencias Naturales.

Oyuela-Caycedo, Augusto. 2004. "The Ecology of a Masked Feast: Negotiating at the Frontier of Identity in the Northwest Amazon." *Baessler-Archiv Band* 52: 54–74.

Reichel-Dolmatoff, Gerardo. 1973. *Desana: Le symbolisme universel des indiens Tukano du Vaupés*. Paris: Gallimard.

———. 1996. *Yuruparí: Studies of an Amazonian Foundation Myth*. Cambridge: Harvard University Center for the Study of World Religions.

Riviere, Peter. 1984. *Individual and Society in Guiana: A Comparative Study of Amerindian Social Organization*. Cambridge: Cambridge University Press.

Romero Moreno, Maria Eugenia. 1993. "Achagua." In *Geografía Humana de Colombia: Región de la Orinoquia* 3, vol. 1: 108–38. Santa Fe de Bogotá: Instituto Colombiano de Cultura Hispánica.

Signi, Alejandro. 1988. *Arte y Vida*. Catálogo de la colección del Museo Etnológico del Territorio Federal Amazonas. Caracas: Editorial Ex-Libris.

Vidal, Silvia M. 2000. "Kuwé Duwákalumi: The Arawakan Sacred Routes of Migration, Trade, and Resistance." *Ethnohistory* 47, no. 3–4: 635–68.

Whitehead, Harriet. 1986. "The Varieties of Fertility Cultism in New Guinea, Part I." *American Ethnologist* 3, no. 1: 80–99.

Wright, Robin. 1998. *Cosmos, Self, and History in Baniwa Religion: For Those Unborn*. Austin: University of Texas Press.

6. Desire in Music

Soul-Speaking and the Power of Secrecy

MARCELO FIORINI

A Bird's Overture

To to ki su´, the white-tailed trogon, began to sing that morning, forcefully and before any other bird. We had been walking for six days in the forest and had camped south of the River of Fire Ants the night before. While crossing the river, we had seen a nearly four-meter-long coral snake skirting an oxbow by a steep bank, clearly visible in the greenish, translucent water. Everyone admired its beauty, danger, and power. But that morning, while Skimpy-Buttocks and other women tried to rekindle the fire, I noticed how Blue-Neck had become rather thoughtful. He seemed to listen to the melancholy bird song carefully. Then, at once, he turned to other people in the camp, some of whom were still lying down. There followed a spate of conversation between Blue-Neck and Bung-Nose, Skimpy-Buttocks's brother-in-law, and his wife, Gangly-Croc. I could feel some urgency in what he said, although I could not overhear it, as I was farther away from the group, jotting notes in a journal. But the next moment, Blue-Neck came up to me and said: "We must turn back home immediately. My father has arrived in the village. He brings news."

The urgency was implicit in the form of the Nambikwara imperative with which he had communicated what he had been musing.[1] I saw that people had started gathering their belongings. No

18. White-tailed trogon, also known as the to to ki su´. Drawing by Anaïs
Chaumeil.

one questioned him. But as we left the camp, I seized the opportunity to ask him: "How do you know your father has come back to the village?" He replied, simply: "Can't you hear to to ki su´ calling? That's what it is saying."

How could a bird tell Blue-Neck that Chief Arm-Strong, his father, had arrived back in the Wasusu village from the town of Vilhena, where he had been for several weeks recovering from a broken arm?

All I could get out of Blue-Neck that morning, as he hastened everyone and quickly picked his way on the trail back home, was that birds sometimes conveyed messages with their calls. They did not only "say their names" (as the Wasusu and other Nambikwara claim birds usually do, when they emit their calls),[2] but birds were able to carry messages between people over great distances. Blue-Neck added it was rather odd that the bird sang with such vigor at that early hour in the morning, in that very place, and its call seemed quite plaintive, insistent. I pressed him for further clarification, but he merely said: "Had that bird sung by the river the evening before, it would be 'saying' something quite different: a child is crying and in need of assistance."

Symbolic Forms and Cultural Objects

Steven Feld (1982) has eloquently written about the relationship between birds, songs and sentiment among the Kaluli of Papua New Guinea. His work has provided me with inspiration for understanding how the Nambikwara link personal emotions and history to socially encoded sentiment expressed (or impressed) in music and myth.[3] Thus, the Nambikwara way of conceiving how bird or animal calls, as well as music, may convey powerful messages between people or between personal entities separated in space or temporal dimensions, appears to extend well beyond their use as means of communication. Bird or animal calls, songs, and flute tunes may ultimately be used as means for changing the course of events while providing personal empowerment. They can therefore be seen as vehicles for the channeling of agency.

I want to borrow a frame of analysis put forth by Ernest Cassirer (1923) in relation to the construction of cultural objects to talk about the dialogical forms of signifying practice implicit in Manairisu (Wã n'ai ri su´) or Nambikwara flute music performance. For Cassirer, three processes may constitute cultural objects: presentation, expression, and signification.[4] Presentation refers to what a cultural object more directly communicates, and it relates to the sphere of language. Expression concerns representation, what a cultural object—either a flute tune or the flute ritual itself—recalls or evokes, and it ultimately relates to the sphere of myth. Finally, signification is highly specific to a cultural-historical scenario; it is perhaps what the ritual or the tune comes to mean in a specific context, and it bears a relation to how a particular phenomenology of knowledge may be articulated at that very moment.

I want to use Cassirer's analysis of the formation of cultural objects as a heuristic device to illuminate some aspects of Nambikwara music. Both flute music and the flute ritual may be seen as operating by processes of expression and representation, presentation and communication, apart from being forms of signifying practice where knowledge can be tested and transformed. All these processes may act concomitantly and should not be thought to preclude one another, but they can also be looked at separately. A person may have a mere aesthetic experience of the music in flute rituals; the ritual itself may be performed in such a way to highlight the beauty of the music, but that does not mean the ritual may not be carrying out other functions or meanings.

If one considers to to ki su´'s call in the forest, one could say that birds (and certain animals) are special beings in the Nambikwara cosmos, since they "say" their names with their songs or calls (e´ na la´). In the terms of Cassirer, this is an instance of presentation relating to the realm of language. This is certainly not an elaborate language like that of human beings, but it is equally used for communication, and its basis is the mimetic. In this case, birds present or identify themselves with their calls. The Wasusu would frequently resort to imitating the birdcall by means of a word in their language—as distant as its phonemes would sometimes dismayingly appear to me—to testify to the fact that a bird "was saying its name." Therefore, to to ki su´ (the white-tailed trogon) is "really saying: *to to to to to to to*," while the w'ai kãu su´ (the white forest falcon) is "saying *w'ai kãu, w'ai kãu, w'ai kãu*."

Sometimes bird songs and calls allegedly express or evoke further moods or sentiments, a quality that may appear in myth as well as being implied in daily interaction. This would more closely fit into Cassirer's notion of representation. As a full-fledged mythical character (pun intended), or in respect to the connotations that its appearance in myths implies: to to ki su´ may express a sense of abandonment or loneliness, tu tu´su´, the hummingbird, may hint at furtiveness and cleverness, while the white forest falcon may recall the sadness caused by a person's disappearance, the yearning to fulfill one's absence, the cantankerousness of the old.[5] In other words, to to ki su´'s call "says its name," it may evince a certain affective response, and it might also signify, in certain contexts (as during our expedition in the forest, if someone like Blue-Neck is so predisposed), something entirely different such as "someone has arrived back in the village" or "a child is crying." At the level of signification, according to Cassirer's terminology, a specific bird call heard in a certain social-historical context may mean, to any knowledgeable person who may interpret such context, something quite different than what it usually does through presentation or expression. It may connect to personal feelings, to the innermost yearnings of individuals, to fears and to dreams.

The Manairisu explain this process by which a bird call may bear such an emotional significance and it may be a vehicle for messages exchanged between people as a form communication

19. Men making flutes. Photo © Marcelo Fiorini.

carried out virtually, between souls. The preferred term I found among the Wasusu at the time of my fieldwork, for whom this signifying level of song or bird call is extremely pronounced, especially when they travel in the forest, was *te le pho na⁀n'ēn'hna´*, a recently coined jargon, owing to the capacity of this kind of communication to carry over great distances, and because of its resemblance to communication by means of telephones. Like the case of to to ki su´s call, this level of signification where messages and emotions are conveyed through bird calls is thought to be a potential yet integral part of the aural sign. It clearly marks the difference between those moments when a bird simply "says its name" and when it is an antenna for personal communication, depending on particular human dispositions or relational scenarios. Pragmatically, Blue-Neck's certainty is indeed not too different from when we think of our own father, the telephone rings, and we call it "telepathy." Among the *cerrado*-dwelling Waka-litesu, where shamans have much more publicly pronounced social roles, this kind of communication is akin to what they call "soul-speaking," the capacity through which shamans "may capture messages at a distance."

I have taken this detour through the song of a bird to show how such empowering communication through birds or animals parallel the uses that flute and vocal music may be put to.

While a flute tune may refer to a bird, such a melody is primarily an expression of a communication with its spirit. Flute tunes may refer to different personae: a human being, an animal, a bird, each of which may further relate to the sphere of myth, but the phatic connection with the spirit (of bird, animal, or person) is already established by the playing of the tune. Presentation, in this sense, precedes representation. The old woman flute tune, for instance, alludes to a character in a myth: a mother who anxiously awaits her son's return from the hunt. But only a fragment of such a relationship is expressed through the tune: "a woman is crying." Beyond this, flute tunes may evoke, for certain people, personal relationships that may be dialogically resignified by connecting them to yet other relationships or circumstances that are part of those people's experience at that particular moment in time. This includes situations or relationships that must be reflected or commented upon, potentialized or transformed. Both signification and expression would therefore appear to be heightened here by presentation, since, by presenting a tune, one is both symbolically alluding to its referent—the old woman, in this case (by means of musical notes)—and expressing a relationship to its spirit. One may therefore claim that flute music may be considered part of the communicative universe of signifying practices, of presenting cultural objects or potentially revealing personal dispositions through them, as well as expressing (or representing) contexts and events, or adding some emotional tone to the latter. By presenting a tune (wordlessly "naming" its referent through a musical tune), or by performing such culturally recognized objects like flute tunes, one is potentially alluding to such relationships and affecting the course of events. The performance of the entire flute ritual itself may be thought of as a form of presenting culturally significant objects, contexts, and personae through a variety of flute tunes. The playing of such tunes itself summons their spirits. In this sense, Chaumeil's assertion (vide infra) that the flute ritual parallels shamanism as a form of communication and management of relationships between people and spirits—and I should add, among people in general, or between people and all recognized categories of persons—may be specially relevant for societies like the Manairisu or the Nambikwara groups of the Guaporé Valley, where the role of shaman is commonly not assumed by any one person, and a "shamanism without shamans" prevails.[6]

But another characteristic pervades Nambikwara ritual flute music or, more specifically, its tunes: they are not usually named. Knowledge of a tune's referent is more commonly enveloped in secrecy, like the ritual itself. Only a specialist musician can say what a tune may refer to: bird or animal, or plant, in some cases, except for a few tunes that refer to people and to their relationships. Ideally, one must verify the referent of a certain flute tune by asking its composer, for whom the flute tune must have appeared in a dream.[7] Or, in the case of a traditional tune, a specialist musician can demonstrate such reference by resorting to vocal music. But this does not mean that flute tunes are actually songs played in the flutes or that flute tunes must have their origins necessarily attributed to vocal music. Specialist musicians among the Nambikwara resort to musical motifs and traditional melodic phrasing so as to "translate" or transpose the flute tune into a vocal song, thereby identifying (through the song's lyrics) its referent as a bird, a plant, or an interpersonal relationship. In this sense, playing a flute tune is still, indirectly, a form of presentation that relates to the realm of language, since one may resort to these song variants to reveal that a particular tune refers to a bird, an animal, an old woman crying, etc. Like the Wauja women's songs that relate to the Kawoká flute tunes (Mello, this volume and 2005), Nambikwara song may refer to a flute tune by transposing it to the sphere of language. But as I have stated, that does not necessarily mean that the tune came from the song; rather, it means that both flute tunes and vocal songs belong to parallel musical traditions that a musician may compare, equate, and relate.[8] Nevertheless, since the origins of vocal song and flute music are established through myths, one could say that flute tunes are already an integral part of expression: they are a way of transforming the everyday into myth.

In sum, while there is no one-to-one relationship between flute tunes and vocal music, the knowledge of a flute tune's referent, or of its sentimental or expressive potential or its significance for a certain historical context, is usually accessible to composers, experienced musicians, and ritual specialists, as well as to any knowledgeable people, including those people who are endowed with spiritual power. Such knowledge has therefore transformative potential, all the more so because of the usual secrecy underlying it. One could argue that the Nambikwara heighten the instance of presentation as well by enveloping the reference in a layer of secrecy. Indeed, the playing itself is considered a powerful act, and it effects change. By withholding reference (presentation), the Nambikwara may also be emphasizing the transformative power of the tune itself.

Among the reasons given for playing the ritual flutes, the Nambikwara reckon the maintenance and preservation of the known universe. Most Nambikwara flute tunes present, or metaphorically refer to, certain referents: birds like tu´hlu´ (the flutist-wren), wa kãn´hlu´ (the great-egret), k'wa s'a su´ (the forest dove); plants like k'wa se su´ (the arrow-vine), or people like ta ka lu su´ (the Old Woman). But apart from "designating" such animals, plants, or people, the flutes produce them, since music is conceived as their spirit. Thus the Nambikwara seem to fit neatly among those groups of people who do not believe in the separation of signifier

20. Men playing the flutes in the garden. Photo © Marcelo Fiorini.

and signified, since the tune is said to be a manifestation of (therefore having an intrinsic relationship to) that which it stands for (Wagner 1981: 106). Apart from this, many of the explanations I have obtained among Nambikwara musicians, about the actual meaning of flute tunes, read like the signifying and at once connative and connotative levels of to to ki su´'s call mentioned at the beginning of this essay, as interpreted by Blue-Neck when we camped in the forest.[9] Such meanings may be translated in short statements such as "my father returns home," "an old woman is crying," "a jealous wife," "a daunting father-in-law," and so on. In this sense, there is an evocative side to instrumental music, in its recalling of myth or its evocation of a mood or sentiment, but even more commonly in the use of that very phenomenology of knowledge that led Blue-Neck to interpret to to ki su´'s call as something other than a mere bird call.

In that particular case, his father had broken his arm only a few weeks earlier. His father's absence and the expectation of his recovery as well as the fact that we had been traveling in the forest for six days certainly made Blue-Neck's feelings resonate with the melancholy mood expressed by the trogon's song. It is not a coincidence that one of the meanings of to to ki su´'s call for the Wasusu is "a child needs assistance." Meaning arises in this case like the interpretation of a reverie, of thoughtfulness, or a wakeful dream. Meaning arises in practice, and it does not preclude agency, since Blue-Neck is not a mere recipient of the message in this case but a participant in the process of its instantiation. In fact, his father was back in the village when we got back, and for Blue-Neck, that was certainly not a coincidence.

Similarly, I recorded an instance where a stray egret appeared by the Wasusu village's stream and showed familiarity with people, just as news was spreading of the death of a Sararé man, whose own village was located a hundred miles away to the south. The egret was said to be carrying the man's spirit to the abode of the spirits, the sacred caves some thirty miles away to the north. A tune designating the great-egret was played in a flute ritual a few days later, announcing the passage of the spirit and the deferential acknowledgment of the man's death.

Keith Basso (1996) has described the performative use of place-names among the Apache as a form of evoking an interpersonal domain instilled with sentiment and as a way of using it for the potential transformation of social relationships. Although Nambikwara place-names preserve a great deal of the local groups' histories, it is their music domain, I would argue, that fulfills this role of inspiring and revamping the interpersonal domain. This is perhaps all the more so because Nambikwara ritual life is spare. Rituals often last not a long time in comparison with other Amazonian groups (except during funerals and times of crises), and they occur sparsely and farther in between. It is music that more closely resembles myth in Nambikwara culture, and it is important to stress here the fact that music first originates in mythical times. But being so much more a part of daily life (as people constantly play flutes, sing, and whistle a tune outside of ritual contexts), music seems to have become a prime domain among the Nambikwara for the evocation of personal wants and desires.

Nambikwara music is thus replete with such possibilities for transforming events or situations into more significant ones for their participants and thereby reinterpreting lived experience or allowing greater agency on the part of the interpreter. A flute tune referring to an "old woman" known as the woman who became a constellation (the Pleiades) in a certain myth, is said to signify, in the context of the flute music, that such a woman is waiting for a son's return from the hunt, hoping he is bringing home game that he must have seized. Therefore, such a tune may reverberate with a number of events ensuing in daily life and a host of desires and feelings emanating from individuals. In other words, one must be attentive, or thoughtful at least, to "tune in" to these meaningful moments, as when a bird sings in the forest and means something quite different than it usually does, when a bird "telephones."[10]

Apart from the aesthetic appreciation of the beauty of a tune, which is inseparable from its cultural, emotional, or historical context, one must therefore consider what flute tunes may come to represent for the relationships of different persons in the Nambikwara universe. In this sense, the tunes played by the gourd trumpets are exemplary, for they point to dangerous relationships, that is, relationships that must be controlled to avoid adversity or disaster. Flute tunes should not be seen merely as poetic vehicles. They are themselves vehicles or channels of power, like the flutes themselves. Chief Arm-Strong, one of the Wasusu elders, once told me that when the white men came, their rifles were also called by the term *ya ˜lĩn su´*, one of the names of the sacred flutes, precisely because of the dangerous power that could be delivered from them. The thundering sound of a rifle implied its power, its "music," or its spirit. In the same way, the spellbinding sight of a coral snake winding its way smoothly in the oxbows of an emerald river may inspire a certain awe toward its being and danger, and its consequent dream may inspire a tune or a song, but what it may signify in the personal space of memory and feeling often pervaded by music may be something quite different.

Engendering Mythical Contests

The fact that Nambikwara music ultimately deals with personal relationships is also implicit in the two different stories given by the Forest Nambikwara as the origin of ritual flute music. Two distinct myths among the Wã n'ai ri su´ refer to the origin of the flutes. The first may be almost called historical, for it narrates how the group played nothing but papaya-tree shoots until they came into contact with the People from the Savannahs (Sa 'mã^le kí'te'su´) an ancestral indigenous group with whom the Nambikwara allied themselves.[11] This myth also reveals an important aspect of the flute ritual: the fact that it entails people's relationships with otherness.

The other myth tells us that the women used to have the flutes and hold them in secrecy. This myth concentrates on the fact that the men, upon hearing their sisters playing, thought the music was so hauntingly beautiful that they were held under its spell. Although they asked to see or play those mysterious instruments, the sisters would not reveal the flutes to them. The sisters invariably told their brothers that if they wanted to listen to the flutes, the sisters themselves would play for them. But as the men perceived that their sisters were keeping the instruments from them, they grew jealous of their own sisters, something quite inappropriate in Nambikwara culture, where brothers and sisters should be nothing but allies who share freely and equally in respect to anything, whether food, material objects, or cultural knowledge. Since the brothers would not let it go and kept insisting on partaking of that music, one day the sisters, giving an example of what is morally correct, told their brothers to be patient, for they would have what they desired. They told their brothers to wait while they withdrew to the forest and started playing the music. Only then, the sisters warned, should the brothers follow them into the forest so that the sisters could show the brothers the instruments and teach them how to play. When the beautiful flute tunes began echoing in the forest, the brothers followed, but they could not find their sisters, as much as they searched for them. They only found the shoots of ya ˜lĭn su´, the taboca bamboo. They realized these shoots were the limbs of their dear sisters. The sisters had transformed themselves into bamboo, and the flute music one hears today is the sisters' spirits. This is why the Wasusu still stop the ends of the bamboo shoots with leaves when they pick them in the forest to make new flutes, so that the breath of the souls won't blow out and away. Music is to the flutes as a spirit is to a living body, and therefore musicians may be seen as being engaged in reconciling spirits to bodies as much as shamans.

The theme of sharing and nourishing, in the sense of satisfying one's desires, is important in the flute's myth, as well as the implicit allusion to envy and sexual tension and desire. But another important aspect of the flutes' embodiment of spirits is that the spirit, yãun ki t'i su´, comprehends a corollary vital principle, 'wa ˜nĭn': one's spirit power or force. These two spiritual aspects of being inhabit the body, concomitantly. The yãun ki t'i su´ preserves the danger and ambiguous power of the spiritual realm, while the 'wa ˜nin' is thought to be the force that can be seized to cure illness or protect people from ill. In the other version of the aforementioned myth, found among the cerrado or savannah Nambikwara, it is the father's abandonment of his son that leads the latter to stray out to the edge of the village and transform himself into the local traditional cultivars and the flutes (thereby creating the first garden). Both of these mythical versions reiterate the themes of sharing, nourishment, and the maintenance of expected relations between people.

The Sacred and the Secret

There are three types of Nambikwara ritual flutes: ta wã´na su´, a straight, four-stop duct flute made of the taboca bamboo (ya ˜lin su´); ha´y'u ha´y'u hlu´, a trumpet made by reversing the native bamboo and fitting a gourd resonator at its opposite extremity, and a speaking/resonating instrument called ti k'a li su´, the Anteater speaking trumpet, also made by reversing the bamboo and splitting it sideways several times along its shaft from a point near the proximal end to a point near the distal end.[12] In the Guaporé Valley, where most Southern Nambikwara-speaking groups traditionally had less than fifteen types of items of material culture and no developed visual representation, ritual flutes made up a fifth of the objects formerly found among them. Instrumental music is thus recognizably an important part of the material culture.

The flute ritual itself subsumes the idea of personal relationships. It subsumes one's relation to one's in-laws, as brothers-in-law gather in the flutes house or village patio to perform, as well as the relationships between men and women and of the living to the spiritual world. But in the latter two cases, the flutes also effect a separation. The ritual process goes from an approximation of the spiritual world to a severance from it, as spirit guardians "come near" the village to hear the sound of the flutes, only to leave it when the playing ceases. As for men and women, the flutes separate them spatially in order to join them in intention, for the women listen to the flutes, often attentively, requesting that the men play them at certain times.[13]

While everyone in the village may appreciate listening to the flutes, one of the reasons Wasusu men told me they played the flutes was because "the women wanted to hear them."[14] I want to emphasize this permissive quality of the flute ritual, as opposed to its visual prohibition for reasons that will soon become clear. For the moment, it suffices to say that there is no imposed penalty for the women seeing the flutes among the Wã n'ai ri su´ and other Nambikwara groups.[15]

Wasusu women explain that they don't want to see the flutes because if they did, their throats would clog up and they would sicken and die. Incidentally, that is an accurate description of a death caused by contact with a spirit. If one recalls the myth of the origin of the flutes, one could say that women are not as jealous of the men as the latter were when the women had possession of the flutes. When the flutes are being played in the village plaza, the women gather inside the houses, and although a curious young woman may watch the men surreptitiously through a chink in the thatch, older women may consider this act reckless.[16] In the myth, the emphasis is not on the action of seizing the flutes, for one should remember there is no theft or violence in the mythical narrative I collected among the Guaporé Valley Nambikwara. The significant part lies instead on the emotions that inform the relationship of brothers and sisters, for it is the men's feeling of jealousy itself that leads the women into the forest and causes the metamorphosis of their bodies into flutes as well as the transformation of their spirits into music.[17]

The present situation is the reverse of the myth: the men are the guardians of the flutes. They keep their knowledge out of circulation and do not share it with women. They also control shamanism and the power to cure. The women find themselves in the position of the mythical brothers: they listen attentively to the men's instruments and find their sound hauntingly beautiful. They may indeed ask the men to play the flutes for them. By giving up possession of the flutes, the women allow the men to control a powerful medium for taking care of people's contact with the world of the spirits, a task for which they see themselves as unfit. Now the men must continue playing the flutes for the benefit of society and particularly of women. As the embodiment of such an agreement, the flutes seal a kind of gender complementariness that symbolically reproduces society in the same manner that women once did in the myth.

In the fully developed ritual among the Wasusu and other Wã n'ai ri su´ groups, the men begin playing the straight flutes in the early evening inside the flutes house, and then pause. They may stop to fabricate the gourd trumpets themselves, a process that may already cause great excitement among the men. At night, they begin playing the flutes again, adding the gourd trumpets (Ha 'yu ha 'yuh lu´) cumulatively, and alternating between straight flutes, gourd trumpets, and their ensemble. After the next pause, the performers playing the straight flutes begin to dance and the gourds accompany them, often in the village plaza. The gourd tunes encompass slight tonal differences and refer to animal species that have a special status in Nambikwara culture—the Jaguar, the Bushmaster Snake, the White Vulture, the Giant Armadillo—usually identified as affinal in myths and evoking elements of danger, death, scatology, or war. The gourds add some raunchiness to the flute ritual, and the atmosphere becomes like that of a men's club. The Anteater speaking trumpet (Ti k'i li su´) arrives much later, and his coming is greatly enveloped in secrecy. Somewhat furtively, he breaks into shouting over the tune, issues forced laughter, speaking in a creaky falsetto. His role in the ritual includes mockery or ribald joking with the participants. This ridiculing involves immorality and social transgression, as the Anteater assumes the role of a tease in a joking relationship, calling the men his "little husbands" and mentioning or hinting at the personal names of participants in the ritual, something that would be out of the question in everyday life, where mentioning a person's name is unacceptable when the person named is present.

Hearing the raucous sound of the gourd trumpets, the women might request that the men stop, and they may simply do as they are told, although occasionally, and specially after the Anteater has arrived, the men are often already too excited to listen to such a request. The greater power of the speaking trumpet is directly associated with its position in the flute ritual as an instrument enveloped in the utmost secrecy as well as being the expression of a moral freedom, as a vehicle for all kinds of licentiousness that are not socially permissible.

I want to put forth here a different perspective on this reserved or "sacred" quality of the flutes, depending more on a creative principle (related to the Greek concept of Eros), than on a

21. The gourd trumpet. Photo © Marcelo Fiorini.

destructive or deadly principle, as in the views postulated in anthropology through the notion of sacrifice (related to the Greek concept of Thanatus). This is not a whimsical shift of anthropological or philosophical stance, or a mere return to a psychoanalytical paradigm where women's power resides in their natural ability to give birth.[18] As something set apart, restricted to a certain time and space, the concept of the sacred has necessarily been pervaded by the idea of secrecy. I would argue, therefore, that the emphasis here is not on a control of death or disease, Thanatus, but on the maintenance of certain dispositions toward life and relationships, which by themselves guarantee the permanence and regeneration of life. One should recall that in the Wasusu myth, the disappearance of the sisters is caused by their brothers' jealousy over a mysterious power. Ultimately, the sisters give custody of the flutes to their brothers so that the latter will continue to have a complementary relationship with them and thus society may be reproduced.

As in many other parts of the world, Nambikwara flutes have also been considered a symbol of masculinity.[19] Nevertheless, the Wã n'ai ri su' do not consider the flutes to be gendered, nor do they have a homoerotic view of them. If the anthropologist insists, ta wã'na su', the straight flutes, are said to be the bodies of the mythical sisters. The Wasusu prefer to equate the various types of flutes with kinship relations. The straight flutes, in this sense, would represent relations between siblings, real or fictive, and are thereby imbued by the notions of alliance or consanguinity; the gourd trumpets represent relations of affinity (same generation), since this instrument is thought to have originated from the transformed body of a brother-in-law in ancient times, during the apocalypse when night first appeared. Finally, the Anteater speaking trumpet, a musical instrument with a similar status as the trumpets, made as well from ya ˜lĩn su' or taboca bamboo, is an ascending generation affine, an age-old spirit who incarnates the trickster of Nambikwara mythology. He is also the guardian of epilepsy, and he may cause the players to feel muscle cramps.[20]

My clue for reconsidering the status of the flutes and their ritual as embodying and regulating a creative, renewing force is more particularly related to certain cultural practices. First of all, since the Wasusu explain the taboo on women seeing the flutes as a physical incapacity, one must perhaps look at other prohibitions that could elucidate what is actually being preserved by institutionalizing them as part of a men-only ritual kept in secrecy. The other major prohibition in relation to the flutes is that they cannot be played after a woman has given birth. This is not only explained by the Manairisu or Guaporé Valley Nambikwara as a way to protect the newborn, but also because of "the blood of women" (or the blood women shed during and after birth and that babies preserve in the reddish color of their skin). Playing the flutes would be harmful to both. Blood is women's contribution to fertility, and the blood of menstruation or parturition must be treated with great care, being considered a veritable source of contagion as well as the sign of a renewal. For the Nambikwara, women contribute the blood to men's semen, and both are the sources of the new life.

Shedding blood applies a series of restrictions that go from alimentary to behavioral or relational. A Wasusu man whose wife is menstruating cannot go out hunting, since he would risk snakebite. Moreover, his condition is so much a part of his physical body that it is equated with and thought to exude a smell that can only bring his misfortune (ñen). Such is the Wasusu's interpretation of the abject, dismal disposition of a man in this situation. He must refrain from eating certain foods or engaging in activities like playing the flutes or working with pointy objects like arrows or the thatch of a house. Such restrictions may also apply to his younger brothers and particularly to his eldest son.

The image of menstruation as a powerful force that must be controlled reappears in many aspects of existence: eclipses of the sun or moon are cataclysmic menstruations and must be cured by singing; otherwise, the sky would fill with blood until it heaved and collapsed. Nose bleeds and nose and lip piercing are forms of male menstruation. Since piercing is the main form of male initiation among the Nambikwara, it is significant that the flutes' tuning is carried out with the same wood instrument, the yu yu´su´, a sharpened thorn of the palm used for making bows, which is used for perforating the septum and the upper lip. The Wasusu actually equate the tuning of flutes with the piercing, and it is thus a direct allusion to a form of male menstruation. The Nambikwara flute ritual seems thus to corroborate the analysis of Stephen and Christine Hugh-Jones (1979) on the importance of menstruation for the conception of male initiation and its creative force in indigenous Amazonian societies.

The ta wã´na su´ flutes are not only conceived, but they are said to be the mythical sisters' bodies. The flutes actually contain the full bodies of the mythical sisters: from the mouth and nose (the mouthpiece and the airstream ducts at the instrument's proximal end, both of which are used for tuning, which is obtained by adjusting the beeswax closing off most of the orifices), to the belly button (a notch found near the flute's distal end), the eyes (the stops), and the anus (the orifice inside at the distal end of the taboca bamboo). But the flutes are not only bodies; they are the tracheas and the esophagi of spirits, and the fact that some Nambikwara groups often blow tobacco or spurt *chicha* (manioc or maize beer) through them makes that even more explicit. Arm-Strong considered these actions unnecessary, for the flute ritual already promotes the consubstantiality of the living with the spirits by the very fact that both partake in the drinking of the chicha set for consumption during the performance. In the ritual, the chicha cannot be drunk immediately, for the spirits must first be summoned to partake in the ritual. Also, no drink needs to be spilled, since the spirits drink through the players' own drinking. For Arm-Strong, as for other Nambikwara of the Guaporé Valley, it sufficed to play the flutes to communicate and exchange substances with the spirits.

Another reason the Wasusu and other Wã n'ai ri su´ give for playing the flutes is "because the flutes are hungry." To say the flutes are hungry indicates that the relationship between the living and their ancestors has to be provided for, and it needs a harmonious form of exchange to guarantee the state of affairs desired by the living and protected by the guardian spirits. The spirits are therefore fed and satisfied in the course of the performance. The flute ritual is conceived as an exchange relationship, and the appeasement of the spirits' hunger and desire implies the relationship's well-being; so much so, in fact, that the Wasusu and Wã n'ai ri su´ see the maintenance of the universe as founded in the social order that any threat to the village may occasion the playing of the flutes. Moreover, hunger must be interpreted as akin to a sentiment and not as a condition for the Nambikwara, for it implies deep shame and a sense of forlornness and despair.

Hunger and the lack of food exchange entail physical weakness and may lead to disease and death.

Blue-Neck explained to me that the sound of the flutes makes the guardian spirits approach and listen to the flutes' performance. The guardian spirits know how to recognize the tunes and what they signify in a certain moment. The shouts given by the players in the village plaza and their echoes reverberating in the forest are expressions of an ongoing communication between the living and the ancestors. Indeed, the Wasusu sometimes attentively listen to the shouts reverberating in the forest and claim they were the spirits' reply to the living. Every flute has its own shouting, and thus they dialogically communicate their own presence. But neither the shouts nor the flute tunes themselves are understood as forms of propitiation. Just as birds and animals emit their calls in the forest, by presenting or designating (metaphorically naming or referring to) animals and plant species as well as the persons being alluded to in other tunes, the tunes already communicate and appease the guardian spirits. They also evoke and express sentiments and perhaps come to signify the transformation of certain events, such as a recent raid the group carried out against an enemy (a farmer who had invaded their land), a celebration for the arrival of friendly visitors, or the hunting of a tapir after a period of scarcity. The healing or the reestablishment of relationships promoted in such situations exemplifies the continuation of the universe and of the Nambikwara way of life.

It is thus difficult to find anything directly sacrificial in the practice of the Nambikwara flute ritual, even if one sees the performance as a counterpart of the practice of shamanism, where interceding with spirits becomes a form of healing and securing the order of things. Perhaps one possible reason that the Nambikwara consider the flutes to be sacred instruments today may be found in how they have come to represent their practice of secretiveness regarding the flutes and their ritual. But I would also argue that this adoption of the term *sacred* is a translation of their practice of secrecy. The flutes have indeed been a point a contention between the group and missionaries in the past, and they have come to represent a form of resistance to the various attempts of missionization that have been carried out by different clerical persuasions working in the Nambikwara region. But it is also the perception of these instruments as vital objects with vital powers that has made them instruments and symbols of resistance to external influences in the first place.[21] If the flute ritual is considered one of the centerpieces of Nambikwara culture, and if it may be regarded as the principal expression of ritual life among the Manairisu or Forest Nambikwara, then one might equate secrecy with the seal of culture, as the expression of that which may be assumed or colluded with in practice, as one's silent articulation of one's culture.

Therefore, I suggest that when the Nambikwara themselves nowadays classify the flutes and the flute ritual as "sacred," they are referring to their distinct character, which results from the practice of holding them in custody or playing them in secrecy, at night, away from the eyes of women but within earshot of both women and guardian spirits, to guarantee life's regeneration through the well-being of such relationships, with such beautiful aural signs that refer, evoke, and subsume the full range of their known universe, of their emotions, and of their own histories.

Notes

1. For the purposes of this essay, I use the term *Nambikwara* for talking about all the indigenous groups belonging to the Nambikwara linguistic family, as established in the anthropological literature (Price 1981), but I do specify where cultural traits were collected or observed. Wã n'ai ri su' (in simplified form: Manairisu) is the cluster of Nambikwara groups, like the Wasusu, the Hahãintesu, the Alãntesu, the Waikisu, and the Sararé, often identified as the Forest or Guaporé Valley Nambikwara. Like the Nambikwara from the cerrado (the savannah-like vegetation on the Chapada dos Parecis in Mato Grosso, Brazil), they speak dialects of Southern Nambikwara (Price 1981, although Sararé has peculiarities that may set it apart as a separate language). The northern Nambikwara (Mamaindê, Negarotê, Tawandê, Tamaindê, Latundê, and Lakondê)

speak dialects of a mutually unintelligible language to the southern group, as do the Sabanê, who speak yet another Nambikwara language that seems well on its way toward extinction. I carried out fieldwork among the Wasusu and Sararé (Forest Nambikwara) in 1986–88 and 1992–95, and I have continued to visit them for shorter stints of research in 1998, 2000, 2001, 2007, 2008, and 2009. In 1995–96, I was an indigenous agent and regional administrator for FUNAI (the Brazilian Indian Foundation) for northwestern Mato Grosso and Rondônia, and was able to get to know all the Nambikwara communities, including some neighboring groups like the Erikbaktsa and Aikanã. In 2006, I also began doing research with the Wakalitesu, the cerrado-dwelling group formerly studied by Claude Lévi-Strauss.

I use a simplified Southern Nambikwara orthography here. Vowels are [i, e, a, o, u], stops [p, t, k, ', ty, kw], resonants [m, n, l/r, s], and semivowels [y, w]. Vowels can be laringealized [_] and nasalized [~] (except [o]), or laringealized and nasalized simultaneously. All consonants can be glottalized. For the purposes of this article, I represent Southern Nambikwara tones as contours after syllables, loosely following the analyses by Lowe and Kroeker published in the linguistic literature, except for the marking of a high tone, which seems more appropriate for Sararé in this system. Thus, the tones are [´] ascending, ['] descending, [^] high, and [ ] (unmarked) for low tone. It is important to note as well that a different analysis of Northern Nambikwara language has been more recently presented by Leo Wetzels, indicating that Northern Nambikwara language may be considered pitch stress language.

2. For a similar case in Papua New Guinea, see Steven Feld 1982.

3. Other authors have compared the Kaluli's cosmology with Amazonian cosmology (see note 2, America and Beyond (América e Alhures) from the Abaeté project site, http://nansi.abaetenet.net/a-onça-e-a-diferença-projeto-amazone/o-solo-etnográfico-do-perspectivismo-1).

4. My inspiration for using Cassirer comes from the work of Jean Lassègue (2003).

5. All of these dispositions are due to these animals' appearances as characters in certain myths, but others, like the giant armadillo's tendency to lie, may be treated as a kind of folklore.

6. Shamanism is much more pronounced in other Nambikwara regions like the cerrado, although this situation is probably related to the loss of shamanic practice among the neighboring Paresis.

7. For another example of the relation between music and dreams among indigenous societies in Brazil, see Graham 1994.

8. This notwithstanding, this ability to transpose instrumental music into

vocal music and vice versa has probably generated the spread of music among Nambikwara groups, and the corpus I collected includes tunes that span language divides like that between Southern Nambikwara (Wasusu) and Northern Nambikwara (Mamaindê).

9. I say connative because the bird call draws attention to itself as an open channel for the transmission of a message, and connotative because it establishes the meaning of such a message as something quite distinct from mere reference to a cultural object.

10. Among the Wasusu, this term was equally applied to the people as well as the bird involved in the communication. And since its significance is already inherent to the call, in the particular context it is produced, one could argue that, for the Nambikwara, the medium is also (or already) the message (McLuhan 1964).

11. One can still identify this mythical indigenous group with the Aruakan Paresis today, who live on the plateau outlying the eastern part of the Nambikwara territory and who possessed a magnificent material culture and a complex civilization in former times.

12. Ta wã´na su´ are also called wãih´lu´ among other Southern Nambikwara groups. The classification used here follows Izikowitz (1935). I classify ha´y'u ha´y'u hlu´ as trumpets, even though no pronounced pursing of players' lips takes place, because its sounds are produced by blowing with the lips pressed against the trumpet's mouthpiece and modulated by the combination of the frequency issuing from the interior orifice of its proximal end and its amplification by the gourd at its distal end (see fig. 21). The Anteater speaking trumpet (ti k'a li su´) is a megaphone in Izikowitz's classification, and it falls under the category of complex trumpets or roarers. Nose flutes, ta tãu su´, are not considered part of the Nambikwara ritual flutes. In most Nambikwara groups, they are thought to be instruments for mere entertainment, although in the cerrados and among the Sararé, there are some associations between them and fertility and war, respectively. The northern Nambikwara possess other types of ritual instruments like double flutes and, together with the cerrado subgroups of the southern Nambikwara, they have adopted the panpipes. Speaking trumpets are also present among the Paresi and the Tupari of southern Rondônia (see Roquette Pinto, 1935 and Caspar, 1956).

13. The flute ritual represents the main type of ritual activity in Nambikwara culture outside of curing, funerary, or certain growth (initiation) rites, and it may be directly related to and often performed during all the latter activities.

14. For a similar point about Amazonian indigenous music, see Seeger (1987).

15. Although the Wasusu acknowledge the existence of women with shamanic power mostly in the distant past, women who could see and play the

flutes, the actual participation of women in such a male ritual event has probably been an impossibility for a very long time: the only case the Wasusu remember of a woman partaking in the flute ritual in the last generations included sexual license between the men and the woman, homosexuality (the woman's), and her eventual killing as a witch.

16. Such instances are extremely rare in any case, for the flutes are rarely played during the day: the only exceptions I found were a traditional fertility ritual among the Wasusu and men's funerals among the Sararé. The ritual flutes are also commonly played at night and inside the flutes house (if one is available), until darkness falls and later at night, and then only men may dance in the village plaza (when the village is fast asleep).

17. Traditionally, in the only context flutes were generally played during the day by the Wasusu, to guarantee the fertility of the gardens, the player's sisters participated more conspicuously, painting their brothers and preparing the chicha, the maize beverage that would have to wait their return to the village for consumption. And yet, as the flutes were brought out, they entered the house.

18. One should not forget that men have a primordial role in the creation of a new life among the Nambikwara because of the importance of the semen in the slow constitution of the fetus.

19. Aytai (1967), for instance, has conjectured that ta wã´na su´ is a male flute, and the gourd trumpet, its female counterpart (for the gourd would represent a womb). My ethnography points to the reversal of these Nambikwara ritual flutes' genders.

20. The cramps are actually thought to be caused by one of its brother spirits that usually accompanies the Anteater.

21. I thank Jean-Pierre Chaumeil for the insightful critique that inspired this passage. One could see similar processes in the constitution of secret (now, so-called sacred) territories among the Nambikwara, as the management of the relationship to the spiritual world, and more recently, as a response to land or cultural encroachment and the necessity of preserving the ritualized, harmonious relations that spiritually powerful people (shamans) may have with the realm of the spirits.

References Cited

Aytai, Desidério. 1967. "As Flautas Rituais dos Nambikuara." *Revista de Antropologia* 15, FFLCH/USP, 67–75.

Basso, Keith. 1996. *Wisdom Sits in Places: Landscape and Language among the Western Apache.* Albuquerque: University of New Mexico Press.

Caspar, Franz. 1956. *Tupari.* London: Bell and Sons.

Cassirer, Ernst. 1923. *Philosophie des formes symboliques 1: le langage*. Paris: Editions de Minuit.

Feld, Steven. 1982. *Sound and Sentiment: Birds, Weeping, Poetics, and Song in Kaluli Expression*. Philadelphia: University of Pennsylvania Press.

Graham, Laura. 1994. *Performing Dreams*. Austin: University of Texas Press.

Hugh-Jones, Christine. 1979. *From the Milk River: Spatial and Temporal Processes in Northwest Amazonia*. Cambridge: Cambridge University Press.

Hugh-Jones, Stephen. 1979. *The Palm and the Pleiades: Initiation and Cosmology in Northwest Amazonia*. Cambridge: Cambridge University Press.

Izikowitz, Karl Gustav. 1935. *Musical and Other Sound Instruments of the South American Indians: A Comparative Ethnographical Study*. Göteborg: Elanders.

Lassègue, Jean. 2003. "Note sur la construction des formes sémantiques en anthropologie et en linguistique: Catégorisation linguistique, parenté, rituel." *Langages* no. 150.

McLuhan, Marshall. 1964. *Understanding Media: The Extensions of Man*. New York: McGraw-Hill.

Mello, Maria Ignez C. 2005. "Iamurikuma: Música, Mito, e Ritual entre os Wauja do Alto Xingu." PhD diss., PPGAS/UFSC.

NANSI (Núcleo de Antropologia Simétrica): http://nansi.abaetenet.net/a-on%C3%A7a-e-a-diferen%C3%A7a-projeto-amazone/o-solo-etnogr%C3%A1fico-do-perspectivismo-1.

Pinto, Roquette. 1935. *Rondônia*. São Paulo: Companhia Editora Nacional.

Seeger, Anthony. 1987. *Why Suyá Sing: A Musical Anthropology of an Amazonian People*. Cambridge: Cambridge University Press.

Wagner, Roy. 1981. *The Invention of Culture*. Rev. ed. Chicago: University of Chicago Press.

Second Movement

Musical Transpositions of Social Relations

7. Archetypal Agents of Affinity

"Sacred" Musical Instruments in the Guianas?

MARC BRIGHTMAN

The central Guianas are not a classic area for the study of sacred aerophone cults, and this is arguably because musical instruments there are not really sacred and the rituals that are associated with them are not really about the instruments themselves (as, say, the property of a given clan), the latter being merely tools in ceremonies that celebrate and renew society itself. There is nevertheless at least one type of musical ceremony found throughout the Guianas that bears comparison with the classic sacred flute cults associated with other parts of Amazonia, even if the instruments are not preserved between ceremonies and are not subject to visual prohibitions. At the risk of reinforcing the impression that the Guiana Caribs do not qualify for entry into the sacred instruments club, I am going to question a few of the categories that have been used to define its members and suggest that the common features of Guianese and northwestern Amazonian musical ceremonies may bring us insight into some pan-Amazonian social themes; in this I take advantage of the tendency for Guianese ethnography to provide simpler and more manageable templates, so to speak, of phenomena found throughout the region (Henley 2001).

In Guianese Amazonia, where collective property is scarce and ephemeral, narratives of myth and ethnicity play an important role in promoting social continuity. However, from a material perspective, continuity is nevertheless symbolized or ensured by the quality of hardness, and this is a theme common to societies throughout the Guianas and in other parts of Amazonia. The high value placed on "hard," long-lasting objects such as beads and bone and feather artifacts, as well as stone house archetypes, represent sociality and controlled power. In the Trio language, for example, people and objects are praised as *karime*, "hard," "strong," or "healthy," or *kurano*, "beautiful" or "desirable"—qualities that often go together, particularly in objects such as glass beads. Rivière writes of "an association between hardness, durability, and invisibility," whereby hard artifacts are copies of primordial archetypes: "in the manufacture of stools the hard wood used is a substitution made by men for the rock out of which a culture-hero carved the prototype" (Rivière 1995: 196). Stools (*kororo*) are also significant because they act (or acted in the past) as symbols of authority, it being the privilege of a leader or shaman to possess and sit upon them.

At funerals, cremations, and burials, it seems that the general rule that all the deceased's possessions are burned or buried with the corpse is more frequently ignored with durable items such as these. For instance, the missionary Art Yohner describes an Akuriyo burial that took place during one of the Akuriyo contact expeditions, at which the son of the deceased kept all of his mother's monkey tooth necklaces, leaving her with "one strand of white beads" (Yohner 1970: 8). Such items are kept safe in a vanity basket and only taken out for ceremonial occasions. Even these items do not seem to be particularly old; I was never shown an object that was said to have been made by anyone longer ago than the previous generation. However, it must be remembered that minimal generational depth is a characteristic of Guianese kinship. In view of this fact, it is perhaps unsurprising that these "hard" items do not usually have personal histories or genealogies attached to them (unlike in northwestern Amazonia, for example). Occasionally they have mythical associations, but these tend to belong only to a type of object (or to its archetype) rather than to one object in particular. In these cases, as in that of the stool, the object is a copy of a mythical original, from which its value is derived analogically.

Musical instruments, which in the Guianas, as elsewhere in Amazonia, are predominantly aerophones of various types, are copies of archetypes in exactly this way. As well as being "hard," especially in the case of bone flutes, Guianese aerophones are used in ritual contexts in which social formations and dynamics are particularly visible. They are highly gendered, and the ability to play well is expected of a leader. As tubes, they both symbolize and provoke transformation, and they are used in rituals that transform and order the knowledge and power of the outside for the benefit of the collectivity. Van Velthem (2001) has convincingly argued that several forms of artifact are regarded as persons by the Wayana and other central Caribs, especially in ritual contexts, and the aerophone-as-tube clearly represents the body in this sense, as in other parts of Amazonia. Their tubularity is also the negation of their genderedness, as Hugh-Jones has pointed out with regard to myths of gender in northwest Amazonia: the body as tube can be seen as a "reflection on the bodies of men and women, on the congruence between the form of their genitals, and on their respective reproductive capacities" (Hugh-Jones 2001: 252).

The role of aerophones in promoting and embodying continuity lies not just in the material object of the instrument but also in the music itself: instrument and sound endlessly represent and reproduce archetypal or prototypical forms.[1] The ritual occasions upon which this takes place bring together otherwise independent family units to form a collectivity and thus structure collective life. This chapter will show that by examining music, we can more clearly see hierarchy and leadership at work, giving order to society, but its scope goes further.

In the context of recent discussions of the typologies of Amazonian societies following Descola's definition of two types of "animist" society, based on principles of reciprocity on the one hand and predation on the other, Rivière claimed that in the Guianas, "the idea that death involves reciprocity between two worlds— that is to say, reciprocity as a mode of regeneration, disguised or not as predation—seems absent. In fact, in a certain sense, it could be argued that, for some peoples in the Guianas, death does not exist, or better, is just an illusion. Like birth, it only consists of a passage between two ways of being" (2001: 39). While agreeing with this, the material presented in this chapter will clarify the discrepancy between the way of death in the Guianas and elsewhere in Amazonia.

At ceremonial feasts, which may be celebrations of the clearing of new gardens, of male and female initiation, or of the Gregorian New Year, visitors from other villages are associated with male affines and game meat, while local people are associated with female kin and the manioc beer that is copiously drunk and, above all, shared. The renewal of society, which takes place through ceremonial feasts, is, in material terms, conceived of as a reciprocal transaction: men come from outside, contributing their very presence to the conviviality and wealth of humanity, and are given beer by women from inside. Outsiders who come to the village for these feasts may be strangers, and strangers are regarded as being potentially non-human—indeed, there is a perceived risk that they may prove to be spirits until their behavior reveals otherwise (Erikson 2000). Here, alterity and kinship are not absolute states; on the contrary, affines can be transformed into kin by human action. Because there is no differentiation between the world of the dead and the spirit world, and because the transformable, ambiguous environment of the outside is the realm of nonhumans and distant affines alike, it is logical to suggest that the dead are in effect brought back to life through these ceremonial feasts.[2] This is only made possible by collapsing the difference between the visitors and hosts, so that the presence of group reciprocity is denied as the groups themselves dissolve into one another. The result of this is that reciprocity does exist as a mode of predation (in the sense that insiders "consume" outsiders and are eventually in turn "consumed" by the spirit world when they die), but it is disguised as sharing, just as trade and other relationships with outsiders exist in daily life despite an ideal of local group endogamy.

The role of music in all this is primarily communicative (Menezes Bastos 1978). Paradoxically, it reveals itself as perhaps even the supremely social mode of communication precisely because of its privileging of form over content. The greater the level of social difference providing the context for a piece of musical communication (on a scale ranging from the intimate relations within the nuclear family to the often tense relations with unrelated members of other groups), the more structured that form of communication appears to be, and in this fact lies the explanation for the importance of music for leadership and political organization. It is true that the formalization of language into ritualized speech, "intonings," or song, and of movement into dance, reduces the amount of "communication" in linguistic terms, arguably allowing ritual to act as an instrument of power (Bloch 1989). But if we do not reduce communication to the verbal expression of rational thought (which would represent a value of Western society), and understand it more broadly as "making common" by diverse means, and encapsulating such things as human substance and vital energy, then we can arrive at a richer and less conspiratorial understanding of its political dimensions. As I present the different musical forms and place each in its social context, I will show how interethnic relations and social continuity are managed through musical rituals.

Trio and Wayana Instruments and Rituals

The Trio and Wayana are Carib swidden horticulturalists who now live mostly on the upper reaches of the main rivers in southern French Guiana, southern Suriname, and across the border in northern Parã state in Brazil. Villages have become larger and more permanent in recent decades since the creation of medical posts and schools, and the economy includes cash and manufactured goods as well as game, fish, forest products, and traditional art objects.

Idioglottal clarinets, known among the Wayana as *waitakala*, used to be played regularly in groups of three players on various ceremonial occasions, including the *toule* and *pono* mourning ceremonies (Crevaux 1993: 322–23) and the *marake* initiation ritual. These clarinets are made with a single piece of green bamboo, into the first knot of which is inserted a single-piece beating (idioglot) reed made of another, thinner length of bamboo. Using the hocket technique (in which melody is created by the rhythmic alternation between instruments), each instrument produces one tone, except the high lead clarinet, which produces two. The only ritual that survives today in which they are used is the marake, the centerpiece of which is the application of *kunana*, stinging mats, impregnated with ants or wasps, to the bodies of candidates. An individual's first marake constitutes a rite of passage into adulthood, but the Wayana consider it desirable to pass it several times, as it is said to harden and humanize the body and thus to nourish a variety of moral as well as physical qualities. As initiation into adulthood, it prepares the candidate for marriage and, in the case of a man, as a hunter; thereafter, it renews him or her as a social person.

At the marake, as at other collective ceremonies in the past, visitors from another village play musical instruments and lead the dancing. These visitors are symbolically associated with hummingbirds, and the forward and backward movement of the dance steps is equated with copulation and with the hummingbird's metaphorical copulation with the flower (Schoepf 1998). As if to emphasize the importance of this, the ceremonial house, or "visitors' house," where all collective ceremonies take place and where visitors sleep, is called the *tukusipan*: "place of the hummingbirds." As the association between visitors and hummingbirds suggests, and as we may expect from comparison with other cases in Amazonia, collective feasts involving visitors from other villages encourage flirtation between the sexes, and the feasts act as catalysts for marriage. They can also be the occasion for conflict between men from different factions or villages. In other words, they put affinal relations to the test, giving them the opportunity to be made or broken. The positive, harmonious side of this is emphasized in the often-expressed formula of complementary exchange: men come from outside bringing music and dance, and local women give manioc beer in return.

A more general theme can be identified at these events: that of fertility and renewal. A myth explaining the origin of waitakala clarinets illustrates this point: The culture hero Alalikama goes hunting and undergoes a transformation that is described as a kind of death. He later hears the sound of clarinets, shouts and cries, and vomiting. A hummingbird appears and says to him, "Do not go into the bamboo or my many children will eat the cartilage ((ë)yetpï) of your bones." The hummingbird is the "master" or spirit of bamboo, and the bamboo culms are therefore his children. Alalikama then becomes a spirit and hears the sound of clarinets again. He sleeps at the place of the yellow-rumped cacique,[3] a bird able to mimic human and animal voices, whose nest is protected by aggressive wasps. The caciques are described as a kind of "master of speech." Alalikama does not sleep, for fear of wild animals, and he hears the Kalau male initiation songs. The cacique birds—whom he sees as humans—vomit and serve drink all night. He sees the olok (feather headdresses) and the kunana stinging mat used for the marake, and hears the ëlemi (spells or charms) for healing (eju) (Chapuis and Rivière 2003: 388–89).

So, following a transformation that changes his perspective, and after transgressing the boundary warned of by the hummingbird, by entering the bamboo grove, Alalikama learns about clarinets and initiations, drinking and vomiting, stinging, and headdresses—in short, he learns about collective rituals, such as the marake. It is in the bamboo grove itself that this forbidden, exotic, powerful knowledge is to be found, and this is consistent with the important role that bamboo aerophones play in Wayana ceremonies: bamboo are the children of the hummingbird, who, it seems, is the archetypal visitor. In visitors' feasts, the roles of man and hummingbird are reversed, and it is the symbolic hummingbirds who come into the human village; only the direction of the transfer of knowledge remains the same. Alalikama's transgression can be seen as a theft of knowledge: he went to another village, but took knowledge instead of giving it; as all knowledge is regarded as being of extraneous origin, the first people had to obtain it in this way, without reciprocity. Significantly, it is the "masters of speech" who are also the masters of ceremonies, the cacique birds, and Trio and Wayana leaders—who are accomplished orators—perform the very same role.

The significance of the hummingbird's warning, "My many children will eat the cartilage of your bones," requires some further background. According to another myth, another culture hero, Kuyuli, impregnates his sister Salomakan with "the sound of his flute" (Chapuis and Rivière 2003: 45), in a clear articulation of the fertile associations of aerophones, music, and breath. Later Salomakan wanders in the form of a tortoise until she is devoured by jaguars. Her children later avenge her by recovering her "bones" or "claws" before killing the jaguar children.

Salomakan's "bones" or claws are the origin of the *kuliputpë amo-hawin* (tortoise claw) and *mëlaimë amo-hawin* (armadillo claw) duct flutes, both of which are also played using the hocket technique, like the clarinets, during the marake ceremony. Another version of this myth remarks that Salomakan's son Mopo plays a tune on his mother's left claw, which causes the wind to blow, and when he blows in her right claw, a strong wind and heavy rain come (Chapuis and Rivière 2003: 87n., H. Rivière 1994).

As Alalikama learns about the marake (Chapuis and Rivière 2003: 395–98), he sees the kuliputpë amo-hawin flute. Meanwhile, there are signs that he has "died" following the humming-bird's warning: at one point he says "never mind if wild animals eat me—I'm already dead" (Chapuis and Rivière 2003: 397). Of course his death is not the end of him, and instead after many more adventures he returns to his village to teach the Wayana all he has learned.

The themes of death and fertility, and the motifs of bones and blowing, are common in stories of this type. Death is portrayed as a transformed state in much the same way as changing clothes in many other Guianese myths. In such transformed states, the stories' protagonists meet spirits and learn about culture from them: they learn all the things that make people human, such as body ornaments, songs, flutes, and dances. As wind brings rain and productive gardens, blowing a flute can bring people into be-ing. Meanwhile, as bones, flutes represent the hard center of the person, the soul (P. Rivière 1994). Exposed, they thus evoke both death and immortality. It is the action of blowing that causes the flute's power to be realized, and this is coherent with the frequently expressed ideas of blowing as the vehicle of shamanic power and wind as the carrier of disease.

Aerophones : Blowing
Death : Fertility

The correspondence between these ideas is strong enough for us to suggest a scheme whereby aerophones are to blowing as death is to fertility. The aerophone is both a symbol of death and an instrument of fertility: through its power, Kuyuli impregnates his sister. The flutes (or claws) blown by Salomakan's son Mopo bring wind and then rain. In the forest environment of the Gui-anas, every rainstorm is preceded by a distinctive cool breeze, and these winds are almost always followed by rain. Most of the celebrations I have described take place during the dry season, the time of clearing in preparation for planting. The Wayana and Trio do not believe that their rituals will magically bring the rains;

instead, by reenacting the events of mythic time that gave order to the universe and to society, they reassert their own place in that order. The hummingbird's children who eat the cartilage of people's bones may do so in order to make flutes, in a mirror image of what people now do in order to make their own transitory "flutes": they go and take the hummingbird's children—the bamboo—and strip them to the bone in order to turn them into clarinets. The effect of this reenactment of Alalikama's transgression is a renewal or reassertion of society—comparable to the social renewal explicitly equated elsewhere in Amazonia with menstruation or snakes shedding their skin (P. Rivière 1994; C. Hugh-Jones 1979; S. Hugh-Jones 1979).

Discussion

In this light, the ritual role of aerophones appears to be as instruments or agents of transformation. Like other kinds of tube, they act as "energy transformers" (Rivière 1969) and convert affines into kin metaphorically if not literally. The ceremonial aerophone, representing neither category of affine nor kin, is able to mediate between these categories. Lévi-Strauss condensed numerous indigenous American myths involving tubes into a formula whereby "(1) the hero's body enters a tube that contains him; (2) a tube that was contained within the hero's body comes out of it.; and (3) the hero's body is a tube either into which something enters or out of which something comes. From extrinsic at the outset, the tube becomes intrinsic, and the body of the hero passes from the state of contained to that of container" (1985: 216, my translation). This is precisely what happens during aerophone rituals. If the aerophone, as the archetypal musical instrument and tube par excellence, has as its principal quality the ability to mediate between inside and outside, consanguinity and affinity, then we can see that in relations with the outside—whether it be the spirit world, the government, the church, or people from other villages—it has a vital role to play.[4] In Lévi-Strauss's terms, the hero, using the flute-tube, transforms the encompassing-outside-affine into encompassed-inside-kin. As we begin to see the different manifestations of this transformative quality, we can see how Guianese aerophones blur some of the distinctions that have been used to categorize sacred musical instrument cults in Amazonia.

For example, the opposition between individual and collective, emphasized by Beaudet (1997), may seem less sharp when actual practice and historical change are considered. Several supposedly individual aerophones are frequently played during collective ceremonies, and they are much more common there than in everyday life. The instrument known in Trio as the *ruwe* (a generic word for both aerophones and the type of bamboo used to make them) or *sawaru ruwe* (tortoise aerophone)—panpipes played in conjunction with a tortoiseshell friction drum—is "traditionally" an individual's instrument in the Guianas, played solo in a similar way to the deer bone notch flute, as Beaudet has pointed out, but in the Trio and Wayana village of Tëpu it seems to have replaced the waitakala clarinet as an instrument played in groups of up to three, using the hocket technique, at collective ceremonies and visitors' feasts.

Another opposition, which other contributors (Hill, this volume) have also shown being blurred by Amazonian musical practice, is that between lexicality and musicality. This is best illustrated with reference to new musical elements that have become important in collective rituals: megaphones, creole music, and church music. Megaphones are now regularly used to amplify chiefly dialogue, in which the speaker uses a stylized, rhythmical form of language that is karime, "hard," "assertive," "strong," or "persuasive."[5] In this speech form, prosody takes over from content; rhythm and tone are given priority over literal meaning, evoking the *no kato* ceremonial dialogue used between non-co-resident affines in the past. Yet the speeches that they amplify also articulate the effect of music: they exhort *sasame*, collective harmony, the very feeling that dissolves difference and promotes social inclusivity. The use of the megaphone can be seen as a performance of the leader's role as mediator between outside and inside, between affine and kin; like flutes or clarinets, megaphones transform energy, bringing knowledge and power from the outside to the local group.

If sacredness is manifested by secrecy or prohibitions, then there is no clear-cut distinction between sacred and profane in the Guianas. Only men make and play flutes and other musical instruments, but this seems to have no significance beyond other aspects of the gendered division of labor. As for gendered prohibitions: in the Guianas, there are no visual prohibitions on aerophones, and although I never saw women or children touch, let alone play, any kind of flute, they are not formally forbidden to do so; it is simply taken for granted that flutes belong to the affairs of men. The "prohibitions" in this case are articulations of hierarchies of value, rather than coercive strategies of oppression.

I have suggested that social renewal and fertility are important themes in collective ritual in the central Guianas. If we consider this in gendered terms, corresponding to the opposition between inside and outside which is characteristic of Guianese cosmology, it is easy to understand why only men play aerophones. Where uxorilocality is the norm, and knowledge and male fertility come from outside the village, men represent the outside and women the inside; by playing flutes or clarinets, men perform the role of visitor who becomes husband and co-resident son-in-law, and produces further kin for the village. Through the musical ritual, affines are transformed into kin, and the shared collective subjectivity of participants is expanded. The music is part of the promotion of the often-expressed ideal of conviviality and of kin living together (Overing and Passes 2000).

On the subject of gender, it should also be remembered that a discussion of musical instruments can give an appearance of male domination, because it privileges the male role in what is a complementary relationship. However, dance is in fact inseparable in practical terms from music, and in dance, at least among the Trio, women take just as active a part. Perhaps even more important, the production and distribution of beer, which is entirely the responsibility of women (although men must create the gardens in which manioc is grown), is an integral element of the rituals we have been discussing, without which musical instruments would not be played at all; in fact, beer is often drunk without music, but music is rarely played without beer.

Similar features of gender roles are also articulated in the recently adopted use of creole music (known as *poku*) such as R&B, reggae, and zouk, which is played on sound systems by young unmarried men (cf. Alemán, this volume) and danced to individually and in couples. The unmarried men have brought urban music to delight and seduce local women, just as they would bring aerophone music from the forest and from other villages in the past.

This suggests in turn that an opposition between tradition and modernity can teach us little about the nature of musical rituals. If we think of these rituals as forms of communication with alterity, then we should remember that different registers may be used to communicate with different categories of spirit (Chaumeil 1997). The same principle applies to relations with human as well as with nonhuman "Others."[6] If in pre-Columbian times, the Trio and Wayana only interacted with outsiders in the form of spirits, animals, and other Indians, they have long had dealings with other social categories: the *mekoro* (maroons), the *karaiwa* (Brazilians), and the *pananakiri* (urban or coastal dwellers, viz. Creoles and white people). Aerophone music is said to come from spirits and other Indians, and playing it serves to transform their energy in a controlled way into a force for social renewal. Creole and church music is used in an analogous way to communicate with the Creole and missionary worlds, respectively.

Although the oppositions I have discussed above may not help us to understand Amazonian ritual music, it is certain that aerophones, both as tubes and as instruments for communicating with nonhumans, do represent and act upon certain other dualities. The flute itself is characterized by an inside and an outside, and it transforms breath into sound. Musical rituals are characterized by their action upon relationships between the inside and outside of the human-lived world, although the form this action takes is articulated in different ways in the Guianas from other parts of Amazonia. As Jean-Pierre Chaumeil has pointed out (1997), the differences appear to correspond to the characteristic forms of kinship system in each of these areas and their associated ways of remembering the dead: the dead in the Guianas, like enemies and affines, are generally homogenized and distanced, but valued nevertheless as a source of knowledge and power. Even culture heroes who may be considered ancestors, although they would perhaps be better described as human archetypes, are not individually brought back to life in collective rituals, and this is consistent with the Guianese relationship with the outside. In contrast with northwestern Amazonia, say, where principles of unilineal descent exist and certain aerophones are held sacred and preserved down through the generations, in the Guianas new instruments are made for each celebration. But in both cases, music acts for the regeneration of society and the reiteration of the hierarchies of value that give it order.

Conclusion

It is clear that some of the formal characteristics used to define Amazonian aerophone rituals highlight differences between those of the Guianas and those of other areas, and Guianese ritual instruments do not quite fit the classic model. But by using myth and ritual practice to understand the purpose of these instruments, we can find some things that are common to such cults throughout Amazonia. My argument is analogous to Leach's famous formula: "what we can usefully compare as between different societies are not these particular ps and qs (regarded as separate institutions) but the ratio of p to q as a mathematical function" (1966: 26).

Here, instead of classifying societies that "have" sacred flutes as distinct from those that do not, I suggest that we focus on comparing the relationship between flutes and rituals and that we do so in the context of comparisons of other sets of relationships. In light of the differences between Guianese and northwest Amazonian or Xinguano concepts of death and funeral practices, for instance, the distinctions between their aerophone complexes seem quite natural, and the relationship between flute ceremony and society appears to have a similar logic whether the flutes are considered sacred or not.

All of the musical forms used by the Trio and Wayana manifest a hierarchical relationship between the bringers and the receivers of music, whether it is brought by male visitors from other villages, by culture heroes from the nonhuman inhabitants of the forest, by cosmopolitan youths from the city, or by church leaders from the world of Christian evangelists, and this relationship allows the renewal of society. Ritual instruments help to mediate these relationships with the outside: as tubes that are both containers and contained, encompassing and encompassed, aerophones are agents that do not fit into either of the opposing categories of consanguinity and affinity or kindred and strangers and that instead act as mediators between these categories; with these qualities they recall what Viveiros de Castro has called the *terceiro incluido* (literally, "included third"), after Peirce's concept of "thirdness" (2002: 152). Their power as agents comes from their archetypal origins, and it is used to manipulate affinity. These seem to be common features of aerophone cults from the Guianas and other parts of Amazonia. In the context of historical change, music can be seen as a means for transforming difference, both temporal and cultural. While the use of music remains the same, its form changes and multiplies, and it thereby constitutes at once the means and the manifestation of both social stability and historical transformation.

Notes

This chapter is based on my doctoral research, funded by the ESRC. I am grateful to Vanessa Grotti, Stephen Hugh-Jones, the editors of the present volume, and the participants in the symposium in which it originated for commenting on earlier versions.

1. Compare Panare male initiation rituals, which promote social continuity by reproducing the activities of "ancient people." Henley (2001: 216) compares the feeling that this produces to the Trio *sasame* (see below).

2. See Bloch and Parry 1982 for several cross-cultural variations on the complementary relationship between death and the renewal of life.

3. *Payakwa*, *cacicus cela*, which nests near wasps and is capable of mimicry.

4. As Hill (2000) has pointed out, tube imagery, especially the umbilical cord, is also associated with bringing people together and building social connections.

5. Although some form of speech-amplifying tube seems to be indigenous to Amazonia, and such instruments are certainly found elsewhere in the region (Izikowitz 1935: 241; J. Hill pers. comm.), in this case the megaphone seems to have been adopted from urban society.

6. Hill (1997) has examined a similar phenomenon among the Wakuénai, showing how "musicalization" of relations with oppressive Others can be employed as a strategy of resistance.

References Cited

Beaudet, J-M. 1997. *Souffles d'Amazonie: Les orchestres "tule" des Wayãpi.* Paris: Société d'ethnologie.

Bloch, M. 1989. "Symbols, Song, Dance, and Features of Articulation: Is Religion an Extreme Form of Religious Authority?" In *Ritual, History, and Power: Selected Papers in Anthropology.* London: Athlone.

Bloch, M., and J. Parry, eds. 1982. *Death and the Regeneration of Life.* Cambridge: Cambridge University Press.

Chapuis, J., and H. Rivière. 2003. *Wayana eitoponpë: (Une) histoire (orale) des Indiens Wayana.* Paris: Ibis Rouge.

Chaumeil, J-P. 1997. "Les os, les flûtes, les morts: Mémoire et traitement funéraire en Amazonie." *Journal de la Société des Américanistes* 83: 83–110.

Crevaux, J. 1993 [1887]. *Le mendiant de l'Eldorado: De Cayenne aux Andes (1876–1879).* Paris: Payot.

Erikson, P. 2000. "Dialogues à vif . . . Notes sur les salutations en Amazonie." In *Les rituels du dialogue: Promenades ethnolinguistiques en terres amérindiennes,* ed. A. Monod Becquelin and P. Erikson. Paris: Nanterre, Société d'ethnologie.

Henley, P. 2001. "Inside and Out: Alterity and the Ceremonial Construction of the Person in the Guianas." In *Beyond the Visible and the Material: The Amerindianization of Society in the Work of Peter Rivière*, ed. L. Rival and N. Whitehead. Oxford: Oxford University Press.

Hill, J. 1997. "Musicalizing the Other: Shamanistic Approaches to Ethnic-Class Competition along the Upper Rio Negro." In *Enchanting Powers: Music in the World's Religions*, ed. L. Sullivan. Cambridge: Harvard University Center for the Study of World Religions.

———. 2000. "The Variety of Fertility Cultism in Amazonia: A Closer Look at Gender Symbolism in Northwestern Amazonia." In *Gender in Amazonia and Melanesia: An Exploration of the Comparative Method*, ed. T. Gregor and D. Tuzin. Berkeley: University of California Press.

Hugh-Jones, C. 1979. *From the Milk River: Spatial and Temporal Processes in Northwest Amazonia*. Cambridge: Cambridge University Press.

Hugh-Jones, S. 1979. *The Palm and the Pleiades*. Cambridge: Cambridge University Press.

———. 2001. "The Gender of Some Amazonian Gifts: An Experiment with an Experiment." In *Gender in Amazonia and Melanesia: An Exploration of the Comparative Method*, ed. T. Gregor and D. Tuzin. Berkeley: University of California Press.

Leach, E. 1966. "Rethinking Anthropology." In *Rethinking Anthropology*. London: Athlone.

Lévi-Strauss, C. 1985. *La potière jalouse*. Paris: Plon.

Menezes Bastos, R. 1978. *A Musicológica Kamayurá: para uma Antropologia da Comunicação no Alto Xingu*. Brasilia: FUNAI.

Overing, J., and A. Passes, eds. 2000. *The Anthropology of Love and Anger: The Aesthetics of Conviviality in Native Amazonia*. London: Routledge.

Rivière, H. 1994. "Les instruments de musique des indiens Wayana du Litani (Surinam, Guyane française)." *Anthropos* 89: 51–60.

———. N.d. *Musique instrumentale des Wayana du Litani* (CD). Paris: Buda.

Rivière, P. 1969. "Myth and Material Culture: Some Symbolic Interrelations." In *Forms of Symbolic Action*, ed. R. F. Spencer. Seattle: University of Washington Press.

———. 1994. "WYSINWYG in Amazonia." *JASO* 25, no. 3: 259.

———. 1995. "Community and Continuity in Guiana." In *About the House: Lévi-Strauss and Beyond*, ed. J. Carsten and S. Hugh-Jones. New York: Cambridge University Press.

———. 2001. "A predação, a reciprocidade e o caso das Guianas." *Mana* 7, no. 1: 31–53.

Schoepf, D. 1998. "Le domaine des colibris: Accueil et hospitalité chez les Wayana (région des Guyanes)." *Journal de la Société des Américanistes* 84, no. 1: 99–120.

Van Velthem, L. 2001. "The Woven Universe: Carib Basketry." In *Unknown Amazon: Culture and Nature in Ancient Brazil*, ed. C. McEwan, C. Barreto, and E. Neves. London: British Museum.

Viveiros de Castro, E. 2002. "O problema da afinidade na Amazonia." In *A inconstância da alma selvagem*. São Paulo: Cosac and Naify.

Yohner, A. 1970. *Contact with a New Group of Akurijo Indians of Suriname.* Washington: Smithsonian Institution Center for Short-Lived Phenomena.

8. *From Flutes to Boom Boxes*

Musical Symbolism and Change among the Waiwai of Southern Guyana

STEPHANIE W. ALEMÁN

Bamboo, bone and turtle shell
sweet songs from the diaphragm expel
dialogs with absent friends
This one was given to me by Ewka
the village leader of Yaka-yaka
This one by Macherawe
the champion flautist of them all
Each tune resonates around the village
reverberating with the memory of its maker
Maruwanaraï, Maruwanaraï
Magnificent magician of the muse
with one note exhaled
conjures up a refrain
then lyric trills, lurid turns
seductive complaints
When will you give up the flute?
When the memory dies
When the tunes die
When the Waiwai become the Wapishana.

    —G. P. Mentore

22. Waiwai aerophones made from deer bone and various sizes of bamboo (*ratu*). Photo by Stephanie W. Alemán.

Flute music has long held a special place in Waiwai expressions of selfhood and identity. As a medium of communication among men and between men and women, its significance persists and is still recognized by all village members. The use of the flute in dialogue, narrative, seduction, and hunting identifies it as a key symbol of Waiwai male personhood. In the case of the Waiwai, the flutes they employ are known from Izikowitz's 1935 typology as notched, or with a special notch carved into the blowing edge (see fig. 22). In addition, references to Waiwai flutes and their use are present in both of the seminal works on the Waiwai by Fock (1963) and Yde (1965).

To orient the reader, the Waiwai are a group of Carib-speaking indigenous Amazonians that inhabit the forests on the upper reaches of the Essequibo River in Guyana (in two villages) and over the border in northern Brazil, with several villages on the Anaua,

23. The voice of the flute, Maruwanarï, at Masakinyarï village in southern Guyana. Photo by Stephanie W. Alemán.

Jatapuzinho, and Mapuera rivers. Their total population on the Guyana side is about 275 and about 1,500 on the Brazilian side.

In the present-day Guyanese village at Masakinyarï (Mosquito Place), one man, Maruwanarï, represents the last of the highly skilled players who continues to offer his tunes on a daily basis to a village that listens attentively for the sound of his expressive notes (see fig. 23). More than just an evening concert, these playing sessions bring to life the sounds and dialogues of animals, stories of magically aided love, desire, and enticement, competitive conversations between men, and prowess in finding and captivating prey.

In addition to these various themes, a Waiwai flute player can also make commentary on current social events and personal actions. Much as Jonathan Hill says in this volume regarding Wakuénai flute music, Waiwai "musical sounds and musicality are densely interwoven with lexical sounds and meaning as well as the sounds and behaviors of natural life forms."

The poem that embellishes the beginning of this chapter was written by our colleague George Mentore after many evening experiences of Maruwanari's flute sessions. As the last flautist in the village at Masakinyarï who continues to play regularly, Maruwanari's expression of male adult personhood continues to represent an autochthonous ideal of musical tradition. People in this village recognize his playing as part of what it means to be Waiwai, but at the same moment, the performance of Waiwai personhood is expanding to encompass other forms of musicality.

The point of change is generational. Young Waiwai men have not taken up the tradition of the flute, stating without exception that it is "hard to blow." For reasons described later in this chapter, young men have embraced a new medium in the form of battery-powered cassette players (boom boxes). In addition, an influx of Brazilian popular music, Guyanese soca and reggae, and American Christian gospel and country music has caused a shift in Waiwai self-expression through the medium of recorded songs. In a completely novel way, young people now express their thoughts, feelings, and desires through the use of specific tunes and appear to replicate the uses the flute formerly performed.

The subject matter of this chapter could be used to follow several trajectories and could also be brought to bear on a variety of relevant issues in terms of representing Waiwai sociality. In this instance, I have chosen to focus on the ways musical expression among the Waiwai allow us to reconsider the ways in which Amazonian people continue to reformulate, modify, and express cultural ideals in the context of modernity. By using flute music and musicality in general as a way of addressing the larger subject of culture change as an inevitable but not necessarily detrimental phenomenon, it is one of my larger aims to develop a representation of the Waiwai (and indigenous Amazonians in general) that does not focus on cultural loss, annihilation, and extinction, but highlights instead a more positive, actively engaged agency that incorporates "outside influences" into internally meaningful symbolic discourses. In fact, what at first may appear to be a "cultural loss" in terms of skill at flute playing is in fact revealed to be yet another example of the Waiwai ability to incorporate change into their expression of core ideals.

The main themes of this chapter, then, are those of internally defined "traditions" juxtaposed with modernity, the nature and quality of intergenerational dialogue and communication, and the imperative to actively re-create society—in this case through emergent, shared understandings regarding the nature of the ambient soundscape. The uses of new modes of musical expression also parallel an understanding of potential sources of power that enhance the social discourse flowing through Waiwai musical expression.

A Dual Competitive Discourse

There are several forms of musical discourse that the Waiwai currently employ. These are represented in the main by (1) the flute, the playing of which is not localized in ritual but integrated into everyday life; (2) the boom box, which parallels the flute in that it is also not ritualized but integrated into everyday life; and (3) the guitar, which represents the third source of Waiwai musicality in the playing of gospel and religious music in the context of religious ceremonies within the Christian Brethren Church. Although these three types of music form a triangular, competitive discourse within the village, the use of gospel music through the playing of guitar and the development of gospel music with Waiwai lyrics has still not approached as high a level of competitiveness within the Waiwai village as the ongoing discourse between the flute and the boom box. For this reason, I will focus more on the simultaneous and competitive discourse formed between the flute and the boom box and explore the addition of other forms of musicality and symbolic musical discourses elsewhere. The additional playing of bamboo and bark trumpets during festival times (see figs. 24 and 25) seems to fall into the

24. Brothers Antony and Warau making music on the large bamboo trumpet (*ratuimo*) that imitates the sound of bush hogs (*poniko*) as they enter the village during Kresmus celebrations. Photo by Stephanie W. Alemán.

25. Hunters returning with large warishis full of smoked meat from a ten-day hunting trip. Some of their catch often adorns the bark trumpets they play entering the village. Here it is a small smoked monkey. Photo by Stephanie W. Alemán.

self-designated category of "traditional" that the flute occupies, but it does not require the same force of shamanic breath as the flute does. Therefore, many of the same young men who play boom boxes shift into other forms of musical discourse during festivals and ritual periods and move through several expressions of musicality, including guitar music.

Two Musical Discourses in Detail

As mentioned above, flute playing (or *ratu poco*) is a specialized skill among the Waiwai that is traditionally part of a man's adult expression of gendered knowledge. Setting aside the actual skill involved in playing the flute, there is the initial knowledge required to make the instruments by transforming power-laden, forest dwelling materials into objects suitable for the containment of the shamanic breath that will "burst" through the flute and into the ears of active listeners.

In discovering a Waiwai sense of "traditional" music, it is necessary to consider the paramount importance of the ability and obligation to hear and listen properly. An emphasis on the necessity to create open and receptive conduits via the senses is embedded in a Waiwai concept of individual human development. The ear as the physical loci for both the reception of sound and a target for the reception of sound is ideally always in a state of achieved openness (Mentore 1993). The successful use of the power inherent in the use of shamanically mediated sound depends on this shared notion of a willingness to hear. This emphasis on hearing and listening as well as the social obligation to perform both with proficiency is shared with other indigenous Amazonian groups and can be seen as a common feature of social life. As Seeger (1981) points out among the Suyá, the verb "to hear" has other referents that include moral sense and morality, knowledge and understanding, acceptable behavior and judgment of others. This is exactly so among the Waiwai. As he relates, "The ear, then, is the receiver and holder of social codes. A fully social person hears, understands, and knows clearly." Turner (1995) discusses the same concept of human development through correct hearing among the Kayapó as part of a larger discussion of the relationship between the biologically individual body and the social dependency of this body for its continued existence. He also emphasizes the relationship between hearing, understanding, and sociality, citing correct hearing as well as the willingness to engage in listening—as it is among the Waiwai—as a sign of the socially informed body.

Into this active, willing state of being among the Waiwai, then, comes the tradition of the flute. As an instrument suitable for cultural expression, a flute is transformed from natural components of the forest, most often bamboo or bone. But the vital energies it contains in its "raw" state must be carefully retained, since it is also learning to garner and master this energy through eloquent performance that gives its player the coercive power to affect those who hear it and to influence their responsive behavior. A partial acknowledgment of this philosophy can be demonstrated by the fact that in this case, the Waiwai word for bamboo, *ratu*, is also the word for flute. (In addition, *ratu poco* can mean either playing the flute or making one from gathered bamboo.) Whereas other culturally transformed material objects also undergo a linguistic change that signifies their transformation (*sheere*, cassava, into *chuure*, cassava bread, or *wotu*, raw, uncleaned meat, into *tuyonho*, raw, cleaned, and cut meat, into *nïye*, cooked meat),[1] the word *ratu* retains its natural designation and thereby signals an acknowledgment that it is both the inherent magical properties of bamboo and the successful human manipulation of a flute made from it that combine to give its potential for power.

The shamanically produced sound emanating from the flute can be directed at several types of listeners. In short, the flute can be used in competitive discourse with other flautists (who are men), and can also be used to magically entice both game animals and women (in this sense, game animals and women as potential or desired lovers are both considered "prey"). With regard to the "nonritual" nature of Carib flute music, the lack of prohibitions on seeing flutes and the daily, rather than ritually punctuated, use of the flute in general, the Waiwai echo some of the information given by Brightman and Beaudet (this volume) on the different ways musicality is grasped and manipulated by indigenous Amazonians from across the Amazonian region. Certainly, the Waiwai would admit similarities in the concepts of hardness as value (in bone, bamboo, beads, and health) such as Brightman outlines for "Guinanese Amazonia" and the larger Amazon. The special quality of tubes as conduits is marked in Waiwai descriptions of both flute playing and the shamanic abilities that derive from the correct manipulation of tubes. Bamboo, as ready-made tube, is filled at several points in Waiwai shamanic lore with magical objects before burying, or it is used extensively as a sort of divination crucible when discerning "who" has caused the death of another Waiwai person. Waiwai flutes (and the flautists) are a felt presence in the village, due to the routine sessions of playing that the village enjoys. In my own case, although I did not see women playing flutes, I played them frequently, attempting to hone some level of skill and also attempting to please Maruwanarï, who seemed very keen on instructing me both in terms of technical skill and the dangers of the use of shamanic power without understanding its intent. Beaudet in this volume also addresses the nature of our gendered experience of flute music as ethnographers, wondering if our perception of the relationships between flutes and gender are more influenced by our own—and not an Amazonian emphasis on gendered hierarchical differentiation. In the case of the Waiwai, it appears that the attainment of personhood requires engagement with flutes and flute music by both men and women, although the role of each is of course different. The passage to personhood for both men and women involved an understanding of the vital energies of persons. Moreover, the idea that Brightman develops regarding flutes as agents of transformation and Riviere's "energy transformers" are both easily discernible in Waiwai philosophies of both being and becoming human, where managing stores of personal vital energies and manipulating the stores of vital energies in others become a social imperative. Beaudet's and Brightman's references to the relationships between the creator of a sound and the fertile are also reflected in the ways in which flutes are used and conceptualized by the Waiwai in Guyana.

Thus when Maruwanari makes music, he seeks to influence other men by engaging them in a relationship in which they, as listeners, are compelled to acknowledge both the message he conveys and his eloquence in conveying it. The resounding notes of individual tunes remind both listener and player of successful alliances with other skilled players, especially when he shifts to compositions he has "traded" and learned from them. These memories of such exchanges underscore his own abilities and enhance their admiration of his skills. Alternatively, some tunes are composed with the specific purpose of enticing game (those with titles such as "Deer, Come and Dance" and "Waiting in My Moonlit Garden" evoke this idea) and performing these serves to remind listeners of an equally admirable skill in hunting. A parallel set of tunes in Maruwanari's repertoire tell tales of their use as irresistible love calls as well as the subsequent success he has had in enticing women for sex. Songs with titles such as "Turtle Has a Necklace," which signifies a lover's acceptance of the flautist through the public wearing of a gift exchanged between couples involved in sexual relationships, and "So, do you think you will like me?" a title asking this question to an already magically enticed lover, underscore the effect of flute music directed to women as listeners, especially as they can be rendered powerless and willingly receptive by hearing his coercive notes. Maruwanari has also been known to express a lively sense of both humor and the relatedness of women to game by switching the tunes in different contexts. Thus he says you can attract game by playing the "So, you think you will like me" and female lovers by playing "Waiting in My Moonlit Garden." In addition, if he was to play "Deer, Come and Dance" to attract a lover, it might work, but the women could possibly really be a deer in disguise.

In all of these musically conveyed messages is the understanding that they represent key aspects of male personhood. Although this suggests that the highly gendered nature of flute music places its use as a form of power to the advantage of men, there is not a sense of antagonism in the concept of the flute and its shamanic aspects. In fact, in an additional parallel found among Caribs, flutes seem to suggest a narrative of gender balance and perhaps gendered obligation but not gendered antagonism. One of Maruwanarï's playing sessions can thus bring to life the sounds and dialogues of animals, stories of magically aided love, desire, and enticement, competitive conversations between men, and prowess at finding and captivating prey. In this same context, Maruwanarï's ability as a flute player allows him to convey his successful achievement of humanness, and as Mentore's poem again suggests, it is a humanness that can only cease to exist when the Waiwai are no longer Waiwai.

Given the depth of meaning flute playing contains in a "traditional" understanding of Waiwai identity, it is especially important to understand how Waiwai persons can achieve humanness if they do not play flutes. If, in this village, Maruwanarï is the only Waiwai man who continues to perform his identity through flute playing, how are other Waiwai men achieving humanness? What modes of self-expression are employed to this end, and can one still look at musicality to find them? This question found the beginnings of a response when I began to focus on the younger generations and their approach to personhood. The use of music by men between the ages of sixteen and thirty-five revealed a symbolically different mode of performance but one that contains the idea of performing for the achievement of similar ends.

The use of the boom box in the Waiwai village at Masakin-

26. Antony and Warau with their boom box—in charge of the music during the long festival days of Kresmus. Photo by Stephanie W. Alemán.

yarï is pervasive (see fig. 26). At any given time of the day, sometimes in direct competition with Maruwanarï's evening playing, boom boxes can be heard. The sound they produce carries so far across the village that often one boom box is allowed to play at a time, so that the music itself—and in some cases the lyrics—can be clearly heard. Often the boom boxes (and the batteries they consume) are given between fifteen and thirty minutes of individual play, followed by a short silence that is then filled with the next player's choice of tunes.

Without exception, the younger Waiwai men describe flute playing as "very hard" and cite their attempt at learning to be unsuccessful. If pressed to try, most men will barely coax a note from a flute or they will fail to make a sound altogether. In truth, it is not that hard to make a sound on a Waiwai notched flute. The young men are actually referring to the proper kind of breath necessary to play flutes. In this case, the proper kind of breath is shamanic.

The statements by younger men involving the playing of flutes may at first seem to be about technical skill and ability, but are actually made in reference to the concept of shamanic breath (for more on this concept among the Waiwai see Mentore 2004). In keeping with the provocative title of this volume, the burst of (shamanic) breath associated with playing the flute is the main feature of its use. In the case of the flute, this further suggests that the breath required for correct and successful flute playing is obtained through shamanic means. Further, the breath required for flute playing is composed of vital energies that must be garnered, using shamanic ability, from the surrounding forest and concentrated through the narrow passage of the flute by shamanically enhanced breath. The nature of shamanism is then more readily described as the ability to control and manipulate vital energies. Moreover, the sound made by a flute is not the same as the sounds made by other things, because the quality of the flute's sound is perceived as resonant, and the sound wave is considered palpable to those who hear it. In some senses, this shamanic ability is not only lacking in the younger men, but is inaccessible to them because of emergent ideologies regarding the inappropriateness of shamanic activity. Although any length of time in the Waiwai village will clearly demonstrate the extent to which animistic and shamanic belief systems still operate in their worldview, the overt practice of shamanism is seen as an antisocial type of behavior. In this context, being "good" at flute playing, or even wanting to be good at it suggests an interest in shamanic performance and knowledge. Waiwai persons would agree that this type of 'showing ones self' is a sure way toward social sanction. Shamanic practice has currently been reduced and reformed to be part of what is known as "family magic" or "revenge magic"—referred to as *erem*. In addition, blowing magic or *tanu* is also considered dangerous and antisocial. Anyone interested in these practices is usually discouraged by the suggestion that attempts to use sources of power with which one is unfamiliar could lead to detrimental consequences. Within the family, it is understood that there are some forms of knowledge and power that may be used to protect and nurture kin. The Christian teachings of the former missionary presence have been integrated into Waiwai discourse and practice, but often these can be seen as merely a veneer that covers deeper ideologies and practices. As a result, one will find the same individuals who play boom boxes also engaged in playing religious gospel music on guitar, as well as participating in traditional Waiwai ceremonial use of bark trumpets, but not playing or learning the flute.

The narrative surrounding the generational shift from flutes to boom boxes is multilayered and complex, but is centered around the idea of finding alternate routes to social power when the traditional route through mastering shamanically aided flute playing is not readily available. The boom box then has become the main mode of musical expression among younger men. The boom box can signal other aspects of male prowess if it is considered as a traded commodity and the pathways to attaining one are traced. A boom box of the kind desired by Waiwai young men is about $100US. This is a significant, but not fantastic amount for a young man to acquire. It may happen as the result of several months of working gold, several weeks of guide work, or through countless exchanges of bead and feather work as well as weaving that eventually add up to the purchase price. Adding to its social value is the necessity to further establish a relationship with someone who will bring one through the trails to the village for you, or to make the journey to the 'outside' world where such things can be purchased. In this sense, a boom box is a rather potent commodity, because it demonstrates many levels of social positioning and engagement. Once obtained, there is the constant need for batteries (constant engagement with trade partners) as well as the choice and maintenance of tape collections to convey the proper messages with via the use of the boom box. Being able to obtain and then maintain a boom box is certainly a viable way to demonstrate expertise in the local economy, and thus, contribute to one's overall attainment of humanness through social interaction. A boom box is a signal of engagement on several levels and thus is a rather special representation of the way in which Waiwai ideals can remain viable while shifting symbolisms to other objects—or indeed-the objects of others.

The use of the boom box parallels the playing of the flute in both the competitive conversations between men and the enticement of lovers (prey) that forms part of the conversation between men and women. An important difference is that boom box music cannot entice game animals, since it is thought they cannot hear this type of music. The reason given for an inability to hear is that both the boom box and the music produced by it were made far away, and not in the forest. The materials were not once in the same habitat as the game-as in the case of bamboo flutes, nor made of parts of game animals themselves (in the case of bone flutes). But the boom box does contain sources of vital energies, although these are of a foreign nature and strength.

In examining the use of the boom box by young men, there is one striking example I will give here that illustrates how the shift from flutes to boom boxes carries with it the same sorts of expression offered by flautists, but uses other means to achieve these expressions. In addition, it is understood that in order for the boom box to have any of the qualities of enticement and coercion that flutes have, there needs to be a shared understanding of the messages it conveys. The fact that there is a generational shift in the ability to interpret the messages in other types of music played on boom boxes is one of the reasons it is successful among the younger generations. Only those with an understanding of outsider forms of knowledge can use and be affected by boom box music.

On an evening like many others in the Waiwai village, I returned from the river after bathing and entered our dark house. While I searched for the matches to light a kerosene lamp, I heard the sounds of reggae music begin from a neighbor's house. The song was "Reggae Physician" by Burning Spear and came from a large collection of cassette tapes I knew my neighbor to possess. On first hearing this tune, I simply enjoyed it as a novelty in the village. But, with the following song, "Night Nurse," by reggae performer Gregory Isaacs, I sensed a pattern in the songs my neighbor was choosing. It seemed interesting that the man playing the boom box had chosen two songs regarding medicine and doctors/nurses. Drifting to sleep that night, I thought of the lyrics to these songs and what the connection might be. The following night, at the same time, my neighbor played the same two songs, only this time I took more notice of the circumstances surrounding them. The man's wife was still coming back from bathing at the river, and I recalled that she had been gone the previous night as well, still at the river when he played the songs.

I had also heard that he was having an affair with another young woman, but had never seen any evidence of this during my time in the village. But, on this night, I also saw the woman in question leave her post in the clinic (which was located on the other side of my house) and take a trail leading to the back of the village. This woman was the apprentice to the CHW—or Community Health Worker. After several repeat evenings, I also discovered that the man playing the music was leaving his house and meeting his lover at a prearranged location outside the village. The tunes he played on the boom box, although they could be heard by the entire village, were serving as a signal to the young health apprentice that she should meet her lover.

When I then made a closer inventory of the repertoire of tunes available to boom box users in the form of cassette tapes, I found that all were either traded copies of tapes, or tapes purchased in Brazilian and Guyanese towns on excursions outside the village. The acquisition of the boom box itself and the access to a constant source of batteries to play it had become a prevalent feature of daily life among the younger men. Of course they were still hunting and fishing and performing other more traditional tasks, but they were also seeking outside work for short periods to gain funds and these were often expended on maintaining their music collections and for more batteries. In other contexts than the example given above, the boom box was used to make social statements about the behavior of certain individuals and in some cases, lyrics were given to songs that did not have them, such as the tune "If I only had more batteries, you would soon be my lover." In fact these boom box songs formed part of a larger discourse of youth in the Waiwai village, which centered on the use of secret slangs, word games and "inside jokes." Many of the instrumental tunes were used when roaming groups of young men would arrive outside the house of another young person, either male or female. The resulting chants were made up on the spot, referring to the person whose house was being serenaded, but using a tune familiar to all. The more I listened, the more I came to understand the boom box as an eloquent use of outside cultural symbolisms and processes of communication to express ideals and play out situations that have long been part of Waiwai life ways. In this context, interaction with outsiders had changed the forms (from flutes to boom boxes) but not the reasoning or hoped for outcome of certain types of social enactment. In contrast for example, to the negative effect cited by Wilbert by the introduction of the fiddle into Warao culture, Waiwai use of the introduced boom box had shifted social meanings, but had also retained substantive ideas and philosophies that did not adhere to the fiddle as used by the Warao (Wilbert 1993).

Instead, the juxtaposition of the flute with the boom box highlights how two different media are achieving the same ends; that is love predation, enticement and conversations about intimacies through seemingly public means. And as the younger men told me "flutes are irresistible, but so are boom boxes if you know the right songs to play"! Thus, boom box knowledge as a source of power has a specialist type of knowledge that is in fact shamanic in its configuration. The ability to operate the mechanics, repair if necessary, create (record) tapes and choose the appropriate tunes on an instrument that was made with powerful, but outside forms of knowledge make the use and possession of the boom box a rising marker of Waiwai male personhood as well in the younger generations. The emergence of a sort of "cassette culture," with objects to trade and messages to convey is similar in some of its aspects to Peter Manuel's study of "new" media and its impact on local experience in areas of north India (Manuel 1993).

In this chapter, I have been concerned to show not only that the Waiwai have been and remain an actively musical people, but that they have endeavored to express this musicality in ways that incorporate the use of outside concepts and material objects to do so. Rather than succumbing to the fate of a defunct social phenomenon, or a mode of expression that is slowly drained of its meaning and falling out of practice, or is infiltrated and overwhelmed by outside influences, music among the Waiwai not only flourishes, but expands as a meaningful, symbol laden system, continually reintegrated and entwined with other core ideals of Waiwai identity through its performance and its intergenerational modification. In fact, Waiwai identity and personhood is formed in part by the ability to understand the use and meaning of all three aspects of Waiwai musical discourse presented here. To be or become a whole Waiwai person, one must possess the knowledge of the use of these various aspects as well as allow one's self to be actively engaged with the messages they convey. The active engagement of listeners with all the musical forms present in the daily life of Waiwai persons is one of the many imperatives of Waiwai social life.

Rather than a distinct form of cultural loss, the use of boom boxes should be seen as a positive native agency. Tradition in the form of the flute and modernity in the form of the boom box coexist in current Waiwai culture as examples of identity formation and projection that employ the sophisticated use of native agency as a tool for perpetuating culture. In this example, Waiwai culture changes, but is not diminished through change. This in turn projects a favorable view of the persistence of their culture and life ways into the future. By contemplating the Waiwai soundscape in but a few of its aspects, and by participating in Waiwai culture through doing so, you are intimately involved in the project of helping them to become and to remain—distinctly Waiwai.

Notes

Special thanks to George Mentore for permission to use his poem for this chapter. *Kiriwanhi oroto Coci okwe!*

1. For the significance of prestation of these variously transformed substances, see Mentore 1995.

References Cited

Fock, Niels. 1963. *Waiwai: Religion and Society of an Amazonian Tribe*. Copenhagen: National Museum.

Izikowitz, Karl Gustav. 1970 [1935]. *Musical and Other Sound Instruments of the South American Indians: A Comparative Ethnographic Study*. Yorkshire, UK: S. R.

Manuel, Peter. 1993. *Cassette Culture: Popular Music and Technology in North India*. Chicago: University of Chicago Press.

Mentore, George P. 1993. "Tempering the Social Self: Body Adornment, Vital Substance, and Knowledge among the Waiwai." *Archaeology and Anthropology* 9: 22–34.

———. 1995. "Peccary Meat and Power among the Waiwai Indians of Guyana." *Archaeology and Anthropology* 10: 19–35.

———. 2004. "The Glorious Tyranny of Silence and the Resonance of Shamanic Breath." In *In Darkness and Secrecy: The Anthropology of Assault Sorcery and Witchcraft in Amazonia*, ed. Neil Whitehead and Robin Wright. Durham: Duke University Press.

Seeger, Anthony. 1981. *Nature and Society in Central Brazil*. Cambridge: Harvard University Press.

Turner, Terence. 1995. "Social Body and Embodied Subject: Bodiliness, Subjectivity, and Sociality among the Kayapo." *Cultural Anthropology* 10, no. 2: 143–70. Special issue, *Anthropologies of the Body*.

Wilbert, Johannes. 1993. *Mystic Endowment: Religious Ethnography of the Warao Indians*. Cambridge: Harvard University Press.

Yde, Jens. 1965. *Material Culture of the Waiwai*. Copenhagen: National Museum.

9. From Musical Poetics to Deep Language

The Ritual of the Wauja Sacred Flutes

ACÁCIO TADEU DE CAMARGO PIEDADE

This chapter discusses some aspects of the ritual of the sacred flutes among the Wauja Indians of the Upper Xingu. The universe of the sacred flutes of the Wauja, known as *kawoká*, is congruent with the "sacred flute complex" observed in other societies of the Upper Xingu and among other peoples of the South American lowlands, as well as among various ethnic groups in other parts of the world. The study of this ritual involves important issues of native cosmology, shamanism, society, and musicality. Following the clues provided by the discourse of the Wauja flutists, my study of the music of this ritual focused on the musical system in action in this repertoire, particularly on its motific sphere, which is understood by the natives as the heart of the flute ritual. At this musicological level, it is clear that the Wauja musicians conduct important operations of variation and other musical processes. At the base of these operations are principles of repetition and differentiation that constitute the native musical thinking, one of the pillars of Wauja cosmology and philosophy. Initially, I will discuss factors pertinent to the Xinguano peoples and their social and ritual system, concentrating on the sacred flutes and the cosmologies. I will then provide a brief description of the Wauja cosmology and discuss the ethnography of the ritual in question. I intend to focus on what I call the musical poetics that are revealed in the interplay of the musical motifs of the Wauja sacred flute ritual. I conclude the article with a general hypothesis.

Xinguano Sacred Flutes

In the Upper Xingu region a single sociopolitical system encompasses the lives of several indigenous peoples. It is notable particularly at moments of intertribal communication, such as rituals, exchange ceremonies, and marriages, as well as in the practice of shamanism and witchcraft. The aesthetic and artistic dimensions are crucial elements in this Amazonian system. The so-called Xinguano ceremonial, which includes all the large rituals realized in the region (such as the *kwarýp*, the *yawari*, and the *iamuri-kuma*), is the principal space where the system is expressed and where the different cultures among the Xinguanos are articulated (Menezes Bastos 1995; Menget 1993). As Franchetto affirmed, these rituals "sew together Xinguano society, a ceremonial circuit that guides alliances and metabolizes conflicts, ritually absorbing alterity" (2001: 149). Xinguano rituals are essentially musical (Basso 1985: 243–61). It is therefore necessary to understand the Xinguano social system through its musicality. The grammar of the Wauja musical system includes a codification of the topics of Wauja life that are the foundation of both its particular identity and Xinguaninity itself, to the degree to which this musical system has a supralocal dimension.

At the heart of Xinguana cosmology are the sacred flutes.[1] They are called *kawoká* by the Wauja and Mehináku, *yaku'i* by the Kamayurá, and *kagutu* by the Kuikúru and Kalapalo).[2] Their centrality is expressed in the spatial dimensions of the "flutes house," where these instruments are stored. This house is also referred to as the "men's house" and is located at the center of the Xinguano villages, a predominately masculine space. The Wauja and Mehináku flutes house is called *kuwakuho* (in Kuikúro *kwakúto*, in Kamayurá *tapùy*).[3] Frequent descriptions have been made in the Upper Xingu that indicate that these structures are now precarious and appear to be nearly abandoned. Because of this situation, the instruments have been maintained in other locations, always hidden and under the guard of their "owner." I observed this in the Wauja village and in other Xinguana villages. Nevertheless, instead of seeing this as a transformation in conditions because of a lack of use or a decadence of the tradition, I see these factors as profound characteristics of the institution.[4] The material fragility of the men's house is an original cosmological condition (Gregor 1985).

The Xinguana sacred flutes consist of a set of three identical flute-type aerophones, nearly always used in a trio. When the sacred flutes are played, both within the men's house or on the plaza of the Xinguana villages, the women stay inside and close their doors to respect the prohibition against viewing. If a woman sees the instruments, she will be raped by all the men of the village. The prohibition against viewing is applied to other sacred instruments associated with the flute complex, such as the bullroarer.[5]

The ritual of the sacred flutes can be intertribal or intratribal. In the first case, it is part of the Xinguano ceremonial and involves a large number of participants; usually all the Xinguano groups are present. Meanwhile, the intratribal sacred flute rituals, at least among the Wauja, are much more restricted and related to a process of curing a sick person, similar to other *apapaatai* feasts.[6] In fact, kawoká is an apapaatai, a dangerous supernatural being.

The centrality of the sacred flutes in the Xinguano sociocultural system is also expressed in the mythology and cosmology. According to Xinguano mythology, the sacred flutes belonged to the women and were taken by the men in a violent attack made more frightening by the sound of the bullroarers. There is, therefore, a connection here with gender relations, which indicates the great importance that sexuality and love have in the sacred flute complex (Mello 1999, 2005). In this way, the sacred flute universe is omnipresent in the Upper Xingu, encompassing the dangerous supernatural world and the fundamental sphere of gender relations.

The Xinguano sacred flutes are the local version of the sacred flute complex, which is found throughout the South American lowlands (Chaumeil 1997) and in other parts of the world, particularly Melanesia.[7] When I studied the Tukano of the northwestern Amazon, I called attention to the Arawakan basis of part of their music, especially the Jurupari sacred flutes and trumpets (Piedade 1997). It is intriguing to imagine that other regions of the South American lowlands and upland regions of the Amazon periphery may also have an Arawakan foundation of their sacred flute complexes. This idea is suggested by a comparison of the distribution of these instruments in South America with those of Arawak-speaking peoples.[8]

The music performed in the sacred Xinguano flute rituals is highly appreciated by the Xinguanos in general, even by the women, who constitute an essential audience. As in all the regions where there is a sacred flute complex, the women cannot see the instruments, but the fact that they are in the village to hear the music is what I have called a cultural edict: although they are forbidden to see the flutes, the women must listen to them (Piedade 1997, 1999). The Xinguano women have a repertory of iamurikuma songs based on the sacred flute melodies, and it can be said that there is a dialogical relationship between the sacred flute ritual and that of the iamurikuma (see Maria Ignez Mello's article in this volume).

The structure of the Wauja sacred flute music denotes tremendous attention to the motific sphere, which constitutes the most significant nucleus of the kawoká musical universe.[9] Some of the musical motifs are considered to be exceptionally valuable, secret, and dangerous (*kakaiapai*). The flutists are warned that if they play badly, they could cause someone's misfortune, illness, or death.

Wauja Cosmology

The Wauja cosmos is inhabited by the apapaatai, beings that are usually invisible and that have a determining role in the lives of humans. Gods, spirits, demons, monsters, divinities, or simply supernatural beings, the apapaatai are not spectres, ghosts, or souls, and they are not immaterial parts of human bodies. They are, first, independent beings endowed with an "existential excess." Franchetto (1996) describes them as "hyper-beings," and Menezes Bastos (1999) translates *mama'e* as "that inexhaustible extreme essence."

According to the Wauja cosmogony, what today is this visible world, this welcoming platform and domain of material phenomenon, this world where humans, animals, and vegetables live, all of this was once the world of a people called *ierupoho* (Mello 1999, 2005; Barcelos Neto 2004). The Wauja were poor proto-human beings who lived in a dark world inside a termite mound without fire or water. They drank their own urine and saw nothing. To end this, the demiurge *kamo* (sun) brought light to the world, allowing the Wauja to become humans and enter this world. The ierupoho, who cannot be exposed to light, had to escape to the forest or to the deep waters, while some, to hide from the light, created masks to hide behind, becoming apapaatai.[10] The apapaatai, therefore, inhabit a world of exile, required as they were to abandon the dimension where they previously lived. Their strongest character is related to a desire for revenge, the impetus to cause harm to humans: the apapaatai seek revenge.

The shamanic discourse affirms, however, that the current world of the apapaatai is not a place different from "right here," nor is it another place. The apapaatai only appear not to be present. But the clairvoyant shamans warn: "Their village is right there."[11] This raises the question of visibility: the world of the apapaatai is real, but it is not open to the view of humans, with the exception of the clairvoyant shamans in trance. In this way, a cosmic inequality is manifest. Only the apapaatai have the ability to see themselves and to see the world of humans. Thus they can exercise vigilance over Wauja society and are capable of perceiving any deviation in behavior, even when this is only a thought, an act that constitutes an entrance channel for disease (Mello 2005).

Note that while in principle they are essentially dangerous and evil, the apapaatai also have various characteristics considered beneficial in their relations with humans. When domesticated by the clairvoyant shaman, or *iakapá*, and tamed by ritual, they act as protectors of the formerly ill person against other apapaatai.

Among the countless apapaatai, the native discourse highlights the kawoká, considered the most powerful and dangerous (*kawokapai*, "dangerous"). It created the flutes and took shelter in them. The masks of the apapaatai are not images or symbols of their creators: in the Wauja theory of representation, masks constitute rather what I call existential extensions, a very part of the ritually activated being. The mask of the kawoká is the flute, and the music is their epiphany.

Wauja Sacred Flutes

The Wauja have various aerophones: the double flutes called *watana* (used typically in the *kwarỳp*), the pan flutes (*iapojatekana*), the clarinets (*talapi* and *tankuwara*), the trumpet (*laptawana*), the bullroarer (*matapu*), the flutes (*kawoká, kuluta,* and *kawokatãi*), and the gourd (*mutukutãi*).[12] The kuluta flutes resemble the kawoká flutes, but are made of lighter wood and shorter pipes, so they are easier to play. The kawokatãi flute (small kawoká) is used for learning the repertoire and is also used in curing rituals (Coelho 1988). Matapu bullroarers are used in the Pequi festival. An instrument that is rarely found today is a type of percussive idiophone: a log drum called the *pulupulu*.[13]

The intratribal ritual of the sacred Wauja flutes is related to illness, curing, and good health. The entire process is initiated, therefore, when someone gets sick. This process, understood as simultaneously ethical and aesthetic (Mello 2005), is related to the direct intervention of an apapaatai in an individual's body and soul. The diagnosis of the shaman *iakapá*, which is only possible through trance and by glimpsing the world of the apapaatai, indicates which apapaatai or group of apapaatai caused the disease. The *iakapá* thus conduct the initial part of the cure with smoke and song, removing the spell of the apapaatai encrusted in the interior of the ill person's body. A relative close to the ill person is chosen as his *kawokalamona* ("body of the kawoká"), and should make a brief theatrical representation in the role of the apapaatai. In addition, the kawokalamona is responsible for preparing the masks of apapaatai. If the apapaatai in question is kawoká, the master of the flutes is contracted to produce a set of flutes for the recently cured individual. When they are ready, there is a ritual performance in which the flutes are played and officially given to the owner. Every person formerly ill from ka-woká becomes a *kawokawekeho* ("owner of kawoká") and must take care of the instruments and participate in kawoká flute rituals for the rest of his life. The kawokalamona should play the flute of his relative until the late afternoon, from the center of the village to the flute owner's house. The owner is the principal flutist of the trio whenever this group of flutes is played in this situation.

In the Wauja village I studied in 2003 and 2004, there were five sets of kawoká flutes. Two were called *mutukutãi*,[14] one was called *kajutukalunau* (frog people), another was called *pejú*, and a final one was called *ianumakanau* (jaguar people). Each set had an "owner," obviously a formerly ill kawoká who had become responsible for keeping his set of flutes in good condition. Among the five owners were two women, and because they could not conduct the maintenance of the instruments because they were forbidden to see them, their care was assumed by a husband or brother. Having a kawoká as an apapaatai ally provides a special position in the cosmic political economy and thus in Wauja society. In fact, there is a factional relationship between the owners of kawoká, the flutists of kawoká, and the shamans *iakapá*.[15]

Musical Factors in the Wauja Sacred Flute Ritual

The music of the kawoká flutes is constructed for two voices and always played in a trio. Two accompanists stand on either side of the master flutist. They play a single voice, in unison, based on long notes, while he plays the principal melody. This is not a technique in alternating style, but a type of prolongation of certain notes based on their enunciation at the beginning of the theme. This prolongation produces an echo effect, a reverberation when a note reaches a frequency at which it reverberates, while the subsequent notes appear without this impact. Recalling the structure of old European Gregorian chants, I feel that the voice of the accompanying flutists is a type of *inverted organum*: the melodies of the long notes produced by the accompanying flutists configure the *cantus firmus*, while that played by the master flutist (*kawokatopá*) functions as a florid counterpoint. But in this case, the counterpoint is the principal voice, while the cantus firmus is a duplicated voice (two flutists in unison) and secondary.

The kawokatopá must be in command of all the melodies because only he has the requisite level of instrumental dexterity. The pieces are short, lasting about two minutes, but must be played without error and in the correct order, with many subtle motifs that mark the differences between one piece and another. The kawokatopá can open to himself the world of the apapaatai in its sonic dimension: he is the only one that can remember the music that the apapaatai play for the humans on certain occasions in their dreams. For this reason, the flute masters are like *iakapá* shaman, except that, instead of being clairvoyant, they are "clairaudient."[16]

The master's greatest attribute is his memory. To achieve memory, a previous understanding of the object is necessary, and he understands and memorizes the musical structures that he hears. He also has great responsibility in the ritual, because any mistake can disturb the apapaatai, who may thus become angry, break the alliance, and cause illness and death. The musical performance of kawoká is, therefore, something extremely serious. Before each piece, the master flutist remains static for a few seconds, recalling the structure and order of the pieces, because he knows no mistake can be made. The kawoká music involves the necessary perfection of the execution of the motifs and of the musical form so that the delicate cosmic equilibrium will be maintained.

In the ethnography of the ritual music of kawoká, considering the importance of the motif, a profound study of the musical text is necessary. For this reason, in my 2004 dissertation, I conducted integral transcriptions of the various pieces. I included all the musical events capable of notation according to the western system: the establishment of a range of notes reasonably congruent with the pitches of the flutes, a staff for each of the three flutes, and a rhythm line for the ankle rattle. I found that some musical phrases were repeated during each piece, while others were simply different in a given detail. The phrases that repeated were the same in all the pieces of a named grouping, which I called a suite, given that the different phrases were unique to each piece. I was able to memorize and perform these standard phrases, but I had difficulty with the unique phrases. It is precisely these unique phrases which constitute what my master indicated were the most valuable and important to know how to play perfectly. This interplay of standard phrases and unique phrases was particular to the constitution of this repertoire. All of the pieces obey this same interplay and its rules.

Thus all the kawoká pieces that I was able to analyze began with the execution of the standard phrases typical of the suite, and only after this were the first unique phrases played. Then there was a return to the standard phrases, after which new phrases were presented. A piece always ends with standard phrases. The unique phrases are only played by the master flutists, while the standard phrases are played by all three instrumentalists. It is these unique phrases that the apapaatai create and donate to humans during dreams or special situations. They must be memorized and executed in pefect order and form. As the flutists say, these phrases constitute the heart of the kawoká music. It is where the apapaatai "sing," while the standard phrases are not sung but "blown." The unique phrases, in turn, are short motifs that are varied by different operations, which is what creates the character of each song. These motifs are like signatures of the piece; they constitute difference from a similar and repeated base. They are strongly present in the sequence of the pieces, emerging from the homogeneous foundation and dialoging with it and each other, in the style of an interplay of microstructures involving formal operations and variational principles.

I have identified the systematic use of a set of operations of motific variation. Some are universal, such as augmentation, diminution, transposition, inversion, inclusion, exclusion, and duplication. Some are unique, which I called fusion, elipse, commentary, reiteration, and compression. A series of mechanisms of native musical thinking are thus involved that become known absolutely by the flutists through practice. They were revealed to me through rigorous practice with the instrument and through musical transcription and analysis of the pieces. Supported by what the flutists themselves said, I believe that these operations are not limited to musical thought. They constitute modes that the Wauja apply to create difference based on an original idea. It is for this reason that they belong to realms other than the phrasal, thematic, and motific. I believe that they represent native forms of thinking about the nature of difference, and therefore I see these principles as part of a philosophy.

Considerations about Musical Poetics in the Music of the Wauja Sacred Flutes

The systematic use of the musical operations referred to above constitutes a type of interplay that, beyond the dimension of sound, points to a series of ideas. It involves a type of artistic manipulation of established formal states that are similar to a poetic procedure, applied here in the motific sphere of instrumental music.

To speak here of poetics, in the context of indigenous instrumental music, is in keeping with what the Wauja flutists say about the "speech of the kawoká." This is a native category for the music of the kawoká, which is seen as a form of speech that sustains an interpretation of the musical themes. As in Kamayurá music, the process of musical signification in the music of the kawoká is basically thematic,[17] characterized by a "construction of a highly redundant, memorial time-space, in which repetition is the fundamental trait" (Menezes Bastos 1990: 519). The thematic construction (the musical idea) and the repetition, in its various forms, are the motors of the interplay of motifs and of the process of meaning construction. That is, they are operations of musical thinking that constitute the poetics of kawoká music. This is similar to the meaning given by Roman Jakobson to the term *poetics*, particularly in relation to parallelism.[18] The basic issue is that in the Wauja musical poetics, repetition is not redundance (in the sense understood by information theory) but an original rational principle present not only in artistic discourses but also in native philosophy and cosmology.[19]

In the Wauja sacred flute ritual, it can be noted, through a careful analysis of the motific level of the musical pieces, that this music expresses an idea about repetition, variation, and difference. I use the notion of "interplay" to speak of an interplay of motifs that are established in this repertoire. I point not to an aspect of permeability or indeterminacy but to the regulatory character of the interplay, to the meaning of the rules of this interaction.

The interplay of motifs functions as a musical poetics ruled by a type of grammatical parallelism that deforms an element in the sense that it makes it different. This music involves a confection of difference, given fundamentally in the axis of time and of existence, or that is in the realm of temporality. I believe that the different musical systems of the world result not only from diverse poetics but also from different forms of perceiving temporality. I have learned, with the Wauja, that musical thought is an expression of cosmology placed in action in music, revealing fundamental concepts of the native philosophy concerning temporality. Therefore, the musical system also has an existential character, because it refers to the forms of temporality conceiving finiteness. In this sense, kawoká music is a strong example of how native temporality establishes possibilities to cut and recombine the temporal structure in a poetic form. It can be said that the music pronounces forms of temporality. When I heard the kawoká flutes at night in the village, I heard the instruments invested with a maximum of meaning, not only for me but certainly for the Wauja. For the flutists, this involves the presentification of the apapaatai. It is he who is speaking, the music is his speech, *kawokagatakoja*, the "speech of the kawoká." The apapaatai pronounces himself through the interplay of motifs, intersecting time in a poetic manner.

Among the Wauja, the word *kãi* means "sound," any sonorous phenomenon. Nevertheless, when it involves musical sounds, they speak not of kãi but of *onaapa* (song). The terms *pitsana* (music timbre) and *watanapitsana* (aerophonic musical-timbre) express songs understood as acoustical images of the voices of animals and other beings. It should be recalled that pitsana and watanapitsana involve instrumental music, which is always aerophonic, while onaapa is used for instrumental or vocal music. Pitsana and watanapitsana, therefore, are internal categories of onaapa, the native word for music, recognizing that for the Wauja, music is song: the lexeme *onaapa* has its roots in the verb *apai*, "to sing." The native meaning of song indicates not only "intoning songs" but "creating a musical statement," producing musical discourse, vocal or instrumental, to pronounce a musical phrase, an idea. The core of the kawoká music, that which makes it music, is the "song" of the kawokatopá, the part of the master flutist, who sings, apai, while the accompanists "blow," *ejekepei*. To pronounce an idea is not simply an action without foundation or consequences: an idea is a possibility, an anticipation of thought.

Final Considerations

Among the Wauja, and it can be generalized, with proper caution, to the other Xinguano peoples, the sacred flutes express a musical poetics through their interplay of motifs. The concern for similar forms is also found in ritual macrostructures. In fact, Menezes Bastos (1990) shows that there is a large-scale spectrum structure in the *yawari* musical ritual among the Kamayurá. The musical form of the ritual, an elaborate interplay of inclusion, exclusion, and reserialization of songs, takes a number of days to be completely realized. This large form exhibits the contours of a thinking that progresses and regresses, extending and compressing time, given that repetition is a fundamental operation in the signification: the yawari is itself a ritual of memory and forgetting. Mello (2005) shows that the feminine iamurikuma ritual manifests a musical thinking very similar to that which operates in the kawoká flutes. In the *kawokakuma* songs of the women, special care is taken with the realm of motif and the fine balance between repetition and subtle variation. The iamurikuma ritual is pan-Xinguano, and it is quite probable that this kawoká-iamurikuma musical poetics is found throughout the region, even in the vocal music. It is thus necessary to understand this Xinguano particularity, which is the existence of a feminine ritual that appears to constitute a second side of the complex of the sacred flutes, and to question whether this ritual dialogue is not expressed in other ethnographic universes, even if in structural terms, hidden by the fact that there are no men's houses or sacred flutes.

Is it possible that the sacred flute complex is a phenomenon of proportions that go beyond the ethnographic universes already studied and known in the literature as societies with sacred flutes? Or is it possible that this complex, understood as a particular manifestation of the institution of the "men's house," is more extensive than imagined and that it may be present in some other form, even in sociocultural systems where there are no sacred flutes? We can offer the hypothesis that the sacred flute complex is generalized in indigenous societies of South America as a collective form of thinking of sensitive points of social existence: the differences and conflicts between the world of men, women, and gods, which always involves the dimensions of mythic narratives and of ritual practices and in particular has music as a *deep language*. Even in relation to a society for which there is no evidence of the existence of a sacred flute complex, the hypothesis in question proposes that the complex may be maintained as a structural position. An extensive and comparative study would be needed to verify that this idea is pertinent.

Notes

1. Note that not all sacred flutes are considered flutes from an organological point of view (as in the case of the Jurupari trumpets; Piedade 1997), and also that the attribute "sacred" is theoretically problematic. Despite this, in this article I will use the term *sacred flutes* without quotes, because the expression is well established in the literature.

2. In terms of technical classification, the sacred flutes made in the Upper Xingu region are duct flutes with stops and are called "plug flutes" because of the deflector that fills almost the entire proximal end of the flute's bore except for the air duct (Izikowitz 1970: 351). In addition, these sacred flutes are made by fastening two halves together with beeswax to form an ellipsoidal barrel.

3. In my 2004 doctoral dissertation, I examined the relationship between the men's house and the sacred flute complex. The men's house is a social institution characterized by the community of all the adult men of a people, involving male initiation rites, the production of warriors, the promotion of secrets among men, and relationships with supernatural beings. This reinforces fraternal ties of male solidarity and creates an opposition in relation to women, who are ostensibly excluded from this community. The existence of the men's house becomes materially evident when there is a building which only men can enter. Therefore, the men's house, as a social institution, is nearly always accompanied by the building known as such, a center for meetings of the men's community. Nevertheless, it involves two ethnographic categories, covered in the literature by the same term, although usually there is a native denomination for the building. Not every society with a community of men has an exclusive space like a men's house, as is the case of the Tukano of the northwestern Amazon,

who also have a sacred flute complex. As a working hypothesis, I suggest that the sacred flute complex is a variation of this more general institution, which we can call the "men's house," marked specifically by the existence of musical instruments, by the prohibition against viewing for women and the fact that they must listen to its music (Piedade 1997), and a specific mythology. I believe that there are possible transformations in this model, being that a society that has sacred flutes may not have a men's house, as is the case of the Tukano mentioned above, or vice versa, as with the Bororo, who have a men's house but do not have sacred flutes.

4. See Karl von den Steinen's observations about the precariousness of the men's houses in the region before 1900 (Steinen 1940, 1942; Piedade 2004: 108–9).

5. I believe that the visual prohibition, as a limit to visibility, can be connected to other spheres of "cannot see," as is the case of the very invisibility of the spirits.

6. The apapaatai feasts involve curing disease and maintaining the health of the formerly ill (Mello 2005; Barcelos Neto 2004). I understand these rituals as a type of "payment of tribute" in the Wauja cosmic economy.

7. Due to the impressive parallels in the sacred flute complex in the Amazon region and in Melanesia, these two regions have been the object of intensive comparative studies for some time (Gregor and Tuzin 2001).

8. For a comparative view of the Amazonian Arawak-speaking peoples, see Hill and Santos-Granero 2002.

9. The motific sphere is the level of the smallest melodic units of musical text.

10. About the *aunaaki* (myth-history) of light, see Mello 1999. About the masks, especially the ritual of the Wauja masks, see Barcelos Neto 2004. Also note that the light that illuminates the primeval world can be interpreted as the fire that, in addition to illuminating the darkness, cooks the food: in the cosmogonic myth of the creation of light, the pre-Wauja had to cook their fish under their arms, through the heat of their bodies. The creation of light can be seen as the origin of cooking fire and therefore as a myth that essentially involves the advent of culture (Lévi-Strauss 1991). For the case of the Wauja, I call attention to the fact that that which led to the emergence of culture (light) at the same time unleashed the invisibility of the spirits.

11. I use the term *shamans* in the sense of "those who can see clearly." In fact, only a special class of Wauja shaman can, through a tobacco-induced trance, see the immediately present world of the apapaatai.

12. For a more detailed description of these and other Wauja instruments, see Mello 1999.

13. Among the Kamayurá, the instruments of this complex maintain a kinship relation, as shown by Menezes Bastos 1999: 223–32.

14. *Mutukutãi* is the name of an apapaatai and also of the globular gourd trumpet.

15. By factional relationship, I mean that there is a relationship between all these male (and female) owners that is valid at the level of the political internal groups (factions), not that they explicitly pertain to the same group, although their interests converge.

16. The idea of clairaudience (Schafer 2001) points to an exceptional ability to hear the sonorous dimension of the apapaatai.

17. As Menezes Bastos has shown, following the category *ipỳ*, "musical theme" (1999: 153).

18. For Roman Jakobsen's view of parallelism, particularly for its anthropological interest, see Fox 1977. In the history of western music, in the final Renaissance period and during all of Baroque, the idea of a musical poetics was in vogue in Europe. It is in this sense that I use the term *poetics*.

19. See Ruwet 1972.

References Cited

Barcelos Neto, Aristóteles. 2004. "Apapaatai: rituais de máscaras no Alto Xingu." PhD diss., USP.

Basso, Ellen B. 1985. *A Musical View of the Universe: Kalapalo Myth and Ritual Performances*. Philadelphia: University of Pennsylvania Press.

Chaumeil, J-P. 1997. "Les os, les flûtes, les morts: Mémoire et Traitement funéraire en Amazonie." *Journal de la Société des Américanistes*, no. 83: 83–110.

Coelho, Vera Penteado. 1988. "Informações sobre um instrumento musical dos índios Waurá." *Revista do Museu Paulista*, n.s., 33: 193–224.

Fox, James J. 1977. "Roman Jakobson and the Comparative Study of Parallelism." In *Roman Jakobson: Echoes of His Scholarship*, ed. C. H. Van Schooneveld and D. Armstrong, 59–90. Lisse: Peter de Ridder Press.

Franchetto, Bruna. 1996. "Mulheres entre os Kuikúro." *Revista Estudos Feministas* 4, no. 1: 35–54.

———. 2001. "Línguas e história no Alto Xingu." In *Os Povos do Alto Xingu: História e Cultura*, ed. Bruna Franchetto and Michael Ieckenberger, 111–56. Rio de Janeiro: Editora da UFRJ.

Gregor, Thomas. 1985. *Anxious Pleasures: The Sexual Lives of Amazonian People*. Chicago: University of Chicago Press.

Gregor, Thomas, and Donald Tuzin, eds. 2001. *Gender in Amazonia and Melanesia: An Exploration of the Comparative Method*. Berkeley: University of California Press.

Hill, Jonathan, and Fernando Santos-Granero, eds. 2002. *Comparative Ar-*

awakan Histories: Rethinking Language Family and Culture Area in Amazonia. Urbana: University of Illinois Press.

Izikowitz, Karl Gustav. 1970 [1935]. *Musical and Other Sound Instruments of the South American Indians: A Comparative Ethnographical Study*. Göteborg: Elanders Boktryckeri Aktiebolag; reprint, East Ardsley, UK: S. R.

Lévi-Strauss, Claude. 1991. *O Cru e o Cozido*. São Paulo: Brasiliense.

Mello, Maria Ignez C. 1999. "Música e Mito entre os Wauja do Alto Xingu." Master's thesis, PPGAS/UFSC.

——. 2005. "Iamurikuma: Música, Mito, e Ritual entre os Wauja do Alto Xingu." PhD diss., PPGAS/UFSC.

Menezes Bastos, Rafael José de. 1990. "A Festa da Jaguatirica: uma partitura crítico-interpretativa." PhD diss., USP.

——. 1995. "Indagação sobre os Kamayurá, o Alto Xingu e Outros Nomes e Coisas: Uma Etnologia da Sociedade Xinguara." *Anuário Antropológico* 94: 227–69.

——. 1999. *A Musicológica Kamayurá: para uma antropologia da comunicação no Alto-Xingu*. Florianópolis: Editora da UFSC.

Menget, Patrick. 1993. "Les Frontières de la Chefferie: Remarques sur le Système Politique du Haut Xingu (Brésil)." *La Remontée de l'Amazonie: Anthropologie et Histoire des Sociétés Amazoniennes. L'Homme* 126–28: 59–76.

Piedade, Acácio Tadeu de C. 1997. "Música Ye'pâ-masa: Por uma Antropologia da Música no Alto Rio Negro." Master's thesis, PPGAS/UFSC.

——. 1999. "Flautas e Trompetes Sagrados no Noroeste Amazônico: Sobre Gênero e Música do Jurupari." *Horizontes Antropológicos* 11: 93–118.

——. 2004. "O Canto do Kawoká: Música, Cosmologia, e Filosofia entre os Wauja do Alto Xingu." PhD diss., PPGAS/UFSC.

Ruwet, Nicolas. 1972. *Language, Musique, Poésie*. Paris: Éditions du Seuil.

Schafer, Murray. 2001. *A Afinação do Mundo*. São Paulo: Editora Unesp.

Steinen, Karl von den. 1940 [1894]. "Entre os aborígenes do Brasil Central." *Revista do Arquivo Municipal*, n. 34–52.

——. 1942 [1886]. *O Brasil Central*. São Paulo: Cia. Ed. Nacional.

10. *The Ritual of Iamurikuma and the Kawoká Flutes*

MARIA IGNEZ CRUZ MELLO

The Wauja and the Xinguano System

The *iamurikuma* ritual, practiced by the Wauja women, is understood as one side of a ritual-musical complex that allows humans to interact with *apapaatai* (spirits), which are considered to be both dangerous sources of disease and creative forces governing the fertility of nature (see Robin Wright's essay, this volume). The other side of the Wauja ritual-musical complex is the world of the *kawoká* flutes, which men play and which women are strictly prohibited from viewing (see Acácio Piedade's and Ulrike Prinz's essays, this volume). The Wauja consider music, through its formalization and the interplay of meanings and proportions, to be the central element of this ritual and to constitute the ideal medium for expressing affect. In this essay, I will discuss some of the various connections of this ritual with cosmology, gender relations, ethics, aesthetics, musicality, and politics, highlighting issues such as the need to control desire, the breaking of reciprocity, and the fundamental role of emotions in Wauja sociality.

In 2002, I found that nearly three hundred Wauja Indians lived in a circular village with eighteen houses, close to Piulaga Lake in the headwater region of the Xingu River, in Mato Grosso State, Brazil. The Wauja are one of ten indigenous groups that are part of what is known in the ethnological literature as the Xinguano peoples, those who inhabit the southern region of the Xingu Indigenous Reserve in Mato Grosso State. There are currently nearly three thousand Xinguano people, living within the reserve, a region where there is great linguistic diversity: the Wauja, Mehináku, and Yawalapití speak Arawakan languages; the Kamayurá and Awetí speak Tupían languages; the Kuikúru, Kalapalo, Matipú, and Nahukuwá speak Carib languages; and the Trumaí speak an isolated language. Despite this linguistic diversity, each group member speaks only his or her own language. Portuguese is spoken by a minority and is the language used to communicate with the world of the white people. Among the Xinguanos, not speaking the language of the other seems to be a question of honor, because even if they understand what the people of another group are saying, they continue speaking their own language, in order to avoid presenting a submissive position. This aspect of monolingualism is an important feature of sociality, since the degree to which the language is spoken is one of the strong diacritical signs of the multiple ethnic identities in the region (see Franchetto 2001). Even so, a discrete polylinguism is present among Upper Xinguanos due to the close kinship ties created by marital alliances between members of different language groups.

The Xinguano people maintain intertribal relations through rituals, material exchanges, and marriages. The relationship between the different groups points, in principle, to a culturally stable and apparently homogeneous region. Nevertheless, there is a logic of internal differentiation, the dynamic of which passes not only through language but also through ethnohistory and technical, musical, and iconographic specializations, articulating an intertribal system of exchanges. This logic includes solidarity and cooperation as well as disputes and conflicts.

The Wauja Rituals

This coexistence with difference stands out to the Xinguano researcher, particularly upon observing the intertribal rituals. It is through these rituals that various peoples of the region meet, fight, sing, and dance, and it is when they dialogue and relate. During these practices, however, a strong tension is expressed: the tension that comes from the need for a communicative acceptability within a framework that produces or accentuates difference and even divergence (Menezes Bastos 2001). During the intertribal rituals, despite the fact that one group does not speak the language of the other, the majority of the songs are sung in the ritual's language of origin. In this way it is legitimate to pronounce a language other than one's own, but only in the musical-ritual context. The large intertribal rituals, such as the *kwarýp*, *iamurikuma*, and *yawari*, constitute the space in which the rules and standards of Pan-Xinguano communicability and sociality are placed in action, promoting the constitution of difference and conflict at the heart of coexistence and solidarity. As noted by Basso (1985: 244), there is little space in Xinguano ritual for speaking. There is a certain economy of symbolic objects; those that exist, however, are highly elaborate. In this context, acts of musical composition and performance, by communicating and expressing profoundly felt ideas, are crucial to the very establishment of the ritual. For this reason, the study of the region's musical systems and rites constitutes an important element of the effort to understand the Xinguano world and the way of life of these peoples.[1]

In general, it can be said that one of the pillars of the Xinguano system is the interplay between similarity and difference. Beyond its meaning at the sociopolitical level, this interplay constitutes a fundamental axis in the cosmologies and in the arts of these groups: it is there, in fact, that difference is constructed in a musical-poetical plane. It is in this sense that Piedade, upon analyzing the ritual of the kawoká flutes, concludes that the "Wauja musical poetics involves a confection of difference, given fundamentally in the axis of time and existence, or that is, in temporality" (2004: 230). If in the Upper Xingu it can be said that the music institutes the ritual, which should be considered musical par excellence (Basso 1985), this is because, by handling proportions, repetitions, and variations, the music establishes the conflict at the same time that it keeps it under control.

In addition to the intertribal rituals, there are a series of intratribal rituals that are a preponderant part of Wauja daily life. The generic term in Wauja for all these practices is *naakai*, with which they refer to several rites, constituted by a set of particular events, each of which belongs to a symbolic complex that is sustained in myths, musical repertoires, dances, masks, and body paintings, that is, in a series of elements typical to each ritual. The ritual moments are considered by the Wauja as spaces ripe with expressivity, change in physical posture, in attitudes, behavior, and mood.[2]

This study is focused in greater detail on the feminine ritual of iamurikuma and its relationship with the male ritual of the kawoká flutes. There is a profound connection between these rituals, which constitute a single musical-mythic-ritual complex. In the intertribal context, these two rituals can be called "gender rituals," understood as rituals in which questions concerning gender relations are emphasized.[3] They also occur in intratribal versions, when only members of the group participate. It is important to highlight that the kawoká and iamurikuma rituals, principally in their intratribal versions, are related to shamanism and, in this way, to those illnesses caused by the action of the apapaatai beings.[4] The apapaatai have the ability to hear the thoughts and desires of humans and can detect dissatisfactions and desires not perceived by people. A state of dissatisfaction allows these beings to penetrate human bodies in an attempt to steal their souls. This condensed explanation serves here to present the metaphysical and ethical dimension in which the rituals are inserted and to cast some light on the Wauja concepts of illness and cure.

Note that there are various rituals promoted to cure diseases caused by the apapaatai. These rituals are mostly intratribal,[5] and their musical repertoire can be both masculine (vocal or instrumental), feminine (always vocal), or mixed, when men and women sing together. According to the native discourse, in reality, there are countless rituals for curing, given that disease is perceived as the result of the action of the apapaatai and these beings exist in an unknown number. The *iakapá*, or shaman, is responsible for discovering which apapaatai has caused the evil that afflicted the ill person, and from this diagnosis, a series of ritual procedures and behaviors will be adopted. For the Wauja, the field of possibilities is always open to the appearance of previously unknown apapaatai and the subsequent creation of new curing rites, despite observing the recurrence of a limited number of festivals.

I emphasize that the interest in ritual is also related to the sphere of social distinctions, because it is a sign of personal prestige to be able to pay for a ritual, sponsoring food for all the participants, and putting various people to work around this construction and the maintenance of distinction. Thus the Wauja ritual is based on the political sphere and has a regulatory role in cosmological terms, ruling in the world of curing and beauty, of ethics and aesthetics, as I will explain below.

The Myth of the Iamurikuma: The Breakdown of Reciprocity between Men and Women

In brief, it can be said that the iamurikuma is a ritual that updates the myth of the iamurikuma women, which describes the transformation of women into powerful and dangerous apapaatai called iamurikuma. In the myth, the women are transformed into these beings after being fooled by the men, who, instead of going on a collective fishing trip as they had said, make masks to transform themselves into various apapaatai, with the intention of killing their wives. In reprisal, these women eat certain fruits that make them "mad" and sing and dance at the center of the village—as normally only the men do. They paint and decorate themselves like the men, abandon the male children inside the large pillars of the village, and cross a great hole in the ground. When the men are alerted about this transformation, they come running to the village in order to dissuade them, but the women continue to sing and then go away. Women from other villages come to follow them on this journey, and they leave together singing until they reach the other side of the sky in *yuwejokupoho*, "the village of the dead," where they establish a village where only the iamurikuma live. A boy follows them to this location to find his girlfriend, but she warns him to go back to his village of origin. Upon returning, the youth tells about everything that he saw and teaches the others the music that he heard sung by the women in the "village of the dead."

The Ritual of Iamurikuma, Music, and Gender Relations

This ritual is conducted nearly annually, but does not have a fixed date, as do other festivals. It is an intertribal ritual—involving guests from other villages of the region—held only for women, except that the village chief often takes part by leading the songs. There are also intratribal versions of this festival, when only members of a single village participate. I accompanied an iamurikuma ritual from August to November 2001 in its intratribal version. Many evenings, a group of women would meet at the center of the village to sing and dance. Sometimes they sang all night. At times the men left for a collective fishing trip because of the festival, and at other times there was arguments between men and women, always tempered and within the limits imposed by local ethics. The motive for the festival was that there were five large wooden pillars in the village that had been made by women in an iamurikuma ritual some ten years earlier. They had made these objects for five men who were sick at that time because of the apapaatai iamurikuma. In 2001, the pillars were already old and rotting, which led the women to conduct a festival to burn them and plan to make new ones.

The theme of the feminine songs revolved around love relations, jealousy, envy, romance, and sex. Many songs made direct references to the myth of the origin of the festival. It was also common to see the women use this ritual space to complain about the attitudes of men through the songs especially composed by them. The women performed nearly two hundred songs, which were organized in four subgenres. In the analysis that follows, I will highlight the two subgenres that are most relevant to the present chapter, the iamurikuma itself (those songs that refer to the myth) and the *kawokakuma*, or songs referring to the melodies of the kawoká flutes.

I sought to understand the connection between the vocal music of the iamurikuma ritual and the instrumental music of the kawoká flutes, because the women maintained that the music of the iamurikuma is "flute music." Since they were prohibited from seeing the flutes, this affirmation did not appear to make sense at first. If a woman were to see these kawoká flutes while they were being played or even when idle, she would be raped by all the men in the village, regardless of whether she broke the rule on purpose or by accident. There is no record, however, that this has occurred in the past forty to fifty years. When the women say that their songs are "flute music," they are not referring to something generic, as if everything that they sang could be "flute music." There are songs, even in the iamurikuma ritual, that are not considered "flute music." In this way, the women are referring to a specific set of songs, all considered kawokakuma, but subdivided according to a typology that maintains a clear relationship with the music of the flutes. These different types of songs follow regulations in relation to typology and chronology, which determine that certain songs can only be executed in certain spaces (the center of the village, inside the houses, etc.) and at specific times of the day. Kalupuku, the principal singer, described for me how she had learned a new song through a dream and that, remembering it upon waking, recognized this new music as being "inside" *sapalá*.[6] It was, therefore, a new song to be included in a sapalá suite. Upon expressing this idea of inclusion, of belonging, and therefore of identity between different songs, Kalupuku makes it clear that she is aware of the subtleties that distinguish one suite from another, which makes sapalá different from the *mututute*, for example.

This description is even more significant if we observe that it presents one of the widely accepted compositional processes: the music comes from dreams.[7] It is said that anyone can dream a new song, but only the masters of music, the *apaiwekeho*, have the ability to memorize it. This information from Kalupuku complexifies a bit more the ritual cycle of songs in which meanings of the pieces of kawoká and of kawokakuma are inserted, because by performing the songs of the kawokakuma in the ritual of iamurikuma, the words to the song aggregate another layer of meaning to the instrumental repertoire of the flutes. This meaning becomes part of the instrumental music and emerges when the men play them. Nevertheless, the fact that the women also compose, bringing new songs to the repertoire, causes this circle to open for both men and women in terms of musical production.

There are two ways in which Wauja women's songs influence the meaning of men's flute melodies. First, Wauja women may learn the songs with the master of flutes. They then create poems, or verbal texts, to sing to the originally instrumental pieces. The meaning of these songs is kept when the piece is played as instrumental flute music. And second, women can dream new songs that will be sung by women and learned by the men, and then they may be played as instrumental flute music in a ritual of kawoká flutes.

The music and dance, through the song of women, are those elements that mark the densest moments of the rite. The choreographic movement varies according to the number of participants, the disposition of the dancers, and their movement along the perimeter of the village. These variables are related to the musical repertoire, thought of here as a script, which, in turn, should adapt to the periods of day (morning, afternoon, night, and early morning) and the specific moments of the rite, such as the men's fishing trip, the opening of the ritual, or its closing. There are different choreographic dispositions during the ritual that point to moments with distinct motivations, thus "framing" behaviors that can range from play to aggression. The ideas that Bateson develops in his theory about play frames help us consider the groups of messages that are in play in each of the contexts during the ritual. There is a background that is given by the difference between men and women, a dispute over space, present in the majority of the declarations from the boys and in the behavior of the girls. The boys constantly say, "Iamurikuma aitsa awojopai," loosely translated as "iamurikuma isn't cool." "Iamurikuma apokapai, peietepei," "iamurikuma is crazy, mean," say the older ones. The women appear indifferent to the provocations, always remaining arrogant and distant, except for the moments in which they resolve, as a group, to attack the men. They can hit, scratch, pinch, or attack sexually, going to their hammocks, also as a group. Bateson calls attention to the fact that there is no clear demarcation between the play, the bluff, and the threat: "Together they form a single and indivisible complex of phenomenon" (1998: 61). It is, however, necessary to adopt the correct frame to not go beyond the objectives.

Part of the musical repertoire of this group, which is classified here as iamurikuma, is like a script for the ritual, based on the narrative of the myth (aunaki). Each song narrates a moment of the myth and can be repeated on different days, which evokes the nonlinearity of the ritual. The nonlinear ordering of performances in Wauja women's iamurikuma riuals is similar to what Menezes Bastos (1990) detected in the yawari as a compression and distention of time. He uses the image of accordion's bellows to evoke the alternation between moments of total withdrawal (thought of as densifications) and of the complete distention of the ritual events. If a part of the musical repertoire is linked to a myth, the other, called kawokakuma, is not; it is linked to passions and is a sonorous bridge between the iamurikuma and the kawoká. These songs, kawokakuma, were more deeply analyzed in my dissertation (Mello 2005). An analysis of a portion of this repertoire found that it is anchored to complex musical operations that demand a high degree of knowledge by the women singers, principally of the central singer-composer.

To achieve the musical classifications presented in the thesis, it was necessary to listen to approximately seventy hours of recordings. From these recordings nearly two hundred songs were classified as belonging to specific musical genres. To reach these subdivisions, it was necessary to make a preliminary transcription of the entire group of pieces and conduct a preanalysis that would help in this initial classification. Unlike the repertoire of the kawoká flutes, always executed in blocks of named suites, the songs of the kawokakuma are sung by alternating songs of different styles. In addition, these songs are interlaced with songs that belong to the iamurikuma. The conclusion that these repertoires consist of different genres, iamurikuma and kawokakuma, can only be reached through such careful listening and transcription. At times, the words of the songs assisted in the identification; at other times, however, in view of the absence of words, it depended solely and exclusively on a careful listening.

In the songs of the kawokakuma, each piece consists of a set of themes and motifs. A motif can have few or many notes, in which case it can be considered a phrase. Depending on the piece, each motif can be short, with few notes, or not so short, nearly a phrase, and have one or more variations each. The variations are understood as applications of the fundamental principles of differentiation in the interior of the motifs and may include operations such as transposition, a small alteration of interval or rhythm at the beginning or end of the motif, or an addition or exclusion of a note. Variations in groups of motifs, understood as phrases that constitute the themes, can be thought of as transformations that occur by mechanisms of inclusion and exclusion of motifs or through the variations in their constituent motifs. The

Aunumana, aunumana	Come here, come here
Patuwato Ukaruwã	Bring (your wife) Ukaruwã
Aunumana, aunumana	Come here, come here
Patuwato Ukaruwã	Bring (your wife) Ukaruwã
Maka aunupa okanato	So we can see her mouth
Itsapai Tupatu okanatu	It looks like the mouth of the *tupatu* (a type of fish)
Ukaruwã	Ukaruwã

TABLE 1. Words to the Song and Its Translation.

difference between one variation and a new motif is the structural response of the sequence of notes organized in the interior of the piece. The motifs (indicated in the transcriptions as a, b, c, etc.), however, are the constitutive parts of the themes. I call them Ⓐ and Ⓑ. There is also a phrase, called in the analysis Ⓚ, which usually rises at the beginning of the pieces, as in the separation of the themes Ⓐ and Ⓑ and even at the end, always corresponding to the tonal center of the songs.

Table 1 is an example of a song of kawokakuma with its respective text and an explanation of its meaning. Note that these explanations are necessary for the Wauja themselves, because the lyrics are often not understandable without the respective explanation by the singers.

Kalupuku, the lead singer, explained the song: "There was a Mehinaku man called Ukaruwã who married a women named Mukura. Perhaps she was a Matipú Indian. The Mehinaku women made a song for this woman about her mouth because when she smiled, her mouth was crooked, like that of the *tupatu*, a fish that has a crooked mouth placed on the side. With this music they want to say, 'Ukaruwa, bring your wife here, so we can see her crooked mouth.'"

The emphasis on the Ⓑ (theme Ⓑ with words added) is what

27. Analytical transcription of the song. By Maria Ignez Cruz Mello.

calls the most attention to this song, because it is repeated various times. There are operations here that were observed in other songs, precisely the fact that it begins with the theme B, that appears twice before A. In B note that (f) is in close dialog with (e), which has a question and response type of alternation. It is probable that the descending interval, which reaches *fa*, carries this characteristic, pointing to the dialogical character between the motifs. The theme A is encompassed in B, and therefore the appearance of A is not surprising. After singing K, A, and once again K K, a large section of B^L begins in which it will be presented four times, given that between the second and third time, A, K, A, K reappear. In this piece, a preponderance of B and B^L is evident, which can be considered a mark of this

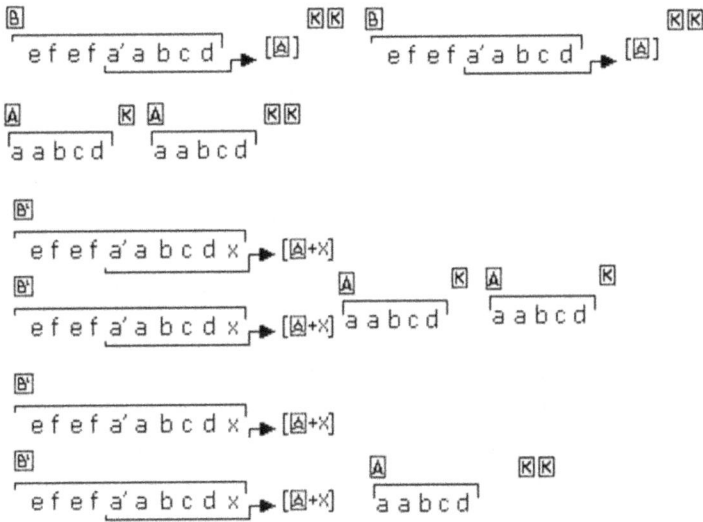

28. Analytic chart of the sequence of motifs and phrases. By Maria Ignez Cruz Mello.

feminine face of the musical genre *kawokakuma-kawoka*. In addition, the words are highlighted here by their humor: the Mehináku women ridicule a Matipú women, who has a "crooked mouth" when she smiles: this is a motif about a physical defect. The singers address this woman's husband, a Mehináku man who married a woman from another group, a fact that is always a reason for reactions of this type, and that, deep down, demonstrates the collective jealousy provoked by interethnic marriages.

In sum, the relation between the themes A and B is dialogical and dialectical. The first theme constitutes the basic material of the piece and the second configures an elaboration of this material in a superior layer (in terms of pitch), generally reaching the highest note on the scale. In this type of transposition, there are often transformations that vary from piece to piece. Another fact observed is the encompassing of A for B: the antithesis elaborates the thesis in such a way as to include it in its termination, at times completely. Also note that the motif K functions as an anchor, indicator, and reinforcement of the tonal center, a vignette of separation between themes and songs. Another important point is the theme of $\boxed{\text{B}^{\flat}}$, which is the theme $\boxed{\text{B}}$ with words added.

Of the musical analyses, various fundamental operations are highlighted in the motific realm of the kawokakuma music: thetic variation, suffixal variation, fusion, neighboring tone type, interplay alternating major and minor thirds, juxtaposed motif of quotation, addition, exclusion, rhythmic prolongment, motif of dissolution, and motif of return. Note the importance of the terminations of motifs, phrases, and themes as well as the *encompassing* of the theme $\boxed{\text{A}}$ by the theme $\boxed{\text{B}}$. In the realm of the words, connections are found between the song, the myth, and the passions, with some recurring themes appearing, such as that of physical defect, in which the singer exposes in the words of the song any defect of the person that she wants to touch through the song. In the relationship between words and music, important factors are noted such as the inversion of the text and the rhythmic flexibility. The distribution of all these compositional operations accentuates the idea that the music of the iamurikuma ritual constitutes not one but two musical genres, iamurikuma and kawokakuma, with the latter being the feminine side of a supergenre, the other side of which is the music of the kawoká flute ritual (see text by Piedade in this volume). A comparative study of the compositional processes of the male and female repertoires would clearly be a stimulating route for future work.

Final Considerations

Men and women use the tactic of mutually provoking each other through song, principally inciting the sentiment of *uki*, "jealousy-envy," and inserting a third person into the situation described by the lyrics. Many kawokakuma songs seek to provoke uki in men or in women who are rivals with the singers. It is through the musical-poetic creation that the conflicts aroused by feelings such as uki are handled. Their positivity or negativity, however, is a question of degree: all the strategies that they have to deal with this feeling—play, myths, and specific rites—are part of the search for an intermediary point in a continuum between an excess and absence of uki.[8] According to the Wauja, jealousy and envy are not something toward which indifference or complete rejection should be shown, unlike feelings such as *kamusixiapa* (anger or hate), which should be quickly placated.[9] To the contrary, uki should be *cultivated*, and one should learn to live with it from an early age. Uki is the spark that incites relationships. As one informant told me, "It's like the pepper that burns, but is good," without which the food would be flat. The merit of knowing how to deal with these feelings is in the right degree of control in provoking and accepting provocations, in knowing the right moment for a reprisal, and in not provoking beyond an acceptable limit. During the play, an evaluation is made of how much the man and woman can take the provocation without reprisal, but a good response at the right time is also expected and even appreciated. It is seen that, through the entire aesthetic-ritual elaboration, detected from the detailed treatment in the motific construction of the songs, passing through the transfer of the kawokakuma songs from one sexual gender to another, and by elaborating on the facts of everyday life that are inserted in the molds of the songs, this entire process only arises during the ritual performance, which winds up making the myth and meaning of the existential questions concrete. The entire ritual creation deals with the demarcation of limits, of establishing proportions, of measuring doses, creating differences, building borders, and creating the human space of agency in the world. This space is established in the ritual where the music is the "statement" that becomes "deed."

Notes

1. In this sense, since the end of the 1970s, studies of the music of the indigenous peoples of the South American lowlands have revealed musical systems and cosmologies that are densely elaborate, with works such as that of Aytai

(1985), Menezes Bastos (1990, 1999), Beaudet (1983, 1997), Fuks (1989), Smith (1977), Travassos (1984), Seeger (1987), Hill (1992, 1993), Ermel (1988), Estival (1994), and Olsen (1996), which respectively analyze the music among the Xavante, Kamayurá, Waiãpi (Beaudet studies on the Guiana Francesa side and Fuks on the Brazilian), Amuesha, Kayabi, Suyá, Wakuénai, Cinta-Larga, Assuriní and Arara, and Warao. Since the late 1990s, there has been growth in this line of study in Brazilian universities, through work such as that of Bueno da Silva (1997) about the music of the Kulina (in Alto Purús); Piedade (1997), about the Tukano; my work about Wauja music (Mello 1999, 2005); Cunha (1999), among the Pankararú; Montardo (2002), about Guarani music; Werlang (2001), about the Marubo; and Piedade (2004), about the kawoká flute music among the Wauja.

2. Peirano (2001: 26) presents a synthesis of the anthropological perspectives that deal with ritual today and uses concepts from Tambiah to escape the rigidity of definitions that impede us from perceiving that the "performative character of the ritual is implied in the relation between form and content which, in turn, is contained in the cosmology." According to Tambiah (1985), ritual is a culturally constructed system of symbolic communication, composed of special events, which are more formalized, redundant, and condensed than those of daily life. He maintains that the effectiveness of the ritual stems from three factors: (1) to say something in the ritual performance means effectively to do something, that is, the statement is a deed (here he is inspired by the ideas of Austin); (2) rituals use various means of communication through which the participants experience the events in an intense manner; and (3) rituals include a profusion of indexable values linked or inferred by the actors during the ritual.

3. Sticking here with this preliminary definition, the question of ritual specifically dedicated to the opposition or complementarity of the sexes receives considerable attention in the anthropological literature of the Amazon and Melanesia (see McCallum 2001; Gregor and Tuzin 2001; Herdt 1982), at times being seen as a war of the sexes (Gregor 1985), as a result of sexual antagonism (Hugh-Jones 1979), as fertility cults (Hill 2001), as a derivation of the deepest issue of maternity (Biersack 2001), or even as an expression of factors of consanguinity and affinity (Descola 2001). I also recall that the very emphasis on the issue of gender can be seen as a result of a western bias (cf. Overing 1986; Piedade 2004 presents a similar position). I emphasize that I understand the iamurikuma-kawoká complex to be simultaneously gender and musical rituals (cf. Basso 1985).

4. The Wauja distinguish the diseases caused by the apapaatai from what they call "white people diseases," which are caused by other processes and can be cured with medicine "from the white man," such as the flu, measles, leish-

maniosis, malaria, etc. This distinction is common among the Xinguanos (see Menezes Bastos 1999).

5. There are some exceptions, as in the ritual of the *Payemeramaraka* (music of the community of the shamans) described by Menezes Bastos (1984–85). On one occasion this researcher observed shamans of various ethnicities gathered in the Yawalapití village to promote the cure of a Kamayurá shaman who lived there and who was very ill.

6. All the kawokakuma songs as well as the melodies of kawoká flutes have a similar native classification, corresponding to groups of songs that have thematic coherence and form named units, such as *kisoagakipitsana, sapalá, mututute*, and others that Piedade (2004) identifies as suites (cf. Menezes Bastos 1990).

7. The Gê-speaking Xavante of Central Brazil also compose songs in dreams. Young men undergoing a prolonged period of initiation into adulthood and living in a special "bachelor's hut" in the center of the village plaza must compose a new song of the genre called *dan'ore* and teach it to their age mates. The new song is then performed in public in the transitional space between the bachelor's hut and the semicircle of domestic family households around the periphery of the village (Graham 1986, 1994).

8. See in Mello 2005 the explanation about the *Pequi* ritual. This festival revolves around disputes between men and women, during which they play games and provoke one another musically.

9. The root of this word, *usixa*, means "to burn."

References Cited

Aytai, Desiderio. 1985. *O Mundo Sonoro Xavante*. São Paulo: USP.

Basso, Ellen. 1985. *A Musical View of the Universe: Kalapalo Myth and Ritual Performances*. Philadelphia: University of Pennsylvania Press.

Bateson, Gregory. 1998 [1972]. "Uma teoria sobre brincadeira e fantasia." In *Sociolingüística interacional: antropologia, lingüística, e sociologia em análise do discurso*, ed. Branca T. Ribeiro and Pedro Garcez. Porto Alegre: Editora AGE.

Beaudet, Jean-Michel. 1983. "Les Orchestres de clarinettes Tule des Waiãpi du Haut-Oiapok." PhD diss., Université de Paris X.

———. 1997. *Souffles d' Amazonie: Les Orchestres "Tule" des Wayãpi*. Nanterre: Société d' Ethnologie (Collection de la Société Française d'Ethnomusicologie, III).

Biersack, Aletta. 2001. "Reproducing Inequality: The Gender Politics of Male Cults in the Papua New Guinea Highlands and Amazonia." In *Gender in Amazonia and Melanesia: An Exploration of the Comparative Method*, ed. T. Gregor and D. Tuzin, 69–90. Berkeley: University of California Press.

Bueno da Silva, Domingos A. 1997. "Música e Pessoalidade: por uma Antropologia da Música entre os Kulina do Alto Purús." Master's thesis, UFSC.

Cunha, Maximiliano W. Carneiro. 1999. "A Música Encantada Pankararu." Master's thesis, Universidade Federal de Pernambuco.

Descola, Phillipe. 2001. "The Genders of Gender: Local Models and Global Paradigms in the Comparison of Amazonia and Melanesia." In *Gender in Amazonia and Melanesia: An Exploration of the Comparative Method*, ed. T. Gregor and D. Tuzin, 91–114. Berkeley: University of California Press.

Ermel, Priscilla Barrak. 1988. "O Sentido Mítico do Som: Ressonâncias Estéticas da Música Tribal dos Índios Cinta-larga." Master's thesis, São Paulo PUC.

Estival, Jean-Pierre. 1994. "Musiques Instrumentales du Moyen Xingu et de l'Iriri (Brésil): Tule Asurini et Musique Rituelle Arara." 2 vols. PhD diss., Université de Paris X.

Franchetto, Bruna. 2001. "Línguas e História no Alto Xingu." In *Os Povos do Alto Xingu: história e cultura*, ed. B. Franchetto and M. Heckenberger, 111–56. Rio de Janeiro: Editora UFRJ.

Fuks, Victor. 1989. "Demonstration of Multiple Relationships between Music and Culture of the Waiapi Indians of Brazil." PhD diss., Indiana University.

Graham, Laura. 1986. "Three Modes of Shavante Vocal Expression: Wailing, Collective Singing, and Political Oratory." In *Native South American Discourse*, ed. Joel Sherzer and Greg Urban, 83–118. The Hague: Mouton de Gruyter.

———. 1994. *Performing Dreams*. Austin: University of Texas Press.

Gregor, Thomas. 1985. *Anxious Pleasures: The Sexual Lives of Amazonian People*. Chicago: University of Chicago Press.

Gregor, Thomas, and Donald Tuzin, eds. 2001. *Gender in Amazonia and Melanesia: An Exploration of the Comparative Method*. Berkeley: University of California Press.

Herdt, Gilbert H., ed. 1982. *Rituals of Manhood: Male Initiation in Papua, New Guinea*. Berkeley: University of California Press.

Hill, Jonathan, ed. 1992. "A Musical Aesthetic of Ritual Curing in the Northwest Amazon." In *Portals of Power: Shamanism in South America*, ed. E. J. Langdon and G. Baer, 175–210. Albuquerque: University of New Mexico Press.

———. 1993. *Keepers of the Sacred Chants: The Poetics of Ritual Power in an Amazonian Society*. Tucson: University of Arizona Press.

———. 2001. "The Variety of Fertility Cultism in Amazonia: A Closer Look at Gender Symbolism in Northwestern Amazonia." In *Gender in Amazonia and Melanesia: An Exploration of the Comparative Method*, ed. T. Gregor and D. Tuzin, 45–68. Berkeley: University of California Press.

Hugh-Jones, Stephen. 1979. *The Palm and the Pleiades: Initiation and Cosmology in Northwest Amazonia*. Cambridge: Cambridge University Press.

McCallum, Cecilia. 2001. *Gender and Sociality in Amazonia: How Real People Are Made*. Oxford: Berg.

Mello, Maria Ignez C. 1999. "Música e Mito entre os Wauja do Alto Xingu." Master's thesis, PPGAS/UFSC. Available at www.musa.ufsc.br.

———. 2005. "Iamurikuma: Música e Mito e Ritual entre os Wauja do Alto Xingu." PhD diss., PPGAS/UFSC. Available at www.musa.ufsc.br.

Menezes Bastos, Rafael José de. 1984–85. "O 'Payemeramaraka' Kamayurá: Uma Contribuição à Etnografia do Xamanismo no Alto Xingu." *Revista de Antropologia* 27-28: 139–77.

———. 1990. "A Festa da Jaguatirica : uma partitura crítico-interpretativa." PhD diss., USP.

———. 1999 [1978]. *A Musicológica Kamayurá: para uma antropologia da comunicação no Alto-Xingu*. Florianópolis: Editora da UFSC.

———. 2001. "Ritual, história, e política no Alto Xingu: observações a partir dos Kamayrá e do estudo da festa da jaguatirica." In *Povos Indígenas do Alto Xingu*, ed. B. Franchetto and M. Heckenberger, 335–57. Rio de Janeiro: Editora UFRJ.

Montardo, Deise Lucy. 2002. "Através do mbaraka: música e xamanismo Guarani." PhD diss., University of São Paulo.

Olsen, Dale A. 1996. *Music of the Warao of Venezuela: Song People of the Rain Forest*. Gainesville: University Press of Florida.

Overing, Joanna. 1986. "Men Control Women? The 'Catch 22' in the Analysis of Gender." *International Journal of Moral and Social Studies* 1, no. 2.

Peirano, Marisa. 2001. "A Análise antropológica de rituais." In her *Dito e Feito*, 17–40. Rio de Janeiro: Relume Dumará.

Piedade, Acácio Tadeu de C. 1997. "Música Ye'pâ-masa: Por uma Antropologia da Música no Alto Rio Negro." Master's thesis, UFSC. Available at www.musa.ufsc.br.

———. 2004. "O Canto do Kawoká: música, cosmologia e filosofia entre os Wauja do Alto Xingu." PhD diss., PPGAS/UFSC. Available at www.musa.ufsc.br.

Seeger, Anthony. 1987. *Why Suyá Sing: A Musical Anthropology of an Amazonian People*. Cambridge: Cambridge University Press.

Smith, Richard Chase. 1977. "Deliverance from Chaos for a Song: A Social and

a Religious Interpretation of the Ritual Performance of Amuesha Music."
PhD diss., Cornell University.

Tambiah, S. J. 1985. *Culture, Thought, and Social Action: Anthropological Perspective*. Cambridge: Harvard University Press.

Travassos, Elizabeth. 1984. "Xamanismo e Música entre os Kayabi." Master's thesis, Museu Nacional–UFRJ.

Werlang, Guilherme. 2001. "Emerging Peoples: Marubo Myth-Chants." PhD diss., University of St. Andrews.

11. Spirits, Ritual Staging, and the Transformative Power of Music in the Upper Xingu Region

ULRIKE PRINZ

This essay aims to develop a better comprehension of the "complex of the secret flutes" in the Upper Xingu region by highlighting their ritual counterpart, the women's music and dance, *iamurikuma* (cf. Menezes Bastos, this volume). The male ritual complex has gained much attention because of its gender exclusivity and the cruel menace of gang rape for women who violate the prohibition against seeing the "secret flutes." This practice is accompanied by myths in which women are said to have been the original owners of the flutes. This has led to some speculations concerning "antagonistic" gender relations in the Upper Xingu region.

The spatial and social segregation of the sexes is common not only in Upper Xingu but also throughout Lowland South America. Gender differences are expressed in the division of the village into separate women's and men's areas as well as the division of labor and social roles. Because the use of aerophones is of special importance for the Arawak-speaking societies of Amazonia (see Wright, this volume), the Arawak-speaking Wauja, Mehináku, and Yawalapití of the Upper Xingu present an ideal field site where the complementary nature of two gendered rituals can still be observed.

Since the beginning of the scientific investigation of Lowland South America, the so-called trumpet cult has taken center stage.[1] The female ritual counterpart, however, remained unknown until the 1970s.[2] Its scientific investigation starts in the 1980s with the works of Ellen Basso (1985) and Aurore Monod Becquelin (1982, 1987), but until recently the significance of the ritual has been quite underestimated. Recent studies (e.g., Mello 1999, 2005; Prinz 1999, 2002) have demonstrated the importance of female ritual and musical traditions and should help to bring about a more balanced perspective of the ritual complex as a whole in the Upper Xingu region. Another recent study (Piedade 2004) has provided a detailed ethnographic documentation and analysis of the music of *kawoká*,[3] the "sacred flutes" of the Arawak-speaking Waujá village, for ethnographic detail (see Mello and Piedade, this volume).

In this essay, I will develop an interpretation of the entire ritual complex by taking into account not only the complementarity and opposition of ritual practices but also the transformative power of ritual and music itself. The playing of the men's "sacred flutes" as well as the women's iamurikuma ritual represent inversions of gender roles, and they both play with alterity that is described not only by the other sex but also by the spirit conditions. This is because during both male and female performances, the participants get into a serious and dangerous play with the *apapaatai*, the powerful mythical beings and producers of uncontrolled transformations and diseases.

For a better understanding of the ritual complex, it is necessary to take a look at the ritual process itself: what occurs when women are acting like men, and what happens to the flute player while playing the music? How does the world of the spirits interrelate with the gender groups, what does it mean for the individual person, and, in a supposed "gang rape," who will be acting, ghosts or men?

In the Mehináku Village "Ukayumai"

In 2000, I had the opportunity to investigate gendered rituals in the village of Ukayumai. The iamurikuma feast had been canceled shortly before my arrival, replaced by the *pühükã*, the piercing of the ears for the boys. After the initiation ritual, Mehináku women, being aware of my curiosity about iamurikuma, sang and danced for me on two occasions. Each time, Mehináku men seemed uncomfortable with the representations and perhaps also with the importance women were gaining with their dancing. So they disturbed the women's dancing and singing, objecting that they were either getting too close to the "house of the spirits" (*casa do bicho*) or that someone in the village was seriously ill.

I was able to attend another ritual belonging to the context of "gender quarrel" rituals: the manioc feast. It includes the manufacturing of manioc sticks and scoops for turning over the *beiju* pancakes. Like the iamurikuma ritual, the manioc feast implicates repeated phases of men and women arguing (*xingar*) about their mutual sexual deficiencies.

About Iamurikuma

The Arawak-speaking villages of Upper Xingu are considered to be the "inventors" of the iamurikuma ritual.[4] The term for the "hyper-woman," *iamuri-kuma-lu*, originates from an Arawak language: *iamuri* means water spirit, the syllable *kuma* modifies the name designating the great and/or supernatural (Viveiros de Castro 1987b: 45ff.), and the syllable *lu* stands for the female form of the spirit.

Iamurikuma is the name of a powerful apapaatai spirit that appears as a woman, causes serious disease, and can bring death. It attacks in the forest or near the water. Etienne Samaine describes iamurikuma as a beautiful dancing woman who provokes an intensively sore throat. For curing, a little piece of wood (about 2 cm long) must be painted red (1991: 226).

A iamurikuma spirit can make its presence known at any time by "catching" a person and provoking a serious corporeal crisis. The shaman recognizes the spirit causing the illness and initiates a curing process. Ritual staging requires women to come together at the village center, and the invoking of *iamurikuma-lu* spirits is part of this curing process. The former patient has to feed the spirit, which means that s/he has to "pay" the women, by dancing. After the performance, s/he takes some spicy fish soup and manioc bread to the center, since "iamurikuma likes to eat." This procedure is repeated until the spirit has "eaten enough" or until women "are ashamed to admit more food from the sponsoring person" (Samain 1991: 226).

The iamurikuma and the *kawoká* ritual are different healing rituals. This process, which is also known as the "taming" of the spirit, will create a kind of tight, almost amicable bond between the sponsor and spirit. The apapaatai are thus part of a twofold and ambiguous process conveying both the illness and the healing process.

On closer examination, the ritual complex can be seen to contain two distinct mythic categories. Both have been recorded by the Villas Boas brothers.[5] One tells of the coming into existence of the iamurikuma women, and the other accounts for the finding of kawoká's "speech" by men. Both of these mythic categories are closely connected, although the related spirits are evoked differently, a fact that is also reflected in the women's singing and dancing.

Female Musical Traditions

While researching female musical traditions, we found several distinct music traditions that had not been previously reported in published ethnographic sources.[6] Maria Ignez Cruz Mello amplifies this finding with her substantial fieldwork carried out one year later in the neighboring Wauja village.[7]

Besides the iamurikuma tradition, Arawak-speaking villages also keep alive the tradition of *tünexakumã*, the "big woman." Both musical representations are related to the women's former ownership of the flutes, although they have different songs (poetry and melody) and dance steps. The melodies of tünexakumã that Mello refers to as *kawokakuma* are also known as *i-haha*, and they directly relate to the music of the kawoká flutes (Mello 2005: 13, 43). Parita, a player of kawoká flute music, affirmed that kawoká melodies originated from and are the answer to the women's (i-haha) songs. While dancing, the women are rhythmically moving their folded hands in front of their bellies.

Parita also affirmed that iamurikuma had a different melody. At the "real" iamurikuma dance, women are brandishing an invisible arrow above their heads. The image of the arrow-swaying woman arouses the image of a disease-bringing apapaatai. When women are performing the "real" iamurikuma dance and songs, "men are not respected," and they run the danger of being mistreated.

"Gender War" in Literature

Interpretations of the "flute complex" and rituals of "gender war" have passed through different conceptualizations. Since Margaret Mead's 1962 writings, feminist anthropologists have questioned "natural" sex roles and provided empirical arguments in favor of gender equity (Di Leonardo 1997: 5ff.). Mead's writings incited studies in the field of sexual antagonism and made it a favorite model of North American anthropology. Coming from Oceanian studies, the concept had been transferred to Lowland South America by Robert Murphy and applied to the Xingu area by Thomas Gregor, where the ritual expression of gender quarrels with its equivalent in analogous myths was taken as an indication of deeply rooted gender conflicts. Both concepts were relevant to the Xingu area, where the topic of female repression and the idea of gender antagonism both figure prominently in scholarly literature.

In the 1980s, feminist efforts at correcting male "bias" and giving proof to the concept of complementarity provoked a gradual reprieve from the antagonism concept and eventually provided the groundwork for a turn to questions of actual research in Amazonian ethnography. For the Xingu area, Aurore Monod Becquelin (1982) and Ellen Basso (1985) placed emphasis on the complementary structures of the gendered rituals, describing harmonious life instead of "gender war." Both researchers especially point to the communicative role of the music in the context of ritual transformation. Monod Becquelin focused on the central theme of female transformation during the iamurikuma ritual, paying relatively little attention to the openly acted out aggressions of the women toward the men. Ellen Basso explored how personal emotions came to their extremes during the transformation. Her emphasis was placed on the ritual process, taking the spirit representations as a kind of projection that need to be acted out during ritual events, without referring directly to everyday life (Basso 1985: 239).[8] Nonetheless, the contradiction of Xinguano peaceful and harmonized everyday life with the sexualized violence during both rituals (the menace of gang rape at the flute ritual and assaults against men during iamurikuma ritual) have yet to receive a satisfactory explanation. In some ways, the "gender wars" live on in the literature as a dichotomy between female British Amazonian studies of love and franco-tupi masculine Amazonian studies of war and predation.[9] The former concentrates on the construction of "sociability" and the "ethos" of everyday life,[10] whereas the latter focuses on cosmology and the dynamics of predation.[11]

Difference and Violence

With the contributions of Cecilia McCallum (1994) and Bruna Franchetto (1999), the discussion of gender and violence regained a new impulse in the 1990s. Besides the model of communication and complementarity, McCallum brings up a question which had been neglected to some extent in the discussions of the 1980s: the merging of sexuality and violence, discussing the delicate question of ritual "gang rape" a phenomenon, that is not restricted to the area of Upper Xingu (Quinn 1977; Jackson 1992).

Due to McCallum, it has been understood that male and female rituals are not so much about sexual hierarchy, as Thomas Gregor (1985) and Joan Bamberger (1974) have argued; rather, the rituals are about constructing gender separateness, providing distance between spirits and humans on the one hand and between men and women on the other (McCallum 1994: 108).[12] McCallum is trying to understand the merging of sexuality and violence in Amazonian myth and everyday life.

Looking at the Xingu, it can be seen how Kauka and iamuri-kuma rituals transfer a potentially excessive and violent sexuality into a secure and socially acceptable status. During the ritual, the productive power of the spirits is extremely dangerous and violent (McCallum 1994: 108). In these ritual performances, it can come to an "enraged" contact between the performers. "The sight of women and the close proximity of men stimulate such untimely and vicious passions in the performers, who act out physically their emotions upon the unfortunate bodies and, sometimes, the making of monstrous spirit children" (McCallum 1994: 102).

McCallum interprets gendered rituals as a process of the "taming" of the spirits. The menace of gang rape on the part of the men can be understood as a measure of precaution to escape the fury of the spirits. "Gang rape is many things: what it is not is a manifestation of a supposed universal male desire to overpower and humiliate women" (McCallum 1994: 110). She reveals this as a western construct of naturalizing sexuality.

McCallum makes clear that it is not male anxiety about women that triggers gang rape, like Gregor assumes, but rather the fury of the flute spirit. However, one question is without reply: what does enrage the spirit? In my opinion, the rage of the spirit cannot be reduced to the level of individual sickness. But it must be seen in the context of the gender-related "agencies" and the process of transformation.

In a reply to McCallum, Bruna Franchetto (1999: 218) discards the concept of gender complementarity in support of irreducible gender antagonism. However, the main divisive arguments between Franchetto and McCallum lie not in the "hard facts" of Xingu ethnography but in the understanding of the ritual process.

McCallum, for example, evokes the "real power" of ritual and their transforming forces (1994: 91), while Franchetto does not concede any importance to the ritual powers. The hyper-world of the spirits for her seems to have no relevance in everyday life. The mythical anti-world of iamurikuma-lu renews itself during the ritual process but does not have any consequences at a personal level. Even though iamurikuma assimilates the theme of difference and takes it to the limit, women fail because of the "biologic imperatives" that inevitably lead to female subordination (Franchetto 1999: 218).

The Power of Ritual

Gaps such as those between the positions of McCallum and Franchetto concerning different evaluations of the ritual level and its relation to everyday life are quite common. One party assumes that symbolic and ritual representation has little to do with actual complementary gender relations (McCallum 1994; Jackson 1992), whereas the other party regards ritual as symbolic expression of a gender ratio of superficial harmony, which is symbolic (Murphy and Murphy 1980) or in fact dominated by men (Gregor 1985; Franchetto 1999).

The dilemma lies in the absence of a coherent framework that accounts for the fact that opposition and antagonism, as well as complementarity, play a major part in gender relations of the Upper Xingu. In a comparison of male-controlled ritual complexes in Melanesia and Amazonia, Hill (2001: 46) argued that "hierarchy is explicitly manifest in male-controlled ritual cults that to a large degree oppose and contradict the egalitarian quality of secular social relations" and that "analysis and comparison of these contradictions and the various local ways of attempting to resolve them opens up the possibility for productive comparative insights." Following this more comprehensive approach allows us to explore complex and shifting relations between gender complementarity and opposition. If the relations between men and women are said to be so harmonious, why would the furious spirit of the flutes, represented by all the village men, rape women in case they violate the prohibition against seeing the flutes? And why should women scratch and attack men if they do not have anything to reproach in everyday life?

Myth, Ritual Performance, and Everyday Life

Like Basso and Monod Becquelin, I depart from the assumption that the performers undergo transformative experiences during ritual. The main theme of iamurikuma myth and ritual is certainly not the failed inversion of social order. Instead, it lies in the renewing process of gendered agencies. Because both gendered rituals play with the agency of the respective other sex, the taming of the spirits not only applies to the theme of sexuality but also should be applied to reversal in ritual roles and the potential for subversion contained therein.

In the interpretation of the mythical complex, I tried to show that myths do not address anxiety about the opposite sex (Gregor 1985) or "eroticized aggressions" (Basso 1985: 239), but deal with the "deceit" concerning gender roles. Myths talk about the takeover of the mighty and extremely increased faculties of the opposite gender group.

If women in iamurikuma ritual act like men, then men, by playing the flutes, are acting like women. Basso reports that men decorate the flutes with the designs of menstruation when playing them and that the mouthpiece of the flute is called a "vagina"; when the flutes are stored at the house of the sponsor, it is said that they "menstruate" (Basso 1985: 304, 305). Men paint with the designs of menstruation while playing the flutes. Menezes Bastos (1999: 229) assume that men "menstruate" while playing the flutes. But what does this mean? An explanation for the visual taboo may be the taking over of female agencies by men during ritual time. Myths remember this takeover of the creative power as a deceit. They may be motivated by bad conscience about the "taking away" of female agency from the women while they were playing something that in reality does not belong to them. This also means that the spirit gets angry not only because of the fraud in itself but in order to prevent its possible detection. The segregation of gender agencies paradoxically is restored by the imposition of phallic power and through some "extreme" or "spirit-state" sense of fertility.[13]

The aggressions arising during this process, however, do not find their explication in an elementary hostile relationship of men and women. The reason for this is simple. If it is thought that the enraged spirits of the flutes or iamurikuma are externalizations of inner aggressive feelings of the one gender group toward the other, then why should they just aim at the opposite sex? Or, to ask more precisely, why should women turn into men in order to express their fear and hatred of them?

The aggressive utterances of women as well as the menace of gang rape during the rituals can hardly ever be reduced only to the sexual feelings of the gender group in question. Myth describes some kind of approximation to alterity that is equated with the other sex. It is not the fear of the opposite gender but the fear of trespassing over the established limits of gender roles and the secret longing for this experience: to get into the opposite gender role and at the same time experience turning into a powerful spiritual being. This is what both gender rituals play with: women take over male functions and play with male "agencies" while men play the flutes to get into a state of femaleness. Men approximate the most valued and, at the same time, the most dreaded attributes of the female condition. This kind of "serious play" also has a serious aim: it is about getting to know the other side and controlling it.

Process and Transformation

In a "breakthrough into performance," Dell Hymes (1975) describes the anthropological attempt to examine the common structures of theater and ritual, constituting an interface between dramatics and cultural anthropology. Shifting interest from the structure of culture to its process, ritual became of special interest and was described as a transformative performance and a "social drama" (Turner 1987). Many studies in Lowland South America focused on the form and aesthetics of dramatic performances as well as the narrative genres initiating studies of "verbal art as performance,"[14] "ethnography of speaking,"[15] "ethnopoetics,"[16] and ethnomusicology.[17] The idea of cultural staging and performative experience opened up a new understanding of myths and rituals. They were no longer read as expressions of social structure in general or as repressed feelings and unconscious drives, but were seen as "performed art" (Basso 1985: 6). The shifting from content to the form of discourse and expressive practices opens up new perspectives und understanding in how meanings unfold in performances.[18]

Recent studies have centered on the ludic element of human activities and their sensual aspects. They analyze bodily aspects of ritual staging as well as the dramatic space and the relationship of the stage, actors, and audience.[19] In order to differentiate between "social" and "dramatic" acting, Köpping prefers the concept of "game" or "play" instead of "performance."[20] This kind of differentiation is crucial for the interpretation of rituals of role reversal because the game contains a potential of transgression (Köpping 1998: 69). The possibility of transgression at the same time permits a confinement opposite to what we would call "carnival" or "burlesque" representation.

Returning to the Upper Xingu, the ritual process in itself and the power of transformation in rituals of role inversion has been valued by Monod Becquelin, Basso, and McCallum. While the "secret flutes" have been looked upon for a long time as phallic symbols, or at least as a symbol of male power,[21] in Upper Xingu, nevertheless, there is more evidence for the contrary explication.

In Amazonia, ritual transformation and the taming of spirits are well known facts. To understand gendered rituals, it is important to remember their ambiguity as well as the different layers of experience contained for the people involved.

It is hard to say to what extent men and women get involved in ritual performance and to what extent they get "transformed." During the iamurikuma singing, for example, the exclusion of the opposite sex is not as strict as it is when the sacred flutes are played. One can speculate about whether this has something to do with the intensity or "authenticity" of the metamorphosis. The menace of gang rape is far more serious than the women's aggressions toward men. During iamurikuma, men must only keep a safe distance from the women, and there is neither a strict visual taboo nor a threat of sexual violence.

A possible explanation for this imbalance would be that women do not perceive such a big deficit concerning gender roles, because they are able to give birth. Men, on the other hand, may feel more deficient when "fertility" is concerned (see Prinz 1999: 271–72). Another explanation would be that women do not dare to "transform" themselves the way men do. It can be interesting to take a closer look at the relation of bodily experience in ritual and transformation.

Subversion and the Corporal Experience during the Iamurikuma Ritual

During iamurikuma ritual, women violate and subvert the strict gender roles common throughout Amazonian cultures of Lowland South America. In this sense, ritual is opening an opportunity to break with the categorical identities of "men" and "women." Ritual breaking out of conventional roles allows women to get into spheres normally prohibited to them.

The ritual performance turns into an amplification of corporeal experience to women. As they are enacting male roles, singing and dancing at the "center," their bodies experience male roles and transform. During the performance, the distinction between "model" (male ritual practice) and its imitation (women's performance) loses its importance and the corporeal process evolves its own dynamics. Iamurikuma singers not only undermine the categories of "men" and "women" but also dissolve the limits between "human beings" and "spirits." Music thereby plays an important part. It unleashes and tames the transformative powers of the spirits.[22] The decoration of the women with masculine objects and the painting with men's colors are designed to transform them and therefore "activate the powers of a different body," as Eduardo Viveiros de Castro puts it (1998: 482). The same is true for men, who approximate to female agencies by playing the flutes.

Another kind of bodily experience becomes clearly exhibited during the favorite men's sport, *hukã-hukã*. After the iamurikuma feast, women get into the arena of the central plaza. As bodily experience, the imitation of hukã-hukã is as real or "authentic" as its prototype. At the same time, the perspective of the male world is closely linked with the spiritual world. The bodies' affects and capacities are alterable, and they can transcend everyday reality. McCallum refers to the "semi-spirit body" to designate this kind of in-between space, during which the real person submits to the transformative powers of ritual.

This gendered performance is more than a simple communication between the sexes or between ghosts and humans because it implies the transformation of the player as a spiritual corporeal experience; it is a dangerous play.

Both Ellen Basso and Aurore Monod Becquelin emphasize the transformational capacities of Xinguano rituals, though in different ways. Basso, assuming an inner transformation of Kalapalo women, demonstrates how their bodies are converted into an important musical instrument that permits them to experience the process of becoming powerful spirits.

Although performers during rituals play with the transformation of the dancers into mythical spirits, an important limitation must be noted: "real" transformation is highly dreaded, and during the ritual process and the reactivation of mythic time, much energy is engaged in *not* trespassing over the limits.

Monod Becquelin in contrast expresses the dangerous side of the transformation and the restrictions. The designs of the Trumaí women differ from the designs described in iamurikuma myths (Monod Becquelin 1988: 557). Mehináku women affirmed that they used male designs, but only at the legs and not at the breast like the men do. They also placed emphasis on the fact that they did not transform themselves. Xingu women are using small but well directed deviations in their ritual techniques to avoid the risk of real transformation. For Mehináku women, ritual is the place where people "only sing" and where there is no real transformation. Despite this serious modification concerning ritual practice, the representation of the opposite sex conveys a corporeal experience of otherness from which women normally seem to be excluded.

Double Reality/Ambiguity and Staging Culture

In the Upper Xingu region, one of the well-known forms of transforming the disease-causing spirits is the act of taming them in order to gain cultural benefits. This process is, in the first place, a dangerous play with the "other," which is only partly described by the characteristics of the opposite sex. As already noted, there are at least two interpretive levels: the one of "gender war" (man-woman) and the spirit level (human-spirit).

The playing of the flutes as much as the singing and dancing of the women is designed to bring the performers in contact with the spirit world, to give musical expression to the powerful spirits and in this way appease them.[23] At the man-woman level it also has the effect of venting one's personal anger and frustrations. Anger and resentments against spouses and lovers are nothing special in a society where harmony is a dictate in everyday life. For example, during the manioc feast Mehináku women and men are disputing while singing and dancing. Women make public the sexual deficiencies of their husbands and lovers. But the rules of the game determine that men must not get annoyed, because women are "only singing" remembering the ritual frame. The same is true for men mocking the women. Ritual opens up a liminal and ambiguous play that blends mythic spirits and everyday personal reality. It is dangerous play because the existence of the frame at the same time comprises the possibility of its transgression. Ritual is, in this context, to be seen as a transformative event, which *empowers* and transforms the body of the performer (Köpping and Rao 2000).

Gang Rape and the Transgression of the Ritual Frame

I will try to point up the ambiguity (Doppelbödigkeit) of ritual performance by focusing on the extreme expression of gang rape during the flute ritual. Men only transform into furious spirits when their transformation becomes visible for women. The rage of the spirits can lead to the true-life rape of a woman. The thin line between the embodiment of the kawoká spirit and the turning into the "other" vanishes and "transgression" takes place (see Köpping 1998: 69). It has to be understood as an extreme, an exceptional event, and neither an "institutionalized" part of ritual nor the expression of everyday gender relations (see Quinn 1977: 216).

Myths of "gender war" show that the acting persons are only transformed due to certain conditions. The reason for metamorphosis does not lie in the inherent hostility of men-women relationships, but in the conjunction of mythical incidents and, above all, in the deception and denial of food and therein the negation of sociability (see Prinz 1999: 273–74).

The offense of the visual taboo can lead to ritual transgression modeled on myth. The rape has to be understood as a state of the men being "beside themselves with rage" and their inescapable transformation into spirits. At the same time, the rape of women happens at the personal level. The spirit condition may "excuse" the uncontrolled, wild acting of the individual person as well as the collective. Only spirits and enraged humans act against society.

This affirms McCallum's findings that the menace of gang rape does not play a role as an instrument of power in everyday life of men and women (McCallum 1994: 110). Therefore, for the Amazonian societies, while it is imperative to prevent transgression, or "real" transformation, it is equally indispensable for the continuity of life and for the taming of the "fertilizing spirits" to play with transgression.

If the taming of the spirits fails, the person gets identified with the spirit and becomes furious. The mythical reality imposes itself, and the rage of the spirits will be acted out.

Visibility and Invisibility

Looking at the ritual process as an intermediary level between mythical and everyday worlds, new questions arise concerning the different levels of performance and the transformative power of ritual.

As the iamurikuma myth tells, the visual seductive power is so strong that men, like women, cannot avert their eyes and must follow the iamurikuma spirits.

> They [the iamurikuma spirits] came into another village. "Don't look at the women that are coming there!" the husbands of the village warned their womenfolk. "I want to look at the women that are coming up there." "Me, too. I want to see these women with my eyes!" The women of the village looked after the dancing women, and they looked at them with their eyes. That was when they heard the call of Yamarikumá and the dancing women. . . . Yamarikumá went through

all the villages. Yamarikumá went there underground following the ways the armadillo was digging. At each village he came up to the surface. When Yamarikumá had passed the village, they were following the underground way until the next village. And so on. A village, the earth hole, that the poor old man, the armadillo, had dug until they came to another village. (Münzel 1973: 245, my translation)

The myth shows the consequences of trespassing against the visual prohibition of the dancing spirits. It shall prevent a real and irreversible metamorphosis. Philippe Erikson (2000) also emphasizes the danger of transformation in relation to visibility and invisibility by means of the utterance of monosyllabic sounds and exclamations of Matis Indians of the Brazilian Amazon. He interprets them as a light form of the "flute complex," so to speak, or as a modification for nonsedentary Indians. Monosyllabic cries are understood as a ritual expression of the "gender antagonism." This, however, does not stand for the dominance of one sex over the other. Erikson points out that gender-specific utterances and the exclusion of one gender group should prevent this group from unintended transformation.

In his musicological study about the Wayãpi of the Guiana, Jean-Michel Beaudet indicates the affinity of the aerophones and shamanic breathing. He interrelates the visibility and audibility of the breathing: music of the aerophones is audible but not visible, whereas shamanic breathing is made visible by means of tobacco and is barely audible. He also explains the visual taboo by a common polarization between the play of aerophones and the ability to give birth. It would be incompatible "souffler dans les instruments et mettre des enfants au monde" [to blow through the instruments and to bring children into the world] (1997: 149). Analogous to the pattern of Xinguano gender complementarity, Beaudet correlates male musical performance with the female manufacture of beer. Male aerophones are equated with female menstruation and political dominance with the ability of women to give birth. Women and aerophones together produce chaos while men order the cosmos with their music (see Beaudet 1997: 150ff.).

There is much evidence about the correlation of flute playing and the female fertility complex. The playing of the flutes parallels the female agency of menstruation and giving birth, which are also connected with a strict visual taboo. Here, then, the visual prohibition of the aerophones as a typical "male ritual" is equivalent to the pan-American precautionary measures concerning the first menstruation ritual for the girls.

Finally, it is the process of transformation that is subdued to visual taboo. It relates to the "real" and extremely dangerous transformative process that women experience during their first menstruation and when giving birth and that men can experience while playing the flutes. Seclusion is the Amazonian way to make bodily transformation invisible. In the Upper Xingu, this process is closely related to shame (*parikú*), as Viveiros de Castro (1987a: 34–35) observes. Perhaps men construct the playing of the flutes as some kind of compensation. In any case, both transformative processes are parallel, and I suppose that both of them are afflicted with shame. The examples of gendered rituals of the Upper Xingu demonstrate that established gender segregation is to be transcended in secret. To what extent these processes can be assigned to other cultures of the Amazonian lowlands remains to be proven in future studies.

Visual taboos, together with the playing of certain aerophones, are part of a ritually restricted role reversal, which at the same time portends a dangerous communication with the spirits and should not be seen as a simple sign of male dominance per se. It makes a difference if men symbolically appropriate women's reproductive capacities or if they play with the agency of the other sex to understand and to control it. The fact that this process in myth is referred to as deceit, in my opinion, does not refer to the suppression of women but rather to a deceit of the gods (in the face of which men pretend to be like women).

This kind of deceit for indigenous Amazonians is not unusual. The deceit obeys the same principles as hunting magic: the approximation toward the other is nothing but an act of mimicry exploring the reality of the "other" and making oneself equal with the "prey."

Therefore, the possession of the flutes is not to be equated with mean possession of (political) power over women, but rather as a "magical" way of approximation of the "other" in at least two ways. It is an approximation to the world of the spirits and at the same time to the world of the other sex. To appease the spirits of the flutes, men must turn into women (or approximate themselves in some spiritual way), and the same is true for the women. Gendered rituals may be something like a performative and an anxious approximation to the "other of itself" and therefore some kind of self-awareness.

Notes

1. The first descriptions trace back to German scientists like Karl von den Steinen (1894) and Max Schmidt (1905).

2. George Zarur (1973) wrote the first short description and put it in the category "rituals of rebellion." See also Coelho 1991–92.

3. In literature, also known as *kauka* flutes.

4. Although this chapter is about both gendered rituals, the focus will be on the female part, because it remains lesser known. See also articles of Mello and Piedade, this volume.

5. Villas Boas and Villas Boas 1991, 116–17, 119–21; Prinz 1999: 230ff.

6. See unpublished research report Grubner/Prinz 2001; Prinz 2002.

7. Mello shows that there are more than two female categories, of which nonetheless, the "real" *iamurikuma* and *kawokakuma* have to be pointed out. See Mello, this volume.

8. Mello (2005) also understands music as the best media of expression for feelings. She notes the prevailing anxious mood of the songs.

9. See Overing and Passes 2000; Calavia 2002: 2. Of course, as Calavia also notes, the frontiers between the two schools are blurred.

10. In her article "The Body That Knows," McCallum shows how sociability is constructed with and through the female bodies, which are "instruments of transformation of the substances that go to building up the body" (1996: 353).

11. See McCallum 1998: 2ff.

12. Earlier, Robert and Yolanda Murphy (1980) pointed out that gender separateness was paramount in ritualized dramatizations of gender differences.

13. Furthermore, the attributes of femaleness, and respectively maleness, would lose their powers at the moment, in which they would be recognized as their own by the other sex. This would account also for the strict secrecy of the flutes, because the more distance that can be kept between men and women, the stronger the powers of the gendered spirit (Prinz 1999: 271–72).

14. Bauman (1977, 1992) and Ben-Amos and Goldstein (1975) developed the idea of performance for the narrative genres. Their analysis focused on mythic symbols not as logic structures but as an interactive process of transaction. See also Basso and Sherzer 1990:14.

15. Among the authors of the first four for Lowland South America were Ellen Basso, Anthony Seeger, Greg Urban, and Joel Sherzer (see, e.g., Basso 1985, 1997; Basso and Sherzer 1990; Seeger 1986, 1987; Sherzer 1992; Sherzer and Urban 1986; Urban 1986, 1991).

16. The main representatives were Stanley Diamond, Dell Hymes, and Dennis Tedlock; in Lowland South America following the approach among others were Mark Münzel (1992), Charles Briggs (1990), and Jonathan Hill (1990).

17. In his essay on ritual curing in the northwest Amazon, Jonathan Hill (1992: 188ff.) points out the key function of music during the transformative healing processes.

18. See Laura Graham's 1995 investigation of the performance of songs, the telling of dreams among the Xavante of Central Brazil, and the transmission of culture. Suzanne Oakdale (2005), investigating autobiographical accounts of the Kayabí, stresses that ritual speaking performance promotes some kind of transformation while it interconnects men with a variety of others—ancestors, spirits, and enemies—who speak through them.

19. See Köpping and Rao introduction (2000).

20. Although Turner (1995) correctly had noted the process of drifting apart of ludic and ritual performance, according to Köpping, one should not neglect the frame of the performative elements, as Schechner (1987) does in mingling theater and temple (Köpping 1998: 69).

21. This interpretation stems from the area of northwest and central Amazonia. See Murphy and Murphy (1974) for Mundurucú.

22. See Robin Wright's article, this volume.

23. This process could also be called "soundscaping the world." See Hill, this volume.

References Cited

Bamberger, Joan. 1974. "The Myth of Matriarchy: Why Men Rule in Primitive Society." In *Woman Culture and Society*, ed. M. Z. Rosaldo and L. Lamphere, 263–80. Stanford: Stanford University Press.

Basso, Ellen B. 1985. *A Musical View of the Universe: Kalapalo Myth and Ritual Performances*. Philadelphia: University of Pennsylvania Press.

Basso, Ellen B., and Joel Sherzer, eds. 1990. *Las Culturas nativas latinoamericanas a través de su discurso*. Quito, Ecuador: Abya-Yala; Rome: MLAL.

Bauman, Richard, 1977. *Verbal Art as Performance*. Rowley, Mass: Newbury House.

———, ed. 1992. *Folklore, Cultural Performances, and Popular Entertainments*. New York: Oxford University Press.

Beaudet, Jean-Michel. 1997. *Souffles d'Amazonie: Les orchestres "tule" des Wayãpi*. Nanterre: Société d'ethnologie.

Ben-Amos, D., and K. S. Goldstein, eds. 1975. *Folklore: Performance and Communication*. The Hague: Mouton.

Briggs, Charles. 1990. "Diversidad metapragmática en el arte verbal: poesía, imaginación e interacción en los estilos narrativos Warao." In *Las Culturas nativas latinoamericanas*, ed. E. Basso and J. Sherzer, 135–74. Quito, Ecuador: Abya-Yala; Rome: MLAL.

Calavia Sáez, Oscar. 2002. Review of Cecilia McCallum, *How Real People Are Made: Gender and Sociality in Amazonia. Mana* 8, no. 2.

Coelho, Vera Penteado. 1991–92. "A festa do pequi e o zunidor entre os índios Waurá." *Schweizerische Amerikanisten-Gesellschaft*, Bulletin 55–56.

Di Leonardo, Micaela. 1991. "Introduction: Gender, Culture, and Political Economy: Feminist Anthropology in Historical Perspective." In *Gender at the Crossroads of Knowledge: Feminist Anthropology in the Postmodern Era*, ed. Micaela di Leonardo, 1–48. Berkeley: University of California Press.

Erikson, Philippe. 2000. "'I,' 'UUU,' 'SHHH': Gritos, Sexos, e Metamorphoses Entre os Matis (Amazônia Brasileira)." *Mana* 6, no. 2: 37–64.

Franchetto, Bruna. 1999. "Women among the Kuikúro." *Revista estudos feministas* (special issue), Instituto de Filosofia e Ciências Sociais IFCS/UFRJ, 205–19.

Graham, Laura R. 1995. *Performing Dreams: Discourses of Immortality among the Xavante of Central Brasil*. Austin: University of Texas Press.

Gregor, Thomas. 1985. *Anxious Pleasure: The Sexual Lives of an Amazonian People*. Chicago: University of Chicago Press.

Grubner, Barbara, and Ulrike Prinz. 2001. "Relatório da pesquisa Mudança de papéis e representação de gênero na festa *yamarikumã* no Alto Xingu." Research report.

Hill, Jonathan. 1990. "El mito, la música, y la história: Transformaciones poéticas de discurso narrativo en una sociedad amazónica." In *Las Culturas nativas latinoamericanas*, ed. E. Basso and J. Sherzer, 71–88. Quito, Ecuador: Abya-Yala; Rome: MLAL.

———. 1992. "A Musical Aesthetic of Ritual Curing in the Northwest Amazon." In *Portals of Power*, ed. J. Langdon and G. Baer. Albuquerque: University of Mexico Press.

———. 2001. "Varieties of Fertility Cultism in Amazonia: A Closer Look at Gender Symbolism in Northwestern Amazonia." In *Gender in Amazonia and Melanesia: An Exploration of the Comparative Method*, ed. T. Gregor and D. Tuzin, 45–68. Berkeley: University of California Press.

Hymes, Dell. 1975. "Breakthrough into Performance." In *Folklore, Performance, and Communication*, ed. D. Ben-Amos and K. Goldstein. The Hague: Mouton.

Jackson, Jean E. 1992. "The Meaning and Message of Symbolic Sexual Violence in Tukanoan Ritual." *Anthropological Quarterly* 65, no. 1: 1–18.

Köpping, Klaus Peter. 1998. "Inszenierung und Transgression in Ritual und Theater Grenzprobleme der performativen Ethnologie." In *Ethnologie und Inszenierung: Ansätze zur Theaterethnologie*, ed. Bettina Schmidt and Mark Münzel, 45–85. Marburg: Curupira.

Köpping, Klaus Peter, and Ursula Rao, eds. 2000. *Im Rausch des Rituals: Gestaltung und Transformation der Wirklichkeit in körperlicher Praxis*. Münster: LIT.

McCallum, Cecilia. 1994. "Ritual and the Origin of Sexuality in the Alto Xingu." In *Sex and Violence: Issues in Representation and Experience*, ed. Penelope Harvey and Peter Gow. New York: Routledge.

———. 1996. "The Body That Knows: From Cashinahua Epistemology to a Medical Anthropology of Lowland South America." *Medical Anthropology Quarterly*, n.s., 10, no. 3 (September): 347–72.

———. 1998. "Alteridade e sociabilidade Kaxinauá: Perspectivas de uma antropología de uma vida diária." *Rev. bras. Ci. Soc.* 13, no. 38. Available from www.scielo.br/scielo.php?script=sci_arttext&pid=S0102–69091998000300008&lng=en&nrm=iso.

Mead, Margaret. 1962 [1935]. *Sex and Temperament in Tree Primitive Societies*. New York: William Morrow.

Mello, Maria Ignez Cruz. 1999. "Música e Mito entre os Wauja do Alto Xingu." Master's thesis, PPGAS/UFSC.

———. 2005. "Iamurikuma: Música, Mito, e Ritual entre os Wauja do Alto Xingu." PhD diss., Universidade Federal de Santa Catarina.

Menezes Bastos, Rafael José de. 1999. *A Musicológica Kamayurá: para uma antropologia da comunicação no Alto-Xingu*. Florianópolis: Editora da UFSC.

Monod Becquelin, Aurore. 1982. "La Métamorphose." *Journal de la Société des Américanistes* 68: 133–47.

———. 1987. "Les femmes sont un bien excellent: vision des hommes, être des femmes dans le haut Xingu." *Anthropologie et Societés* 11, no. 1: 121–36.

———. 1988. "Der dekorierte Mensch: Körpermalerei bei den Trumai des Alto Xingu (Zentral-Brasilien)." In *Die Mythen Sehen*, ed. Mark Münzel, 533–79. Frankfurt am Main: Museum für Völkerkunde.

Münzel, Mark. 1973. *Erzählungen der Kamayurá: Alto Xingú Brasilien*. Wiesbaden: Franz Steiner.

———, ed. 1988. *Die Mythen Sehen: Bilder und Zeichen vom Amazonas*. 2 vols. Frankfurt am Main: Museum für Völkerkunde.

———. 1992. "Die Kreativität einer Guaraní-Mythe." In *Mythen im Kontext: Ethnologische Perspektiven*, ed. Karl-Heinz Kohl, 79–105. Frankfurt-Main: Edition Qumran im Campus Verlag.

Murphy, Yolanda, and Robert F. Murphy. 1974. *Women of the Forest*. New York: Columbia University Press.

———. 1980. "Women, Work, and Property in a South American Tribe." In *Theory and Practice: Essays Presented to Gene Weltfish*, ed. S. Diamond, 179–94. The Hague: Mouton.

Oakdale, Suzanne. 2005. *"I Foresee My Life": The Ritual Performance of Autobiography in an Amazonian Community*. Lincoln: University of Nebraska Press.

Overing, Joanna, and Alan Passes, eds. 2000. *The Anthropology of Love and Anger: The Aesthetics of Conviviality in Native Amazonia*. New York: Routledge.

Prinz, Ulrike. 1999. *Das Jacaré und die streitbaren Weiber: Poesie und Geschlechterkampf im östlichen Tiefland Südamerikas*. Marburg: Curupira.

———. 2002. "'Wer die Flöten hat, hat die Qual': Vom Streit um die gender-Repräsentationen am Alto-Xingú." *Anthropos* 97: 397–411.

Piedade, Acácio Tadeu de C. 2004. "O canto do Kawoká: música, cosmologia e filosofia entre os Wauja do Alto Xingu." PhD diss., PPGAS/UFSC (www.musa.ufsc.br).

Quinn, Naomi. 1977. "Anthropological Studies on Women's Status." *Annual Review of Anthropology* 6: 181–225.

Samain, Etienne. 1991. *Moroneta Kamayurá: Mitos e Aspectos da Realidade Social dos Indios Kamayurá (Alto Xingu)*. Rio de Janeiro: Lidador.

Schechner, Richard. 1987. "Drama." In *Encyclopedia of religion*, vol. 4, ed. Mircea Eliade. New York: Macmillan.

Schmidt, Max. 1905. *Indianerstudien in Zentralbrasilien*. Berlin: Reimer.

Seeger, Anthony. 1986. "Oratory Is Spoken, and Song Is Sung, but They Are All Music to My Ears." In *Native South American Discourse*, ed. J. Sherzer and G. Urban, 59–82. Berlin: De Gruyter.

———. 1987. *Why Suyá Sing: A Musical Anthropology of an Amazonian People*. Cambridge: Cambridge University Press.

Sherzer, Joel. 1992. "Ethnography of Speaking." In *Folklore, Cultural Performances, and Popular Entertainments*, ed. R. Bauman, 76–80. New York: Oxford University Press.

Sherzer, Joel, and Greg Urban, eds. 1986. *Native South American Discourse*. Berlin: De Gruyter.

Steinen, Karl von den. 1894. *Unter den Naturvölkern Zentral Brasilien: Reiseschilderung und Ergebnisse der Zweiten Schingú-Expedition 1887–1888*. Berlin: Reimer.

Turner, Victor. 1987. "The Anthropology of Performance." In *The Anthropology of Performance*, ed. Victor Turner. New York: PAJ.

———. 1995 [1982]. *Vom Ritual zum Theater: Der Ernst des menschlichen Spiels*. Frankfurt am Main: Fischer.

Urban, Greg. 1986. "The Semiotic Functions of Macro-parallelism in the Shokleng Origin Myth." In *Native South American Discourse*, ed. J. Sherzer and G. Urban, 15–57. Berlin: De Gruyter.

———. 1991. *A Discourse-Centered Approach to Culture: Native South American Myths and Rituals*. Austin: University of Texas Press.

Villas Boas, Orlando, and Cláudio Villas Boas. 1991 [1971]. *Xingu: los indios, sus mitos*. Quito: Abya-yala.

Viveiros de Castro, Eduardo B. 1987a. "A fabricação do corpo na sociedade Xinguana." In *Sociedades indígenas e indigenismo no Brasil*, ed. João Pacheco de Oliveira Filho, 31–41. Rio de Janeiro: UFRJ Editora Marco Zero.

———. 1987b. "Alguns aspectos de pensamento yawalapíti (Alto Xingu): Clasificações e transformações." In *Sociedades indígenas e indigenismo no Brasil*, ed. João Pacheco de Oliveira Filho, 43–83. Rio de Janeiro: UFRJ Editora Marco Zero.

———. 1998. "Cosmological Deixis and Amerindian Perspectivism." *Journal of the Royal Anthropological Institute* 4, no. 3 (September): 469–88.

Zarur, George. 1973. *Parentesco, Ritual, e Economia no Alto Xingu*. Brasilia: FUNAI.

12. An "Inca" Instrument at a "Nawa" Feast

Marubo Flutes and Alterity in Amazonian Context

JAVIER RUEDAS

This chapter explores the connections between flute use and concepts of alterity in Amazonia by analyzing a Marubo headman's comments on flute use. The Marubo, a Panoan society of the Javari River basin in western Brazil, do not have sacred flutes, but their youths play flutes in informal settings such as manioc beer feasts. During one such feast at Maronal, a village on the upper Curuçá River, the headman explained to me that flutes were Inca instruments and what we were attending was not a Marubo event but rather a *nawa* (distant stranger, white man) feast. I will analyze Marubo concepts of identity and alterity (otherness) to show the importance of nawa and Inca in Marubo thought and, more broadly, in the constitution of Panoan (including Marubo) social forms. I then will use ethnographic observations to point out that the Marubo associate youths with alterity (the nawa) and elders with Marubo identity. Youths incorporate nawa elements into Marubo rituals, while a core set of ritual actions organized by elders remains central to the Marubo self-definition. The Marubo preserve identity by associating youth with alterity.

Marubo flutes, used by youths and defined as "Inca," reproduce the broader Amazonian connection between flute use and concerns with alterity. Although they are not sacred and occupy a marginal place in Marubo ritual, the comparison with sacred flute complexes "may bring us insight into more fundamental

Amazonian social themes" (see Brightman, this volume). Throughout Amazonia, the connection between flutes and discourse on alterity reveals the ways in which different Amazonian peoples worry about what they perceive to be the dangerous other and then set about socializing or domesticating the danger or, in the Marubo case, turning it into an object of laughter. Although the ritual and discourse surrounding most Amazonian flute use exhibits a concern with sexual difference or with affinity, Marubo flute use reflects the Panoan concern with the radical otherness of those who represent distant states—the Inca and the white man.

The Headman Says Flutes Are Inca Instruments

In September 1997, a new *shovo* (longhouse) was completed at Maronal, and this event occasioned a feast. The longhouse belonged to the headman's son-in-law, Mayãpa, and was built to house him and his wife and son as well as his three brothers and their wives and children. Because these brothers were all members of the Varináwavo section, the longhouse was called the Varináwavo shovo.[1]

The occasion for the longhouse's inaugural feast arose on October 4, 1997, when an *ako* was heard to sound in Maronal. An ako is a hollowed-out log drum that is found in almost every Marubo longhouse. The ako is used mainly during feasts that involve multiple longhouses. It was once used as a warning that enemies had been sighted. Its main nonceremonial use was to signal that a herd of white-lipped peccaries had been located. As soon as the ako sounded, all the hunters in the village dropped whatever they were doing and gathered to discuss their strategy. They sent spotters out to keep track of the herd, while the bulk of hunters waited for the next day. Early the following morning, twenty-eight hunters surrounded the herd and forced it through a gauntlet of shotgun fire. Forty-three peccaries were killed. The bulk of the meat was given to the Varináwavo brothers so they could host their inaugural feast.

On the day after the hunt, young men all over the village rolled up their hammocks and went to the Varináwavo shovo to eat grilled peccary.[2] The older men stayed in their own longhouses. Accompanying a group of elders, I visited the new longhouse on October 7. In addition to grilled peccary, the Varináwavo brothers' wives had made a large batch of the slightly fermented corn beer, *waka*. We ate to our heart's content and then I returned with the elders to the center of the village, where I lived.

On October 8, the remaining inhabitants of the longhouse compound where I lived returned to Mayãpa's shovo for breakfast. This morning, however, the feast had changed in quality. As we approached, I saw many splotches of a congealed white semi-liquid substance all around the edge of the new swidden clearing surrounding the longhouse. I asked what this was and was told that the feast organizers had finished brewing manioc beer. The young men had been drinking and had vomited in order to continue drinking.

Along with the elders that I had accompanied, I sat on the *kenã* benches that flanked the shovo entrance and ate peccary, corn beer, plantains, manioc, and banana porridge. The young men of the village were coming into the shovo, filling cups from a large pot of manioc beer, and drinking deeply, then going back outdoors. Outside, one young man carried a radio playing a cassette of Brazilian dance music, while another young man banged on a handheld peccary-skin drum and others played plastic flutes.

After eating, the elders went outside to sit on a log and watch the proceedings. I sat with them and elicited oral histories from the headman, Alfredo. The histories ranged from the arrival of the first government officials in the 1970s, through his youth, to the story of his father's family during the rubber boom (c. 1890–1910) and its aftermath. During the rubber boom, he said, several women in his family were kidnapped by Peruvians. He then explained that what we were watching was a *festa nawa*. The predominant contemporary meaning of *nawa* in Marubo is "white man," synonymous with the Portuguese term *o branco*. I asked Alfredo what made this a festa nawa. He responded that the skin drum, the flutes, and the radio playing dance music were nawa. He said, "This is not our way, it is another." Referring to the flutes, he said, "This is not Marubo, it is Inca."

While the elders and I returned to the village center to work and sleep, the youths continued drinking manioc beer—without sleeping—for the second night in a row. I was told that, during that last night of drinking, a conflict arose when a young man from another village tried to persuade his host affines to let him take his wife into virilocal residence. I also heard that a young man came to blows with a young woman. By the time I returned the next morning, the manioc beer was finished, but many youths were still awake and still playing flutes and drums. While Mayãpa served food to the elders and me, the youths dug a pit outside, filled it with water, and began to throw mud at each other and attempt to tackle one another in the pit. The young men and women irreverently threw mud at the headman, who sat in immutable dignity during this process. Noticing my efforts to avoid the mud, a group of mud-covered women seized me, covered me with mud, and threw me into the pit. I escaped, bathed in a nearby rivulet, and left with the elders. With the end of the manioc beer, the inaugural feast for Mayãpa's shovo ended that day.

The events described above raise a number of important questions. Is it significant that the participants in this feast were all youths, while the elders were observers? Why is this feast classified as festa nawa, and why is the flute considered an Inca instrument? What can this tell us about Marubo and Panoan concepts of identity and alterity, and how can this shed light on flute use in Amazonia more generally?

Nawa, Inca, Yura: Marubo and Panoan Concepts of Identity and Alterity

Nawa is a category of alterity found in nearly all Panoan societies (Erikson 1986, 1996). The term *nawa* is often glossed as "stranger," but can also mean "people." When used as an affix, nawa generates ethnonyms, descent group names, or the names of other internal groups. In this sense, it is often used in combination with the pluralizer *vo*. The Marubo descent groups, for example, have names such as Iskonáwavo, "oropendola people," or Varináwavo, "sun people." Similar internal group names are found among the Katukina-Pano (Coffaci 1994) and Amahuaca (Russell 1964). This morpheme is also commonly found in Panoan ethnonyms, often exogenous such as the insulting *Kashinawa*, (bat people). However, as a free morpheme, *nawa* is used by Panoans to refer to the outermost limits of alterity: the Inca and the white man (Keifenheim 1990, 1992). In this sense, *nawa* refers to peoples who originate beyond the forest, belong to powerful states, and create metal tools and merchandise. Alfredo's statement that the youths were conducting a nawa feast thus meant that the festivities belonged to this furthest conceivable realm of alterity, consisting of elements imported from—or created in imitation of— the white man and the Inca.

The presence of the Inca in Panoan mythology and concepts of alterity has occupied the attention of scholars for some time (Roe 1982, 1988; Melatti 1985, 1986; Lathrap et al. 1985, 1987; DeBoer and Raymond 1987; Erikson 1990; Harner 1993; Kensinger 1993; Calavia 2000; McCallum 2000; Cesarino 2008; see also Bardales Rodriguez 1979). Julio Cezar Melatti was the first to draw attention to the particular place of the Inca in Marubo mythology and cosmology. For Melatti's informants, the Inca and the white man were thoroughly fused into a single category. In the Marubo creation story (Melatti 1986), the first people emerge from the ground and learn to have sex by watching capuchin monkeys. Although the ancestral leaders know to have sex only with cross-cousins, some of the people have sex indiscriminately with forbidden categories of kin. When the people reach a wide river spanned by a living caiman bridge, the leaders tell the people who have proper sex to cross first. Then, when the incestuous transgressors are crossing, they cut the bridge, and the transgressors fall into the water to be eaten by piranhas and catfish. Some women take the water with the blood of the dead into their mouths and blow it to the west. The blood goes to a place called Roe Inka (Inca Axe), where it becomes the white man and the Inca and where, according to Melatti's informant, the axe factory is. Another of Melatti's informants described Roe Inka as being inhabited by "a tribe of whites, Americans, over there in the West, where the axe factory is" (Melatti 1985: 53), again equating the Inca with the white man and metal goods. More recently, Cesarino (2008) has translated a Marubo myth describing a journey by the Marubo ancestors to Roe Inka to obtain stone axes.

Melatti (1985: 80–85) argued that the "Inca" in Marubo myth and cosmology could refer to any of three groups. First are the actual subjects of the Inca empire, with which some ancestors of the Marubo probably had contact. Second are Quechua speakers associated with the Spanish colonization of the upper Amazon, including missionaries, traders, and soldiers. Finally, Quechua speakers entered the Javari River basin during the rubber boom. Melatti argues that the figure of the Inca in Marubo mythology most likely originates in contact with the pre-Hispanic Incas, but has been reinforced and altered by subsequent regular contact with other "Incas." Cesarino's translation of the Marubo myth Inka Roe Yõka seems to indicate at least some pre-Hispanic contact, because it portrays the Marubo ancestors as obtaining stone axes, whereas colonial and postcolonial Quechua speakers would have owned metal axes. On the other hand, Melatti's informants associated the Inca with metal tools and equated the Inca and the white man, indicating a postconquest reformulation of the "Inca" category. Furthermore, whereas the Inca seems to have once been the paradigmatic representative of the category of distant stranger (nawa), that position has more recently been occupied by the white man. In contrast to the Shipibo (Bardales Rodriguez 1979) or Kashinawa (Kensinger 1993), among whom the Inca occupies a central position in mythology, in Marubo mythology the Inca is a marginal figure whereas the white man is the subject of considerable speculation (Melatti 1985).

The Marubo Inca is a variant of the generalized Panoan Inca and of the Panoan theories of alterity that are represented in the varying definitions of the category of nawa. For example, for the Kashinawa, the Incas and white man also originated in the crossing of a bridge consisting of a living caiman (family Alligatoridae). However, in the case of the Kashinawa, those who cross become the Inca, while those who stay behind become the Kashinawa. In this myth (Deshayes and Keifenheim 1994: 168–70), the ancestral Huni Kuin (the Kaxinawa autonym) are upset because they have no stone or metal. Deciding to travel, they reach the wide river bridged by the caiman. The caiman allows families to cross in return for gifts of meat. However, when one family brings a gift of caiman meat, the caiman is offended and refuses to allow any more crossings. Those who had already crossed reached the land of metals and became the Inca; the white man is the son of the Inca. Thus, for the Kashinawa, the Inca and the white man also fall into the same category of alterity, characterized by possessing metal. Renard-Casevitz et al. (1986: 100) also report a Kashinawa myth collected by Deshayes and Keifenheim in which the Kashinawa travel to work for the Inca in return for metal but, receiving nothing for their hard work, plan to kill the Inca and return to their own villages. Calavia (2000: 11–12) discusses the Kashinawa myths of the Inca collected by Capistrano de Abreu and by Tastevin, in which the Inca is a powerful figure controlling both natural forces and cultural knowledge. This is similar to the Shipibo Inca (Bardales Rodriguez 1979; Lathrap et al. 1985; Roe 1988), which, though not a single figure but rather a multiplicity of distinct characters, is almost always a culture hero that controls essential cultural knowledge. In contrast, the Marubo Inca is neither a culture hero nor a co-resident of the Marubo, nor does the Marubo go live near the Inca; rather, the Inca is a distant owner of stone and metal tools and of the knowledge of their production.

Although there are clear indications that the Marubo Inca has its roots in pre-Hispanic contacts, there is also little doubt that it has been reformulated over time to account for new contacts with Quechua, Spanish, and Portuguese speakers (cf. Calavia 2000).[3] The rubber boom, in particular, seems to have brought Quechua speakers into direct contact with the immediate ancestors of the Marubo (Montagner Melatti and Melatti 1975: 22). My informants stated that during and after the rubber boom, several Marubo who worked as rubber tappers spoke "Inca" fluently. One of the most prominent Marubo elders during my fieldwork was nick-named "Kuraka," the Quechua term for chief, and several other Marubo words are Quechua in origin (Cesarino 2008). The rubber boom contributed to reinforcing and changing the position of the Inca in Marubo categories of alterity, but also to fusing the Inca and the white man together in the category of nawa, the attractive but dangerous metal-owning representatives of the distant and mysterious state.

Although Alfredo called the manioc beer feast of October 1997 a festa nawa, much of this event was indigenous and Panoan in form and content. The occasion was the inauguration of a new shovo, it was preceded by a communal peccary hunt, the peccaries were distributed by an elder, the entire village was invited to the feast, and all guests were offered cooked peccary meat and corn beer. This was followed by the consumption of a batch of manioc beer, which was the scene for the expression of tensions between affines and between people involved in sexual relationships, very much like the informal feasts of the Brazilian Yaminawa (Calavia 2004). Among the clearest Panoan components of the feast was the mud fight, which is one of the sequence of semiformal inter-generic insults preceding the biannual Kachanaua fertility ritual among the Kashinawa (Kensinger 1995: 70–71).

Within this generally Panoan context, Alfredo identified specific ritual elements as nawa: the stereo playing Brazilian music, the skin drum, and the flute, this latter more precisely identified as Inca. The stereo and the Brazilian music are relatively recent incorporations into the Marubo cultural repertoire and self-evidently originate in the world of the white man. Although there are some known Panoan aerophones, they are clay transverse aerophones with resonating chambers (Erikson 1996: 263–70), whereas the flute identified by Alfredo as Inca was a plastic end-blown flute. The skin drum is found among the Shipibo, but there it is called *tampora*, a cognate of the Spanish word *tambor* (Roe 1982: 100, 321n45), indicating a nawa origin. The Marubo skin drum and flute ensemble used at the manioc beer feast so closely resembles the highland Quechua *flauta y caja* ensembles (Olsen 2004: 304–305) that, as a preliminary hypothesis, we can take at face value the emic identification of the instruments as Inca, incorporated into the Marubo repertoire during and after the rubber boom when the Marubo were in contact with Quechua-speaking Peruvians. Thus imported ritual elements are being consciously embedded within the framework of a Panoan-style ritual.

If the category of nawa, with its Inca subset, represents the outermost band of alterity, Marubo identity is represented by the category *yura*. *Yura* is a Panoan cognate generally meaning "body" (Erikson 1996: 75). Among some Panoans, in combination with a morpheme meaning "other," it can be used to refer to the intermediate band of alterity occupied by other Panoans (e.g., Dole 1979: 35). Although most Panoans use some variant of the proto-Panoan *oni* as an autonym (Erikson 1996: 73), the Marubo (as well as some Amahuaca) use the corporeal metaphor *yura*. The Marubo are the result of the fusion of Panoan groups in the immediate aftermath of the rubber boom (Melatti 1977: 92 and 1986: 30–37; Ruedas 2003, 2004), and today consist of nine intermarried exogamous matrilineal units. In its most limited usage, the Marubo use *yura* to refer to themselves, that is, any member of the nine matrilineal units that survived the rubber boom by hiding together between the Ituí and Curuçá rivers from about 1895 to 1965.[4] However, *yura* is also applied to any Panoan group with an ethnonym containing the morphemes *nawa* or *vo*, and it can also be applied to any indigenous peoples, in which case it forms part of a dualistic opposition with nawa (Montagner Melatti and Melatti 1975: 3). The categories of yura and nawa are frequently opposed in Marubo discourse, as when the elders complain that youths listen to *nawã vana* (white man's words) instead of *yurã vana* (Marubo words, meaning the elders' formal discourses; Ruedas 2002). The yura and nawa categories are also opposed in the classification of feasts, as will be described below.

This analysis of the Marubo concepts of identity and alterity evoked by Alfredo in his explanation of the manioc beer feast shows that Marubo flute use is described in terms of the principal categories of distant alterity, nawa and Inca. The close connection between flutes and alterity that is common throughout Amazonia thus holds for the Marubo, albeit in a rather different form from that found in classic Amazonian sacred flute complexes. Among the Marubo, ritual flute use is one part of the insertion of non-Panoan motifs in indigenous Panoan ceremonies. To understand this phenomenon, it is necessary to examine, first, what the Marubo consider a "Marubo" feast as opposed to a festa nawa, and secondly how the categories "youth" and "elders" correlate with the distinction between Marubo and nawa ritual.

Youth Is to Inca as Elder Is to Marubo

The principal feasts that are considered "Marubo" are the *akoya* and the *tanamea*. The akoya is the feast held to celebrate the construction of a new hollowed-out log drum, or ako. These drums are considered by the elders to be the only authentic yura instrument (other than the human voice). All Marubo shovo should have an ako hung next to the benches lining the front entrance. The absence of an ako is considered a sign of poverty or laziness. When a new longhouse is constructed or an old ako is damaged, longhouse owners seek the opportunity to hold an akoya. The ako is constructed by a group of youths supervised by elders. While it is being constructed, a communal hunt takes place, often of a spider monkey troop or a peccary herd. The ako is carried back to the longhouse where it will be placed. A group of strong young men carry it by hanging it from a long pole. Along the way, they stop repeatedly to play it. While they play the ako, women playfully poke their cross-cousins in the ribs. Arriving at the longhouse, they hang the ako, play it, and eat. Subsequently, one or more elders begin to sing *saiti* (myth songs), and the youths walk around the open space in the center of the longhouse repeating the elders' verses in a call-response format. This lasts until dawn, when the ritual ends. The two akoya that I observed at Maronal involved the entire village (twelve longhouses at that time). The ako, the akoya, and the saiti are all considered "Marubo" by the elders.

The second major feast that the elders considered "Marubo" is the tanamea. The tanamea takes months of planning and involves the entire village in organizing to host several other villages. During the single tanamea that I observed from beginning to end, multiple longhouses cooperated to assemble enough food for the feast. Plantains, bananas, and manioc were brought from swiddens around the village. After a one-day ceremony called the *vina atxia* (wasp-grab), the young men in the village went hunting. Simultaneously, two elders set out to invite other Marubo villages to the feast. One crossed the forest to the Ituí River, where he went from longhouse to longhouse issuing formal invitations in ceremonial dialogues. The other went downstream to another village on the Curuçá. The Curuçá guests arrived first, bringing baskets of turtle eggs and smoked game. Once the guests had arrived, young men began to play the ako and elders began to sing saiti while young men walked around the longhouse center repeating the verses (see Ruedas 2003 and Cesarino 2008 for more details on saiti). When enough guests had arrived, the singing was moved outdoors to the longhouse patio; eventually singing took place simultaneously indoors and outdoors. When the Ituí guests arrived, they staged an invasion of the host village, tearing up pepper bushes, chopping down fruit trees, churning up the pristine patios, and chopping down the ako of the host longhouse, severely damaging it. (This, of course, necessitated the celebration of an akoya a few months later.) The guests then took over the inside of the host longhouse to sing. They sat down to eat smoked meat, turtle eggs, manioc, plantains, and banana porridge, and offered presents of arrows, feathered headdresses, and spears.

Several youth-led events took place in conjunction with the elder-led feast. In the days leading up to the feast as well as in its immediate aftermath, Alfredo's son took advantage of the presence of elders from other villages to hold political meetings to discuss land rights, education, health care, and economic development. These meetings were initiated and led by the young political activists in the village, not by the elders. On the night that the tanamea ended, the electric generator was turned on, a stereo system was activated, and a festa nawa lasted all night, involving Brazilian and Spanish American music, pharmaceutical alcohol, and nonindigenous dancing. The following day, a soccer tournament was held pitting the various villages against one another. A similar festa nawa was held at the end of a tanamea on the Ituí River a few months later. Thus the incorporation of imported elements into traditional feasts is itself something of a tradition. This aspect of Marubo ritual highlights the distinction between generations, because it is always the elders who organize and direct the ritual elements that are defined as Marubo (or yura), while it is the youths who organize and direct the ritual elements that are defined as nonindigenous, or nawa.

The associations between elders and yura ritual, on the one hand, and between youths and nawa ritual, on the other, make sense if we consider the economic and political activities that are culturally appropriate for these categories of Marubo. Alfredo's personal history exemplifies these associations. Alfredo's father had been headman before him, prior to official contact with the Brazilian government in the mid-1970s. Alfredo, however, was not the eldest of his father's sons; his brother Zacarias was considerably older. According to Alfredo, as his father got older he first passed the duties of headman to Zacarias, but Zacarias did not know how to organize labor. Alfredo did, he said, and so he assumed the role of headman. When Alfredo said this, he also emphasized that, prior to marrying, he had been to Rio Branco, Manaus, and Brasília. This accords with a comment later made to me by Zacarias, namely, that Alfredo was nawa chief while he himself was yura chief, implying that Alfredo was leader in terms of relations to nonindigenous people, while he himself was leader in traditional matters. In fact, Zacarias was not residing at Maronal during the year of my fieldwork; he was attending to pension paperwork in a village closer to Brazilian government offices. Alfredo was the headman of Maronal in all respects, not only in the realm of relations to nonindigenous people. He coordinated labor for projects of communal interest such as trading logs for a generator, cutting and maintaining an airstrip, or maintaining and operating radios; he engaged in healing rituals and issued lengthy sermons on proper social behavior, behaving in every way as the embodiment of oft-stated ideals for leaders' behavior (Melatti 1981; Ruedas 2001). But it is interesting to note that this highly traditional leader had, in his youth, visited far-distant nawa cities and that this was considered a positive factor in evaluating his worthiness to lead a village (Erikson 1996: 80–82).

The cyclic nature of orientations toward tradition and toward the nonindigenous world are further revealed in considering the way Alfredo's son, Alfredinho, spoke of his father. Alfredinho once told me that it was important for youths such as himself (meaning bilingual and politically active youths) to "present ideas to the elders" and to "present the reality of the situation" to the elders. Otherwise, he said, the elders just wanted to plant new swiddens, order hunting to take place, and organize traditional feasts. But the youths, Alfredinho said, "have been to the city and returned. They have seen the reality and learned." Only if they present ideas to the elders will the elders take steps in directions such as education and economic development; otherwise, they focus only on "traditional" goals. Alfredinho attended political meetings, frequently traveled to cities, communicated with indigenous political organizations, conveyed news of the outside world to his father and to the other elders, and called meetings of elders. Alfredo was perfectly content with this state of affairs. But it is interesting to note that Alfredinho's behavior was not so different from the behavior of his father when the latter had been young. The older Alfredo had also once traveled to the cities and been considered nawa-oriented, only to turn into a traditional leader who delegated the responsibility for nonindigenous affairs to his own son. Four years after my initial fieldwork, I heard that Alfredinho was married and was traveling less; it is possible that he was beginning his own transformation into a traditional leader whose children would handle relations with nonindigenous people.

Similar relationships between youth and elders were discernible in the family of my host, José (Alfredo's brother). José had traveled to the cities in his youth, learned some Portuguese, and worked as a rancher and logger. After his marriage he engaged in rubber tapping and continued to travel to towns, now with heavy balls of rubber on his back. But during my fieldwork he almost never left his village and refused to travel to cities. His son Manoel was bilingual and worked first as secretary-treasurer for the indigenous political organization CIVAJA and later as an agent of the Brazilian government Indian agency, FUNAI. Manoel once gave me a speech almost identical to Alfredinho's about how young people needed to learn about the nonindigenous world and influence the elders on policy toward the nawa.

There is thus evidence that the emphasis of youth on nonindigenous affairs and of elders on tradition is a cultural tendency based on age and not an idiosyncrasy based on individuality. Young men tend to focus on nonindigenous affairs, both political and economic, but eventually diminish their emphasis on these affairs as they marry and raise a family. By the time they have grown sons, the same men who once focused entirely on nonindigenous affairs at the expense of tradition have morphed into traditional elders. The focus of youth on nonindigenous affairs therefore seems to be a long-standing tradition and a very old one, considering its presence in the myth in which young men travel to obtain Inca stone axes. The association of youth with the external and of elders with the internal is clearly established in the cultural expectations concerning the social behavior and interactions of these two categories of Marubo people, the *vevoke* (those who came anciently) and the *txipoke* (those who came afterward).

The associations of youth and elders to forms of social behavior are reflected in their ritual behavior. Thus, while the elders lead youths in ceremonial activities considered "Marubo" or "traditional," the youths insert imported elements into the framework of the traditional feasts. A festa nawa, led and attended exclusively by youths, follows the end of the traditional tanamea feast, and the next day a soccer tournament is organized by the same youths. On the symbolic and ritual level, this completes the analogy of elder:yura::youth:nawa, which already exists on the level of social behavior.

Conclusions

The Marubo system of permitting youths to contribute imported elements to the structure of indigenous rituals is a variation on the general Panoan concern with the absorption of alterity (Erikson 1996). "The great Panoan rituals have been analysed as episodes of assimilation of otherness, or more precisely as the constitution of the social self through this assimilation" (Calavia 2004: 164). But although this is a pan-Panoan process, its specific consequences vary from group to group. Among the Yaminawa, the leaders organize feasts in which nonindigenous elements such as *cachaça, forró,* and exotic commodities predominate (Calavia 2004). In the Marubo case, the assignment of otherness to youth prevents the imported elements from permanently changing the definition of Marubo-ness, which appears quite rigid. Elders delegate relations with nonindigenous peoples to the youths who, many years later, delegate nonindigenous affairs to their own children. Elders, by definition bearers of what they consider to be authentic Marubo culture, have undergone a transition from youthful fascination with alterity to sober orthopraxy. A core set of ritual actions remains central to the Marubo self-definition (emically phrased as "yura," not "Marubo"), while ceremonial activities imported from other groups remain defined as nawa even when, as in the case of the flute and skin drum, nearly a century has passed since their introduction to the Marubo cultural repertoire. The Marubo use flutes in ceremonial contexts, but flutes remain excluded from the definition of Marubo-ness by this long cultural memory concerning what youths have brought from outside and by the equations of youth with otherness and of elders with indigeneity.

The presence of flutes in an informal, youth-led ritual that the elders specifically define as non-Marubo seems very distant from flute use in Amazonian contexts where flutes are considered sacred, but it highlights themes common to the region. Piedade (this volume) writes that "even in sociocultural systems in which there are no sacred flutes, the sacred flute complex is generalized in indigenous South American societies as a collective form of thinking about sensitive points in social existence." Indeed, flute use in Amazonia is embedded in cultural reflections on otherness, and its analysis reveals important regional differences in systems of thinking about alterity. Hill (2001) has pointed out that the classic ritual cults of Amazonia fall in a spectrum from "marked" to "unmarked." In marked fertility cults, "ritual power is exercised in ways that define masculinity in opposition to femininity," while in unmarked cults "the dominant theme is the building of male-female complementarity" (Hill 2001: 49). The Xinguano flutes described by Piedade and Cruz Mello in this volume are used in "rituals in which questions relative to gender relations are emphasized." In contrast, in the Wakuénai *pudáli* ceremony, musical meanings are "rooted in beliefs and attitudes about the potential problems created by social 'others,' or affines" (Hill 2004: 35). The pudáli deals with male-female relations, but in an overall context of concern with affinity, a situation fitting Descola's 2001 argument that, although some Amazonian societies—those with what Hill calls marked fertility cults—exhibit a cultural concern with sexual differences as dangerous alterities, in most of Amazonia the concern with gender is subsumed within a broader concern with affinity, and affinity is the really dangerous otherness that must be, in Piedade's terms, collectively thought about. Among the Marubo, flutes seem linked to generational difference rather than to gender or affinity, but generation, as explained above, stands in here for a bigger problem: ethnocultural otherness. The Panoan case thus suggests a third option within Amazonia: the concern with ethnocultural otherness as the dangerous alterity that must be ritually absorbed or, at least, contained.[5]

In the Marubo case, the concern with absorption of otherness is not surprising: Marubo ethnogenesis involved the coming together of several groups, speaking at least two (and possibly more) languages (Ruedas 2001: 709–41). The elders who managed this process had to think carefully about how best to effect this fusion, and they left behind a series of rituals in which internal oppositions are dialectically opposed and then converted into alliance and reciprocity (cf. Hill 2004). Although Marubo feasting is very much concerned with affinity, informants told me that they considered all members of the nine Marubo lineages, including affines and potential affines, to be kin (Portuguese *parentes*; Marubo *wetsama*, "not others"). But beyond the concern with internal difference, there is a concern with radically different otherness, the nawa—after all, the cause of Marubo ethnogenesis, via the violence of the rubber boom—and the methods for coping with its presence. This concern is shared with other Panoans: "among all Panoans, the assimilation of the exterior is perceived as a sine qua non condition for social reproduction" (Erikson 1996: 78). This takes different forms among different Panoan groups. The Matses captured women from other groups in order to ensure their own survival (Fields and Merrifield 1980; Romanoff 1984), while the Shipibo have absorbed not just individuals but the entirety of the Conibo, Shetebo, and perhaps other ethnic groups (Morin 1998). For the Yaminawa, "the internal social order requires the incorporation of the powers of the society of the 'others'" (Townsley 1986: 24), while the Matis "aim for the symbolic incorporation of alterity rather than its exclusion from the human category" (Erikson 1996: 77). Erikson (1996: 79) argues that conceptualizing the nawa is not just about incorporating their qualities, but also about finding oneself in them, so that the nawa is not only an antagonist but also a self-reference.

The Marubo are unique within the Panoan continuum in that, whereas in many Panoan societies the incorporated other is central to self-definition, the Marubo system ensures that the incorporated other does not alter the definition of yura. Marubo flute-playing is a form of incorporating the other, but it takes the form of youthful play, and men stop playing flutes as they become the elders whose behavior defines what it means to be a yura. The Marubo use of "Inca" flutes domesticates the predatory outsider—the powerful nawa—within a symbolic economy of alterity (cf. Wright, this volume, on Arawakan flutes) in which this domestication is a fundamental process of constituting the social body (yura), for if the nawa are not properly managed, the yura cannot exist. The Marubo manioc beer feast thus contains a distinctively Panoan variation on the Amazonian connection between flutes and alterity, one in which neither the woman-as-threat nor the affine-as-threat constitute the focus of collective thought, which is instead the powerful representatives of the distant and dangerous state.

Notes

1. There are nine Marubo matrilineal units, each with two denominations that alternate each generation. For example, the child of a Varináwavo woman is Tamaoavo, and vice versa. Melatti (1977) called the units formed of two denominations "matrilineal units" and the alternating-generation groups within each unit "sections" by analogy with the Kariera type of kinship. In this chapter, I follow his terminology.

2. In transcribing Marubo words such as *shovo*, I have rendered their bilabial fricative with the letter *v*. In addition, for this paper I have ignored the difference between the retroflex fricative and the palato-alveolar fricative, which is a phonemic distinction in Marubo. In his earlier writings on the Marubo, Melatti (1977) transcribed the bilabial fricative with the letter *b* and distinguished the retroflex fricative by transcribing it *sr* instead of *sh*. In his later writings, Melatti (1986) shifted to a *v* for the bilabial fricative and ignored the *sr/sh* distinction. I follow his later model.

3. There is an ongoing debate among Panoanists concerning the existence and extent of contacts between Panoans and highland Quechuans in pre-Hispanic times. Lathrap et al. (1985) utilized evidence from archaeology and the analysis of myth to argue that Quechua-speakers lived among riverine Panoans in pre-Hispanic times, establishing a ruling class and dominating the area for a time. This argument was refuted by DeBoer and Raymond (1987: 130), who suggested the presence of the Inca in Panoan myth is a postconquest phenomenon, noting that "use of the generic term 'Inca' to refer to the peoples of the Andes is a Spanish practice." Melatti (1985) has argued that the Inca as represented in Marubo myth could only be derived from experience with pre-Hispanic Andean peoples, and Cesarino's translation of a Marubo myth has the Marubo trading for stone axes rather than metal axes, which strongly suggests a pre-Hispanic context. Calavia (2000: 8) discusses the idea that the presence of the Inca figure in Panoan myth may result from missionaries using Quechua as lingua franca and leaders of messianic movements acting as descendants of the Inca or spokespersons of Indianist nationalisms, who have all updated and altered the meaning of "Inca" in regional discourse over time. Calavia notes that recognition of pre-Hispanic contacts between Andean elites and Panoan peoples is compatible with the idea of a constant reformulation of the Inca figure during postconquest history, a position I agree with. The extent and nature of pre-Hispanic contacts between Panoans and Quechuans remains very much an open question.

4. The traumatic nature of contact between native Amazonians and rubber workers during the rubber boom (see, e.g., Taussig 1987 and Reeve 1988) was

a crucible for ethnogenesis in the Panoan area (cf. Erikson 1996). According to oral histories gathered by Montagner Melatti and Melatti 1975, Coutinho 1993, and this author, some ancestors of the Marubo sought isolation from the rubber workers by migrating to a remote area near the headwaters of the Arrojo River by the 1890s. Various Panoan groups joined these original migrants over the next forty years, and it is from these people that the contemporary Marubo are descended. The exogenous term *Marubo* has only recently become an autonym. The concept of ethnogenesis is one that has been receiving increasing attention in Amazonian studies in the past decade (Hill 1996; Hornborg 2005).

5. While Panoanists have long noted the tendency of Panoans to absorb the cultural other in a variety of ways, Arawakanists (Santos-Granero 2002: 28–32) have noted the process of "Panoization" whereby some Arawakan neighbors of Panoan groups—notably the Piro—tend to undergo a form of transethnic change whereby they come to resemble Panoans more than other Arawakans in a number of ways including clothing, pottery, and specific practices of warfare.

References Cited

Bardales Rodriguez, Cesar. 1979. *Quimisha Incabo ini yoa: leyendas de los Shipibo-Conibo sobre los tres Incas*. Yarinacocha: Instituto Lingüístico de Verano.

Calavia Saez, Oscar. 2000. "O Inca Pano: mito, história, e modelos etnológicos." *Mana* 6: 7–35.

———. 2004. "In Search of Ritual: Tradition, Outer World, and Bad Manners in the Amazon." *Journal of the Royal Anthropological Institute* 10: 157–73.

Cesarino, Pedro de Niemeyer. 2008. "Oniska: A Poética da Morte e do Mundo entre os Marubo da Amazônia Ocidental." PhD diss, Universidade Federal do Rio de Janeiro.

Coffaci de Lima, Edilene. 1994. "Katukina: história e organização social de um grupo Pano do alto Juruá." Master's thesis, Universidade de São Paulo.

Coutinho, Walter. 1993. "Brancos e Barbudos na Amazônia: Os Mayoruna na história." Master's thesis, Universidade de Brasília.

DeBoer, Warren, and J. Scott Raymond. 1987. "Roots Revisited: The Origins of the Shipibo Art Style." *Journal of Latin American Lore* 13: 115–32.

Descola, Philippe. 2001. "The Genres of Gender: Local Models and Global Paradigms in the Comparison of Amazonia and Melanesia." In *Gender in Amazonia and Melanesia: An Exploration of the Comparative Method*, ed. Thomas A. Gregor and Donald Tuzin, 91–114. Berkeley: University of California Press.

Deshayes, Patrick, and Barbara Keifenheim. 1994. *Penser l'autre chez les Indiens Huni Kuin de l'Amazonie*. Paris: L'Harmattan.

Dole, Gertrude. 1979. "Pattern and Variation in Amahuaca Kin Terminology." *Working Papers on South American Indians* 1: 13–36.

Erikson, Philippe. 1986. "Altérité, tatouage, et anthropophagie chez les Pano: la belliqueuse quête du soi." *Journal de la Société des Américanistes* 72: 185–209.

———. 1990. "How Crude Is Mayoruna Pottery?" *Journal of Latin American Lore* 16: 47–68.

———. 1996. *La griffe des aïeux: marquage du corps et démarquages ethniques chez les Matis d'Amazonie.* Paris: Peeters/Centre National de la Recherche Scientifique.

Fields, Harriet, and William Merrifield. 1980. "Mayoruna (Panoan) Kinship." *Ethnology* 19: 1–28.

Harner, Michael. 1993. "Waiting for the Inca God: Culture, Myth, and History." *South American Indian Studies* 1: 53–60.

Hill, Jonathan D., ed. 1996. *History, Power, and Identity: Ethnogenesis in the Americas, 1492–1992.* Iowa City: University of Iowa Press.

———. 2001. "The Variety of Fertility Cultism in Amazonia: A Closer Look at Gender Symbolism in Northwestern Amazonia." In *Gender in Amazonia and Melanesia: An Exploration of the Comparative Method*, ed. Thomas A. Gregor and Donald Tuzin, 45–68. Berkeley: University of California Press.

———. 2004. "Metamorphosis: Mythic and Musical Modes of Ceremonial Exchange among the Wakuénai of Venezuela." In *Music in Latin America and the Caribbean: An Encyclopedic History*, vol. 1, ed. Malena Kuss, 25–47. Austin: University of Texas Press.

Hornborg, Alf. 2005. "Ethnogenesis, Regional Integration, and Ecology in Prehistoric Amazonia: Toward a System Perspective." *Current Anthropology* 46: 589–620.

Keifenheim, Barbara. 1990. "Nawa: un concept clé de l'altérité chez les Pano." *Journal de la Société des Américanistes* 76: 79–94.

———. 1992. "Identité et altérité chez les Indiens Pano." *Journal de la Société des Américanistes* 78: 79–93.

Kensinger, Kenneth M. 1993. "When a Turd Floats By: Cashinahua Metaphors of Contact." *South American Indian Studies* 2: 37–38.

———. 1995. *How Real People Ought to Live: The Cashinahua of Eastern Peru.* Prospect Heights IL: Waveland.

Lathrap, Donald, Angelika Gebhart-Sayer, and Ann Mester. 1985. "The Roots of the Shipibo Art Style: Three Waves on Imiríacocha or There Were 'Incas' before the Incas." *Journal of Latin American Lore* 11: 31–119.

Lathrap, Donald, Angelika Gebhart-Sayer, Thomas P. Myers, and Ann Mester.

1987. "Further Discussion of the Roots of the Shipibo Art Style: A Rejoinder to DeBoer and Raymond." *Journal of Latin American Lore* 13: 225–71.

McCallum, Cecilia. 2000. "Incas e nawas: produção, transformação, e transcendência na história Kaxinawá." In *Pacificando o branco: cosmologies do contato no norte-amazônico*, ed. Bruce Albert and Alcida Rita Ramos, 375–401. São Paulo: Editora UNESP.

Melatti, Julio Cezar. 1977. "Estrutura social Marubo: um sistema australiano na Amazônia." *Anuário Antropológico* 76: 83–120.

———. 1981. "Os patrões Marubo." *Anuário Antropológico* 83: 155–98.

———. 1985. *A origem dos brancos no mito de Shoma Wetsa.* Brasília: Universidade de Brasília, Trabalhos de Ciências Sociais, Série Antropologia Social, 48.

———. 1986. *Wenía: a origem mitológica da cultura Marubo.* Brasília: Universidade de Brasília, Trabalhos de Ciências Sociais, Série Antropologia Social, 78.

Montagner Melatti, Delavair, and Julio Cezar Melatti. 1975. *Relatório sobre os Índios Marubo.* Brasília: Universidade de Brasília, Trabalhos de Ciências Sociais, Série Antropologia Social, 13.

Morin, Françoise. 1998. "The Shipibo-Conibo." In *Guía Etnográfica de la Alta Amazonía*, vol. 3, ed. Fernando Santos-Granero and Frederica Barclay, 225–435. Quito: Abya Yala.

Olsen, Dale A. 2004. "Aerophones of Traditional Use in South America, with References to Central America." In *Music in Latin America and the Caribbean: An Encyclopedic History*, vol. 1, ed. Malena Kuss, 261–325. Austin: University of Texas Press.

Reeve, Mary-Elizabeth. 1988. "*Cauchu Uras*: Lowland Quichua Histories of the Amazon Rubber Boom." In *Rethinking History and Myth: Indigenous South American Perspectives on the Past*, ed. Jonathan D. Hill, 19–34. Urbana: University of Illinois Press.

Renard-Casevitz, France-Marie, Thierry Saignes, and Anne-Christine Taylor. 1986. *L'Inca, L'Espagnol, et les sauvages: Rapports entre les societes amazoniennes at andines du XVe au XVIIIe siècle.* Paris: Editions Recherche sur les Civilisations.

Roe, Peter. 1982. *The Cosmic Zygote: Cosmology in the Amazon Basin.* New Brunswick NJ: Rutgers University Press.

———. 1988. "The Josho Nahuanbo Are All Wet and Undercooked: Shipibo Views of the Whiteman and the Incas in Myth, Legend, and History." In *Rethinking History and Myth: Indigenous South American Perspectives on the Past*, ed. Jonathan D. Hill, 106–35. Urbana: University of Illinois Press.

Romanoff, Steven. 1984. "Matses Adaptations in the Peruvian Amazon." PhD diss., Columbia University.

Ruedas, Javier. 2001. "The Marubo Political System." PhD diss., Tulane University.

———. 2002. "Marubo Discourse Genres and Domains of Influence: Language and Politics in an Indigenous Amazonian Village." *International Journal of American Linguistics* 68: 447–82.

———. 2003. "Social Context and Creation of Meaning in Indigenous Amazonian Performances of Myth and Oral History." *Journal of Ritual Studies* 17: 35–71.

———. 2004. "History, Ethnography, and Politics in Amazonia: Implications of Diachronic and Synchronic Variability in Marubo Politics." *Tipití: Journal of the Society for the Anthropology of Lowland South America* 2: 23–64.

Russell, Robert. 1964. *Un estudio del sistema de parentesco amahuaca*. Lima: Instituto Lingüístico de Verano, Información de Campo 22.

Santos-Granero, Fernando. 2002. "The Arawakan Matrix: Ethos, Language, and History in Native South America." In *Comparative Arawakan Histories: Rethinking Language Family and Culture Area in Amazonia*, ed. Jonathan D. Hill and Fernando Santos-Granero, 25—50. Urbana: University of Illinois Press.

Taussig, Michael. 1987. *Shamanism, Colonialism, and the Wild Man: A Study in Terror and Healing*. Chicago: University of Chicago Press.

Townsley, Graham. 1986. "La sociedad Yaminahua y sus 'otros.'" *Extracta* 5: 21–26.

13. Arawakan Flute Cults of Lowland South America

The Domestication of Predation and the Production of Agentivity

ROBIN WRIGHT

This chapter presents a comparative view of the centrality of aerophones in the cosmologies and ritual lives of five Arawak-speaking societies of Amazonia: (1) the Wauja of the upper Xingu among whom aerophones, masks, and manufactured objects are attributed agentivity in distinct ritual contexts, many of which are related to the curing of sickness provoked by predatory spirits, called *yerupoho*; (2) the Enawene Nawe of the upper Juruena among whom the complex set of aerophones representing the clans, *yãkwa*, are played during seven-month-long rituals in which the Enawene Nawe "domesticate" the predatory *yakayriti* spirits, who control all food production. The yãkwa flutes thus transform a predatory relation into one of reciprocity between humans and the spirits of nature; (3) the Apurinã of the Purus River whose complex *kamatxi* rituals, which are no longer celebrated, were clearly linked to the spirits of the dead and the production of warriors, similar to the flute cults of the northwest Amazon; and (4) the northwest Amazon Arawak (Baniwa, Tariana, Warckena) who celebrate the rituals of Kuwai, which combines themes of male and female fertility, sacred flutes and trumpets believed to be the "body" of the first ancestor, generative relations among humans and the spirits of nature, and agentivity in interethnic relations of political alliance and warfare in history; (5) other northwest Amazon Arawakan societies, such as the Yukuna, Kabiyari, and Matapi, are briefly compared, although more in-depth analysis awaits a future paper.

To begin to understand the meaning of the sacred flutes in these diverse Arawak-speaking societies, I shall place each within the context of a larger theoretical model that seeks to explain the dynamics of socioreligious formations of indigenous Amazonian societies and their historical transformations. In this way, I shall focus on comparisons and contrasts in rituals based on the use of aerophones and their critical importance for the historical reproduction of these societies.

A Model of Historical Transformations in Amazonian Socioreligious Formations

Recent anthropological research on the social and religious lives of indigenous peoples of the South American Lowlands highlights, on the one hand, the importance of aesthetics and emotional life which are intimately linked to knowledge and moral value and in which there is an expressed ideal of "harmonious conviviality," that is to say, a deliberate effort in indigenous communities to promote an ethic of sharing and caring among relatives. This ideal, however, is at the same time described as a constant struggle, a "sisyphus syndrome," in which every effort to establish this ideal of harmony runs up against negative forces such as sorcery, symbolic or physical violence, and conflict that prevents the realization of the ideal. So, in fact, two models have been proposed for understanding the social and religious lives of Amazonian indigenous societies: one, the so-called moral economy of intimacy (represented by British social anthropologists, led by Joanna Overing and her students; see e.g., Overing and Passes 2000), in which societies seek to establish harmonious conviviality among consanguineal kin groups by restricting the abuses of power, for example; and the second that has been called the "symbolic economy of alterity" (represented by the Brazilian anthropologist Eduardo Viveiros de Castro and his students), which emphasizes the relative importance of the social category of affines (in-laws) as a potential source of conflict and hence as a dynamic force in social and religious processes (see, e.g., Viveiros de Castro 1996, 2002). The second model concentrates on processes of symbolic exchange and above all those in which predation is a central theme: warfare and cannibalism, hunting, shamanism, and funerary rites.

These theoretical tendencies are not necessarily exclusive, and an exponent of the first school has found both socioreligious idioms, differentially defined, within a single ethnic group (the Arawak-speaking Amuesha of the eastern Peruvian Amazon, about whom Fernando Santos-Granero has written an important monograph, *The Power of Love*).[1]

Now, all Amazonian indigenous societies, we must recognize, have suffered transformations, often catastrophic, since at least the beginning of the colonial regime (epidemics, demographic collapse, atrocities) so severe that it is hardly imaginable that these have taken place without leaving deep and structural traces within their cosmologies and socioreligious processes as we have come to know them. So what are called "relations of predation" between humans and the natural world, as well as among human groups with all its connotations of (potential) violence in Viveiros de Castro's model cannot be addressed without reference to the historical realities of colonial violence and its social structures. I argue that predatory images in cosmology are amplified due to the extent to which the spirits of the dead have multiplied while the populations of living peoples have diminished.

Indeed, the historical trajectories of Amazonian societies are marked by profound crisis, social and environmental "predation," against which they have activated their structural mechanisms, transforming their socioreligious formations through such processes as prophetic movements and even the more recent movements of conversion to evangelical pentecostal denominations.[2]

This reaction to crisis clearly cannot be thought of without relating it to processes of the surrounding society, with its analogous historical and structural movements, like colonialism or development on a global scale.

So how can we understand the dialectics of internal harmony and external predation, dispersion and concentration while taking into account historical transformations? We suggest that both dialectics may be subsumed in a single model composed of a series at the ends of which are two socioreligious formations: one which we may call "particularist"; and the other, "universalist." Evidently, different from the way these terms have been used since Weber, we argue that both formations are inherent in Amazonian cosmologies and social structures, and both can be seen to articulate with external historical and ecological circumstances. That is, these formations are generative of, and are influenced by, historical dynamics; specific external historical influences may intensify or exacerbate one or the other indigenous formation. Both necessarily involve relations of humans to nature as defined by indigenous cosmologies. In both formations, flute cults have a central role in processes of cosmological and historical reproduction. In the following, I examine each of these formations more closely.

Particularist socioreligious formations are marked on the social level by their emphasis on local kinship ties, conflicts with affinal or "other" groups considered non-kin, and mediation with spiritual and natural resources through religious specialists such as shamans. Likewise, on the religious level, the cosmologies of traditional tropical forest agricultural societies are marked by life-generating (ritual) violence. The core idea in these cosmologies is the centrality of death and regeneration, violent acts, as in the common motif of the killed and dismembered deity or primordial being, out of whose body parts sprout the important food plants, which is periodically reenacted in rituals. This ideology with its implicit and explicit violence allows us to understand rituals such as head hunting and cannibalism, but also fishing, hunting, and planting all reiterations of the primordial act of killing. Translating these ideas into contemporary ethnological theory, one would expect the idiom of predatory violence to be predominant, though evidently not excluding harmonious conviviality.

The universalist socioreligious formations, on the other hand, are characterized by the following elements: first, political and religious identity are constructed over greater social distances and involve universal constructs of identities (notions such as "all we people," nation, indigenous people, etc.) These constructs supersede localized kingroup membership. Second, supra-local religious and political authorities (such as priests, prophets, federations, pan-indigenous organizations) seek to stimulate an effective integration of extensive religious, political, and social units. Third, access to spiritual and material resources becomes immediate, superseding the mediation characteristic of particularistic formations. Priestly specialists certainly do mediate between humans and the divine, but individuals and family groups, through prayer, also have direct access to divine assistance and experience of divinity.

The distinction between particularist and universalist socioreligious formations has been used by Kapfhammer (2004) to discuss Sateré-Mawé conversion to evangelicalism (in Wright 2004); I have extended this distinction to contemporary Arawakan-speaking societies about whom we have fairly complete ethnographies (Wright 2008). The distinction is broader than that which is commonly used in the literature between "shamanic" and "priestly" societies. Through it, we seek to understand more global processes that characterize the cosmologies of each formation and the historical transitions from one to the other. Here, we focus on the place of the flutes in these historical processes.

It is likely that many historical Arawakan-speaking societies were of the universalist kind, such as the Taino of the Antilles; the Achagua of the savannahs (whose masked dances were called *Chuway*); and the Maypure of the upper Orinoco River. Hill and Chaumeil have noted in the introduction to this volume that one of the Jesuit sources of the eighteenth century on the Orinoco likewise noted the centrality of flute cults, sometimes related to treatment of the dead, sometimes as in the case of the Maypure related to a "cult of the serpents" with the name of *Cueti* (cognate to the Arawakan word for the flutes, Kuwai): "*Cueti* means animal. The Maypure believe that the serpents come from time to time into their villages, that they drink with them, and that they enjoy dancing with the men" (Gilij, *Ensayos*, 2: 235–36, cited in Wright 1981: 111).[3]

In his travels on the upper Rio Negro in the late eighteenth century, for example, the naturalist Alexander von Humboldt noted the great importance of the sacred flute cults located on the upper Guainía where it joins the Tomo River. This is exactly in the territory of the Baniva. According to von Humboldt, "There are but a small number of these trumpets. The most anciently celebrated is that upon a hill near the confluence of the Tomo and Guainía" (1907: 362–63) The flutes and trumpets were a central institution in religious and political life. According to von Humboldt, had colonization not destroyed indigenous societies in the early eighteenth century, then *"the botuto cult of Tomo could have been of some political importance, where the guardians of the trumpets would become a ruling caste of priests, and the oracle of Tomo could gradually form a link between bordering nations"* (364, my emphasis). He described the playing of the sacred flute instruments under palm trees "to secure their fertility." He also noted that they represent "the ancestor" and, more specifically, the ongoing relationship between humans and their ancestors. The relationship is creative and dynamic, for it sustains the periodicity that is vital to the growth of the harvest. The ancestral flute cults, in short, promoted the growth of the harvest as they provided for the growth of social groups.

For the Amazonian peoples to whom we will refer, contacts with non-indigenous society are today more or less established: the Wauja of the Xingu Park in central Brazil; the Enawene Nawe of the upper Juruena River, to the southwest of the Xingu; the Apurinã of the upper Purus River to the south of the Amazon; and the Baniwa of the Içana River and its tributaries of the northwest Amazon; and the Yukuna of the Caquetá and Miriti rivers. All are Arawak-speaking peoples; the first two are relatively small groups (populations around 300 people), while the population of the Apurinã is around 2,400; the Baniwa/Wakuénai/Curripaco, around 12,000; and the Yukuna, about 500.[4]

The Wauja of the Xingu

Among the Wauja, according to anthropologist Aristóteles Barcelos Neto, predation occurs between the primordial spirits, called *yerupoho*—zoomorphic, anthropomorphic beings—and humans, and between humans and animals.[5] They speak of primordial predation of the spirits on humans who were forced to live inside termite hills. This situation was reversed when the Sun put on a powerful mask and forced the yerupoho spirits to assume a hidden existence in nature. Many of the yerupoho fabricated masks, flutes, and other ritual artifacts with which they hid themselves from the power of the Sun. Others jumped into lakes where they remained as monstrous, cannibalistic predators. Others assumed the forms of animals. The yerupoho "dressed" themselves as plants, animals, domestic artifacts, and musical instruments.

The yerupoho today are said to have an enormous curiosity for human life, wish to live with them, make human beings into their own images, incorporate them into their own population, animalize them. There is danger in this approximation, for they may rob human souls, and the more dangerous yerupoho may practice monstrous cannibalism on humans. In stealing human souls, they provoke sickness, although it is said that they don't do so intentionally and, if a person falls sick, they are the first ones to help in curing. Humans, on the other hand, have every interest in domesticating these spirits, for sickness to the Wauja signifies an imbalance in the desires of the soul, which is what attracts the yerupoho in the first place and makes them want to take the souls of humans away. By domesticating the yerupoho, that is, overcoming the fear that the sick have of the yerupoho transforming that relation into one of friendship and intimacy humans can later use their power to prevent further attacks by other yerupoho. So humans summon the yerupoho spirits, in the form of giant masks (some of them nine feet in diameter) and aerophones (or flutes and clarinets), celebrating their presence, in ritual dances in order to reestablish the balance through cure between the sick and the social. Thus the predatory power of the yerupoho is domesticated or transformed into harmonious conviviality through ritual.

We should remember, too, that the Wauja today have recovered socially, politically, and demographically from a critical reduction of their population in the 1960s due to epidemics, a period in which their ritual life was intensified, according to Wauja ethnographers. That is, the Wauja did not abandon the use of their musical instruments, which were still seen to have great power, during the period of demographic loss. To the contrary, the Wauja and their sacred instruments seem to have controlled the predation of sickness-giving spirits and thus averted catastrophe. As is mentioned in several places in this volume, the curative power of the flutes among the Wauja "suggests a direct and ancient relationship between shamanism and the flute rituals, whose "breath" or music (or the simple act of seeing them) had the power to cure certain illnesses" (introduction, 9; see also articles by Mello and Piedade). The *kawoká* flutes, in particular, are made to commemorate the shamanic healing of individual men and women, who then become the flutes' owners when they are played in later rituals. This in turn provides collective protection from the predatory spirits.

The Enawane Nawe of the Juruena River

The Enawene Nawe, studied by Márcio Ferreira da Silva, formed part of the larger group called Paressi who were contacted in the eighteenth century by the slave-runner Antonio Pires de Campos.

An ethnohistory of these peoples since these first contacts has yet to be written; nevertheless, I believe it is possible to suggest that the Enawene Nawe either were close relatives of the Paressi or were a Paressi subgroup that separated early in contact and thus were able to maintain their autonomy until they were contacted by Catholic missionaries in the 1960s.[6]

The excellent ethnographies by Marcio Ferreira da Silva of Enawene Nawe social life and cosmology clearly show how the group has cultural features which link them to the Xinguan Arawaks (the Wauja) and, I suggest, to the Arawak-speaking peoples of the southwest and northwest Amazon. As, for example, in the elaborate sets of flutes and trumpets that are so central to Enawene Nawe religious life. I will first briefly discuss their cosmology and ritual life in order to come back later to the question of the domestication of predation through the ritual use of flutes.

The Enawene Nawe say they inhabit the intermediate layer of the cosmos between the spheres of the celestial ancestor spirits (whom they call "grandparents"), described as immortal, beautiful, generous, playful, healthy, who live in a world of plenty, an architecturally perfect village surrounded by a bountiful natural world, where everything grows and flourishes without having to be cultivated and the subterranean spirits who are described as ugly, implacable, greedy, lazy, perverse, insatiable, asocial (that is, in contrast to the ancestral spirits, these are considered non-kin, "others," who provoke sickness and death among humans). The world of humans is thus the imperfect specter of the celestial layer, inescapably vulnerable to the capriciousness of the subterranean spirits.

These subterranean spirits called *yakayriti* "own" or at least are intermediaries between humans and almost all of the resources found in nature. Since these spirits control natural resources, the Enawene Nawe depend on them for food production and for the reproduction of social life. The subterranean spirits demand that humans produce food for them as well, during the rituals dedicated to them. If the Enawene Nawe don't, these spirits will become so furious as to kill all humans with sickness (in the Enawene Nawe idiom, the yakayriti throw pieces of their flutes into the bodies of humans, which provokes pain and sickness here again, we find the association between sickness and pieces of the spirits' flutes which must be sucked out in shamanic rituals. Whenever an Enawene Nawe gets sick or has a problem, s/he attributes it to the yakairiti spirits, who are angered at something and threaten to take the individual to the other world. Enawene Nawe mythology is full of catastrophes produced in the past by these spirits. They are supposed to have provoked a series of catastrophes that almost decimated all humans. The few survivors, guided by the celestial spirits of their respective clans, went one by one to a designated ancestral village. When they got there, they went to the house of the clans where they left their flutes in a certain position which is exactly the position in which the flutes of those clans are placed today. Each of the survivors taught the others some peculiarity of their clan's customs; altogether, the customs created the cultural tradition of the Enawene Nawe. Here, we have an indigenous understanding of their own cultural formation in history, in which clan identity is intimately associated with each flute.

The Enawene Nawe, like the Wauja, have an extraordinarily elaborate ritual life which involves a complex set of aerophones/flutes, representing the various clans. There are rituals associated with the *Enore*, the celestial spirits and ancestors of the clans, and those associated with the yakayriti, the subterranean spirits. The sacred flutes are always played during the seven-month-long rituals called *Yākwa*, which refers both to the clan ancestors and to the flutes of the yakayriti. In these rituals, a relation of reciprocity is established between humans and their ancestors with the yakayriti: the latter provide the Enawene Nawe with abundant quantities of smoked fish, and in exchange the Enawene Nawe provide the spirits with plant salt and other foods.

The Yākwa is the longest and most important of the Enawene

Nawe rituals. Performed annually between January and June, it begins with the harvest of the new corn and ends with the planting of the collective manioc garden. The ritual groups are organized along paternal lines, and each ritual group is associated with a specific group of ancestral spirits. The Enawene Nawe believe that the ancestral spirits are themselves organized in groups as well and inhabit their own territory (a real physical space), which is part of their traditional territory.

The generic name of the ritual groups is Yãkwa; they are, in reality, the Enawene Nawe clans. They bear the names of the groups of origin that in mythical times came from distant points of the territory and united to form the Enawene Nawe. Each ritual group (Yãkwa/yakayriti) is related to a specific set of musical instruments.

In the first part of the ritual, in January, the village divides in two: the hosts, called *hari kare*, and the men who will go off on a fishing expedition and come back as the yakayriti spirits. Initially, the whole village prepares by making canoes and fishtraps and harvesting manioc. The first offerings of food, chants, and dances to the yakairiti spirits are then performed. The men also prepare the first plant salt, an essential exchange and food item for the yakayriti who in turn are said to obtain the fish for the Enawene Nawe during the ritual period.

In the second part of the ritual, the men leave for the smaller waterways, where they build one or more dams and catch and roast fish for a period of up to two months. At the conclusion of this period, the men become the yakayriti spirits, painting and adorning themselves according to the image the Enawene Nawe have of these spirits. When they return to the village, there is a mock battle between the yakayriti and the hosts demonstrating the intensely ambivalent relation that exists between these spirits and humanity. Then, the most important part of the ritual begins, which lasts four months, during which there are profuse exchanges of food, as well as chants and constant dances with all of the nine sets of flutes in the patio of the village. At the end, the ritual participants fabricate masks that represent the manioc spirits. With the end of the planting, the *yakwa* cycle comes to an end and the following ritual cycle begins.

Thus, like the yerupoho spirits, the yakayriti are dramatized in the masks and ultimately domesticated during the course of the rituals. This involves a complex process in which the village is divided into hosts, hari kare, and men dressed as yakayriti who enter the village bringing an abundance of fish which they give in exchange for plant salt and other food and beverages. Everything is done with the intention of following the traditional ways and satisfying the yakayriti, in order to prevent these spirits from threatening life in the village and, on the other, to uphold the harmony of the world. All of the predatory danger that these spirits represent is thus transformed in the course of the ritual into a celebration of harmonious conviviality.

The music of the flutes played by the human hosts is melodious, harmonious, accompanied by highly cadenced dance formations. The "music" and dance of the yakayriti is burlesque, that is, bawdy, humorous entertainment full of grotesque exaggeration. The two styles counterbalance each other, producing a harmony that nevertheless has to be renewed constantly every cycle.

In the cases of both the Wauja and the Enawene Nawe, we may thus speak of symbolic economies of alterity involving the spirits and humans in which harmonious conviviality is constructed through collective rituals in which the sacred flutes are the centerpiece counterbalancing the tyranny and excesses of predation.[7]

The Apurinã of the Upper Purus River

In contrast to the Wauja and Enawene Nawe, the Apurinã of the upper Purus River, as well as both the Yukuna and the Baniwa of the northwest Amazon region have experienced relatively long and brutal histories of contact, the Apurinã and Yukuna since at least the mid-nineteenth century and the Baniwa since the mid-eighteenth century. For the Apurinã and Yukuna especially during both rubber cycles; for the Baniwa, from the period of indigenous slavery down to the second rubber cycle. As one would expect, such traumatic contacts have marked indigenous cosmologies. We could say that and this is the important point in these cases, the peculiar characteristics of the particularist socioreligious formations have become exacerbated/intensified by their articulations with historical circumstances. How, and why?

The recent ethnography of the Apurinã unfortunately does not allow us to explore fully the kinds of questions for which we are seeking answers. Although the Brazilian ethnographer Juliana Schiel has taped and transcribed a great many Apurinã narratives, there is very little exegesis on cosmology and human/nature relations that would permit a deeper understanding of the flutes and ritual life as it was in the past.

The earliest written sources on the Apurinã describe them as being a numerous, formidable, and warlike tribe. "Constantly engaged in war, and mainly against those of their own tribe" (Schiel 2004: 52). They stood in contrast with the Piro, a neighboring Arawakan people, among whom trade was their principal manner of relating to other peoples. So important was war as a dynamic that Schiel concluded that "war and internal vengeance had and have a great importance for the Apurinã and are constitutive both of their external image and their self-image" (2004: 52).

Apurinã cosmogonic myths begin with a cataclysmic destruction of a preexisting world and monstrous beings of nature against whom the culture hero Tsura seeks vengeance. Vengeance is thus a predominant theme as well in Apurinã cosmogony. In their history of contact, when the Apurinã were not fighting off the whites during the rubber boom, their wars were often waged among themselves, and the principal motives for war or vendettas were vengeance, seemingly endless cycles of retribution among families as though, coupled with the predation of the whites on them, the Apurinã destroyed themselves.[8] We could say that here, external historical circumstances, coupled with the warrior ethos of the Apurinã as defined in myth, have intensified internal predation to the extreme.

As in all Arawakan societies, Apurinã shamans had significant power to visit other worlds below the earth and in the sky where the deity Tsura is. The stronger the shaman, the fewer limitations to his soul's travel; and as in life, so it was in death, for the shamans, several Apurinã said, "do not die" but become "enchanted" (*encantados*) *kamatxi*. At the moment of their deaths, it is said, one heard the sound of thunder. Reportedly, the shamans of the distant past even gave instructions as to how they should be buried so that they could leave their tombs. In some cases, their tombs were kept clean; in others, the souls of deceased shamans were seen among bands of animals, such as wild pigs (*queixadas*). Most, however, went after death into the north.

The Apurinã recount stories of great migrations in the mythic past when their ancestors left a place of origin in the south and migrated to a place in the north where death does not exist. Only an elect group succeeded in reaching this "sacred land," while most Apurinã decided to remain in the middle of the way, in a land which they came to know as the "land where many deaths occur" (Schiel 2004).

The sacred flutes of the Apurinã, called *Kamatxi*, "enchanted beings" or spirits, were played during the festivals of the same name when the *Kamatxi* spirits, who were the "chiefs" or "owners" of the buriti palms and who lived inside the buriti palm trees (*Mauritia flexuosa*), would come and play the flutes with the men. The shamans would go out to bring the Kamatxi to the festivals, but these were prohibited for the women to see. Women had to remain secluded during the presence of the Kamatxi in the villages. In this respect, the Kamatxi flutes were similar to the sacred flutes of the northwest Amazon, to which early travelers such as Ehrenreich and Steere compared them. In some sense, also, they were connected with the spirits of deceased warriors.[9] Sources during the second rubber boom stated that these festivals were no longer practiced, though elder Apurinã men today remember the festivals of the "Enchanted Spirits" (*Encantados*), the meaning they have given to the Kamatxi. It is plausible to conclude that here, once again, we find the close association between the shamans and the sacred flutes, through the mediation of the breath; the association between the sacred flutes and the fertility of the fruit trees; and the association between the sacred flutes and the identity of warriors. Finally, the prohibition against "seeing" the flutes (as opposed to "hearing" their music) is explicitly stated in contrast with both the Wauja and the Enawene Nawe.

The Yukuna of the Miriti River

Slightly north of the Amazon, on the tributaries of the Caquetá and Miriti, lies the southern fringe of what might be called the "classic" area of the "Yurupary complex." While some of the earliest documents from the Japurá River region and its tributaries suggest the existence of sacred flutes and trumpets among the Arawakan Yumana, Passe, and Resigaro, those societies suffered drastic reductions and relocations in the eighteenth and nineteenth centuries. The Yukuna, Kabiyari, and Matapi, however, have received far better ethnographic treatment by anthropologists such as Pierre-Yves Jacopin (1988), Elizabeth Reichel Dussan (1987), and Augusto Oyuela-Caycedo (2004).

The Yukuna ritual of sacred flutes traditionally lasted seven days during which men played the famous trumpets (*wakaperi*: "bad eagle") and women were forbidden to see and have contact with them. This was followed by a fast lasting three to eight weeks, at the end of which the *wera* festival brought kin and affines together in a common celebration of the newly initiated boys and girls with the drinking of buriti (*Mauritia flexuosa*) and Umari (*Puraqueiba selicea*) chicha, a lightly fermented beverage.

The rite corresponds to the same ceremony among the Tukanoan-speaking peoples to the north. Summarizing from Jacopin's lengthy description of a Yukuna ritual in which he was an initiate, the young boys are gathered in the longhouse and wait to hear the trumpets approaching. Children and women take refuge inside the house. The trumpets surround the longhouse and play their music for all to hear; eventually the women and children are pushed outside the house and the trumpets enter. The initiates, whose heads are covered in blankets, are frightened. The next day, the men and initiates go into the forest where they fast and stay for seven days. The initiates then see and learn how to play the trumpets and memorize the creation myth. They are secluded and protected from the rays of the sun. The women are forbidden to see their children for fear that this would harm the children. At the end of the fast, the children catch, cook, and eat their first animal food. Shortly after, the headman schedules the final closing festival in which the participants drink umari beer. Finally, men and women perform the "dance of the snakes" and then return to the community.

Jacopin relates that had he not discovered the "eagle of Yurupary" (*wakaperi*) during his research on Yukuna myths, he would have never witnessed the ritual, for the Yukuna had not performed the ritual for many years. According to the story, the eagle brought a deadly fire to the four creator-heroes, Kahipu-Lakeno, who were resting in heaven after creating the world. The four creators learned that Yurupary—the powerful spirit whose body became the sacred flutes and trumpets—could only be destroyed by this fire. So the four took Yurupary's fire from his sister's vulva and burned him to death. Jacopin surmises that the meaning of the story has to do with the irreversible passage from life to death.

Yet because women give birth, they are able to reverse the irreversible. Similarly, by means of the Yurupari, men (in particular shamans) are able to make boys men born again. So the Yurupari is a ritual of the inversion of daily life; this is why, for example, Kahipu-Lakeno get their lethal fire from Yurupari's sister, a woman who gives birth to fire. (Jacopin 1988)

Reichel Dussan says one of the purposes of the ritual is to make the initiates "see beyond the eyes" (1987: 196), that is, to understand the "other" side of visible reality, the laws of social structure, and the symbolism of material culture. They are blindfolded until the time they "see" the flutes and trumpets, although both they and the women "hear" the music from inside the house. (According to the story, the women were their primal owners in matriarchal origin times, but after the trumpets were taken away by the men, the women were forbidden to see them.)

From this, one of the key points that emerges from the comparisons thus far has to do with the importance of bodily senses, especially the "seeing" versus the "hearing" the music of the sacred flutes as it is being played. And, more than the flutes themselves, the powerful being(s) whose body(-ies) they are. For those societies who prohibit the women and children from "seeing" the flutes, which would result in their death by sorcery (a form of extreme predation by the shamans), to "hear" the music is not at all prohibited. It is in fact considered good for all to hear the songs and melodies of the flutes/spirits as they sing, for this promotes growth and harmony. To "see" the body of "Yurupary"—without mediation—results in immediate death, but to "hear" the melodies promotes physical and spiritual growth.[10]

The Baniwa of the Aiary River

Finally, we turn to the case of the Baniwa Indians of the border of Brazil, Venezuela, and Colombia, whom I have researched since 1976. Again, since the Symposium has brought together the three main ethnographers of the Baniwa/Kuripako/Wakuénai people (Hill, Journet, and myself), I will limit my remarks to the associations we have been trying to explore here between predation and conviviality and the flutes as agents of both.

Among the Baniwa, we may see more clearly a dialectical model of "particularist" and "universalist" socioreligious formations at work. In "The Wicked and the Wise Men" (2004), I showed that, during the time of the second rubber boom, which was marked by violent conflicts between the Baniwa and the rubber bosses, assault sorcery increased disproportionately, provoking a grave internal crisis that the traditional mediators, the shamans, were unable to control. Like the Apurinã, internal predation intensified as a result of external processes.

In their mythology, the Baniwa have the figure of Kuwai, who is the great spirit "Owner of Sickness" from whom all sickness-giving spirits of nature, called Yoopinai, came into being. Kuwai is considered to be the "Owner of Sicknesses," for his body is said to be exceedingly poisonous; yet the sacred narrative of his life and death recounts how his body, full of holes, produced the most beautiful songs. After his sacrificial death in an enormous conflagration, from the ashes of his body emerged the sickness-giving spirits Yoopinai, but also a giant tree from which the sacred flutes were made, and it is with these flutes that traditionally the men initiated boys and girls in the major rituals held at the beginning of the rainy season.

So the relation of Kuwai to humanity is marked by paradox: the source of social reproduction, he is also the source of the treacherous assault sorcery and sickness that can destroy society. It was from Kuwai's body that the world of humans was made, which the shamans call a "sick place," a place of pain, a rotten place recalling the Apurinã "land where many deaths occur." It is people, shamans say, who have made this world "bad"; the shamans say that the only "good place," where people do not die, is that of the Creator. Significantly, one of Kuwai's numerous manifestations in the story is the white man, whose historical economy has most preyed on the Baniwa. Baniwa cosmogony, like that of the Apurinã, includes the theme of catastrophic predation by cannibalistic animal spirits on humans, but the primordial animal spirits are a source of power that may be internalized into society, that is, domesticated, and actually become the source of future generations of adults.

Alternatively, these dangerous sources of power may be rejected, explicitly abandoned in favor of the much desired state of harmonious conviviality. History has shown how such ruptures take the form of conscious decisions that indigenous peoples have made to put an end to the destructiveness of predation. (For example, the Baniwa recount a story of how their ancestors abandoned warfare by burying all of their war-making instruments at the bottoms of streams.) Not all is predation, for in all cases, there are spaces (such as the sacred earth of the Apurinã) where to live morally is to live in harmony.[11]

Universalist socioreligious formations are characterized among the Baniwa by priestly functions having to do with management of the dead and the ancestors. An example of this would be the lengthy sets of chants that Baniwa *kalidzamai* chanters must perform during the initiation rites, in which they voyage, in their thoughts, to all known ancestral places of the earth in order to sacralize the world with the music of the sacred flutes and to prevent the ancestors from doing any harm to the newly initiated.[12] Unlike the shamans, who are considered to be jaguar-spirits, the essential function of the Baniwa chanters is that they must know the entire litany of places associated with deceased ancestors. Through "their thought," a priestly, canonical knowledge, they create a universal construct of Baniwa identity. As they manage the souls of dead ancestors, so they create the conditions by which all of society is reproduced.

Second, in their prophetic functions, involving the divinely sanctioned idea of "world transcendence," typically negating the reality of death (by assault sorcery). A great deal has been written on prophetic movements (the most recent work is my book,

2005). Just in the northwest Amazon region, they have been interpreted from many angles: as rebellions against colonial oppression; as grounded in mythological themes of world destruction and renewal; as historical traditions and not merely outbursts of reaction to domination; in terms of the spiritual dimensions of prophetic eschatology; and in opposition to the characteristic social scientific "explanations" of such phenomena in political, economic, or military terms. Most recently, I have directed attention toward the sorts of internal conflicts that characterize particularistic socioreligious formations specifically, conflicts which have been translated into sorcery accusations, vested with mythological significance, and exacerbated by historical circumstances. In these contexts, the mediatory functions of the jaguar becomes "heated up" (to use an expression of Viveiros de Castro, 2002), that is, expanded, in the sense of transcending local differences and the limitations of mortality (i.e., they are immortal figures). In this context, prophets or "wise men or women" have emerged.[13] Indigenous histories of these movements often pit the particularist socioreligious formations directly against the universalist formations (sorcerers vs. the "wise men") without necessarily arriving at a definitive resolution. That is, prophets have not necessarily resolved the problem of sorcery. But not for that reason can we conclude as social scientists have often done that prophetic (or messianic or millenarian) movements have "failed." To argue this once again ignores the vibrant historical struggles of indigenous religious traditions to come to terms with the internal dilemmas posed by their ontologies when articulated with historical circumstances.

A third way in which universalist formations may be seen is in conversion movements to evangelical Protestantism, and Pentecostalism, with its "immediatist" cultism. In fact, there has been little investigation of the reception of evangelical forms of Christianity in the indigenous societies of Amazonia and none at all of their effects on human-nature relations.[14] Nevertheless, it may be useful to reflect on how the music of the sacred flutes that is, the "speech of Kuwai," transformed into the "speech of God," as the evangelicals say. It is inadequate to say that the evangelicals simply wiped away or made a clean slate of Baniwa religious identity by burning the flutes in public. In some fashion, the "speech of God" transformed the "speech of Kuwai" and vice versa in the process of forging a new identity.

In the discourse of the evangelicals today, the history of the cosmos has been reformulated to be more coherent with their current political projects of creating a united front to enter the market of sustainable development projects. In this reformulation, it is interesting to see how they justify their conversion to evangelicalism by referring to shamanic visions and the mythology of the primordial times. The evangelicals state that the shamans foresaw the coming of the first evangelical missionary before she arrived in the area. One young evangelical leader told me that, according to the shamans, the history of the cosmos can be divided into three "worlds": in the first, there was only one being, called Hekwapi ienipe, about whom very little is known, but he lived in a sort of "paradise" in which everything was possible: the gardens grew by themselves, food was never lacking, etc. That world came to an end when the great tree of Kaali, a primordial Tree of Nutition, the source of all food, was cut down. After that, only the shamans had access to the primordial world through their use of *parika*, a psychoactive "fruit" that was found in a hole on top of this tree. The second epoch transpired as Nhiaperikuli created and transformed all things in this world, preparing life for the Walimanai, that is, for future generations. There are numerous stories about this epoch. This period came to an end when, at the end of the first rituals of initiation, Nhiaperikuli killed Kuwai, his son, by pushing him into a huge bonfire that destroyed the world. From the ashes of the fire, another huge tree burst forth, which was the transformed body of Kuwai, a second axis mundi that connected the earth to the sky. Nhiaperikuli cut this tree down and transformed the pieces of it into the sacred flutes and trumpets with which the men were to initiate all future generations of children. Humanity lived in the third epoch until Sophie Muller, the first evangelical missionary, came and instructed them to do away with their ancient culture, the ways of the past. Before her coming, shamans had foreseen that great transformations were imminent, their stories said. For that reason, the Baniwa abandoned the traditions of their ancestors. It was a rupture foreseen from the past like the other ruptures in the history of the world; indeed, in some Baniwa communities, this rupture was marked by the burning of the flutes on the plazas of their villages. The fiery transformations which had, in primordial times, produced the second world tree connecting the Other World of the ancestors with the present world of humans was then destroyed in the bonfires that consumed the sacred flutes. From then on, the connection to God would be immediate through the songs of the *crentes*.

Today the Baniwa on the Brazilian side of the border are divided into evangelicals and nonevangelicals, each asserting the truth of distinct cosmological histories. For the evangelicals, it was Sophie Muller who "saved the world" from perdition; for the nonevangelical, "traditionals" who still abide by the shamanic point of view, it was Nhiaperikuli who saved the world from the ferocious monsters that once tried to destroy humanity and that can eventually reappear in the form of sorcerers.

The evangelicals, however, did not simply lose the "speech" that was once transmitted through the knowledge of Kuwai in songs, flute music, chants, etc. The evangelicals became literate in their own language and learned how to read the New Testament translations that Sophie Muller had done and sing hymns. All of this formed the basis of a new Baniwa evangelical identity, opposed to the old "traditional" Baniwa identity based in Kuwai-speech. Thus the converted Baniwa (today, approximately 70 percent of the population of Brazil) understand that the process of conversion reestablished their communitarian way of life, which had been ruined by the extractivist regime.

People ___* ___ Features	Wauja	Enawene Nawe	Apurina	Baniwa/ Wakuénai/ Curripaco	Yukuna
Ancestors		X	X	X	X
Fertility of fruits			X	X	X
Warriors			X		
Body(ies) of Primal Being(s)	X			X	X
Male/female Initiation		X		X	X
Sickness & Shamanic Healing	X	X	X	X	
Gender Antagonism			X	X	X

TABLE 2. Arawakan Sacred Flutes: Meanings in Comparative Perspective.

Final Reflections

Concluding, I have tried to show how, in each case, the flute complexes intimately intersect with the predominant socioreligious formations. The flutes are instruments of the reproduction of human and non-human beings; they are the body of the great spirit "Owner of Sickness," Kuwai, and the omnipresent spirits of sickness, Yoopinai, that most afflict humans with sickness. Like shamanic powers, the sacred flutes ambiguously may provoke lethal harm while they propitiate growth. Such is the power of their agentivity and generativity. Summarizing these features schematically in table form, we have:

The key theoretical presupposition of the model I have developed in this essay of Arawakan socioreligious formations is that the sacred flutes and instruments are icons that empower people to transform predation into the peace of harmonious conviviality. This clearly is important for understanding processes that interested Max Schmidt (1917) in the "expansion of the Arawak" throughout South America, the Caribbean, and what is now southern Florida. It is also critical to understanding how northern Arawak-speaking peoples transformed the externally imposed changes that have occurred in their lives over the centuries, enabling them to keep their traditions alive while they established clear boundaries with non-Arawak-speaking peoples.

Notes

1. See also Santos-Granero 2007.

2. As far back as my 1981 doctoral thesis, I have argued for a historical understanding of cosmological processes. Based on archival and field research, I showed there how Arawakan flute cults of the northwest Amazon, specifically among the Baniwa of the Aiary River, were critical mediating elements in historical transformations, as seen in prophetic movements based in the mythology of Kuwai, the "Owner of Sickness," whose body became the sacred flutes and trumpets.

3. The reference to the Maypure is interesting because they once inhabited an area of the Uaupes River and possibly around the Aiary River where there are petroglyphs covering a huge boulder that at highwater look very much like a serpent emerging from the river.

4. The ethnographies of these societies are uneven, however: several essays in this volume are on the Wauja and the Wakuénai, Baniwa, and Curripaco. There are several published articles on the Enawene Nawe by the anthropologist Marcio Ferreira da Silva, to whom I am grateful for sending copies. Information on the Apurinã are by the linguist Sidi Facundes, to whom I am likewise grateful for his observations, and a doctoral thesis by Juliana Schiel defended in 2002. On the Yukuna, I am grateful to Augusto Oyuela-Caycedo for sending several articles relevant to this paper.

5. Since the Symposium included several excellent papers on Xinguan and specifically Wauja musicology, I will limit my remarks to a few brief points about their cosmology relating predation/conviviality to the ritual use of flutes.

6. See Max Schmidt's 1917 description of a Paressi-Kabixi "large trumpet-like instrument with a gourd for resonance and a small pipeflute." These represented the "evil male serpent demon and his wife." Consistent with both the northwest Amazon Arawaks and the Apurinã, women were prohibited from seeing these flutes. Both instruments are also found among the Enawene Nawe.

7. At the time of this writing, the Enawene Nawe are engaged in a violent struggle to defend their lands from the encroachments of several hydroelectric dams, which if completed would totally destroy the ecological balance which

the Indians have maintained for centuries, provoking irreversible damage to the eco-ritual system in which the sacred flutes are a centerpiece.

8. The Apurinã have a ritual called Xingane that is like a representation of war. The guests arrive armed, painted, and adorned. They approach the village shouting. The hosts go to their encounter likewise armed. When they meet, they begin a ceremonial speech, spoken loudly and quickly with their weapons always pointed directly at the hearts of their opponents. When they lower their voices, they simultaneously lower their weapons.

9. The tiny drawing of one of the Kamatxi "trumpets" published by Ehrenreich (in Schiel 2004: 189) only permits us to see that they were most likely made from buriti bark wrapped in a cone-like fashion. Ehrenreich said the Kamatxi represented the dead warriors and ancestors, which is very close to the meanings attributed to them by the peoples of the northwest Amazon. For a drawing of an Ipurina bark trumpet, see a reproduction of Ehrenreich's original 1891 drawing (¹/₉ scale, fig. 47) in the *Handbook of South American Indians* (Steward 1946–59).

10. See Santos-Granero 2006 for a further discussion of the implications of different perceptions for the theory of indigenous Amazonian "perspectivism."

11. The Arawak-speaking Tariana of the middle Uaupes River may form a counterpoint to the previous examples. In their long history of contact (Andrello 2004), they have frequently been allies of the white men as a strategy to appropriate key symbolic and material elements of their culture or "civilization": paper, clothing, and names. According to Andrello, this is the equivalent of ontological predation, or the incorporation of external power as a means to attain social reproduction. The Tariana thus have classified the white men in the same ontological position as the "fish-people," spirits of the waters, and other traditional enemies from whom humanity derived ancestral power in the forms of names and ceremonial ornaments. A lengthier discussion of the Tariana would have to consider the connection between the *Jurupary* or *Kue* [*sic*] flutes, which were important instruments for the warriors, forming part of war dance rituals, and the sacred masks, called *Izi*, which were made of woven monkey fur and the hair of girls at first menstruation. Again, the rich iconography of the flutes in the context of an ensemble of cultural meanings points to the themes of social reproduction and the domestication of predation.

12. These chants, called *kalidzamai*, have been interpreted by me for the Hohodene (1993), Hill for the Wakuénai (1983, 1993), Vidal for the Piapoco (1987), and Gonzalez Ñañez (1986) for the Warekena. What nearly all authors have observed is a correlation between the geographical areas covered by these chants and the historical migrations of the peoples of the northern Arawakan

language family. For discussion of this, see the articles by Hill, Wright, Vidal in Hill and Santos-Granero 2002.

13. I do not agree with Stephen Hugh-Jones or Eduardo Viveiros de Castro, who argue that the northwest Amazon prophets were generally of the "horizontal" type shaman, as opposed to the "vertical" type priestly specialist. The distinction of horizontal/vertical ultimately draws from Hill's 1984 discussion of ecological diaphasia in the northwest Amazon region, which corresponds to an alternation in sociopolitical regimes. While Hugh-Jones correctly attributes this notion of process to Hill's analysis (1984), he incorrectly associates the mid-nineteenth-century Baniwa and Tukanoan prophets with the "horizontal," egalitarian type of shaman. In my 1998 book, I challenge this association, for the power to be in constant communication with the principal deity in the Baniwa cosmos is attributed to the highest form of specialist, who is both a jaguar shaman and a priestly chanter. Viveiros de Castro's suggestion of a "heating up" of the horizontal shaman is true as far as it goes, but he fails to recognize the importance of both the kalidzamai priests and healing shamans to the reproduction of Baniwa society.

14. The principal works on the indigenization of Christianity by Amazonian societies are the two volumes I have edited, *Transformando os deuses* [Transforming the gods] (1999 and 2004), and Vilaça and Wright, *Native Christians* (2009).

References Cited

Albert, Bruce. 1998. "O Ouro Canibal e a Queda do Céu: Uma crítica xamânica da economia política da natureza." *Série Antropológica* 174. Universidade de Brasília, Depto. de Antropologia.

Albert, Bruce, and Alcida Rita Ramos, eds. 2001. *Pacificando o Branco: Cosmologias do Contato no Norte-Amazônico*. São Paulo: Editora da UNESP, Imprensa Oficial SP: Institut de recherche pour le développement.

Andrello, Geraldo L. 2004. "Iauareté: transformações sociais e cotidiano no rio Uaupés (alto rio Negro, Amazonas)." PhD diss., Universidade Estadual de Campinas.

Barcelos Neto, Aristóteles. 2004. "Apapaatai: rituais de máscaras no alto Xingu." PhD diss., Universidade de São Paulo.

Chandless, W. 1866. "Ascent of the River Purus." *Journal of the Royal Geographical Society* 36: 86–118.

Dussan, Elisabeth Reichel. 1987. "Astronomia Yukuna-Matapi." In *Etnoastronomías americanas*, ed. J. A. de Greiff and E. Reichel Dussan, 193–231. Bogotá: Universidad Nacional de Colombia.

Ferreira da Silva, Márcio. 1998. "Tempo e Espaço entre os Enawene Nawe." *Revista de Antropologia (São Paulo)* 41, no. 2.

Gonzalez Ñañez, Omar. 1986. "Sexualidad y Rituales de Iniciación entre los indígenas Warekena del Río Guainía-Negro." *Montalban* 17: 103–38.

Hill, Jonathan. 1983. "Wakuénai Society: A Processual-Structural Analysis of
Indigenous Cultural Life in the Upper Rio Negro Region of Venezuela."
PhD diss., Indiana University.

———. 1984. "Social Equality and Ritual Hierarchy: The Arawakan Wakuénai
of Venezuela." *American Ethnologist* 11, no. 3: 528–44.

———. 1989. "Ritual Production of Environmental History among the Arawakan Wakuénai of Venezuela." *Human Ecology* 17, no. 1: 1–25.

———. 1993. *Keepers of the Sacred Chants: The Poetics of Ritual Power in an
Amazonian Society.* Tucson: University of Arizona Press.

———. 2002. "Shamanism, Colonialism, and the Wild Woman: Fertility Cultism and Historical Dynamics in the Upper Rio Negro Region." In *Comparative Arawakan Histories: Rethinking Language Family and Culture
Area in Amazonia*, ed. Jonathan Hill and Fernando Santos-Granero, 223–
47. Urbana: University of Illinois Press.

Hill, Jonathan, and Fernando Santos-Granero, eds. 2002. *Comparative Arawakan Histories: Rethinking Language Family and Culture Area in Amazonia.* Urbana: University of Illinois Press.

Hugh-Jones, Stephen. 1996. "Shamans, Prophets, Priests, and Pastors." In *Shamanism, History, and the State*, ed. N. Thomas and C. Humphrey, 32–75.
Ann Arbor: University of Michigan Press.

Humboldt, Alexander de, and Aimé Bonpland. 1822. *Personal Narrative of
Travels to the Equinoctial Regions of the New Continent during the Years
1799–1804.* 2 vols. Trans. Helen Maria Williams. London: Longman, Hurst,
Rees, Orme, and Brown.

Jacopin, Pierre-Yves. 1988. "On the Syntactic Structure of Myth, or the Yukuna
Invention of Speech." *Cultural Anthropology* 3, no. 2: 131–59.

Kapfhammer, Wolfgang. 2004. "De Satere Puro (Satere Sese) ao Novo Satere
(Satere Pakup): Mitopraxis no Movimento Evangelico entre os Satere-
Mawe." In *Transformando os Deuses*, ed. Robin Wright, 2: 101–40. Campi-
nas: UNICAMP.

Metraux, Alfred. 1963 [1948]. "Part 4: Tribes of the Western Amazon Basin:
Tribes of the Jurua-Purus Basin." In *Handbook of South American Indians*, ed. J. Steward. BAE Bulletin 143: 657–86.

Overing, Joanna, and Alan Passes, eds. 2000. *The Anthropology of Love and
Anger: The Aesthetics of Conviviality in Native Amazonia.* New York:
Routledge.

Oyuela-Caycedo, Augusto. 2004. "The Ecology of a Masked Dance: Negotiating at the Frontier of Identity in the Northwest Amazon." *Baessler-Archiv* 52: 55–74.

Santos-Granero, Fernando. 1991. *The Power of Love: The Moral Use of Knowledge amongst the Amuesha of Central Peru*. London: Athlone.

———. 2006. "Sensual Vitalities: Noncorporeal Modes of Sensing and Knowing in Native Amazonia." *Tipiti* 4, no. 1–2: 57–80.

———. 2007. "Of Fear and Friendship: Amazonian Sociality beyond Kinship and Affinity." *Journal of the Royal Anthropological Institute*, n.s., 13, no. 1: 1–18.

Schiel, Juliana. 2004. "Tronco Velho: Histórias Apurinã." PhD diss., Universidade Estadual de Campinas.

Schmidt, Max. 1917. *Die Aruaken: Ein Beitrag zum Problem de Kulturverbrietung*. Leipzig: Veit.

Steward, Julian, ed. 1946–59. *Handbook of South American Indians*. 7 vols. Washington DC: Government Printing Office.

Vidal, Silvia. 1987. "El Modelo del Proceso Migratorio Prehispánico de los Piaposo: Hipótesis y Evidencias." Master's thesis, Centro de Estudios Avanzados, Instituto Venezolano de Investigaciones Científicas.

Vilaca, Aparecida, and Robin M. Wright, eds. 2009. *Native Christians*. Burlington VT: Ashgate.

Viveiros de Castro, Eduardo. 1996. "Images of Nature and Society in Amazonian Ethnology." *Annual Review of Anthropology* 25: 179–200.

———. 2002. *A Inconstância da Alma Selvagem*. São Paulo: Cosac & Naif.

Whitehead, N. L., and Robin M. Wright, eds. 2004. *In Darkness and Secrecy: The Anthropology of Assault Sorcery and Witchcraft in Amazonia*. Durham NC: Duke University Press.

Wright, Robin M. 1981. *The History and Religion of the Baniwa Peoples of the Upper Rio Negro Valley*. Ann Arbor MI: University Microfilms.

———. 1993. "Pursuing the Spirit: Semantic Construction in Hohodene *Kalidzamai* Chants for Initiation." *Amerindia* 18: 1–40.

———. 1998. *Cosmos, Self, and History in Baniwa Religion: For Those Unborn*. Austin: University of Texas Press.

———, ed. 1999, 2004. *Transformando os deuses*. 2 vols. Campinas: Editora da Unicamp.

———. 2002. "Prophetic Traditions among the Baniwa and Other Arawakan Peoples of the Northwest Amazon." In *Comparative Arawakan Histories: Rethinking Language Family and Culture Area in Amazonia*, ed. J. D. Hill and F. Santos-Granero, 269–94. Urbana: University of Illinois Press.

———. 2004. "The Wicked and the Wise Men." In *In Darkness and Secrecy:*

The Anthropology of Assault Sorcery and Witchcraft in Amazonia, ed. Neil Whitehead and Robin Wright, 82–108. Durham NC: Duke University Press.

———. 2005. *Historia Indigena e do Indigenismo do Alto Rio Negro.* Casmpinas: Mercado de Letras.

———. 2008. "As Formas Sociorreligiosas da Amazonia Indígensa e suas Transformações Históricas." *Revista Ciencia & Cultura.* São Paulo: SBPC.

———. n.d. "Mysteries of the Jaguar Shamans of the Northwest Amazon." Ms.

Coda

Historical and
Comparative Perspectives

14. Sacred Musical Instruments in Museums

Are They Sacred?

CLAUDIA AUGUSTAT

In the South American collections of the Museum of Ethnology in Vienna, there are ten ritual musical instruments from the Amazon. Their presence in a museum collection is remarkable, or perhaps even disturbing, because of the way they are culturally constructed: they are regarded as a community's most meaningful possessions. Being sacred, they play a role in important rituals and as such construct and fortify the identity of a community. Their meaning is emphasized and strengthened through secrecy, making them taboo for the uninitiated and for women.

They are inalienable objects, and consequently in their handover to the collectors their transformation into a commodity is inherent. This transformation illustrates Arjun Appadurai's argument that "things have no meanings apart from those human transactions, attributions, and motivations endow them with" (1986: 5). In analyzing the collecting history of the objects, I will be building upon Appadurai's insights by exploring the social life of the sacred musical instruments from the Amazon and showing that selling them does not mean that they have lost their meaning in general but that they were moved between different regimes of value. But first I will explain the connection between the sacred and the inalienable with reference to Maurice Godelier's *Enigma of the Gift*. Here he explains that the sacredness of an object lies in its ability to connect people with the origin of society: "It is these objects which give them an identity and root this identity in the Beginning, in the time of the (imaginary) order of things, the time when the cosmic and social order was first established" (1999: 121).

But this order was not created by men. Rather, the world first came into being when culture heroes gave the most powerful and significant cultural elements and things to the mythic ancestors of contemporary people. Like Marcel Mauss, Godelier argues that things exchanged to constitute social relations were extensions of people, and people identified with the things they possessed and exchanged. In this case, an object stays in touch with the donor, and its value is grounded in this connection. Correspondingly, objects with a mythical origin are an extension of the cultural heroes preserving their power and connecting the mythical time of creation with the present during ritual. In this case, the musical instruments of the northwest Amazon connected with the Yuruparí ritual are very good examples because they are not only an extension of the ancestors but also a transformation of them. They were created from the body of the mythical anaconda (Tukanoan groups) or, alternatively, from the palm that sprouted from the burned body of an ancestral spirit (Arawakan groups). In the former case, the totality of the ritual instruments of the Yuruparí is said to represent the different parts of the body of the anaconda and in this sense the totality of the ancestors of different sibs (Kapfhammer 1992: 118). The incorporation of the instruments kept by different sibs in ritual creates a positive effect and benefits the future of the community. In the case of the Arawakan groups, a palm tree grew from the ashes of the ancestral spirit connecting the world of human descendants and the ancestors, and the flutes made of the palm trees transmit this connection in ritual. In Godelier's sense, the musical instruments are gifts of the gods and as such they are sacred and excluded from exchange.[1] They are the inalienable possessions of the group. As Annette Weiner (1985: 210) explains, "The primary value of inalienability, however, is expressed through the power these objects have to define who one is in a historical sense. The objects act as a vehicle for bringing past times into the present, so that histories of ancestors, titles, or mythological events become an intimate part of a person's present identity."

Thus the preservation of sacred objects is the preservation of identity, and the loss of the objects has a fatal impact on the feeling of identity. Or again in the words of Annette Weiner: "but a loss may indicate a perceived weakness in a group's identity and therefore in its power to sustain itself for future generations. Such a loss is a destruction of the past, which ultimately weakens the future" (1985: 212).

With this in mind, the existence of the sacred musical instruments or sacred objects in general in museum collections could seem like a symbol of a dying culture. If indigenous sacred objects move as commodities in external markets, it is often explained as a loss of their traditional functions and that they are not manufactured for use in local rituals anymore. Thus they seem to be without meaning and can be easily transformed to a new function as commercial goods. During my fieldwork about the commodification of sacred masks that are part of the Warime ritual among the Piaroa in Venezuela (see the article by Mansutti in this book), I came to realize that this story is more complicated and that the sacred meaning of an object can still be relevant and in the consciousness of people even if its material manifestation is transformed into a secular commodity (Augustat 2006). To understand this kind of transformation, it is important to focus on the moment of the acquisition of a sacred object because it is not inevitably characterized as a loss of meaning and culture, as the following reconstruction and analysis of the acquisition of sacred musical instruments from the Amazon will show.

The Acquisition of Sacred Musical Instruments:
An Act of Commodification?

My first example is a bark trumpet from the Apurinã collected by Paul Ehrenreich in 1888 (Museum of Ethnology Vienna, No. 47.688). The trumpet was originally part of the collection at the Ethnological Museum in Berlin and came into the museum in Vienna through exchange in 1893. Another example is still in Berlin.

Ehrenreich visited the Apurinã in February 1888 at the Rio Aciman. There he had the opportunity to see the *kamatxi* dance where the sacred trumpets were played. The following description is based on his article in *Globus* (1892). The *kamatxi* are spiritual beings with a body covered with feathers or fine hair. They are living in a lagoon, and only some of the shamans know their home. At the beginning of the *kamatxi* feast, the shaman picked up the trumpets at the lagoon or manufactured them. Only the initiated men were allowed to see and play them. For women, their view was dangerous because a *kamatxi* could get into her stomach and burst it. There were between fifteen and twenty trumpets with different pitches depending on their length. When the men playing the trumpets approached the village, the women hid in the house. The musicians were called "wild pigs," and they were imitating the behavior of these animals. During the playing of the trumpets, the women reached out through the walls of the house with dishes and drinks for the *kamatxi*. After being played, the trumpets were hidden in the forest, and then men and women celebrated together with the many guests who came to a feast that could last for several days. Unfortunately, the feast was terminated after two days because of conflicts among the Apurinã, so Ehrenreich's description is incomplete. But Ehrenreich recognized the relationship between the *kamatxi* feast and the Yuruparí ritual common in the northwest Amazon. In this case the trumpets are conceived as temporary dwellings for the spirits, and the voices of the *kamatxi* spoke out of them.

When Ehrenreich tried to acquire some of the trumpets, his request was refused. However, the Apurinã promised him that they would make some especially for him when they brought him back to the *criollo* town. They kept their promise, although it seems that Ehrenreich had to put pressure on them because he wrote, "Finally it worked out to get the magic trumpets from them" (Ehrenreich 1892: 330, my translation).[2] That he resorted to such tactics seems all the more likely in light of the fact that Ehrenreich also pressured indigenous people in other cases when he wanted to get one of their special objects and that he sometimes got his way despite the later regrets of his indigenous hosts (Kraus 2004: 348).

The example of the Apurinã trumpets shows that the sale of the trumpets used in ritual was impossible at this time. But the Apurinã found a solution to grant Ehrenreich's wish. It is likely that they did not consider the trumpets they manufactured for Ehrenreich to be sacred objects. But the fact that their manufacture took place in the *criollo* town and not in their own village could be a sign that even the making of "copies" was not uncomplicated. For example, among the Piaroa in Venezuela, there are different opinions about the meaning of masks made for sale which are a transformation of the sacred masks used during the Warime ritual. On one hand, the masks for sale are considered "false copies" that could be sold because they were not made under ritual circumstances and were not used in ritual. On the other hand, the "copies" are esteemed as symbols of a secret cultural knowledge, and selling them is an unacceptable exposure. In the case of the Piaroa masks, different concepts of one object are part of two different strategies for dealing with the outside world. These strategies include the participation in political organizations and the presentation of culture to strangers, but also segregation and secrecy. The mask as symbol of identity is a powerful instrument used by both parties: one side attempts to gain acceptance through adjustment, whereas the other wants to keep control over cultural knowledge and uses distance as a means of self-assertion.

In the case of the Apurinã, it is important to note that they both rejected Ehrenreich's request to purchase the ritually used trumpets and also found a solution for the problem. The Apurinã took an active part in the negotiation, and they showed their ability to design similar objects in different regimes of value. Perhaps this transfer across regimes was possible because the trumpets were conceived as only a temporary dwelling of the spirits and acquired their sacred meaning only through and in the ritual process. But because of the scarce information we have about the Apurinã, we can only hypothesize about their understanding of the trumpets as "copies." It is also quite possible that the Apurinã were uncertain about the identity of Ehrenreich himself. They believed that the *kamiri*, or spirits of the dead, could be very dangerous for the living, and a murderer had been killed by the *kamiri* of his victim only a short time before Ehrenreich arrived in the village (Ehrenreich 1891: 68). Thus it is likely that the Apurinã saw him as potentially dangerous and thought it wise to comply with his request.

But there was also a real threat in refusing to comply with the request of European visitors whose expeditions were supported by nation-states.[3] For example, Theodor Koch-Grünberg applied political pressure to collect sacred flutes from the Siusi, one of the Baniwa (or Curripaco) phratries of the Upper Rio Negro region. At first the Siusí told him that they did not have any such flutes. But after Koch-Grünberg argued that the governor in Manaus would be very disappointed because he really wanted to see them, the Siusí told him that they kept three flutes and gave them to him (Koch-Grünberg 1910: 186). The handover took place under secrecy at the beginning of the night, and in the middle of the night the flutes were brought to the boat and hidden in its hull. Koch-Grünberg also purchased some sacred Yuruparí flutes among the Tariana along the Rio Caiaray-Uaupés. In both cases, the instruments were still in use, and the deal had to be made with great care and in secrecy so that the women did not recognize anything. The men were concerned that the women could see the instruments during their transport to the harbor or whenever the boat had to be reloaded. This was clear evidence that the flutes did not lose their meaning through the trade. Webb Keane (2001) stated with reference to Annette Weiner (1992) that the distinction between the alienable and the inalienable is central for the creation of political hierarchies. The example of Koch-Grünberg also shows that a political hierarchy based on other values could blur, but not truly destroy, the border between the inalienable and the alienable.

A third example demonstrates what is in my opinion something that typifies the acquisition of sacred objects in general: the decision to give them away comes often from an individual and not from a whole community. This is true in the case of the Yuruparí instruments from the Makuna in the collection of the Museum for Ethnology in Vienna (see fig. 29). It is a complete set existing of two bark trumpets and two flutes. They were collected between December 1971 and October 1972 by Fritz Trupp and Wolfgang Ptak, two Austrian ethnologists, during their field study of the mythology of the Makuna. Ptak writes in his dissertation that collecting myths among the Makuna was not easy because many myths contain elements that are taboo for women. Interviews could only be conducted in midmorning when the women were in their gardens (Ptak 1976: 5f). In a maloca at the Caño Jotabeyá, they could see a Yuruparí ritual and were allowed to record the music. They obtained sacred instruments in another maloca along the same river from an informant they characterize as "shifty," and they note that he had a bad reputation in the other villages (Trupp 1974: 23). This leads to questions of individual personality and calls attention to the fact that values are not always or even usually shared by the whole community, especially under circumstances of rapid cultural change. Or as Webb Keane said: "One common site in which to locate the sources of value is the desire of the individual person" (Keane 2001: 66).

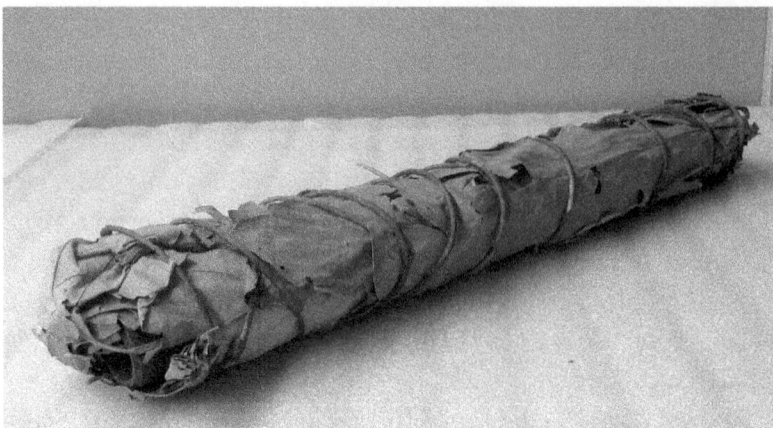

29. Parts of a Yuruparí flute of the Makuna (Coll. Trupp/Ptak 1971/72) covered in leaves and kept in storage at the Museum of Ethnology in Vienna. Photo by Claudia Augustat, 2006.

And the result of cultural change can be that the personal desires are no longer constrained by ancestral requirements. Godelier also said that even if the selling of sacred objects to outsiders, tourists, and collectors has a profane character, "there is often one individual willing to steal them from his own clan and secretly sell them for a few francs or a fistful of dollars" (Godelier 1999: 236). The meaning of an object comes from the social interaction in which it is involved, and it is probable that the secularization of a sacred object is much easier for individuals who are marginalized within their own communities.

All three examples have one thing in common: the collectors were explorers and/or anthropologists on their field trips and they were dependent on the cooperativeness of the indigenous communities. Kraus describes how many of the anthropologists working around 1900 in the Amazon were able to establish a friendly and sometimes close relationship with their indigenous hosts through reciprocal gift-giving and that they exchanged not only material things but also food, stories, dances, and songs (Kraus 2004: 290ff.). These early anthropologists were able to participate in indigenous networks of reciprocity and exchange that established and consolidated social relationships. But the wish to purchase sacred musical instruments created a demand that had not existed before. And as Appadurai (1986: 4) argues, "the demand, as the basis of a real or imagined exchange, endows the object with value."

As the above examples show, the responses to the demand were very different: the objects were sold, they were sold only under pressure, the wish to purchase sacred objects was rejected, and copies were made. It is difficult to analyze under which circumstances each response took place. More research has to be done about the contact between indigenous peoples and European ethnologists in specific times and places. Nevertheless, the three cases presented here already provide some important insights into the social life of the sacred musical instruments: they were transformed into alienable commodities only for a very short time because as museum objects they again became inalienable despite their occasional exchange with other museums, which was common around 1900 but is no longer practiced. Moreover, the transformation belongs only to a special trumpet or flute and not to sacred musical instruments in general. Another important fact that may have supported the indigenous decision to give the sacred instruments away is that they did not exist as a commodity in the source community because they left it immediately and in all examples with respect to indigenous values under the strict observance of the rule of hiding them well from the view of women and children. And this means that their commodity phase was not known by a part of the community. If my analysis is correct, the sacred instruments were never seen as a real commodity by their indigenous makers but only by the collectors, once again pointing to the existence of two parallel but distinct regimes of value. At the time of the instruments' acquisition, the objects did not so much switch from one regime to the other so much as exist in both regimes of value, depending on the point of view.

Out of the Amazon: Sacred Musical Instruments in Museums

This short exploration of European acquisitions of indigenous South American sacred musical instruments shows us that there are "copies" as well as ritually powerful instruments in the collections and that in both cases their presence in the museums has nothing to do with a general loss of meaning. Especially with regard to processes of revitalization in the source communities, curators have to think about how to deal with these sensible objects. In recent years there has been a rethinking in regards to the preservation and exhibition of sacred objects and human remains in museums. Particularly in countries where there are many indigenous visitors in museums, the objects were removed from display and in some cases were repatriated to the source communities (see, e.g., Gulliford 2000). In 1990 the United States passed the Native American Graves Protection and Repatriation Act as a legal framework for mandating and regulating this procedure. Until now in Europe these issues have not been broadly discussed. But from my perspective as a curator in a European museum, it is important to think about what I would like to impart if I show the sacred musical instruments in an exhibition, even if there are only a few indigenous visitors. In the case of the sacred musical instruments from the Amazon discussed above, it could be argued that a "copy" like the one from the Apurinã could be shown in public because it is not a real sacred object and there are no cultural prohibitions to be respected. But the example of the sacred masks from the Piaroa has shown that a clear definition of "fake" or "real" is not so easy to make. This case shows that asking "the people" is important but that it could also obfuscate the apparent border between the sacred and the secular.

At the Museum of Ethnology in Munich, two sacred flutes from the northwest Amazon are on display in the permanent exhibition.[4] The accompanying text gives no information about the flutes' origin or in what context they were used. Instead, visitors

can read only that the instruments are "Bark trumpets for ceremonies. Made for special occasions, not to be in a museum" (my
translation).[5] This makes no sense at all. The visitors do not even
know what they are seeing because there is no explanation. One
could argue that this lack of contextual information is good because if visitors do not know that there is a secret connected to the
object, then it is not possible to reveal the secret. But then it makes
little or no sense to put the object on display and risk hurting the
feelings of indigenous visitors. And the statement that the object
was not made to be in a museum raises more questions than anything else. The majority of objects kept in ethnographic museums
were not made for the purpose of becoming objects for display in
museums. But without any further explanation, this information
is meaningless at best. However, to keep the trumpets and flutes
in storage is not a solution either, since they are such important
objects and deserve some form of recognition and appreciation.

Perhaps there is a way to navigate between the extremes of either showing the sacred instruments in violation of indigenous
South American restrictions or not displaying them at all. As curator of the South American Collection at the Museum for Ethnology in Vienna, I am planning a new exhibition that will be focused on the Amazon.

The concept of the exhibition is based on the role that objects
play in the construction of space and society. There will be two
rooms: one will be "the forest" and the other "the village." In
the "forest," the main subject is the perception and appropriation of the environment through the indigenous societies of Amazonia; mythical landscapes are represented by photos showing
how the environment is used and modified for and through subsistence using objects for hunting, fishing, and gardening. Mask
costumes will visualize spirits, demons, and ancestors, which are
an invisible part of nature affecting the life of people. The connection between people and spirits/ancestors in ritual is essential for the welfare of a community, and the rituals are in most

cases performed in the village. Thus in the center of the "village" room where in many Amazonian societies rituals are performed and which is often a sacred space, there is an installation with objects connected to shamanism, the mask costumes, and the sacred musical instruments that are used to bring the voices of the spirits and ancestors into the human world. The showcase is to be made of milked glass. Thus visitors can experience first in a sensual way and second in an intellectual way through a text that restricting visual access to an object creates a border between groups of people. In connection with a sound installation, they can also realize that being excluded from seeing an object does not mean that they are excluded in all ways. The installation will also convey the idea that the sound is more important than the object itself and that the sound is the real materialization of the invisible.

In the exhibition on the Amazon, I will use the sacred musical instruments more to demonstrate ideas about the visible and the invisible than to explain the concept of inalienability. The latter will be explored in a thematic exhibition about gifts, exchange, and money in the permanent galleries of our museum.[6] As of this writing, the opening date has not been determined, and the concept is still a work in progress. But we all agree that inalienable objects as gifts of the gods will be an important subject of the exhibition. Other subjects to be addressed in the exhibition include exchanges between people and spiritual beings and the role of bartering, markets, and the introduction of money. In our opinion it is important to demonstrate how these different kinds of exchange can appear at the same time in a society and to display themes like commodification and regimes of value as dynamic processes. Here an object from the collection of Trupp and Ptak can be very useful: two parts of a Yuruparí flute wrapped in leaves (fig. 29). They were prepared in this way to hide them from the view of women and the uninitiated when they were brought to the boat of the anthropologists who bought them. Never unpacked, they seem to be still in transition, and it depends now on us to see them as sacred objects or alienable possessions.

Notes

My special thanks go to Jonathan Hill for his important comments on the first version of this article and a deeper understanding why the musical instruments are inalienable possessions of groups.

1. But in ritual they lead to an exchange between humans or between humans and spirits (see Chaumeil, Hill, and Brightman in this volume).

2. "Es gelang uns, von ihnen *endlich* die Zaubertrompeten zu erhalten."

3. It is important to remember that the period of the late nineteenth and early twentieth centuries was the culmination of the Rubber Boom, a time when the expansion of nation-states into the Amazonian rainforests coincided with horrific campaigns of forced labor backed by torture and other forms of violence, including genocide (Guss 1985; Hill and Wright 1988; Taussig 1987; Stanfield 1998; Hill 1999).

4. It is not clear if the trumpets are "copies" or if they were used in rituals.

5. "Rindentrompeten für Zeremonien jeweils für den Anlass gemacht, nicht für Museen gedacht."

6. This exhibition is a team project in which I collaborated with Christian F. Feest (director of the museum), Christian Schicklgruber (curator for Southeast Asia), and Gabriele Weiss (curator for Oceania).

References Cited

Appadurai, Arjun, ed. 1986. *The Social Life of Things: Commodities in Cultural Perspective*. New York: Cambridge University Press.

Augustat, Claudia. 2006. *Entmachtete Gegenstände? Zur Kommerzialisierung sakraler Tanzmasken der Piaroa in Venezuela*. Veröffentlichungen zum Archiv für Völkerkunde Bd. 12. Ed. Christian F. Feest. Vienna: LIT.

Ehrenreich, Paul. 1891. Beiträge zur Völkerkunde Brasiliens. Veröffentlichungen des Museums für Völkerkunde II. Berlin: Spemann.

———. 1892. "Südamerikanische Stromfahrten." In *Globus* 62, no. 3: 326–31.

Godelier, Maurice. 1999. *The Enigma of the Gift*. Chicago: Polity Press and the University of Chicago.

Gulliford, Andrew. 2000. *Sacred Objects and Sacred Places: Preserving Tribal Traditions*. Niwot: University Press of Colorado.

Guss, David. 1985. "Keeping It Oral: A Yekuana Ethnology." *American Ethnologist* 13: 413–29.

Hill, Jonathan. 1999. "Indigenous Peoples and the Rise of Independent Nation-

States in Lowland South America." In *The Cambridge History of Native Peoples of the Americas: South America*, vol. 3, pt. 2, ed. F. Salomon and S. Schwartz, 704–64.

Hill, Jonathan, and Robin Wright. 1988. "Time, Narrative, and Ritual: Historical Interpretations from an Amazonian Society." In *Rethinking History and Myth: Indigenous South American Perspectives on the Past*, ed. Jonathan Hill, 78–106. Urbana: University of Illinois Press.

Kapfhammer, Wolfgang. 1992. *Der Yuruparí-Komplex in Nordwest-Amazonien*. Münchener Amerikanistik Beiträge Bd. 28. Ed. Matthias Laubscher. Munich: Anacon.

Keane, Webb. 2001. "Money Is No Object: Materiality, Desire, and Modernity in an Indonesian Society." In *The Empire of Things: Regimes of Value and Material Culture*, ed. Fred R. Myers. Santa Fe: School of American Research.

Koch-Grünberg, Theodor. 1910. *Zwei Jahre unter den Indianern: Reisen in Nordwest-Brasilien 1903-1905*. Berlin: Ernst Wasmuth.

Kraus, Michael. 2004. *Bildungsbürger am Amazonas: Die deutsche ethnologische Amazonienforschung, 1884–1929*. Reihe Curupira Bd. 19. Marburg: Völker und Ritter Druck GmbH.

Ptak, Wolfgang. 1976. "Mythologische Aspekte der Macuna und Maku SO-Kolumbiens." PhD diss., University of Vienna.

Stanfield, Michael. 1998. *Red Rubber, Bleeding Trees: Violence, Slavery, and Empire in Northwest Amazonia, 1850–1933*. Albuquerque: University of New Mexico Press.

Taussig, Michael. 1987. *Shamanism, Colonialism, and the Wild Man: A Study in Terror and Healing*. Chicago: University of Chicago Press.

Trupp, Fritz. 1974. "Beiträge zur Ethnographie und Mythologie der Makuna in SO-Kolumbien." PhD diss., University of Vienna.

Weiner, Annette B. 1985. "Inalienable Wealth." *American Ethnologist* 12, no. 2: 210–27.

———. 1992. *Inalienable Possessions: The Paradox of Keeping-While-Giving*. Berkeley: University of California Press.

15. Mystery Instruments

JEAN-MICHEL BEAUDET

Translated by Marc Brightman

I

The following essay takes the form of commentaries upon the chapters of this volume. Grounded in the rich ethnography and the high quality analysis in these texts, I permit myself a degree of temerity in my interpretations. The commentaries that follow are written from the point of view afforded by my experience of Wayãpi villages: from the visual and auditory perspective of a male ethnomusicologist who works closely with the Wayãpi women and men of the upper Oyapock, on the frontier between Brazil and (still) French Guiana. I will also suggest several points of comparison based on my brief ethnographic exchanges with the A'uwe-Shavante, Kali'na, Chacobo, and Mashakali.

This perspective is distant from central Amazonia. It is true that the Wayãpi are a people of Tupi language and culture, who migrated from south of the Amazon toward the Guianese plateau in the eighteenth century. This was a migration of both survival and conquest during the course of which they acquired cultural features of Guianese peoples, notably Caribs. Moreover, the Guianas do not seem to be the region of secret musical instruments.[1] The perspective of these commentaries is therefore a distant one inasmuch as the Wayãpi do not have sound instruments that the members of certain social categories (women, the uninitiated) do not see. However, the paradigm of "secret wind instruments" is not alien to them. Indeed, Wayãpi women can see all of the aerophones, but they do not play any of them. As elsewhere, the Wayãpi have a story of an ancient time when women occasionally played certain aerophones.

On another note, Hill and Chaumeil as well as Menezes Bastos rightly draw attention in this volume to the problems of classification of the instruments in question: they are not always flutes, and can be other types of aerophones, or even idiophones, as among the Kamayurá or the Wauja. The question of relations between different types of instruments and what they produce, in terms of signification or agency, during the course of rituals, remains unresolved, and it seems to me that it is up to those ethnomusicologists fortunate enough to work among peoples using several types of secret musical instrument to develop this theme. Of course this is not just a question of formal typology: playing techniques as well as acoustic parameters can turn out to be significant.

Through this subjective introduction, I simply wish to say one thing to begin with: "secret flutes" should be included in the wider ensembles of secret aerophones and of aerophones in general: the fact that, among certain Amazonian peoples, women do not see certain aerophones should be understood in the context of the overwhelmingly widespread fact that, among the Amerindian peoples of the three Americas, women do not play any aerophones, apart from the exceptions that prove the rule, such as the Jalq'a of the southern Andes (R. Martínez 1992, 1994; Beaudet 1997). The geographical extent of this mystery that is also found on other continents, notably in Oceania, suggests that it occupies a fundamental place in these acts or processes through which the women and men of these different cultures define themselves as civilized people.

In any case, if in order to understand secret aerophones it is necessary to extend the analysis to all wind instruments, including those that are not of a ritual nature, it is also important to associate them, in the framework of a comparative analysis, with the presence or absence of a men's house. The civilizations of lowland South America can combine these features as follows: presence of a men's house with secret aerophones (Wauja) (see essays by Cruz Mello and Piedade, this volume), secret aerophones without a men's house (Barasana),[2] a men's house without secret aerophones (Akwê Shavante) (Maybury-Lewis 1967), absence of secret instruments and absence of a men's house (Wayãpi) (Beaudet 1997). In all cases, the polarization "men-women" through musical instruments remains.

The second characteristic that colors these commentaries is that I am a man, one among the eleven male authors and the four female authors of this volume. Does this disproportion signify that women carry three times as much weight as men? Is it representative of the "sex ratio" among ethnomusicologists or amazonianists? Or else, are we all asexual? Must western scientific discourse, in order to be recognized as such, present itself as asexual and apolitical? The neutral exteriority and self-affirmed neutrality of western science, which appears as a standard masking a quite distinct philosophical and political position and orientation: this "essentialization and naturalization of the sciences [belongs to the] fiction of an uncontestable 'science-pure knowledge' that is only responsible to itself" (Pestre 2002: 433). This brief epistemological digression is not really such a long way from my argument. Indeed, the dialectical drama that interests us at present (hearing-seeing, uninitiated-initiated, women-men, alcoholic drink–music) seems to trouble our perception and our definitions of sociality, of the social differentiation of the sexes: although the "gendered division of labor," the differences of costumes, of headdresses, of voices, etc., have been documented by anthropologists, there is a significant terminological imprecision in most of our writings. "To control," "to punish," "masculine power," "shamanic power," "rape," and "forbidden" are all terms whose definitions are not given and whose pertinence is not demonstrated. And, not without reason, in none of the texts in this volume is an ideology and an ensemble of actions related in such a way as to establish a hierarchy between the sexes. Thus, in no way is a system of social domination, structured upon a functional inequality, described or even sketched. The ritual acts which concern us cannot therefore be understood through such a framework. Let us begin with the word "forbidden": among the Wayãpi, as among other Amazonians, one never sees a man peeling or grating manioc (although among the Kali'na Caribs from the Guiana coast it does occur, and this is not an exceptional case). However, nowhere have I read that in these cultures it was "forbidden" for men to grate manioc. Why is this term employed for aerophones, or for incest (which, incidentally, seems to confirm that aerophones and incest are in a similar sense "civilizational," or that both are equally foundations of society)? More simply, few will disagree that in this example men make themselves men, and distinguish themselves from women, by going hunting and fishing, by cutting down trees . . . and by not grating manioc. For their part, women make themselves women, and distinguish themselves from men, by grating manioc, serving alcoholic drinks . . . and by not playing aerophones. Why see in these ritual acts a "coercion" rather than an assumed fabric, deliberate on the part of all the actors, the fabric of a constituent alterity (Erikson 1996), not this time between regional or "ethnic" groups but between two social categories internal to one and the same community, women and men?[3] If a woman saw secret aerophones, she would be "punished by collective rape." Can we tell whether this refers to an actual rape, a punishment, or even just a threat? I would like to propose another explanation: if a woman saw the secret aerophones, quite simply, she would no longer be a woman, she would exclude herself from society, and "all the men," that is to say, not exactly all, but rather any man could have sex with her. This being who would have seen the secret instruments would be indeterminate from the point of view of sex and from that of kinship. The only recorded case, as it is told by the Kamayura chief Takumã (Menezes Bastos, this volume), seems to me to confirm this interpretation.[4] Let us recall that the act by which a woman or women would leave the society of "people" appears in myth in the story of the Yamurikuma and in ritualized form among several peoples, notably Gê (e.g., A'uwe-Shavante, Mashakali). If, as I have already noted (Beaudet 1997), an uncontestable violence is at work in the mythico-ritual definition of the sexes, then it seems to be above all in the domain of the imagination or of dramatization and not to result from social coercion. I will return to this point later, upon which the debate can certainly not be resolved in a few brief phrases.

2

The foundational centrality of these mythico-ritual fabrics also appears through the multiplicity and complexity of the themes dealt with by the different authors of this book. First of all, let us try to extract a preliminary schematic view of this wealth of ethnography. In the cultures of tropical lowland America, including those without secret sound instruments such as the Wayãpi, it seems that eroticism, the regenerative forces, and fertility are associated with a particular relationship between sight and hearing. These two languages of the senses are articulated according to two characteristics: quantity (much/little sound, light) and relative discrimination. Moreover, the polarization between men and women or between initiated and uninitiated is produced in the same ritual gesture as the polarization between sight and hearing. These mythico-ritual acts comprise two sides which correspond to each other: on one side the music of men, on the other side the music or beer of women. This polarization is operated and articulated by sonorous breath, with ritual musical instruments as living and dangerous beings.

It is good to bear in mind an obvious point: if women do not see ritual aerophones, this means that men and aerophones do not see women. This is more of a schematic logic than a reality to be observed in each case: if the aerophones are hidden, for their part, women are also hidden, out of sight of men. This screen, more or less opaque according to each ethnographic case, and the occasional presence of "auditory masking devices" (Hill and Chaumeil, this volume) suggest that these rituals can also be analyzed as masquerades, with or without masks. This screen corresponds, partially and in very different cultures, to carnival masks. This helps to understand the liberty of tone and the sexual content of sonorous exchanges (Curripaco, Nambikwara, Piaroa, Wakuénai, Wauja, Yagua). This reference to European or American Creole carnivals is not as strange as it might at first appear. Indeed in the Andes the musical-calendar period known as Carnaval draws together these different elements in the same semantic constellation: disorder, eroticism, fecundity. Along with sonorous disorder, visual nondiscrimination is a major signifier in the Andes of the space-time of these forces at once of chaos and fecundity (R. Martínez 1992, 1994). In the lowlands, fecundity in its association with secret aerophones is mentioned by several authors (Nambikwara, Piaroa, Yagua, Wakuénai). This association is also present where there are no secret aerophones (Trio, Wayana, or Wayãpi among whom, in the myth of twins, the flute of the creator hero Yaneya impregnates his terrestrial wife, while the flute of one of the twins provokes sexual disorder among women).[5] This fecundity concerns, according to cultures, women, gardens, the forest, or these three domains at the same time. Reading these texts, one can observe another very interesting proximity between the Andes and the lowlands. The eroticism played out in these rituals is not serious or refined. The exchanges between women and men are composed of pleasantries, provocations, teasing, laughter, and sometimes burlesque scenes (the Jalq'a in the Andes, the Wayãpi in the eastern Guianas). Humor, social criticism (for example, by Wauja women of their husbands),[6] and sexual and social disorder are sometimes explicitly considered as favoring fertility. But I think that the sounds themselves, joyful sounds, are also fertile.

Laughter, exclamations of pleasure, the peal of trumpets among the Wayãpi, sonorous euphoria in its entirety, are, in Amerindian cultures, agents of fertilization (see essay by Brightman, this volume). Let us also remember the very strong link between ritual aerophones and female menstruation: among the Barasana, it is secret aerophones that brought about menstruation (Hugh-Jones 1979), whilst among the Wayãpi or the Kali'na, and numerous other Amazonians, shamans cannot make love to a woman during her menstrual period, at the risk of making one or the other seriously ill.[7] Thus a Wayãpi shaman who had transgressed this rule could not play ritual aerophones for several years. Several essays in this book evoke sounds in terms of quantity (Kamayura, Waiwai, and Yagua). Menezes Bastos and Chaumeil place sonorous quantity in an inverse relationship to the capacity to see. A study of the economy of these rituals might allow us to understand what the quantity of sounds means or does (see Seeger 1987). Let us observe first of all the aesthetic value often attributed by the musicians and their listeners to the quantity itself, and that also in Andean music, quantity of sound is a very important value (R. Martínez 1992, 1994). I nevertheless suggest two hypotheses for development, or two lines of interpretation that, as we will see below, are not separate. The quantity of sound may on the one hand be a factor of fertility, and on the other hand it may represent the capacity to attract outsiders.[8]

Sonorous discrimination or nondiscrimination should also be analyzed in terms of its relationship with visual discrimination. Thus the Wayãpi, for their fish dances, make six different types of aerophone: a clarinet, two types of trumpet, and three types of flute. These instruments are clearly distinct from a visual point of view. Most often, about fifteen instruments of five types are played together, and it is then impossible to distinguish the sounds of the flutes. This acoustic amalgam constitutes the Wayãpi's principal music, and is very highly valorized in the ensemble of their musical aesthetic.

This mixture remains visually a composition of different objects or beings. It is a nondiscrimination made up of distinctions. We seem to have in the Wayãpi fish dances two values: one of nondiscrimination, produced by a sonorous language, and one of discrimination, produced by a visual language. Thus this rich question of the relationship between visual and sonorous brings at least the confirmation that in indigenous America musical instruments are not *only* sonorous instruments. Even secret instruments, such as the famous Bororo bullroarers, have a form, colors, designs, by which they are defined (Lévi-Strauss 1955). Finally, this defining place of the visual in music is not of course restricted to America. Let us propose the following formula: numerous peoples, particularly in indigenous America, give visual characteristics to their sonorous instruments which constitute an integral part of the musical system. This formulation therefore implies the following general rule: a musical system can include nonsonorous elements (visual, motor, verbal, olfactory). Or, to put it another way, negatively: to reduce the musical system to its sonorous elements is generally inappropriate. At the same time, and inversely, a choreographic system can include nonvisual or nonmotor elements (sonorous, verbal, or olfactory). The instruments are distinguished by their sounds, their visible features (visibility, form, dimensions, colors, and ornaments), as well as by their position and their movements: among the Wayãpi the presentation and movements of instruments differ from one dance to another, but also according to the sequences of one dance, and between the types of instrument of one dance orchestra. In "musical gesture," certain movements are intended to produce a sound of a certain quality, while others do not have a sonorous purpose; these may present a visual image of the musician (here also a dancer), or a visual image of the instrument itself. One hypothesis may be that, at least among the Wayãpi, these distinctions, from one repertoire to another, and in the framework of one musical-choreographical event, constitute in themselves a mise-en-scène, a dramaturgy that contributes among other things to defining musical instruments as living beings and as beings with power.

Most of the essays in this book agree in showing that these rituals consist of a masculine part and a feminine part that are indissociable. But at this stage of research, be it in terms of music, of words, or of performance, to be understood as complementary or opposed, it remains difficult to decide whether these relations are of a cooperative or a competitive type. The musicological analyses proposed by Cruz Mello and Piedade on Wauja rituals seem to lean toward a complementarity made up of comings and goings within the process of composition itself. Nevertheless, it is probable that in a more general manner, these different dialogical modalities are not exclusive and are at work, in a dynamic and changeable manner, at the heart of any one ritual.[9]

With sight on the one hand and hearing on the other, it is sonorous breath that operates this sexualization of society and of the cosmos. Thus, although the Waiwai do not have secret instruments, Alemán's essay on their music (this volume)[10] is important because it draws our attention to this "third way" thanks to which the ritual is perceived by its actors. Indeed, breath can also be understood as proprioceptive, as the motor experience of the man who blows. It is by this experience of blowing, by this mode of knowing through the senses, that men enter into the world of extraordinary beings. If one adds schematically the data relative to breath included in the texts in this volume, one sees on the one hand that breath is an agent of fecundity, and on the other hand that breath, sight, shamanism, and masculine sexuality constitute one and the same constellation of meaning and agency.[11] Among the Guiana Caribs, flutes, like other artifacts, are living beings (Van Velthem in Brightman, this volume), and in a similar manner, for the Nambikwara, flutes are bodies, tracheae, and digestive tubes: they are animate beings. Finally, the Wauja say that their secret aerophones are extraordinary beings.[12] Thus, in a very concrete manner, for the uninitiated and for women, secret aerophones are invisible animate beings, an ensemble to which extraordinary beings also belong. Also, the fact that aerophones are artifacts, objects made and manipulated by men, changes little insofar as these sonorous instruments remain dangerous beings (especially if they are in contact with women's blood). And the fear shown by women and the pleasure that they take from this fear suggest that after breath, laughter, and the quantity of sounds, risk is also fertile and is, in these rituals, an agent of fertilization.

3

The musical instruments that are the subject of this book are ritual instruments heard during ceremonies. That is to say, their sounds, their dramatization, and the myths that accompany them all, including the burlesque and the ambiguous, constitute official discourses and acts. These official discourses and acts are concerned with sexuality and reproduction. Clearly, these mythico-ritual ensembles produce knowledge, sensual and verbal, to do with sexual identity, with same sex relationships and cross-sex relationships, to take up the useful categories proposed by Marilyn Strathern (1988). As we have just seen, these instruments speak also of the fertility of women, gardens or the forest, or of sometimes non-sexual reproduction as the *deetu* flutes of the Wakuénai remind us (Hill, this volume). Finally, these instruments explicitly fabricate social reproduction when they are played during the initiation rituals of young people.

We have also seen that these aerophones, mostly tubular, symbolize in a banal way the phallus and are considered to have a capacity of fertilization. If women played aerophones, it would be as though they had phalli, and they would be autonomous from the point of view of reproduction. They would no longer be women, but would have two sexes at once, and so they would no longer be people (this, in the Xingú, corresponds to the image of the Yamurikuma). One might ask whether the fear that the ritual aerophones evoke among women ("genuine fear" among

Kamayura women, as Menezes Bastos tells us in this volume) is the fear of the "flute-beings" themselves or the fear of becoming sexual monsters.[13]

As for sensory experience, the motion of the man who blows in the aerophones, the discovery of the secret instruments by the newly initiated, the fear of these sonorous beings experienced by women and the uninitiated: clearly, in these rituals, identity is to be considered not as a state but first as an experience and then as a dialogue.[14] These rituals with aerophones or with men's houses repolarize the groups women/men, and at the same time, they play out the unresolved questions of sexual identity. Strathern describes the historical transformation of ethnology which in 1950 claimed that initiation rites transformed boys into men, while confirming a superiority, a hegemony, of men over women. In 1980, anthropology had changed and one could say, "what myth and ritual really disguise are men's deep doubts about their maleness" (Strathern 1988: 56) so that "not just women are a problem for men but men are a problem for themselves" (Herdt and Poole 1982 in Strathern 1988: 56). Strathern continues with an observation pertinent to the Amazonian ritual configurations that concern us: "male rituals make warriors [rather than men]" (63).[15] The Shavante, for example, do not to my knowledge have secret instruments, but they have a men's house, and they create other ritual spaces outside the village, reserved for men. I have observed that certain very elderly women were able to join men there, and Maybury-Lewis mentions that during the wai'a ritual a woman goes there to make love with several men. He describes the whole of this important rite as a "ritual of ferocity," uses the term "rape," analyzes different combinations of sexuality and ritual aggression, and speaks of "ritual aggression against women" among the Shavante, the Kayapó, and the Sherente (Maybury-Lewis 1967: 265–66, 306). Meanwhile, in certain of their masquerades, the Tikmũ'ũn Mashakali,[16] another Gê group, act out a collective copulation between a woman and extraordinary beings, the *yãmĩy*, which come from the forest (all played by young boys). Maybury-Lewis tells us that he was unable to be present at the ritual collective copulation, and the term *rape* is not based on a direct observation. Furthermore, again among the Shavante, ritual aggressions also concern men among themselves, from one age class to another.[17] Finally, the most spectacular ritual aggressions between men and women among the Shavante and among the Mashakali are systematically to the advantage of women, and men are in these cases the object of laughter for the community as a whole.

All the same, even if there can be no doubt that these secret instruments contribute to the polarization of relations between men and women, this interpretation remains incomplete. Indeed, it is striking that a significant number of the texts in this volume mention the place of outsiders in this musical theater (Baniwa, Ipurina, Kamayura, Marubo, Nambikwara, Siusi, Waiwai, Wauja, Guiana Caribs). The story of Takumã, the Kamayura chief and shaman, which is reported and analysed by Menezes Bastos in this volume, is particularly intense and interesting, in that it confirms metaphorically that the motif of secret instruments also concerns non-Amerindians, and that a "distanced," "scientific" gaze is difficult to hold. This founding story makes our gaze unstable. The asociability of a "white man" in a community taken in a colonial context is nothing exceptional. The mythification of this character by colonial society is no more exceptional. On the other hand, such a concise destruction of this image is of a strength proportional to its rarity. We find ourselves here in a reversed invasion: the Kamayura enter like an arrow into the colonial imagery of the benevolent father (the Jesuit reducciones, for example). In a more general sense, the actors in these rituals weave a triangle with the outsiders: women men outsiders. The protagonists, those who welcome the ethnographer, for example, say: you can witness this ritual, but we have a secret, and you must not divulge it to the women. You can share it with the exterior, among your own people, but do not show it to the women. Here, our secret founds us as "people," as "us." To respect our secret is to respect what "we are." It is to participate in our (auto) definition.[18] A famous version of this triangle is the description of the Bororo bullroarers by Lévi-Strauss (1955: 259).[19] Two texts in this volume, that of Menezes Bastos and that of Wright, seem to show that non-Amerindians, Others in general, the dead and the extraordinary beings represented by the aerophones, can all occupy the same position in this triangle. Brightman in this volume takes up Viveiros de Castro's category of "thirds" and adapts it to musical instruments "as agents which do not fit into either of the opposing categories of consanguinity and affinity or kindred and outsiders, and which instead act as mediators between these categories." Thus it seems to me that in addition to "absorbing" alterity,[20] these musical instruments can also fabricate difference.[21] But to be more precise, they are engaged in processes that are sometimes ambivalent and that can even sometimes fabricate or absorb alterity from one ritual sequence to another or do both at the same time. If women played flutes, there would be no more affinity. In terms of ritual dramatization, it is enough that there should be a conjunction between women and flutes, notably in certain ritual systems, and that women see flutes and so flutes see women, that is to say make love with them, for there to be no more affinity. In other words, music is kinship.

4

To hear and not to see; one might say that the secret contains the polarizations of men women and initiated uninitiated. Certainly as far as the Mashakali, Shavante, and Wayãpi ceremonies that I have been fortunate enough to witness are concerned, I prefer to say that it is the other way around: the polarization men-women allows the fabrication of secrecy. Secrecy is indeed explicitly valorized, and one might say that it is a character, an actor in these rituals. The centrality of this secret, as meaning and agency, is sometimes represented visually and socially, by the spatial centrality of the "aerophones house" or "men's house," as among the Wauja (Piedade, this volume). But this house can be decentered (Shavante, Mashakali), and it can also be provisory or fragile. Among the Mashakali, the "men's house" or "house of songs" is sometimes constituted by an old covering stretched between two pegs or of a rudimentary roof of palm leaves (see Figure 1). It can be made up of one or two cardboard panels. It is nonmonumental and fragile like the secret itself, the secret threatened by "female curiosity" and the uncouthness, even the aggressivity of outsiders.[22] And yet this uncertain composition is enough to polarize the entire public space, to make a ritual space out of it and to create its dramatic tension. As we have seen, the secret may be of flutes, or other aerophones, or even of sonorous objects that are not aerophones. Or even nothing. Among the Mashakali, for example, the house of songs conceals only costumes, the concrete acts which permit the masking of the actors and the sounds, the relationships between men, a ritual camaraderie, a masculinity in the making, and in the course of redefinition. In a general sense, as we know, the secret is not so much an object as a making, a relation. What one hears and what one can or cannot see is breath. Musical breath is first of all a link, like the shaman's breath, which allows one to see or to hear, one might even say to concretize, the exchange between the shaman and the ill person, between the shaman and extraordinary beings. And the secret aerophones, despite the force with which it is sometimes asserted that women and the uninitiated must not see them, are a good argument in favor of this nonsubstantivist conception of the secret, which can be summed up with a play on words: the secret is just hot air.

What does this secret achieve? The Curripaco, and the very convincing interpretation of their rituals that Journet offers in this volume, tell us that beyond the distinctions of gender and kin-

30a and 30b. Mashakali women offering food to the yãmîy po'op (extraordinary monkey being) through the wall of the kuxex (house of songs). Photos by Eduardo Pires Rosse, Vila Nova, Territorio Indígena Pradinho, Minas Gerais, Brasil, 2010.

ship, secret breath creates and re-creates at each ritual a particular modality of relations between the initiated and the uninitiated, between men and women. This relation produces doubtful
forms of knowledge, characterized by uncertainty and ambiguity. The secret ritually produces ambiguity. *Tem coisa!* "There is
something! What is it?" This recurring motif of Mario de Andrade's famous epic *Macunaïma* corresponds to the effect of the
secret carried by these aerophones. A noise in the forest, behind
the vegetation: we hear that there is something, but we cannot
know with certainty what it is before seeing it (cf. Journet in this
volume). This creates knowledge of a certain form and also a certain state of the person, here a particular collective state of the
different actors of the ritual. I believe, with near certainty, that
this ambiguity is itself fertile in terms of knowledge, and that it
is perceived and thought of as fertile by the different actors in
these rituals. It is concerned with the fertility of women, of gardens or of the forest, as well as with social reproduction and the
reproduction of symbolic wealth. Let us recall that we were able
to interpret the principle of polarization at work in these rituals
as a response to the sexual ambiguity of the initiation candidates,
whether this sexual identity has not yet been determined or fixed
(Menget 1984; Beaudet 1997), or whether it is "suspended [. . .]
provisionally contaminated by the feminine" (Cruz Mello 1999:
163). Thus, just as a caiman is an amphibian of the physical environment, the shaman is an amphibian of species, while the initiation candidate is an amphibian of gender. Would the amphibian constitute an equivalent of ambiguity? This opens before us a
perspective upon veridictory and epistemic modalities. Viveiros de
Castro, in *Le marbre et le myrte*, insisted on the instability of Amazonian beliefs as they were seen by the first Catholic missionaries (Viveiros de Castro 1993). For his part, Gabriel Martínez had
begun to describe and to analyse for the cultures of the southern
Andes what he calls "the epistemic hesitation of humor" (1996).
He has interpreted these modes of belief as deliberately creating,

in and through ritual, an indistinct, undecided space. When sound comes out of aerophones, men act "as if" they were extraordinary beings, although they know that they made the instruments and play them themselves, thus bringing into play the veridictory modalities (appearance and truth). But when this same sound, passing through the screen that hides them from the women, comes to be heard by them, the women act "as if" it came from extraordinary beings (veridictory modalities) and act "as if" they believed it (epistemological modalities), although according to numerous accounts, behind the fear which they show, the women know the reality of the aerophones that are hidden from them. To take up the terms of Gabriel Martínez again, in these ritual dramas music contributes strongly "to realizing the determinations of a modality (of veridiction) which defines the appearance of actions as real, although in reality they are simulated programs."[23]

In fact, within the descriptions and analyses collected in this book, it seems that we must distinguish two registers of ambiguity: relations between "others" and "us" are marked at once by domestication and by predatory violence, as Wright reminds us in this volume, while cross-sex relationships are marked at the same time by polarization and eroticism. Second, what is seen and heard produces nondiscrimination. Analyzing the secret aerophones of the Yagua, Chaumeil (this volume) qualifies their music as "heterophony," or a "multiplicity of 'dissonant' sounds and 'voices' [that] were an effort to separate off the constitutive elements of language that would only be found harmoniously together in humans." This differential analysis, which is similar to that of Hill, is important. Nevertheless, it employs a negative vocabulary ("cacophony," "discordant") and is based on the perspective of the coherence of ordinary speech. In light of the aesthetic appreciation of musicians of a number of these cultures, we can also take a different perspective: in these forms of music, coordination, discrimination, and coherence are no more valorized than noncoordination, amalgamation, and dissociation. So we can see that this musical theater is the creation, or the re-creation, of another space-time (chaos in the Andes) and that the pleasure of the actors, especially of women, is to live this space-time full of uncertainties, risk, and eroticism (R. Martínez, 1992, 1994; Beaudet 1997). Wauja women express this ambiguity in a remarkable manner when they affirm the necessity of jealousy.[24] This jealousy seems in certain cases to be intimately linked to the practice and meaning of music. Thus the Chacobo, a Panoan group from southwest Amazonia, have neither secret aerophones nor a men's house. For certain sequences of their great ceremonies, the hitting of *shashu* posts by women responds to the music of men on the *bisto* panpipes. One great musician told me, "Men play panpipes for women," and another man, using a grammatical construct which is ambiguous in itself, explained that "women hesitate to play these posts out of modesty, or rather they would like to have the modesty not to play them, because it provokes jealousy among men and in the couple" (see Beaudet, Erikson, and Jobet 2001).

To sum up, it will already be clear that I interpret these *rituals with hidden sonorous sources* as rituals for the sexualization of the cosmos (and of the society of people in particular), rituals which create affinity, as well as rituals of fertility. This collection permits a panoramic vision of these religious forms and shows a great variability, from one people to another, of ritual intensity. The polarization "sight-hearing" varies from the Guiana region, for example, where women can see all the musical instruments, to certain cultures of the Xingú or western Amazonia, where women must emphatically not see certain sonorous sources. Moreover, one can also observe, outside ritual, a great variability in the sexual division of activity. In certain cultures, men do not process manioc or carry water, while in others it is certainly possible for them to do so. Here, women never touch their men's weapons (or footballs).[25] Elsewhere, it can happen. All the same, it is neither evident nor even conceivable that the variability of the intensity of the polarization seeing-hearing, of the sexual polarization during rituals, and of the daily sexual polarization, are established systematically in the same manner. We thus find different ritual modalities, covering and producing similar contents, notably the triangle, "women, men, and Others." Let us also recall that according to different peoples there is a great variability of the rule itself, or rather of respect for the rule. This varies from Kamayura women who express their fear of the mere possibility of seeing the flutes, to certain Nambikwara women who try to see between the cracks in the walls of the house where they are gathered,[26] to certain young Mashakali women, who, caught up in the general excitement during certain phases of the rituals, can even step over the boundary of the men's house.

Finally, let us draw up the inventory of what is aphrodisiac and fertile, knowing that both are relations rather than substances, in this case ritual in nature, knowing too that from one culture to another, from one ritual to another, the elements of this inventory vary as much in their semantic charge as in their active combinations. Above all, we find ambiguity, as we have seen. Indeed, what we learn from the Curripaco is that clear distinctions are fabricated by ambiguous means. To be more exact, the sonorous indistinction contributes to the fabrication of distinction sexual, social, and cosmic. Then there is risk, or rather the fear, which is a dramatic construction, a *mise-en-scène* of danger inscribed on the ritual program. There is the quantity of sound and laughter; laughter which, like a sonorous balloon, circulates between women and men. And lastly, there is dangerous breath, the sound of aerophones, which sexualizes the cosmos and fabricates (and sometimes absorbs) difference. In a more general manner, and whether it be during rituals or outside them, sound is sexual, and sound is fertile.

5

During a short fishing trip on the upper Oyapock, where we were only among men, I had told a version of the story of the Yamurikuma to my friend Luc Taitetu.[27] When I came to the point in the story at which the men are among themselves on a fishing trip, deep in the forest, and when they stay there among themselves to eat the fish without returning to the village, he asked me the right question: "But then, how did they manage for *tukupi*?" Tukupi is manioc juice prepared in such a way as to serve as a condiment. A condiment indispensable for any meal and which, here, in Luc Taitetu's question, was a metaphor for the feminine part of the meal, that is to say, all manioc products. Thus to eat like civilized people is not possible except through the complementarity of women and men; men bring proteins, while women bring the stable energy base as well as flavor.[28] In the same way, to reproduce as civilized people takes place with the pleasure of laughter, the ambiguous flavor of jealousy, and the eroticism of a mysterious sound.

Notes

1. See Chaumeil 1997 for a map of the areas where these instruments are present, and also Brightman in this volume.

2. In fact, the Barasana house, the *maloca* in the regional language, is permanently gendered, even in daily life, having a women's door and a men's door, and at certain phases of the ritual, it is dramatized in such a way as to become a men's house (Hugh-Jones 1979).

3. Integration into the society of people, and at the same time making this society of people, occurs through "taking gender," an act that is renewed each day and at each ritual by playing or not playing aerophones. The processes of social differentiation are, as we know, one of the major themes of Amazonianist anthropology and of anthropology in general. My wish here is not to criticize previous models, but simply to point out that these wind instruments contribute to social differentiation rather than social inequality.

4. Similarly, in their myth of the origin of the moon, the Wayãpi do not say that the boy who made love with his sisters is "punished," "covered with opprobrium" or with "shame." Simply, and dramatically, he goes away and becomes Other.

5. See the essay by Brightman, this volume, for a similar case in Wayana myth.

6. See Cruz Mello, this volume. A space of social criticism, of women with regard to men and taken in a constituted musical form, is present in numerous

cultures around the world. I am thinking in particular of the grindstone songs of Lobi women in Burkina Faso (Lacherez, personal communication).

7. On the relationships between shamanism, sexuality, and femininity, see Colpron 2006.

8. For example, the Wayãpi of the upper Oyapock, in 1977, after the ceremony of the *wasey* palm (*Euterpe oleracea*), which had lasted three days, thought that they recognized the traces of isolated people in the forest, who had come to listen to them during the ritual. In this case, it was indeed the quantity of the sound of the almost continuous music over three days and the exceptionally high level of sound in the village as a whole that was supposed to have attracted these outsiders.

9. Brightman, in this volume, notes that the feminine part is often drink, and that in focusing our research on music, we tend to minimize this part and thus to give these rituals an unbalanced treatment from the point of view of gender.

10. See also the film *Shodewiko* on the Waiwai rituals (Caixeta 1998).

11. When Wayãpi men say that they have "seen" a woman, it can mean that they have made love to her. There is a similar semantic association among the Inuit (Saladin d'Anglure 2006).

12. I prefer to use the terms *extraordinary being* or *monster* rather than *spirit* because the latter suggests a transcendence which is far from having been demonstrated among Amazonian cultures. One might also, in the light of perspectivism, regard these beings as relations and indeed, following Bachelard, define them as activities: "For a while, one would propose a Heisenberg principle for the life of dreams. Fairies are then extraordinary dream activities" (Bachelard 1948: 24).

13. On the notion of the monster, see Luciani 1975: 5–7: "in the most general sense, the monster escapes the normal. . . . The monstrous would be a separation from the usual reality, either by addition or subtraction of its constituent parts, or by modification partial or total of its dimensions . . . more generally, the monstrous would be a denatured nature. Hence the interest of the notion of mutation: often monsters are defined as the menace of change, the birth of suspense, with this strange implication that the living, due to its continuous metamorphoses, turns out to be monstrous. . . . The etymology suggests one last point. In monster there is the idea of 'showing,' and therefore of 'seeing'; so, to 'see': monster implies spectator, voyeur."

14. On identity as experience, see Strathern 1988: 63. The definition of identity as dialogue seems to me very well to suit these rituals that comprise a feminine and a masculine face; it corresponds here to the perspective that Gabriel Martínez proposes on ethnic identity: "to consider ethnic identity as an object

of analysis, and not 'in itself' of course as dialogue, at times visible, at times hidden, of differential systems of signification between two or more neighboring groups, which seem to constitute a set of ethnic distinctions and which express an identity" (Martínez 1994: 12).

15. These rituals do produce a collective identity, in contrast, it seems to me, with sexual identity as known to the Inuit (Saladin d'Anglure 2006).

16. I had the opportunity to visit the Mashakali during two research trips on the invitation of the Laboratorio de etnomusicologia de l'Universidade Federal de Minas Gerais in 2002 and 2003.

17. *Predu* against *ritaiwa* in the *wai'a* ritual; *predu* against *wapte* in one of the phases of initiation.

18. For this interpretation I rely on my own (albeit limited) knowledge of Mashakali rituals.

19. See also, among numerous other examples, Maybury-Lewis 1967: 263.

20. Franchetto, quoted in Piedade, this volume.

21. Cf. Caixeta, 1998.

22. According to an anecdote reported by Gourlay (1975), in Papua New Guinea, Christian priests deliberately showed secret flutes to women to try to break the indigenous religion; similar incidents have been reported in Amazonia.

23. G. Martínez 1996: 24. For a famous psychoanalytical approach to this question, see Mannoni 1969. This question of epistemic and veridictory modalities is not incompatible, once again, with a perspectivist view of these rituals. The latter create a space-time in which different perspectives can meet: women, men, uninitiated, initiated, extraordinary beings; these multiple exchanges between beings of different "species" playing with the real, acting out the doubtful.

24. Cruz Mello, this volume.

25. As among the Chacobo of Bolivia.

26. Fiorini, this volume.

27. A Kamayura version, this story is absent from current Wayãpi mythology.

28. In fact, in cooking, much of the flavor comes from chili peppers. The chili pepper is a plant cultivated near the houses, but it could easily represent the third term, the uncultivated point of the triangle (women, men, the uncultivated).

References Cited

Bachelard, Gaston. 1948. *La Terre et les rêveries du repos*. Paris: Corti.

Beaudet, Jean-Michel. 1997. *Souffles d'Amazonie: Les orchestres tule des Wayãpi*. Nanterre: Société d'ethnologie.

Beaudet, Jean-Michel, Philippe Erikson, and Philippe Jobet. 2001. *Tapaya: Une fête en Amazonie bolivienne*. Film. Paris: CNRS.

Caixeta de Queiroz, Ruben. 1998. "Les Waïwaï du Nord de l'Amazonie (Brésil) et la rencontre interculturelle: Un essai d'anthropologie filmique." PhD diss., Nanterre.

Chaumeil, Jean-Pierre. 1997. "Les os, les flûtes, les morts: Mémoire et traitement funéraire en Amazonie." *Journal de la Société des américanistes* 83: 83–110.

Colpron, Anne-Marie. 2006. "Chamanisme féminin 'contre nature'? Menstruation, gestation, et femmes chamanes parmi les Shipibo-Conibo de l'Amazonie occidentale." *Journal de la Société des Américanistes* 92, no. 1–2: 203–35.

Cruz Mello, Maria Ignez. 1999. "Musica e mito entre os Wauja do Alto Xingu." Master's thesis, Universidade Federal de Santa Catarina.

Erikson, Philippe. 1996. *La Griffe des aïeux: Marquage du corps et démarquage ethnique chez les Matis d'Amazonie*. Paris: Peeters.

Gourlay, Ken. 1975. "Sound Producing Instruments in Traditional Society: A Study of Esoteric Instruments and Their Role in Male-Female Relations." *New Guinea Research Bulletin 66*.

Hugh-Jones, Stephen. 1979. *The Palm and the Pleiades*. Cambridge: Cambridge University Press.

Lévi-Strauss, Claude. 1955. *Tristes tropiques*. Paris: Plon.

Luciani, Gérard. 1975. "Les monstres dans *la divine comédie*." *Circé 5*.

Mannoni, Octave. 1969. "Je sais bien, mais quand même." In *Clefs pour l'imaginaire ou l'autre scène: Le théâtre et la folie*. Paris: Seuil.

Martínez, Gabriel. 1994. "Jalq'as y Yamparas Gente arriba y gente de abajo." In *Indios de arco y flecha Entre la historia y la arqueologia de las poblaciones del norte de Chuquisaca*, ed. Rossana Barragan Romano. Sucre: Ediciones ASUR.

———. 1996. "L'Humour, le sacré, et la musique: Les modalisations véridictoires et épistémiques dans la musique jalq'a une approche sémiotique." In Actes du colloque, *Penser la musique, penser le monde*, 17–28. Paris: CNRS.

Martínez, Rosalía. 1992. *Bolivie: Musique calendaire des vallées centrales*. Livret et disque. CNRS-Musée de l'Homme. Le Chant du Monde LDX 274938.

———. 1994. "Musique du désordre, musique de l'ordre: le calendrier musical chez les Jalq'a (Bolivie)." PhD diss., Nanterre.

Maybury-Lewis, David. 1967. *Akwê-Shavante Society*. Oxford: Clarendon Press.

Menget, Patrick. 1984. "Delights and Dangers: Notes on the Sexuality in the Upper Xingu." In *Working Papers on South American Indians 5*, ed. K. M. Kessinger. Bennington VT: Bennington College.

Pestre, Dominique. 2002. "Science, philosophie des sciences et politique: Le constat d'une myopie." *Critique* 661–62: 432–42.

Poole, Fitz John P., and Gilbert H. Herdt, eds. 1982. "Sexual Antagonism, Gender, and Social Change in Papua New Guinea." *Social Analysis* 12 special issue.

Saladin d'Anglure, Bernard. 2006. *Être et renaître inuit, homme, femme, ou chamane*. Paris: Gallimard.

Seeger, Anthony. 1987. *Why Suyà Sing? A Musical Anthropology of an Amazonian People*. Cambridge: Cambridge University Press.

Strathern, Marilyn. 1988. *The Gender of the Gift: Problems with Women and Problems with Society in Melanesia*. Berkeley: University of California Press.

Viveiros de Castro, Eduardo. 1993. "Le marbre et le myrte: De l'inconstance de l'âme sauvage." In *Mémoire de la tradition*, ed. Aurore Becquelin and Antoinette Molinié, 365–431. Nanterre: Société d'ethnologie.

The Contributors

Stephanie W. Alemán has been assistant professor of anthropology and ethnobotany at the University of Wisconsin–Stevens Point since 2007. She has done extensive fieldwork among the Waiwai of southern Guyana for over a decade. Her ongoing work with the Waiwai includes explorations of identity, shamanism, globalization, and community relationships with the ambient environment. She is currently engaged with understanding the emergent use of internet and communicative technologies among the Waiwai in the projection and maintenance of identity. She is co-editor, with Neil Whitehead, as well as a contributor in *Anthropologies of Guayana: Cultural Spaces in Northeast Amazonia* (University of Arizona Press 2009) and has forthcoming works involving the Waiwai, including a study of their social responses to natural disaster as well as an exploration of medical pluralism in their search for magically aided healing.

Claudia Augustat (PhD, Ethnology, Johann Wolfgang Goethe University, Frankfurt a.M., Germany, 2004) has taught at Freie Universität Berlin and is currently head of the South American Collection at the Museum of Ethnology in Vienna. She has curated exhibitions at Ethnologisches Museum Berlin, Ledermuseum Offenbach, and Museum für Völkerkunde Frankfurt a.M. She has done anthropological fieldwork with the Piaroa of Venezuela and is author of several published essays.

Jean-Michel Beaudet is professor of anthropology at l'Université Paris X–Nanterre and a member of the Centre de Recherche en Ethnomusicologie of the CNRS in Paris. He is the author of *Souffles d'Amazonie: Les orchestres tule des Wayãpi* (Société d'Ethnologie, 1997) as well as numerous articles on music and dance, and coauthor, with Jacky Pawe, of *Nous danserons jusqu'à l'aube: Essai d'ethnologie mouvementée en Amazonie* (Comité des Travaux Historiques et Scientifiques, 2010). He has done extensive fieldwork among the Wayãpi of French Guiana and produced an LP and two CDs of their music. He is currently working with the Wayãpi and the Parikwene of French Guiana and has worked with the Chacobo of Bolivia and the Kanak of New Caledonia.

Marc Brightman (PhD, Cambridge University, 2007) is Marie Curie Fellow at the Graduate Institute of International and Development Studies in Geneva. He has carried out extensive field research among the Trio, Wayana, and Akuriyo of Surinam and French Guiana. Notable publications include *Animism in Rainforest and Tundra: Personhood, Animals, and Non-Humans in Contemporary Amazonia and Siberia* (Berghahn, forthcoming), of which he is coeditor, and "Creativity and Control: Property in Guianese Amazonia" (*Journal de la Société des Américanistes*, 2010).

Jean-Pierre Chaumeil is a senior researcher at the Centre National de la Recherche Scientifique (CNRS), a member of the EREA Center of the Laboratoire d'Ethnologie et de Sociologie Comparative at CNRS and University of Paris Ouest Nanterre–La Défense, and professor at the Universidad Nacional Mayor de San Marcos and at the Pontificia Universidad Católica del Perú in Lima. He has done extensive fieldwork with the Yagua of eastern Peru and is author of *Voir, Savoir, Pouvoir: Le chamanisme chez les Yagua de l'Amazonie péruvienne* (Georg éditeur Collection ethnos, 2000) and numerous articles and chapters on indigenous South American shamanic ritual and music. In addition, he is coeditor of *La politique des esprits: Chamanismes et religions* *universalistes* (Société d'Ethnologie, Recherches thématiques 7, 2000) and *Chamanismo y sacrificio: Perspectivas arqueológicas y etnológicas en sociedades indígenas de América del Sur* (Banco de la República–Fundación de Investigaciones Arqueológicas Nacionales–IFEA, 2005).

Marcelo Fiorini (PhD, New York University, 2000) has taught in the Department of Anthropology and Sociology at Hofstra University and is currently an invited research director at the Laboratoire de Sociologie et Ethnologie, Université Paris X–Nanterre. He is the author of articles in *L'Homme* and *Visual Anthropology* as well as a book, *Sound Symbolism: The Expression of Emotions in Nambikwara Discourse* (Publications of the Research School of Asian, African, and Amerindian Studies [CNWS], Leiden University, forthcoming).

Jonathan Hill is professor of anthropology at Southern Illinois University and conducted extensive fieldwork with the Wakuénai (also known as Curripaco) of Venezuela in the 1980s and 1990s. He is the author of *Keepers of the Sacred Chants: The Poetics of Ritual Power in an Amazonian Society* (University of Arizona Press, 1993), *Made-from-Bone: Trickster Myths, Music, and History in an Amazonian Community* (University of Illinois Press, 2009), and numerous articles and chapters on music, myth, and history in Lowland South America. In addition, he is editor of *Rethinking History and Myth: Indigenous South American Perspectives on the Past* (University of Illinois Press, 1988) and *History, Power, and Identity: Ethnogenesis in the Americas, 1492–1992* (University of Iowa Press, 1996) and coeditor of *Comparative Arawakan Histories: Rethinking Language Family and Culture Area in Amazonia* (University of Illinois Press, 2002).

Nicolas Journet is an editor in social sciences and an associate member of the EREA Center of the Laboratoire d'Ethnologie et de Sociologie Comparative at CNRS and University of Paris X. He has done fieldwork with the Curripaco of Colombia and is author of *La Paix des Jardins: Structures Sociales des Indiens Curripaco du Haut Rio Negro, Colombie* (Institut d'Ethnologie, Musée de l'Homme, 1995) and "Dialogues chantés chez les Curripaco," in *Les rituels du dialogue*, ed. Aurore Monod Becquelin and Philippe Erikson (Société d'Ethnologie, 2000).

Alexander Mansutti Rodríguez is profesor titular of anthropology at the Centro de Investigaciones Antropológicas de Guayana, Universidad Nacional Experimental de Guayana, and has done extensive fieldwork with the Piaroa and other indigenous peoples of Venezuela. He is the author of *Los Piaroa y su territorio* (CEVIAP, 1990), *Warime: La Fiesta. Flautas, trompas y poder en el noroeste amazónico* (Fondo Editorial UNEG, 2006), and numerous articles and chapters.

Maria Ignez Cruz Mello (1962–2008) conducted fieldwork among the Waura of the Upper Xingu region in Brazil and wrote a master's thesis titled "Music and Myth among the Wauja from the Upper Xingu" (Federal University of Santa Catarina, 1998). In 2004 she became an assistant professor in the Department of Music at the Universidade Estadual de Santa Catarina, where she developed innovative research on music and gender in Brazil and taught courses on music perception and training, musicology, and ethnomusicology. In 2006 her dissertation, "Iamurikuma: Music, Myth, and Ritual among the Wauja from the Upper Xingu" (Federal University of Santa Catarina, 2005), won honorable mention in the National Association of Postgraduate Studies and Research in the Social Sciences (ANPOCS) and revealed the musicality of the iamurikuma ritual, which is performed only by women. She had written essays published in *Revista Antropológica* (2006), *OPUS* (2006), and *The Encyclopedia of Popular Music of the World* (2005), and was working on several others when she became sick. One year after her diagnosis she peacefully passed away on Women's International Day, March 8, 2008, in São Paulo.

Rafael José de Menezes Bastos is associate professor of anthropology and ethnomusicology at the Federal University of Santa Catarina in Florianópolis, and researcher (1B) of the Brazilian National Authority for Scientific and Technological Development (CNPq). He has written extensively on the ethnology and ethnomusicology of Lowland South America; music, culture, and society in Brazil and Latin America; anthropological and ethnomusicological theory; and political anthropology. Since the 1970s he has studied the Xinguano Indians, particularly the Tupian-Guarani Kamayurá, and Brazilian popular music. He is the author of *A Musicológica Kamayurá: Para uma Antropologia da Comunicação no Alto-Xingu* (2nd ed., Federal University of Santa Catarina Press, 1999) and coeditor of *Pesquisas Recentes em Estudos Musicais no Mercosul* (Federal University of Rio Grande do Sul Press, 2000).

Acácio Tadeu de Camargo Piedade (PhD, Universidade Federal de Santa Catarina, 2004) has done fieldwork with the Yepamasa of northwestern Amazonia and the Wauja of the Upper Xingu region of Brazil. He currently is an associate professor at the Universidade Estadual de Santa Catarina and is author of several articles on music and anthropology.

Ulrike Prinz (PhD, Philipps University, 1999) has taught anthropology at the Ludwig-Maximilians Universität in Munich and worked as a consultant at the Goethe Institute in Munich (2005–2006). She is coeditor of "Dossier: Arte y Música en una América Latina en globalización" (*Indiana* 2004-2005) and author of several articles and book chapters on myth and music of the Upper Xingu peoples of Brazil. Currently she is chief editor of the *Humboldt Magazine* (www.goethe.de/humboldt).

Javier Ruedas is a researcher at the University of New Orleans who has done field research among the Marubo in western Brazil and who specializes in the ethnology and history of the Panoan peoples of western Amazonia. His most recent anthropological field-work was a language documentation project with the Marubo. He is coeditor of *Politics and Religion in Amazonia* (special issue of *Tipití*, 2003) and author of articles in *International Journal of American Linguistics*, *Journal of Ritual Studies*, and *Tipití*.

Robin Wright taught anthropology at the Universidade de Campinas for twenty years in the 1980s and 1990s and is currently professor of religion in the Department of Religion, University of Florida. He has done many years of fieldwork among the Baniwa of northwestern Amazonia and is author of *Cosmos, Self, and History in Baniwa Religion: For Those Unborn* (University of Texas Press, 1998) and *History and Religion of the Upper Rio Negro* (Mercado de Letras, 2005); editor of *Transformando os Deuses*, vols. 1 and 2 (UNICAMP Press, 1999, 2004); and coeditor, with Neil Whitehead, of *In Darkness and Secrecy* (Duke University Press, 2004) and with Aparecida Vilaça, of *Native Christians* (Ashgate, 2009).

Index

Amahuaca, 305, 309

Ámaru (also Amaru) (mother of Kuai), 102, 142

Amazonia: aesthetic and artistic dimensions of, 240; alterity in, 301–2, 318; anthropologists' relationship with indigenous communities in, 364–65; characteristics of aerophone rituals in, 214–15; classification of cults in, 316–17; communication with spirits in, 49–50; continuity of sensorial experience in, 34; corporeal dissociation and reintegration in, 54; cultural ideals about modernity in, 222–23; deceit in, 294–95; definition of *spirit* in, 391n12; ethnogenesis in, 309–10, 319n4; ethnographic research in, 4, 8; evangelical Christianity in, 344–46; expression of cultural ideals in, 222–23; flutes and alterity in, 310; flutes as body parts in, 31–32; gender relations in, 282; gender rituals in, 272n3, 284, 288; gender roles in, 288, 374; instability of beliefs in, 386; instruments from in museums, 357; instruments in, 10–19; interethnic relations of, 37; kinship groups of flutes in, 31; length of rituals in, 181; menstruation in, 377; migratory and trade routes through, 19, 23; museum display on, 367–68, 369n6; musicality and lexicality in, 211, 228; myths of sexuality and violence in, 283, 291–92; outsiders' aggression regarding secret flutes in, 392n22; prohibitions regarding sacred instruments in, 124, 159; resources on Christianity in, 350n14; ritual configurations regarding gender in, 381; rituals of Arawak-speaking societies in, 325–26; sacred flutes in, 242, 316–17; seclusion in, 294; secret aerophones in, 372; significance of aerophones in, 277; social relations in, 201–2, 226; sociopolitical regimes in, 350n13; socioreligious formations in, 326–31; Spanish colonization of, 306; typologies of societies in, 203–4. *See also* northwest Amazon; southwest Amazon

Amerindian peoples, 5, 372, 377

Amuesha, 327

anaconda, 153, 164, 165, 358. *See also* Ojuodaa (tapir-anaconda being); snakes

Anaua River, 220

ancestors: Arawakan instruments from spirits of, 358–59; of Baniwa, 343, 346; and collection of sacred instruments, 364; communication of Nambikwara, 192; in cultural soundscaping, 93, 94; of Enawene Nawe,

333–36; flute rituals as cult of, 9; in Guianese society, 214; and inalienable objects, 358–59; in *kamatxi* rituals, 349n9; in kwépani, 101; of Marubo during rubber boom, 309–10, 320n4; migration of Apurinã, 338; power of, 358; relationships with through aerophones, 3, 21, 25–26; sacred instruments as, 330; in sacred object display, 367–68; of Tariana, 349n11; in universalist socioreligious formations, 343; voices of, 106, 115. *See also* dead; elders; kin and kinship groups; mythical beings; primordial beings

Andes, 9, 26, 319n3, 372, 376, 377, 386–88

Andrade, Mario de, 386

Andrello, Geraldo L., 349n11

Anduze, Pablo, 153

animal masters, 49, 55

animals: and aerophone classification, 17–19; as affines of Made-From-Bone, 97; in Apurinã mythology, 338; in Baniwa mythology, 343; communication with, 2; in cultural soundscaping, 94; and Curripaco sacred flute sounds, 141–43; and dissonant sound, 65n4; and instrument spirits, 33; instruments representing in Yagua ritual, 56–58, 65n3; Kamayurá aerophones similar to skinned, 77, 78; and kwépani instruments, 101; language of, 51; music as life force of, 98; myths about creation of, 23; in Nambikwara flute tunes, 178–79, 187, 192; in Nambikwara mythology, 175, 194n5; as outsiders in Trio and Wayana societies, 213; power in Warime ritual, 157–58; and pudáli duets, 110, 114; relationships with through aerophones, 21, 26; representation in ensembles, 27; shamans' communication with spirits of, 24; socialization of, 93; sounds from plant materials, 41n7; Waiwai connection to instruments, 41n8, 221, 230; and Wakuénai, 98, 100, 114–15; in Warime ritual, 154, 158, 160, 164–65; and Wauja, 243, 331; Wayãpi imitation of, 28. *See also* aquatic fauna; birds; fish; game; Mara Reyo; *specific animals*

"animist" society, 204

anteaters, 41n8

Anteater speaking trumpet, 185, 187, 189, 195n12, 196n20

Antilles, 329

Antony (Waiwai), 224, 231

ants, biting, 154. *See also* insects

anup, 82
Apache, 181
apai ("to sing"), 250. *See also* singing
apaiwekeho (masters of music), 264
apapaatai spirits: and dancing, 281; feasts of,
241, 253n5; hearing of, 246, 254n16; in
iamurikuma rituals, 257, 261, 279; kawokatopá in world of, 246; musical text of,
247; in sacred flute complex, 278; visibility
of, 253n11; and Wauja, 22, 29, 242–45,
260–61, 272n4. *See also* danger; *mutukutāi*;
spirit-human relations; spirits; supernatural
beliefs
aphrodisiac, 389
Appadurai, Arjun, 357, 365
Apurinã (Ipuriná): aerophones and cosmologies
of, 325; bark trumpets of, 12, 360–62, 366;
on collection of instruments, 35; comparison
to Baniwa, 342, 343; contact with nonindigenous society, 331; on death, 342; manufactured objects of, 361, 362; migrations
of, 338; outsiders at rituals of, 382; sacred
flute complex of, 336–39; Xingane ritual of,
349n8. *See also* Arawak-speaking groups
apùy (nostrils), 78
aquatic fauna, 57, 77, 160. *See also* animals;
fish
Arawak region, 7–8, 10
Arawak-speaking groups: aerophones and
cosmologies of, 325–26; agentivity in flute
complexes of, 347; "catfish" trumpets of,
119n19; contact with non-indigenous society,
330–31; creation of musical soundscapes,
93; description of, 95; ethnographic research
on, 348n4; evidential system of, 133, 137;
expansion of population, 347–48; flutes of,
164–65; history of, 325; history of Yuruparí
rituals, 147; instruments from ancestral bodies, 358–59; invention of iamurikuma, 279;
meanings of sacred flutes, 347; migratory and
trade routes of, 19, 23, 349n12; Panoization
of, 320n5; Piaroa among, 148; prohibitions
regarding flutes, 348n6; research on, 4;
sacred flutes of, 19, 41n9, 242, 325–26, 347;
significance of aerophones to, 277; similarities of, 333; social relations of, 3; socioreligious formations of, 329–30; at Xingu
Indigenous Reserve, 258. *See also* Apurinã
(Ipuriná); Baniwa; Enawene Nawe; Kablyari;
Matapi; Tariana; Wauja; Werekena; Yukuna
Arawak Yawalapití, 70

The Archive of the Indigenous Languages of
Latin America (AILLA), 38, 119n16
arikamo horns, 77, 82
armadillo, 165, 187, 194n5, 208
Arm-Strong, Chief (Wasusu), 173, 182, 191
Arrojo River, 320n4
artifacts, 54, 202–3, 331. *See also* cultural
objects
Aruakan Paresis, 195n11
Asháninka, 41n9
Atabapo River, 148
augmentation, 248
Augustat, Claudia, 34–35, 395
aunaki, 265
A'uwe-Shavante, 371, 375. *See also* Shavante
Awetí, 258
ayahuasca vine, 58
Ayanama (Kamayurá demiurge), 81
Aytai, Desidério, 196n19

Bachelard, Gaston, 391n12
Bactris gasipaes palm, 54. *See also* palm trees
Bakairi, 7
Bamberger, Joan, 283
bamboo, 184–85, 206–8, 210, 211, 220, 227,
228
bamboo trumpets (*ratuimo*), 223–26, 224. *See
also* trumpets
Bananal Island, 87n17
bananas, 311, 312
Baniva: territory of, 330
Baniwa: aerophones and cosmologies of, 325;
on collection of instruments, 35; collection
of sacred flutes from, 362; communitarian
life of, 346; contact with non-indigenous
society, 331; dissonant sounds of, 28; evidential systems of, 133, 137; flutes of, 17;
history of contact, 336–37; history of Kuwaí/
Kuwai myth, 342; on music recording, 38;
outsiders at rituals of, 382; prophetic movements among, 350n13; sacred flute complex
of, 341–46, 348n2; sacred flutes of, 343,
345–46; school of, 38–39; shamanism of,
23, 24; social relations of, 27, 29–30; trumpets among, 12. *See also* Arawak-speaking
groups; Coripaco; Curripaco
Barasana, 124–25, 132, 373, 377, 390n2
Barcelos Neto, Aristóteles, 87n20, 331
bark trumpets: association with birds, 56;
collection and display of, 360–63, 366–67;
drawing of Apurinã, 349n9; geographic

bark trumpets (*continued*)
distribution of, 12; of Kuwaí/Kuwai, 101, 118n10; Tukano associations with, 58; of Waiwai, 223–26, 225, 233; in Yagua male initiation ritual, 54, 64. *See also* Rúnda; trumpets

Basso, Ellen, 259, 278, 282, 285, 287, 289–90, 296n15

Basso, Keith, 181

Bateson, Gregory, 265

bats, 154, 158. *See also* Kashinawa (bat people)

Bauman, Richard, 296n14

Beaudet, Jean-Michel, 19, 40n6, 211, 228, 229, 293, 396

beer, 375. *See also* manioc beer; *waka* (corn beer)

beiju pancakes, 279

Ben-Amos, D., 296n14

Berlin, 360

Beti (Cameroon), 129–30

birds: calls of, 171–77, 179–80, 182; communication with, 2; and instrument spirits, 33; Kuwaí/Kuwai's body as, 100; myths about creation of, 23; as Nambikwara flute tune referents, 178–79; saying of name, 174–76; sound in instruments, 19, 58; Yagua instrument association with, 56. *See also* animals; *specific birds*

birth, 23, 98, 113, 188, 288, 293–94, 340–41. *See also* maternity; regeneration

bisto panpipes, 388. *See also* panpipes

"blowers" (*sopladores*), 20–21

blowing: difficulty of, 37–38, 222, 231–32; in Guianese myths, 209; magic of Waiwai shamans, 232; Marc Brightman on, 25; owners of in Piaroa hierarchy, 150; as ritual dialogue, 381; of tobacco smoke, 20–21; of Wauja, 250

Blue-Neck, 171–73, 175, 176, 180–81, 192

bocachico fish, 108–9, 113, 119n20. *See also* fish

body (bodies): Amazonian aerophones as, 203; in Amazonian socioreligious life, 328; apapaatai spirits as part of, 243; in Arawakan flute complexes, 347; dissociation and reintegration of, 24, 53–54, 62–63; in gendered rituals, 287–90; instruments as, 24–26, 115, 289–90, 379; of instrument spirits, 31–32; invisibility of, 294; in Kamayurá culture, 82; of Kuwaí/Kuwai in Baniwa myth, 342, 347,

348n2; of Kuwaí/Kuwai in kwépani, 101, 104–5; in Kuwaí/Kuwai rituals, 325; molítu as symbol of, 102–4; as musical instruments, 289–90; Nambikwara flutes as, 190–91; representation in ensembles, 27; reproduction in Yagua ritual, 61; ritual instruments from, 358; sociability through, 282, 295n10; sounds from Kuwaí/Kuwai's, 23, 98–100; and tubes, 203, 210–11; in Wayana ritual, 206; of Yurupary, 341. *See also* genitalia; yura

body ornaments, 190, 209. *See also* ornaments

body paintings, 260, 261, 289

Bolivia, 11

bone(s), 24, 25, 50, 55, 62–63, 208–10, 227, 228, 234

boom boxes, 37–38, 222–26, 230–31, 231, 233–36. *See also* cassette tapes; musical discourse; stereos

Bororo, 253n3, 383

botuto cult, 8, 330

botuto trumpets, 7–8. *See also* trumpets

Boyer, Pascal, 129

Brasília, 313

Brazil: Baniwa on border of, 341, 346; cassette tapes in, 235; clarinets in, 15; contact with non-indigenous society in, 330; evidential system in, 133; informal feasts in, 308; kawoká flute ensembles in, 29; Marubo in, 301, 313, 314; Matis Indians in, 293; music of, 36, 38–39, 222; music of at Marubo feasts, 303–4, 309, 312; poetics of ritual power in, 2; shamanism in, 24; social relations in, 3, 27; vocal art forms in, 65n2; Waiwai in, 220–21; Wauja Indians in, 257–58; Wayápi near, 371; Xavante in, 273n7, 296n18. *See also karaiwa* (Brazilians); Mato Grosso, Brazil; Pará, Brazil

Brazilian Air Force, 84, 86n6

Brazilian Indian Foundation (FUNAI), 194n1, 314

breath and breathing: curative power of shamans', 6–7; fertile associations in Wayana mythology, 208; and secret instruments, 379, 384–86, 389; in shamanic musicologies, 20–21, 23–24; significance to indigenous groups, 19; transformation into sound, 214; in Wauja rituals, 332, 380; in Wayápi ritual, 375; in Yagua male initiation ritual, 61

Briggs, Charles, 287, 296n16

of music in, 296n17; of Nambikwara, 184, 195n13; Piaroa prayers for, 164; sound and vision in shamanic, 24, 41n10; through aerophones, 3; through kawoká flutes, 22; of Wauja, 244–45, 325; in Wayana ritual, 207; yerupoho spirits' role in, 331–32. *See also* illness; shamans and shamanism

Curripaco: ambiguity of, 389; description of, 95; dissonant sounds of, 28; ethnography of, 341; and evidential systems, 133–34, 136; exchange of instruments, 32; flutes of, 17; lies, secrets, and dissimulation of, 130; and molítu flutes, 105, 119n15; on music recording, 38; mutual flogging of, 139, 142, 144; mystery of Kuai ritual, 125; poetics of ritual power, 2; population of, 331; prohibitions regarding sacred flutes, 124–29, 137; secrecy of, 137–40, 384–86; sexual content of sonorous exchanges of, 376; shamanism of, 23, 24; similarity to Tatuyo, 130; social relations of, 27, 29–30; trumpets among, 12. *See also* Baniwa; kapetiapan; Wakuénai

Curuçá River, 301, 310, 311

Daa, 151–53, 158, 164, 165
daapa trumpets, 141. *See also* trumpets
dabacuri flute rituals, 10. *See also* flute rituals
Dance of Pijiguaos (*Bactris gassipaes*), 165
Dance of the Puppet, 165
dancing: of Achagua, 329; Brazilian music for, 303–4; communication through Guianese, 205; contact with spirit world through, 290–91; and exchanges of anthropologists and indigenous hosts, 364–65; in female musical tradition, 280–81; in gendered rituals, 293; in Guianese myths and rituals, 209, 212–13; historical time-space through, 116; in iamurikuma rituals, 261–62, 264–65, 280; in Jurupari feasts, 127; Kamayurá rattles for, 77; in kwépani, 101; in pudáli, 30, 100, 107, 109–13, 119n20, 120n23; study of ceremonial songs for, 117n2; at tanamea, 312; for Wakuénai socializing, 97–98; in Warime ritual, 154, 158, 165; in Wauja rituals, 22–23, 259, 260; in Wayana marake ritual, 206–7; of Wayãpi, 28, 377–79; at *wera* festival, 340; in Yagua rituals, 59–60; in Yãkwa ritual, 335, 336; and yerupoho spirits, 332. *See also* mádzerukái; performance
danger: in Arawakan flute complexes, 347; in Baniwa mythology, 343; in gendered rituals,

289, 291, 294; of gourd trumpets, 182; of *kamiri*, 362; in Nambikwara mythology, 187; and nupa, 126–27; of secret aerophones, 380, 389; in Warime ritual, 161; in Wayãpi ritual, 375; for women in *kamatxi* ritual, 360; in Xinguano sacred flute complex, 242; of yerupoho spirits, 331. *See also* apapaatai spirits; violence

dan'ore, 273n7
dápa (paca) bark trumpets, 101, 118n10. *See also* bark trumpets
daytime, 157–58, 161, 163, 186, 196n16, 196n17. *See also* light; night and sleep
dead: in Amazonian socioreligious life, 327, 330; in Guianese society, 214; in *kamatxi* rituals, 325; relationships with through aerophones, 21, 25–26; in ritual triangle, 383; social relations with, 3; in universalist socioreligious formations, 343; village of in iamurikuma rituals, 262. *See also* ancestors
Dea'ruwa. *See* Piaroa
death: and Amazonian socioreligious life, 328–29; in Apurinã mythology, 338; Baniwa on, 343; caused by apapaatai, 246; in Guianas, 204; and Kuai taboo, 128; mystery of, 123; and Nambikwara rituals and mythology, 181, 185, 187, 188; origins of, 97; in Piaroa hierarchy, 151; and shamanic breathing, 25; in Warime ritual, 159, 166; in Wayana marake ritual, 207, 209; witches and mama'e's involvement in, 87n16; and Xinguano, 215, 242; Yukuna passage to, 340–41. *See also* illness
DeBoer, Warren, 319n3
deer bone aerophones, 211, 220. *See also* aerophones
"Deer, Come and Dance," 229, 230
déetu flutes, 28, 109, 116, 119n21, 380. *See also* flutes; insects
déetu insects, 113–14, 119n22. *See also* insects
de Haan, Ferdinand, 134–35
deities. *See* divinities; God; gods
demons, 242, 367. *See also* devil; spirits
Desana, 10, 132
Descola, Philippe, 203–4, 317
Deshayes, Patrick, 307
desires, 182, 184, 221, 222, 230, 257, 260, 331–32
devil, 5–6, 40n1. *See also* demons
dialogues: of Curripaco women with flutes, 139, 142–43; of Marubo feast invitation,

fossilized psychological categories, 136, 137

Franchetto, Bruna, 240, 243, 282–84

Frazer, Sir James George, 69, 73

"free" aerophones, 12, 40n4. *See also* aerophones

French Guyana, 21, 25, 27, 120n24, 205–6, 371. *See also* Guianas

Friedrich, Paul, 117n2

Fritz, Samuel, 6

frogs, 19, 155

fruit, 59, 127, 152, 158, 160, 345

FUNAI (Brazilian Indian Foundation), 194n1, 314

funerals, 7, 195n13, 196n16, 202, 215, 327. *See also* mourning ceremonies

game: transformation of, 41n7; in Trio and Wayana economy, 206; Waiwai enticement through music, 37, 227–30, 234; Wakuénai hunting of, 95; Xinguano taboo concerning, 88n27; and Yagua male initiation ritual, 54, 55, 60, 61. *See also* animals; food; hunting; meat

Gangly-Croc, 171

gardens and gardening, *103*, 196n17, 204, 209, 213, 367, 376, 380, 386. *See also* agriculture; planting; plants

gender: of Barasana maloca, 390n2; complementarity, 106–14, *108*, 281–85, 293–95, 316–17, 379, 390; description of rituals, 260–61, 272n3; in fertility cult classification, 316–17; in Guianese society, 203, 204, 212–13; inversion of roles through ritual, 285–88, 294–95; of molítu flute playing, 106; of Nambikwara flutes, 189, 196n19; of Piaroa flutes, 153, 164–65; polarization in secret instrument rituals, 373, 375–88; and prohibitions regarding sacred flutes, 124–25, 212; reciprocity in iamurikuma, 261–62; roles in Lowland South America, 288; seclusion in rituals, 294; and social differentiation, 373–75, 390n3; and Waiwai, 226, 228, 230; in Warime ritual, 158–66; in Wayãpi fish dances, 379; of Yagua instruments, 57, 63–64. *See also* iamurikuma rituals; kawoká flutes; men; women

gender relations, 241; antagonistic, 277, 279, 281–86, 288, 290–91, 293; in iamurikuma rituals, 257, 260–70, 272n3, 292–95; of Kamayurá, 75–76, 80–82, 87n18; in kawokakuma songs, 270–71; myth of, 285–86;

of Nambikwara, 183–90; negotiations of, 3; in *pequi* ritual, 273n8; of Piaroa, 148–51, 161–63, 166–67; in ritual cults, 316–17; in sacred flute complexes, 277–78, 281–82; and transgression in rituals, 291–92; in Wauja rituals, 29. *See also* men; women

generational bonds and shifts, 31, 37–38, 222, 223, 230–34, 345–46, 359. *See also* elders; youth

genitalia, 25, 31, 102–4, 380. *See also* body (bodies)

German researchers, 4, 8

Gê-speaking peoples, 4, 36, 82, 273n7, 375. *See also* Tikmu˜'u˜n Mashakali

Gilij, Felipe Salvador, 7

Globus, 360

God, 345, 346. *See also* gods

Godelier, Maurice, 357–58, 364

gods, 242–43, 294, 358, 368. *See also* divinities; God

The Golden Bough (Frazer), 69, 73

Goldman, Irving, 161

Goldstein, K. S., 296n14

Gómez-Imbert, Elsa, 130–32, 134–36

good-bye ceremony, 137–38

gospel music. *See* religious music

gourds, wax, 125

gourd trumpets, *188*; of Arawak-speaking societies, 348n6; classification of, 195n12; description of, 184–85; gender of, 196n19; significance of tunes on, 182; in Wasusu ritual, 186–87, 189; of Wauja, 244, 254n14. *See also* trumpets

Gourlay, Ken, 392n22

Gracian, B., 123

Graham, Laura, 117n2, 296n18

grandparents, 333–36

Greek concepts, 187–88

Gregorian New Year, 204

Gregor, Thomas, 281, 283

grindstone songs, 391n6. *See also* songs

Guainía River, 95, 110, 124, 330

Guaporé Valley Nambikwara, 178, 185, 186, 189, 191, 193n1. *See also* Nambikwara

Guaraní, 11

Guaricaya ritual, 6

Guaviare River, 148

Guiana Caribs, 201, 379, 382. *See also* Caribs

Guianas: aerophones and shamanic breathing in, 21, 293; archetypes in, 202–3, 214, 215; beer and music in, 213; characteristics of,

Guianas (*continued*)

201–2; dualities of, 213–14; exchanges between men and women in, 376–77; historical change in, 215; inside and outside in, 212–14; Kali'na Caribs of, 374; kinship in, 202, 204, 214; musical ceremonies in, 201, 203; musical instruments in, 201–3, 209–14; mythical associations of artifacts in, 202–3; purpose of ritual instruments in, 214–15; reciprocity in, 204–5; research in, 1; social relations in, 3; women's viewing of instruments in, 388. *See also* French Guiana

guitars, 223, 226, 233

Gumilla, José, 7

Guyana: cassette tapes in, 235; musical traditions in, 37–38; Waiwai in, 220–21

Guyana Shield region, 15

Guyanese soca, 222

Hahãintesu, 193n1

Handbook of South American Indians (Steward), 10, 349n9

hardness, 202, 203, 209, 211, 228

hari kare, 335, 336

harmony: in Amazonian socioreligious life, 326, 328, 329; in Arawakan flute complexes, 347; in Baniwa mythology, 343; collective, 211–12, 216n1; in Enawene Nawe ritual, 336; of everyday life, 282, 291; flutes as agents of Baniwa, 341

harvest, 330, 335. *See also* agriculture; planting

hawks, 58

ha' y'u ha' y'u hlu' trumpets, 187. *See also* gourd trumpets

head hunting, 328. *See also* hunting

healing. *See* curing

hearing, 140, 226–27, 234. *See also* seeing and hearing

He concept, 124–25

héemali bark trumpets, 118n10. *See also* bark trumpets; fish

heemari trumpets, 141

Heisenberg principle, 391n12

Hekwapi ienipe, 345

heteroglottal instruments, 15

hierarchical society: and collection of sacred instruments, 363; and cult of botuto, 8; and gender relations, 284; in Guianas, 203, 212, 214, 215; of Piaroa, 148–51, 154, 166–67; and Waiwai flute music, 228; of Wayãpi, 21. *See also* leadership; social order

Hill, Jonathan: biography of, 397; on classification of instruments, 372; classification of ritual cults, 316–17; on creativity of music, 141; on dissonant sound, 387; on ecological diaphasia, 350n13; ethnography of Baniwa/Kuripako/Wakuenai, 341; on flutes as body parts, 31; on gender relations, 284; interpretation of chants, 349n12; on "musicalization" of relations, 216n6; on socioreligious life on Orinoco, 329–30; studies of, 287, 296nn16–17; on tubes, 216n4; on Waiwai musicality, 221–22; Wakuénai musical dialogues, 59; on Wakuénai shamanic chanting, 64; on Warime ritual, 162

hocket style, 26, 55, 58, 108, 206, 208, 211. *See also* ensembles

Hohodene, 349n12

hoka'ù (water's house), 78

Holy Communion, 140

Holy Trinity, 123–24

homosexuality, 196n15, 380. *See also* sexuality

Hornbostel, Erich von, 10–11

Hornbostel-Sachs classification system, 69, 85nn1–2. *See also* Hornbostel, Erich von; Sachs, Curt

hotatap (fire's house), 78. *See also* fire

Houseman, Michael, 129–30

"house of songs," 384, 385. *See also* men's houses

howler monkeys, 51–52, 58, 153, 155, 164, 165. *See also* monkeys

Hugh-Jones, Christine, 190

Hugh-Jones, Stephen, 58, 124–25, 190, 203, 350n13

hukã-hukã (men's sport), 289

human remains, 366

Humboldt, Alexander von, 7–8, 330

hummingbirds, 175, 206–7, 208, 210

humor, 59, 187, 229, 236, 311, 336, 376–77, 386–87. *See also* laughter

Huni Kuin, 307

hunting: in Amazonian socioreligious life, 327–29; of Curripaco, 145; and deceit, 295; fragmentation of spirits of, 24; Maruwanari's sounds of, 221, 229; of peccaries, 302–3, 308, 311; in sacred object display, 367; at tanamea, 311; of Waiwai, 220, 225; of Wakuénai, 95; and Warime ritual, 156, 160, 162; of Wasusu, 190, 192; and Wayana rituals, 206, 207; during *wera* festival, 340; of Yagua, 27, 51, 58, 60, 63. *See also* game

Huottoja. *See* Piaroa
hydroelectric dams, 36, 348n7
Hymes, Dell, 287, 296n16

iaathe flute, 141
iakapá, 243–46, 261. *See also* shamans and
  shamanism
iamurikuma rituals: description of, 279–80;
  gender relations in, 257, 260–70, 272n3,
  292–95; importance of music in, 289; musical thinking in, 251; musical transformations
  in, 89n26; music as inside, 263; myth of,
  261–62, 285–86; relationship with kawoká
  flute ritual, 260; sexuality and violence in,
  283, 284; songs of, 29, 242; subversion of
  corporeal experience during, 288–90; transformation during, 282, 288, 289; in Ukayumai, 278–79; in Upper Xingu region, 277;
  visibility and invisibility in, 292–93; Wauja
  and Xinguano systems of, 257–58; wooden
  pillars in, 262; and Xinguano society, 240,
  259. *See also* gender; kawokakuma songs;
  sacred flute complexes; Wauja; women
ianumakanau flutes, 245
Iapirikuri, 142
iapojatekana, 244
Içana River, 133, 137, 331
identification, 72–73
identities: of Apurinã, 337; of Baniwa, 343,
  345–46; of communities through sacred
  instruments, 357; creation of local, 93;
  expressions of Waiwai, 220, 222, 226,
  228–29, 230, 237; in gendered rituals, 295;
  human in dzawírra duet, 112; individual and
  collective Wakuénai, 115; of Marubo, 39,
  301, 304–10, 315–16, 318; through musical
  performances, 36–40; through rituals, 380,
  381, 386, 391n14; through sacred objects,
  358, 359, 361; and visual evidentials, 135–
  36; of Wayãpi, 22; of Xinguano, 240. *See
  also* collectivity; individuals
idioglottal instruments, 15, 206. *See also*
  waitakala idioglottal clarinets
idiophones, 11, 70, 85n2, 151, 244, 372
ierupoho, 243
i-haha, 281. *See also* kawokakuma songs
Illness: among Baniwa, 342, 348n2; among
  Enawene Nawe, 334; in Arawakan flute complexes, 342; caused by apapaatai, 243, 246,
  257, 260–61, 272n4, 273n5, 279; caused by
  yerupoho spirits, 331–32; curing of Wauja,

244–45; in iamurikuma rituals, 262; and
  Kuai taboo, 128; and menstruation, 377;
  in Nambikwara mythology, 188; and nupa,
  126; origins of, 97; in sacred flute complex,
  278; in Xinguano sacred flute complex, 242.
  See also curing; death; shamans and shamanism
"immediatist" cultism, 344
Imu Chuvo, 153, 154, 158, 164, 165. *See also*
  Chuvo
inalienability, 357–59, 363, 365, 368–69
inamanai voices, 142
Iñapirríkuli. *See* Made-From-Bone (trickster-
  creator)
Inca, 304–10, 319n3
"Inca" flutes, 3–4, 39, 301–4, 318. *See also*
  flutes
incest, 374. *See also* sexual relations
India, 237
individuals, 35, 115, 211, 226–27, 261, 363–
  64. *See also* identities; social relations
initiation rituals: of Baniwa, 343; corporeal
  dissociation and reintegration in, 24, 62–63;
  in evangelical history of cosmos, 345–46;
  Guayakí, 41n11; Guianese ceremonial feasts,
  204; historical time-space in, 116; in kwépani, 102–6; mystery of, 123; of Nambikwara, 190, 195n13; of Panare, 216n1; playing of *karökö* during, 33; secrecy in, 129–30,
  139–40, 141–45; of Shavante, 382, 392n17;
  and social reproduction, 380; and songs from
  dreams, 273n7; sound examples from, 116;
  in Ukayumai, 279; Wakuénai myths about,
  119n22; Yagua flutes for, 17. *See also* children; kapetiapan; marake ceremonies; men;
  ña; puberty; uninitiated
Inka Roe Yõka, 306
insects, 114–15. *See also* ants, biting; coconut
  palm weevils; déetu flutes; déetu insects
instrumental music, 250, 263–70
Internet, 38–39
interplay, 249, 251, 257, 259, 270
intimacy, 326, 327, 332
Inuit, 392n15
inverted organum, 246
invisibility, 367, 368, 380. *See also* seeing and
  hearing
ínyapakáati dzéema, 20–21. *See also* tobacco
  smoke
Ipuriná. *See* Apurinã (Ipuriná)
ipý, 249, 254n17

cal factors of, 245–47; poetics of, 248–50, 259; and sexuality and violence, 283; and shamanic healing, 332; speech of, 249; study of, 278; and thematic construction of ritual, 249, 254n17; and transgression in ritual, 291; and women's songs, 179. *See also* gender; kawokakuma songs; sacred flute complexes; sacred wind instruments; Wauja

kawokakuma-kawoka, 269

kawokakuma songs: classification of, 263, 266–70, 273n6; description of, 29, 263; feelings aroused in, 270–71; in iamurikuma rituals, 264–66; motif and balance in, 251; relationship to kawoka flutes, 281; transcriptions and translations of, 267, 268, 269; variation in, 251, 266–67. *See also* iamurikuma rituals; kawoká flutes; songs

kawokalamona, 245

kawokatãi flutes, 244

kawokatopá (master flutist), 246, 247

kawokawekeho ("owner of kawoká"), 245

Kayabí, 86n5, 296n18

Kayapó, 36, 227, 381

Keane, Webb, 363

Keifenheim, Barbara, 307

kin and kinship groups: in Amazonian socioreligious life, 326, 328, 329; of Enawene Nawe, 325, 333–35; and gender rituals, 272n3; in Guianas, 202, 204, 214; of Kamayurá instruments, 76–78, 77, 89n25, 244, 253n13; knowledge in Waiwai, 233; of Marubo, 305, 311, 317; music as, 383; relationships with through instruments, 3, 26, 115; ritual flutes as, 31–32; and secret wind instruments, 374–75; transformation through wind instruments, 25, 30, 210–12, 215; of Wasusu flutes, 189; of Wayana, 117n5; at *wera* festival, 339; and Xinguano languages, 258; Yuruparí instruments kept by, 358. *See also* affines; ancestors; elders; matrilineal units

knowledge: in Amazonian socioreligious life, 326; ambiguity of, 386; copies as symbols of cultural, 361; cultural in Kashinawa myths, 307; gendered Waiwai, 226; Guianese affines as source of, 214; in Guianese rituals, 203; and hearing, 226; and Nambikwara music and myth, 174, 179, 180; through Guianese musical instruments, 212; Waiwai of outsiders, 233–34, 236–37; in Wayana marake ritual, 208

Koch-Grünberg, Theodor, 8, 35, 362–63

Köpping, Klaus Peter, 287, 296n20

kororo, 202

Kraus, Michael, 364

Kresmus celebrations, 224, 231

Kroeker, 194n1

Kuai (sacred flutes and trumpets): description of sounds, 141–42; in *piamaka* rituals, 127; taboo and secrecy of, 124, 126–30, 137–45. *See also* kapetiapan; mythical beings; sacred wind instruments; trumpets

kuakutu, 7. *See also* trumpets

Kuawayamu (wife of Wajari), 162

Kue flutes, 349n11

Kuemoi (Wajari's father-in-law), 160

Kuikúru, 240, 258

kuliputpë amo-hawin (tortoise claw), 208

kulirina trumpets. *See* kulirrína (also kulirina) trumpets

kulirrína (also kulirina) trumpets: Curripaco prohibitions regarding, 140; description of, 119n19; in pudáli, 101, 107, 108, 110, 113, 114; sound examples of, 116; transition to mythic space through, 28. *See also* catfish; trumpets

kuluta flutes, 244

kunana stinging mat, 206, 207

"Kuraka" (Marubo elder), 308

Kuripako. *See* Curripaco

Kurupira spirit, 51

kuruta flutes, 77, 78

Kutamapù, 73, 75, 76, 84–85, 86n7, 87n11

Kuwái-dance. *See* kwépani ceremonial exchanges

Kuwái/Kuwai: aerophones and cosmologies of, 325; in Baniwa mythology, 342, 345, 346, 348n2; conception of, 98; creation of sacred flutes through, 23; and *Cueti*, 330; evangelical Christians on, 345; flutes as body of, 31, 342, 347, 348n2; in kwépani, 101; and molítu, 102–5; narrative about life cycle of, 98; as plant species, 41n7; representation in ensembles, 27; sacred instruments of, 17, 101, 118n10; secrecy of sacred flutes, 104–5; and shamanic chanting and singing, 23; sound of, 116; stealing of sacred flutes of, 102; Wakuénai myths about, 98–100, 119n22. *See also* primordial beings; spirits

kuwakuho, 240. *See also* flute houses

Kuwé, 163

kuxex. *See* "house of songs"

manioc, fermented, 160
manioc gardens, 95, 97, 104, 335
manioc juice, 390
manioc processing, 374, 388
manioc pulp, 101, 106–7
manioc spirits, 336
manioc tuber, 127
Manoel (José's son), 314
Mansutti Rodríguez, Alexander, 398
Manuel, Peter, 237
Mapuera River, 221
maracas, 151, 153
maraka'ùp (music master), 76
marake ceremonies, 120n24, 206–10. *See also* initiation rituals
marana flutes, 151
Mara Reyo, 154, 158, 160, 161, 163. *See also* animals
Le marbre et le myrte (Viveiros de Castro), 386
marimu, 156
marital exchanges, 158. *See also* marriages
Maronal, 301–4, 310–15
marriages, 10, 154, 206, 207, 240, 258, 267–70. *See also* marital exchanges
Martínez, Gabriel, 386–87
Martius, Friedrich von, 8
Marubo: categories of youth and elders, 310–15; concepts of identity and alterity, 304–10; creation story, 305–6; cultural repertoire of, 309, 312, 316; descent group names, 305; economic activities of, 312, 315; ethnogenesis of, 309, 317–18, 319n4; flute use of, 301–2; headman on Inca instruments, 302–4; musical traditions of, 39; outsiders at rituals of, 382; social relations of, 3–4, 315–18; transcription of words of, 319n2. *See also* Panoan society
Maruwanarï, 219, 221, 221, 222, 228–31
Masakinyarï (Mosquito Place), 221, 222, 230–31
Mashakali, 371, 375, 381–84, 385, 389, 392n16. *See also* Tikmu~'u~n Mashakali
masked peccaries, 152–55, 157, 158, 165. *See also* peccaries
masks and masking: of apapaatai, 244, 245, 261; auditory, 22, 376; comparison to Wayãpi auditory masking, 376; dances using, 329; flutes as, 87n20; of Mashakali, 384; sacredness of Piaroa, 359, 366; in sacred object display, 367, 368; of Tariana warriors, 349n11; in Warime ritual, 154–60, 162, 165;

166; of Wauja, 22–23, 260, 325; in Yãkwa ritual, 336; of yerupoho spirits, 331, 332
master chanters (*malikái limínali*), 20. *See also* chanting
master flutist. *See* kawokatopá (master flutist)
masters of music. *See* apaiwekeho (masters of music)
Matapi, 326, 339. *See also* Arawak-speaking groups
matapu, 244
Mataveni River, 148
maternity, 272n3. *See also* birth; women
Matipú, 258, 267–70
Matis Indians, 293
Mato Grosso, Brazil, 1, 65n2, 193n1, 257–58. *See also* Brazil
matrilineal units, 302, 309–10, 319n1, 341. *See also* kin and kinship groups; women
Matses, 318
Matsiguenga, 41n9
Mauritia, 153
Mauss, Marcel, 82, 358
mawá, 105. *See also* molítu flutes
máwi flutes, 96, 107; comparison to déetu flutes, 109; construction of, 107–8, 119n18; in dzawírra duets, 110–12; geographic distribution of, 17; lengths of, 107, 119n17; making of, 95; in pudáli, 30, 107–9, 113; transition to mythic space through, 28. *See also* flutes
Mayãpa (Marubo headman's son-in-law), 302–4
Maybury-Lewis, David, 381, 382
Maypure, 7, 329, 330, 348n3
McCallum, Cecilia, 282–84, 287, 289, 292, 295n10
Mead, Margaret, 281
meat: at Guianese ceremonial feasts, 204; at Marubo feast, 311, 312; as nupa, 125; in pudáli, 100, 101, 106–7, 110; transformation of, 41n7; in Yagua male initiation ritual, 57, 59, 60. *See also* food; game
megaphones, 211–12, 216n5
Mehináku, 3, 17, 240, 258, 267–70, 277–79, 290
mekoro (maroons), 213
mëlaimë amo-hawin (armadillo claw), 208
Melanesia, 242, 272n3, 284
Melatti, Julio Cezar, 305–6, 319nn1–3, 320n4
membranophones, 11. *See also* drums

Nambikwara (*continued*)

exchanges, 376; shamanism of, 24, 178; signification of, 179–80; songs of, 178–79; women's viewing of flutes, 389. *See also* Guaporé Valley Nambikwara; Wasusu

names: birds saying of, 174–76; of flute tunes, 178; of instrument spirits, 32–33; of places, 181–82; of pudáli duets, 110; Tariana appropriation of whites', 349n11; in Wasusu ritual, 187; in Yagua flute ritual, 56, 65n3. *See also* musical naming power

Ñañez, Gonzalez, 349n12

Native American Graves Protection and Repatriation Act (1990), 366. *See also* tombs

Native Christians (Vilaça and Wright), 350n14

Native South American Discourse (Sherzer and Urban), 117n2

natural soundscaping, 93–95, 100, 104, 112–15. *See also* soundscapes

nawa, 39, 304–10, 317–18. *See also* alterity; outsiders

nawa feasts, 301, 303–4, 308–10, 312, 315, 316. *See also* feasts; outsiders

ndusu/kachuno monkey. *See* kachuno monkeys

Neeripan, 124, 144

Negarotê Nambikwara, 193n1

New Guinea, 81

New Testament translations, 346

Nhiaperikuli, 345–46

night and sleep, 97, 158, 163, 189, 193, 196n16. *See also* daytime

"Night Nurse" (Gregory Isaacs), 235

Nimuendajú, Curt, 8

no kato ceremonial dialogue, 211

non-indigenous people. *See* outsiders

Norón (Yagua spirit), 51

North American anthropological model, 281

northwest Amazon: aerophones and cosmologies of, 325–26; collection of instruments in, 4; comparison of flutes to Kamatxi, 338; contact with non-indigenous society in, 331; cultural features of, 10, 333; Dance of Pijiguaos in, 165; descent of instruments in, 214; flute and mask rituals in, 166; gender politics of, 159; kinship in, 202; language in, 130–34; myth of gender in, 203; prohibitions regarding flutes in, 348n6; prophetic movements in, 344, 350n13; research in, 1; ritual instruments' meaning in, 358; sacred flute complex in, 242, 252n3; secret flutes in, 6; women and children's participation in

feasts in, 127; Yagua male initiation ritual in, 54–59. *See also* Amazonia

nose flutes, 195n12

notiu, 57. *See also* turtles

nupa, 125–27

Oakdale, Suzanne, 296n18

o branco, 303. *See also* nawa feasts

Oceania, 281, 372

Ojuodaa (tapir-anaconda being), 154, 156, 160, 161, 163. *See also* anaconda

okenap (door), 78

Oliveros, Felix, 105

olok (feather headdresses), 207

onaapa (song), 250

* *oni*, 309

oral traditions, 38

origins, 76, 87n19. *See also* ruptures

Orinoco region, 1, 7–8, 147, 148, 162–63, 329–30

ornaments, 349n11, 378. *See also* body ornaments

other and otherness: ambiguity of, 387; among Enawene Nawe, 333; of Baniwa ancestors, 346; disease-causing spirits as, 290; and exclusion from society, 390n4; mimicry of, 295; in Panoan society, 317, 320n5; production through natural soundscaping, 93; in Warime ritual, 158; and Yurupary, 341. *See also* alterity; outsiders

outsiders: in Amazonian socioreligious life, 328, 330–31; Apurinã contact with, 336–37; and boom boxes, 233–34, 236–37; and collection of sacred instruments, 362, 368; communication with, 213, 216n6; Curripaco secrecy from, 138, 140, 145; dialogue with Curripaco sacred flutes, 141; in Guianese society, 204–5, 214, 215; and indigenous musical traditions, 36–40; Marubo associations with, 313, 314; men as in Guianese society, 212–13; negotiation of relationships with, 3; and Piaroa, 149, 361; in ritual triangle, 382–83, 389; sale of sacred objects to, 364–65; and secret wind instrument rituals, 382–83; and sound quantity, 377; as threat to secrecy, 384, 392n22; in Wayana rituals, 206–8, 211; Wayãpi attraction of, 377, 391n8. *See also* alterity; caraíbas; nawa; nawa feasts; other and otherness; researchers; rubber boom; uninitiated; whites

Overing, Joanna, 326

Oyapock River, 15, 371, 389
Oyuela-Caycedo, Augusto, 339

pákamarántakan, 105, 109, 116, 118n7
pakanupaka, 126
palm (*Astrostudium schomburgkii*), 95, 96, 119n18. *See also* máwi flutes
palm (*Bactris gasipaes*), 54
palm boards, 127
palm, buriti (*Mauritia flexuosa*), 338, 339
palm fruits, 97, 102
Palm Grove spirits, 51. *See also* spirits
palm, macanilla, 118n10
palm trees, 118n12, 330, 358–59. *See also* trees
palm, *wasey*, 391n8
palometa fish, 141, 142. *See also* fish
pananakiri (urban or coastal dwellers), 213
Panare, 216n1
pan flutes, 244. *See also* pan pipes
panguana bird, 52
Panoan society, 304–10, 315–18, 319n3, 320n4, 320n5. *See also* Chacobo; Marubo
Pano-speaking peoples, 39, 41n10, 309, 320n4
pan pipes, 26, 195n12, 211, 388. *See also* pan flutes
papaya-tree shoots, 183
papeeku rinupa, 125–26. *See also* nupa; purification
Papua New Guinea, 173, 392n22
Pará, Brazil, 206. *See also* Brazil
parapara bullroarers, 77, 81
Paresi Indians, 194n6, 195nn11–12
Paressi, 332–33. *See also* Enawene Nawe
Paressi-Kabixi trumpet-like instrument, 348n6
parika, 345
parikú (shame), 294. *See also* shame
Parita (player of kawoka flute music), 281
particularist socioreligious formations, 328–29, 337, 342, 344, 347
Passe, 339
Patagonia, 11
patrilineal lines, 335. *See also* kin and kinship groups
payakwa, cacicus cela. See yellow-rumped cacique
Payemeramaraka, 80, 273n5
peach-palm fruits, 97
Peba-Yagua linguistic family, 65n1
peccaries, 19, 57, 80, 152–55, 157, 158, 165, 302–3, 308, 311

peccary-skin drums, 303–4, 309, 316. *See also* drums
Peirano, Marisa, 271n2
pejú, 245
Pentecostalism, 344. *See also* religion
People from the Savannahs (Sa 'mãˇle ki'te'su'), 183, 195n11
peppers, 125, 392n28
pequi fruit rattles, 77–78
Pequi ritual, 87n19, 244, 273n8
Peirce, 215
performance: cultural identity through, 36–40; with déetu flutes, 109; ethnographic research on, 117nn2–3, 287, 296nn14–20; exchanges in, 296n14; myths and mythology in, 287; recordings of Wakuénai, 119n16; Richard Schechner on, 296n20; rituals as, 260, 272n2, 283, 287, 292, 295, 296n12, 296n14, 296n20, 376, 378–80, 382–83, 386–88, 392n23; social change in, 41n12; speech in, 287; of Tupí-speaking peoples, 36; and Wakuénai myths and mythology, 95–102, 115–16, 119n16; of Xavante, 36. *See also* dancing; dzawírra; flute rituals; play
Peru, 2, 11, 24, 41n10, 327
Peruvians, 303
phallus. *See* genitalia
phlegm (*worapóndi*), 53
piamaka rituals, 127–28, 137–38
Piapoco (Vaupès), 133, 349n12
Piaroa: characters of cultural world of, 160, 164; cultural art of, 162–64; description of, 147–48; gender relations of, 148–51, 161–63, 166–67; masks for sale, 361; musical instruments of, 151–53; poetics of ritual power, 2; predation of animals, 165; sacredness of instruments of, 35; sacredness of masks to, 359; sexual content of sonorous exchanges, 376; social organization of, 148–51; spirit voices of, 33; trumpets of, 12
The Picture of Dorian Grey (Wilde), 9
Piedade, Acácio Tadeu de Camargo, 23, 65n4, 87n20, 259, 316, 317, 379, 399
pigs, wild, 338, 360
Pires de Campos, Antonio, 333
Piro, 320n5, 337–38
píti whistles, 28
pitsana (music timbre), 250
Piulaga Lake, 257
place-names, 181–82
plantains, 311, 312

planting, 335, 336. *See also* agriculture; gardens and gardening; harvest

plants: in Amazonian socioreligious life, 328, 329; animal sounds from, 41n7; communication with, 2; cults to, 7–8; in cultural soundscaping, 94; and dissonant sound, 65n4; and instrument spirits, 33; music as life force of, 98; and Nambikwara flute tunes, 178–79, 192; names in Yagua flute ritual, 56, 65n3; and Wakuénai, 95, 115; in Wauja cosmology, 243; Yagua shamans' use of hallucinogenic, 52–53; yerupoho spirits as, 331. *See also* agriculture; gardens and gardening; trees

plant salt, 334–36

play, 271, 286, 289–92, 318. *See also* performance

Pleiades, 182

plug flutes, 17, 252n2. *See also* flutes

poetics, 2, 248–51, 254n18, 259, 287

poetry, definition of, 117n2

poku. See creole music

politics: and Amazonian socioreligious life, 329, 330; in Arawak-speaking societies, 325; and cult of botuto, 8; of ethnomusicologists, 373; of evangelical Christians, 345; in gendered rituals, 293; of Guianese society, 205; in iamurikuma rituals, 257; and instrument collection, 35, 362, 363; of Marubo, 312, 314, 315; of Piaroa, 361; study of oratory of, 117n2; of Wauja, 261, 332

polyphonic music, 33. *See also* dissonant sounds

pono mourning ceremony, 206

Portuguese language, 258, 314

power: in Amazonian socioreligious life, 326; of Baniwa primordial animal spirits, 343; of boom boxes, 234; of cultural elements, 358; in gendered rituals, 284–85, 287–88; of Guianese, 203, 212, 214; in iamurikuma rituals, 261; of inalienable objects, 359; Tariana incorporation of external, 349n11; of Waiwai flutes, 227, 229, 232–33; of Wayãpi musical instruments, 379. *See also* disempowerment; empowerment

The Power of Love (Santos-Granero), 327

prayer, 150, 329

predation: in Amazonian socioreligious life, 327–29; ambiguity of, 387; in Apurinã mythology, 337–38; in Baniwa mythology, 343; domestication through ritual flutes, 30, 333; in Enawene Nawe ritual, 336; flutes as

agents of Baniwa, 341; in gendered rituals, 282; in Guianese rituals, 204; and Tariana, 349n11; by Wauja spirits, 325, 331–32

predu, 392n17

presentation, 174, 175, 177–78

Preuss, Konrad Theodor, 8

priestly societies and specialists, 329, 343, 350n13, 392n22

primordial beings, 17, 27, 93, 115, 328, 331–32, 343. *See also* ancestors; Kuwái/Kuwai; mythical beings

primordial space-time. *See* mythic space-time

"The Primordial Times" (Úupi Pérri), 95–97

Prinz, Ulrike, 399

prophetic movements, 343, 344, 348n2, 350n13. *See also* divinities

Protestantism, 344. *See also* religion

Ptak, Wolfgang, 35, 363, 368

puberty, 23, 71, 79, 86n8. *See also* initiation rituals; youth

pudáli ceremonial exchanges: access to mythic space-times through, 97; and déetu insects, 119n22; dissonant sounds in, 28; female-owned ceremonies in, 110, 120n23; gender complementarity in, 106–13, 108, 317; as mádzerukái, 100–101; and molítu, 104; nonsexuality in, 114; social transformations during, 29–30; sound examples from, 116. *See also* exchanges

pühükă, 279

pulupulu, 244. *See also* log drums

purification, 3. *See also* papeeku rinupa

Puruna (husband of Chejeru), 164

Purus River, 325, 331, 336–39

Quechua, 11

Quechua *flauta y caja* ensembles, 309

Quechua speakers, 306, 308, 319n3

ramanujú, 58. *See also* howler monkeys

rape: David Maybury-Lewis on, 381, 382; in gendered rituals, 282–83, 285, 286, 288, 291–92; and iamurikuma rituals, 263, 277; by Kamayurá, 73, 75–76, 78, 84; and viewing of secret aerophones, 374; by Xinguano, 241. *See also* violence

rattles, 11, 77–78, 153, 247

ratu, 220, 227. *See also* bamboo

Raymond, J. Scott, 319n3

reciprocity: of anthropologists and indigenous communities, 364–65; in Enawene Nawe ritual, 325, 334; of gender in pudáli, 114; in Guianese rituals, 204–5; in iamurikuma rituals, 257, 261–62; and Kamayurá, 75–76, 85; in Marubo rituals, 317; in Wayana marake ritual, 208. *See also* exchanges

recordings, 8, 38–39, 88n21, 89n26, 222, 363

regeneration: and Amazonian socioreligious life, 328–29; in Arawakan flute complexes, 347; in Guianese ceremonial feasts, 204; in lowland cultures, 375; of Nambikwara flutes, 189, 190, 193; Nambikwara men's role in, 196n18; in Wayana marake ritual, 207. *See also* birth; life force; reproductive behavior; social renewal and reproduction

reggae, 222, 235

"Reggae Physician" (Burning Spear), 235

Reichel-Dolmatoff, Gerardo, 10, 161

religion: in Amazonia, 326–31; in Arawak-speaking societies, 326; of Baniwa, 341–46; Christian priests' attempt to break indigenous, 392n22; of the devil, 5–6; of Enawene Nawe, 333; in Lowland South America, 326–31; mystery of, 123–24; ritual wind instruments in American Indian, 5; in secret aerophone rituals, 388. *See also* Catholic religion; Christianity; cosmology; religious music

religion of the devil, 40n1

religious music, 38, 211, 213, 222, 223, 233

Renard-Casevitz, France-Marie, 307

renewal. *See* regeneration; social renewal and reproduction

repatriation, 366

repetition, 239, 249, 251, 260

representation, 174, 175, 177, 182, 244

reproductive behavior, 94, 112–14. *See also* fecundity; fertility; regeneration; sexual relations; social renewal and reproduction

reré shells, 151, 153

researchers, 3–5, 364–65, 368. *See also* outsiders

Resígaro, 339

revenge, 73, 75–76, 232, 243, 337–38

rifles, 182

rimitiu'. See Wirisihó

rinupa, 126

Rio Aciman, 360

Rio Branco, 313

Rio Caiaray-Uaupés, 362–63

Rio Negro area: Arawak-speaking groups along, 148; bark trumpets in, 12; collection of sacred flutes in, 362; creation of musical soundscapes in, 93–95, 115–16; evidential

systems in, 133, 137; languages in, 132–33; music as life force in, 98; practices of playing sacred instruments in, 81; sacred flute cults in, 330; singing and chanting in, 20, 23; social relations in, 29–30

Rio Negro Indians, 9

ritaiwa, 392n17

ritual cults, classification of, 316–17

riverine ecology, 94–95. *See also* ecology; water

River of Fire Ants, 171

Rivière, P., 202, 229

roarers, 12. *See also* bullroarers

roars, 56, 58, 63, 64

Roe Inka (Inca Axe), 306

Roncador-Xingu expedition, 87n10

Rondônia, 195n12

rubber boom: Alfredo on, 303; Apurinã during, 337, 339; effect on Baniwa, 342; effect on Marubo culture, 308–10, 318, 319n4; and expansion of nation-states, 362, 369n3; Quechua speakers in Javari basin during, 306. *See also* colonialism; outsiders

Ruedas, Javier, 399–400

Rúnda, 56, 58, 59, 63. *See also* bark trumpets

ruptures, 76, 84. *See also* origins

ruwe, 211. *See also* aerophones

ruwode. See men's houses, in Warime ritual

Sabanê, 194n1

Sachs, Curt, 10–11. *See also* Hornbostel-Sachs classification system

sacred flute complexes: comparisons of Arawakan, 347, 347–48; comparison to Marubo feast, 310; description of Xinguano, 241–42; differentiation in, 239; gender wars in, 281–82; in Lowland South America, 242; men's houses in, 252n3; pervasiveness of, 251–52; and social life, 316; in Upper Xingu region, 277; of Yukuna, 339–41. *See also* ensembles; iamurikuma rituals; kawoká flutes; sacred wind instruments

sacredness: of flute and mask rituals, 166; of flutes in Amazonia, 316–17; in Guianas, 201, 212, 215; and inalienability, 357–58; and Kuai taboo, 128; of Nambikwara flutes, 187–88; and nupa, 126; of Piaroa masks, 359, 366; preservation of identity through, 359

sacred wind instruments: acquisition of, 4, 34–36, 359–66; character of, 34–37; classification of, 1, 17, 69–70, 252nn1–2; collection and display of, 362, 366–69; historical

social relations (*continued*)
  musical transpositions of, 2–3; as Nam-
    bikwara flute tune referents, 178–79; in
    Nambikwara mythology, 184, 188; and
    Nambikwara ritual life, 181–82, 185–86,
    192; and secret wind instruments, 374–75;
    of sexes, 373–75; and Waiwai flute music,
    229; Wakuénai dances for, 97–98; and Wauja
    sacred flute complex, 252; and yerupoho
    spirits, 332. *See also* collectivity; communi-
    ties; individuals
social renewal and reproduction: of Baniwa,
    342–43; elements of, 390; of Enawene Nawe,
    333; in secret aerophone rituals, 386; of
    Tariana, 349n11; through Guianese musical
    ceremonies, 201, 206, 207, 210, 212–15;
    through ritual instruments, 380; of Waiwai,
    223. *See also* regeneration; reproductive
    behavior
social space: naturalized, 93, 100; and natural
    soundscaping, 94–95; regeneration through
    aerophones, 19, 25–30; of Waiwai, 38. *See
    also* communities; space
society: in collective musical performances,
    41n12; gender categories in, 374, 390n2;
    of Guianese, 201–3, 205, 216n1; and lim-
    ited sensorial experience, 34; role of sacred
    objects in construction of, 367; in sacred flute
    complex, 239; sexualization in secret instru-
    ment rituals, 379, 388, 389; and Xinguano
    ceremonial, 240
socioreligious formations. *See* particularist
    socioreligious formations; religion; social
    relations; universalist socioreligious forma-
    tions
solos, 28–29, 76. *See also* duets; ensembles;
    trios
songs: Baniwa connection to God through,
    346; communication through Guianese, 205;
    from dreams, 264, 273n7; drinking, 105,
    109, 116; education about shamanic, 39;
    exchanges of anthropologists and indigenous
    hosts, 364–65; in female-owned pudáli cer-
    emony, 120n23; in Guianese myths, 209; for
    Kalau male initiation, 207; of Kuwaí/Kuwai
    in Baniwa myth, 342; at Marubo feast, 311;
    memorization of, 264; in Warime ritual,
    158; of Wauja women, 29, 178–79, 262–63,
    280–81; in yawari ritual, 251. *See also* birds,
    calls of; *crentes*; grindstone songs; kawo-

kakuma songs; shout songs (*akía*); singing;
    vocal music
sorcery, 127, 129, 326, 341–44, 346. *See also*
    witches and witchcraft
soul-speaking, 176–77
souls, stealing of, 260, 331–32
sound: essays on natural, 1–2; of molítu flutes,
    106, 116; monosyllabic in gendered rituals,
    293; in natural soundscaping, 94; in pudáli,
    107–9, 111, 116; quality of Waiwai flutes',
    232; quantity and discrimination of, 375,
    377–80, 387, 389, 391n8; in sacred object
    display, 368; and social reproduction, 390;
    of Wakuénai musical performances, 119n16;
    in Wakuénai mythic narratives, 97–98; of
    Wauja, 250; in Yagua male initiation ritual,
    63; in Yagua spiritual communication,
    49–53. *See also* seeing and hearing
soundscapes, 93, 117n1, 223. *See also* cultural
    soundscaping; natural soundscaping
The Soundscape (Schafer), 117n1
Southern Illinois University, 117n4
southwest Amazon, 333, 388. *See also* Ama-
    zonia
space, 367. *See also* flute houses; men's houses;
    social space
space-time, 387–88, 392n23. *See also* mythic
    space-time
Spanish American music, 312
Spanish colonization, 306
speaking tubes, 54–57, 64. *See also* Wirisihó;
    Yagua, flutes of
speech: in Guianese society, 205; of kawoká,
    249; in kwépani, 101, 104, 118n13; "mas-
    ters of" in Wayana marake ritual, 208; and
    molítu flutes, 105, 106, 118n15; in ritual
    performance, 287; in shamanic rituals,
    93, 117n2; transformation through, 287,
    296n18; of Wajari, 157; in Yagua male initia-
    tion ritual, 56, 63. *See also* language; lexical-
    ity; *malikái*; voices
spider monkeys, 311. *See also* monkeys
spirit-human relations: in Amazonian socioreli-
    gious life, 328; in Arawakan flute complexes,
    347; and breath and breathing, 21, 24; of
    Enawene Nawe, 325, 333–36; and food
    exchange, 32; and gendered rituals, 283,
    290–91, 294–95; of Guianese, 209, 213–14;
    in iamurikuma rituals, 257, 289–90; lan-
    guage in, 50–51; of Nambikwara, 185–86,
    191–93, 196n21; in sacred object display,

367–68; through flute tunes, 177–78, 184; of Yagua, 49–53, 60–64. *See also* apapaatai spirits; spirits

spirits: anger in gendered rituals, 283, 285, 286, 288, 291–92; communication with owners of, 2; dwelling in instruments, 358–59, 362; entry of realm through music, 33; at Guianese ceremonial feasts, 204; guidance of Enawene Nawe, 334; of instruments, 31–35; invisibility of, 253n10, 292–95; in *kamatxi* rituals, 360; in Nambikwara flute rituals, 192, 193; taming of, 30, 289–92, 333; and visual evidentials, 134; Yagua communication with vegetable, 52–53. *See also* apapaatai spirits; demons; extraordinary beings; *kamatxi* rituals; Kuwaí/Kuwai; mama'e; monsters; Palm Grove spirits; spirit-human relations; yakayriti; yerupoho spirits; Yoopinai; "Yurupary complex"

Spix, Johann Baptist von, 8

stamping tubes, 11

Steere, 338

Steinen, Karl von den, 8, 277, 295n1

stereos, 309, 312. *See also* boom boxes; cassette tapes

Steward, Julian, 10, 349n9

stone, 306, 307, 308, 319n3

stools (*kororo*), 202

Strathern, Marilyn, 380, 381

stringed instruments, 11. *See also* cordophones

subiya flutes, 151

sucking and vomiting, 109, 113, 154, 157, 207, 303

Sullivan, Lawrence, 41n11

sun, 331, 340

supernatural beliefs, 124, 134, 241. *See also* apapaatai spirits

Suriname, 120n24, 205

surubí (catfish) trumpets, 12, 32, 119n19. *See also* catfish; trumpets

Suyá, 38, 65n2, 82, 86n5, 117n3, 226

symbols and symbolism: of alterity among Enawene Nawe and Wauja, 336; of alterity among Matis, 318; of alterity in Amazonian socioreligious life, 326–27; boom boxes as, 233–34, 236–37; cultural objects as, 173–84; in dzawírra duets, 112–13; in gendered rituals, 284; of Guianese authority, 202; "Inca" flutes as, 318; initiation rituals as collections of, 123; molítu frogs as, 102; in narrative genre performances, 296n14; and prohibi-

tions regarding sacred flutes, 124–26; sacred objects in museums as, 359; in Wauja rituals, 260, 272n2; of wealth, 386; of white men among Tariana, 349n11; in Xinguano rituals, 259; in Yurupary, 341

ta'angap flutes, 81

táari (white bocachico), 119n20. *See also* bocachico fish

taboca bamboo, 24, 182, 184

taboo, 124, 126–29, 189–90, 292, 294, 357, 363. *See also* seeing and hearing

Taino, 329

Taitetu, Luc, 389–90

ta ka lu su' (Old Woman), 179. *See also* flute music, old woman

Takumã (Kamayurá chief), 70–72, 74, 86n8, 86n9, 375, 382

talapi, 244

Tamaoavo, 319n1

Tambiah, S. J., 271n2

tampora, 309

tanamea, 310–12, 315. *See also* feasts

Tanimuka-Letuama language system, 132–33. *See also* language

tankuwara, 244

tanu, 232

Tapajos River, 15

tapir, 165, 192. *See also* Ojuodaa (tapir-anaconda being)

tapu. See taboo

tapùy, 72, 73, 78–80, 240. *See also* flute houses

tapùyatapiã people, 79

tarantula spiders (*Avicularia avicularia*), 165

tarawi, 77

Tariana, 133–73, 325, 349n11, 362–63. *See also* Arawak-speaking groups

Tastevin, 307

ta tãu su,' 195n12

Tatuyo language, 130–32, 134–37

Tatuyo modalities, 140, 144

ta wã' na su flutes, 184, 189–91, 195n12, 196n19

Tawandê Nambikwara, 193n1

Tedlock, Dennis, 287, 296n16

te le pho na' ˜n'˜en 'hna', 176

"telephones," 182, 195n10

Tëpu, 211

terceiro incluído (included third), 215, 383

termite hills, 331

Thanatus, 188

threat, nature of, 124

thunder, 51, 56, 58, 338

ti k'a li su.' *See* Anteater speaking trumpet

Tikmuˉ 'uˉn Mashakali, 381–82. *See also* Gê-speaking peoples; Mashakali

tirite (*Ichnosiphon spp.*), 153

tjujaturuwa ("owners of the people"), 149–50

toads, 141–43, 153

tobacco smoke, 20–21, 31, 32, 191, 293

tombs, 338. *See also* Native American Graves Protection and Repatriation Act (1990)

Tomo River, 330

tortoise, 208, 211. *See also* turtles

to to ki sú (white-tailed trogon), 171–75, 172, 180–81, 195n9. *See also* birds

toucans, 27, 101, 152, 164, 165

toule mourning ceremony, 206

Transformando os deuses [Transforming the gods], 350n14

transformations: of Alalikama, 207; in Amazonian socioreligious formations, 326–31; of animals, 41n7; in Arawak-speaking societies, 326–27, 347–48, 348n2; Baniwa shamans on, 346; in gendered rituals, 282, 284, 287–94, 295n10; of gender ethnology, 381; and globalization, 36–40; and Guianese aerophones, 203, 210–11; in iamurikuma rituals, 261; of Kamayurá identifications, 73, 85; of Kamayurá into mama'e, 80; in kawo-kakuma song, 269; of meaning and value of music, 36–40; of museum objects, 359, 365; musical expression of, 28; and Nambikwara music and myth, 179, 182, 185–86, 192; of Piaroa masks, 361; in sacred flute complex, 278; of sacred instruments into commodity, 357; of seeing and hearing ritual wind instruments, 34; through cult of botuto, 8; through death, 209; through musicality and musical sounds, 93–94; through ritual process, 287–90; through ritual wind instruments, 25, 358; through shamanic musical configurations, 29–30; through speech, 287, 296n18; and traumatic contact, 337–38; and Waiwai flutes, 227–29

Tree of Nutrition, 345–46

trees, 23, 339, 342, 345–46. *See also* palm trees; plants

trickster figures, 23, 33–34. *See also* Made-From-Bone (trickster-creator)

Trio, 3, 202, 205–11, 213, 215, 216n1, 376

trios, 241, 245–46. *See also* duets; ensembles; solos

Trumaí, 86n5, 258, 290

trumpet cult, 277–78, 295nn1–2

trumpets: along Japurá River, 339; in Amazonian socioreligious life, 330; animal sounds of, 141; bamboo, 223–26, 224; of Baniwa, 345–46; Barasana prohibitions regarding, 125; as body parts, 24; classification of, 12, 118n10, 195n12; cult of in Lowland South America, 277–78; curative power of, 7; Curripaco prohibitions regarding, 124; in Enawene Nawe religious life, 333; in ensembles, 27; exchange of, 32; in Jurupari sacred flute complex, 242; in Kamayurá sacred flute kin groups, 77, 88n23; of Kuwaí/Kuwai, 23, 102, 104–6, 325; in kwépani, 101, 106, 118nn11–12; made from plants, 41n7; in mádzerukái, 100, 118n9; and migration and trade routes, 23; of Nambikwara, 184–85, 195n12; natural soundscaping through, 93; as primordial beings' bodies, 115; role in Yagua ritual, 59–63; as sacred flutes, 252n1; sounds of, 2, 116; transition to mythic space through, 28; of Wauja, 244; in Wayãpi fish dances, 377–79; at *wera* festival, 340; in Yurupary, 341. *See also* aerophones; bark trumpets; botuto trumpets; complex trumpets; gourd trumpets; Kuai (sacred flutes and trumpets); kulirrína trumpets; *surubí* (catfish) trumpets

Trupp, Fritz, 35, 363, 368

truth, 123–24, 130–31, 134, 135, 137–38, 144, 387

tsak, 82

Tsura (Apurinã culture hero), 337, 338. *See also* divinities

Tuatuari River, 86n7

tubes, 25, 203, 210–11, 213–15, 216n4, 228

Tucanoan languages, 132, 133, 137. *See also* language

tucano bird, 141, 142

tu 'hlu' (flutist-wren), 179

Tukano, 58, 242, 252n3

Tukanoan-speaking peoples, 130–31, 340, 350n13, 358

Tukano Vai Mahse, 163

Tukano Yuruparí, 164–65

tukupi, 390

tukusipan, 206

tünexakumã, 280

Apurinã, 339; cosmology of, 242–44, 247, 249–50, 253n5, 253n10, 257, 261; description of, 257–58; flute houses of, 240–41; flutes as extraordinary beings to, 379–80; gender relations of, 277, 379; health of, 244–45, 253n5; humans in cosmology of, 243–44; iamurikuma ritual of, 257–58; inter- and intratribal rituals of, 241, 244–45, 260; jealousy of, 388; kawoká flute ensembles of, 29; male and female flutes of, 89n26; manufactured objects of, 325; men's house of, 384; musical poetics of, 248–51; musical text of, 247–48; outsiders at rituals of, 382; population of, 332; rituals of, 258–61; sacred flutes of, 17, 239–40, 244–48, 331–32; secret wind instruments of, 373, 376; sexual content of sonorous exchanges, 376; shamanism of, 22–24; social relations of, 3; study of female musical tradition in, 280–81; study of sacred flutes of, 87n20; temporality in sacred flute ritual, 249–50; women's songs, 29, 178–79, 262–63, 280–81. *See also* Arawak-speaking groups; iamurikuma rituals; kawoká flutes; Xinguano

Wawitihó, 17, 57–59, 64

wawitiu, 58

Wayana: adulthood rites of, 206; on artifacts as persons, 203; art objects of, 206; claws in mythology of, 208; fertile associations with music in mythology of, 208; instruments and rituals of, 12, 15, 117n5, 205–11; interactions with outsiders, 213; marake ceremonies of, 120n24, 206–10; musical forms of, 215; and secret aerophones, 376; shamanism of, 25; social relations of, 3

Wayãpi: aerophones and shamanic breathing of, 293; attraction of outsiders, 377, 391n8; breath and breathing of, 21; clarinet suites of, 27–29; eroticism, regeneration, and fertility among, 375; fish dances of, 377–79; forbidden activities of, 374, 390n4; gender relations of, 373, 376–77; hiding of aerophones, 375–76; migration of, 371; musical instruments of, 371–72; mythico-ritual gestures of, 375–76; polarization in secret instrument rituals of, 383; research on, 4–5; sexual meaning and agency of, 391n11. *See also* Tupí-speaking peoples

weapons, 388

Weber, Max, 328

Weenhayek, 11

Weiner, Annette, 359, 363

Weiss, Gabriele, 369n6

Wenner-Gren Foundation for Anthropological Research, 117n4

wera festival, 339–41

Werekena, 325. *See also* Arawak-speaking groups

Western imagination, 5–10, 373

Wetzels, Leo, 194n1

whip lashing. *See* flogging

whistles and whistling, 20, 28, 41n8, 49, 51, 53

whites: in Baniwa Kuwaí/Kuwai myth, 342; contact with Tariana, 349n11; diseases of, 272n4; in Marubo creation story, 306; Panoans' referral to, 305; predation on Apurinã, 337–38; rifles of, 182; at secret instrument rituals, 382; social category of, 213; Xinguano communication with, 258. *See also* caraíbas; colonialism; nawa feasts; outsiders

White Vulture, 187

wichótu, 57. *See also* turtles

"The Wicked and the Wise Men" (Wright), 342

Wilbert, Johannes, 236

Wild, Oscar, 9

Wind, 51

Wirisihó, 56–57, 59, 64. *See also* speaking tubes

Wirö, 147. *See also* Sáliva peoples

witches and witchcraft, 82, 87n16, 98, 196n15, 240. *See also* sorcery

wiwito tree, 153

"a woman is crying." *See* flute music, old woman

women: ambiguity in ritual, 387–88; association with manioc, 390; and collection of sacred instruments, 362–63, 368; communication of Waiwai, 220; control of Kamayurá sacred flutes, 81; criticism of men, 376, 390n6; in cultural and natural soundscaping, 115; curing by sacred flutes, 7; in Curripaco flute threesome, 141; factional relationship with Wauja men, 245, 254n15; fear of secret aerophones, 380–81, 387, 389; and feeding of instruments, 32; Kamayurá treatment of, 73–74, 78; in kwépani, 100–106, 118n9; Makuna taboo for, 363; Mashakali, 385; musical traditions of, 280–81, 295n7; opposition to men in sacred flute complex, 252n3; in Piaroa hierarchy, 151; pregnant, 118n9;

women (continued)

prohibitions in *kamatxi* ritual, 360; prohibitions in sacred flute complex, 253n3; prohibitions in Yuruparí feasts, 6; prohibitions of Apuriná, 338; prohibitions of Curripaco, 124, 127–30, 138–45; prohibitions of Kamayurá, 73, 75, 79–81; prohibitions of Piaroa, 151, 152, 155, 156, 165, 166; prohibitions of Wayãpi, 21–22; prohibitions of Xinguano, 241, 242; prohibitions of Yagua, 54; prohibitions of Yukuna, 339–41; prohibitions, Oscar Wilde on, 9; prohibitions regarding instruments, 2, 365, 374–75; prohibitions regarding kawoká flutes, 257; in pudáli, 30, 100–101, 106–12, 118n9, 120n23; relationships with through aerophones, 26; representation of inside in Guianas, 212–13; in ritual triangle, 382–83, 389, 392n28; role in ritual, 379, 391n9; role in Warime, 155–65; role in Wayana marake ritual, 207; role in Yagua ritual, 59–60; sacred instruments as taboo for, 357; in secret aerophone rituals, 384–86; secret aerophones to Wauja, 379–80; sexual relations of Kamayurá, 71–72; shamanic powers of Wasusu, 195n15; songs of Wauja, 29, 178–79, 262–63, 280–81; space-time for, 387, 392n23; in twin myth, 376; viewing of flutes, 185, 193, 384, 392n22; Waiwai enticement through music, 37, 220, 227–30, 234; Wakuénai narrative about humanness of, 98; as Wauja flute owners, 245, 280; and Wayãpi musical instruments, 371–72, 375–76; in Yagua male initiation ritual, 59. *See also* feminine elements; gender; gender relations; iamurikuma rituals; maternity; matrilineal units

Worá, 33, 151, 152, 154–56, 158, 160–65

"The World Begins" (Hekuápi Ikée-ñuakawa), 95, 97

world hearing, 82

"The World Opens Up" (Hekuápi Ihmée-takawa), 95, 98

Wright, Robin M., 30, 161, 342, 350n14, 383, 387, 400

Xavante, 36, 273n7, 296n18

Xingane ritual, 349n8

xinguanization, 80, 88n27

Xinguano: cultural edicts in sacred flute complex of, 242; death and funeral practices of, 215; description of, 257–58; etiquette of,

87n13; flute houses of, 78; gender relations of, 293, 317; iamurikuma ritual of, 257–58; identifications of, 72–73; importance of ritual instruments in mythology of, 81; instruments of, 69–70; inter- and intratribal relations of, 240, 241, 258–60; musical poetics of, 251; musical-ritual complex of, 258–60; sacred flutes of, 240–42; and sexual antagonism, 281–82; shamans of, 82; stealing of Kamayurá music, 88n21; study of sacred flutes of, 87n20; transformation of, 80, 289–90. *See also* Kamayurá; Upper Xingu region; Wauja

Xingú: prohibitions regarding women's viewing of instruments, 388; on sexuality and reproduction, 380

Xinguano Indigenous Reserve, 258

Xingu Detachment, 84

Xingu National Indian Park, 70, 82, 86n6, 330

Xingu River, 15, 36, 71, 86n6, 87n10, 257, 331–32. *See also* Upper Xingu region

Yagua: feeding of instruments, 32; flutes of, 17, 49–65; language of, 49, 65n11; male initiation rituals of, 27, 54–61, 63; natural resources management of, 50; nonverbal communication through flutes, 49–50; poetics of ritual power, 2; sexual content of sonorous exchanges, 376; shamans of, 24, 49–54; sound of aerophones of, 387; on sound quantity, 377; tongue scraping by shamans, 53; use of roarers, 12

Yajo, 151, 152, 154, 158, 164

Yakarep, 86n6

yakayriti, 325, 333–36. *See also* spirits

yakokoakamitù, 77

yaku'iare'ùy kin group, 77

yaku'i flutes, 17, 30, 37, 73–80, 79, 82, 84–85, 87, 240. *See also* flutes; sacred wind instruments

yaku'i people, 31, 73, 74, 85. *See also* Kamayurá

yãkwa, 325. *See also* kin and kinship groups

Yãkwa, 334–36

ya ˉlĩn su.' *See* taboca bamboo

Yameo, 65n1

Yaminawa, 308, 315–16, 318

yãmĩy, 382

yãmĩy po'op, 385

Yamurikuma, 375, 380, 389–90

Yanesha, 41n9